Wrasses
& Parrotfishes

REEF FISHES SERIES · BOOK 5

You'll want to own all nine books in Scott Michael's authoritative
Reef Fishes Series as soon as they become available:

  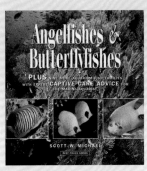 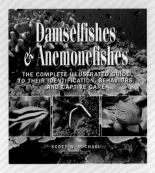

**Moray Eels, Lionfishes
& Anthias,** plus Frog-
fishes, Squirrelfishes,
Seahorses, Dwarf Sea-
basses, and more.
REEF FISHES 1

**Basslets, Dottybacks &
Hawkfishes,** plus
Jawfishes, Grammas,
Cardinalfishes,
Tilefishes, and more.
REEF FISHES 2

**Angelfishes & Butterfly-
fishes,** plus Sweepers,
Goatfishes, Drums,
Remoras, Snappers,
and more.
REEF FISHES 3

**Damselfishes &
Anemonefishes,**
the definitive reference
on a diverse mainstay
marine aquarium family.
REEF FISHES 4

**WRASSES &
PARROTFISHES
REEF FISHES 5**

**BLENNIES
& DRAGONETS
REEF FISHES 6**

**GOBIES &
DARTFISHES
REEF FISHES 7**

**PUFFERS, TRIGGERS
& SURGEONFISHES
REEF FISHES 8**

**THE REEF FISHES
ENCYCLOPEDIA
Omnibus Edition**

Front Cover
All photographs by Scott W. Michael, except where noted.
Background: Tropical Western Pacific reef scene. Photograph by Fred Bavendam.
Left: Bluestreak Cleaner Wrasse (*Labroides diamidiatus*) cleaning parrotfish (*Scarus* sp.), page 238.
Center: McCosker's Flasher Wrasse (*Paracheilinus mccoskeri*), page 288. Photograph by Takamasa Tonozuka.
Right: Cheeklined Maori Wrasse (*Oxycheilinus diagrammus*), page 94.
Back Cover
Top: Blue Flasher Wrasse (*Paracheilinus cyaneus*), page 283.
Middle: Bloody Fairy Wrasse (*Cirrhilabrus sanguineus*), 149. Photograph by Hiroyuki Tanaka.
Bottom: (*Scarus frenatus*) Bridled Parrotfish, 376.

Wrasses & Parrotfishes

THE COMPLETE ILLUSTRATED GUIDE TO THEIR IDENTIFICATION, BEHAVIORS, AND CAPTIVE CARE

Text and principal photography by

SCOTT W. MICHAEL

REEF FISHES SERIES · BOOK 5

Photographic Contributors

Dr. Gerald R. Allen, Fred Bavendam, Ned DeLoach, Tomonori Hirata, John P. Hoover, Paul Humann, Keisuke Imai, Larry Jackson, Rudie H. Kuiter, Tomoshibi Mizutani, Robert F. Myers, Hiroshi Nagano, Alf Jacob Nilsen, Yasuhiro Morita Ogasawara, G. Ogawa, Dr. John E. Randall, Andre Seale, Roger Steene, Keoki Stender, Hiroshi Takeuchi, Hiroyuki Tanaka, Takamasa Tonozuka, Toshio Tsubota, Fenton Walsh, Kiyoshi Yanagiba.

MICROCOSM

tfh

PROFESSIONAL SERIES™

Contents

Paracheilinus filamentosus, Filamented Flasher Wrasses: males cluster on reef in Milne Bay, Papua New Guinea.

Halichoeres hortulanus, Checkerboard Wrasse: vivid markings and flamboyant color contrasts characterize many wrasses.

Preface

THE INFORMATION IN THIS BOOK is designed to assist anyone interested in these fishes to maintain them in peak condition in the aquarium. This book is also part of a larger effort—a multivolume reference tool for marine aquarists as well as divers, snorkelers, and underwater naturalists with an interest in fish species associated with the coral reefs of the world. Each book is designed to be used and enjoyed individually as well as in the series. **A final, comprehensive *Reef Fishes Encyclopedia* will provide a full photographic index to all species covered in the set.**

Acknowledgments

I T IS IMPOSSIBLE TO IMAGINE CREATING THIS SERIES of books without the help, expertise, contributions, advice and unfailing encouragement of a great many generous people in many disciplines and many countries. The following acknowledgments are painfully incomplete, and I apologize to any of you who have contributed and whose assistance is not noted here.

I must begin by expressing my gratitude to an international group of scientists and reef fish experts who have unselfishly aided my efforts to identify fishes, gather photographs and ecological information, and provide behavioral observations on many species. These include Dr. Gerald R. Allen, Dr. Bruce Carlson, Dr. Martin Gomon, Keisuke Imai, Rudie H. Kuiter, Robert Myers, Richard Pyle, Dr. John E. Randall, Roger Steene, Dr. Hiroyuki Tanaka, and Fenton Walsh. Dr. Hiroyuki Tanaka deserves special recognition as he is the *Cirrhilabrus-Paracheilinus* guru. There is no one that knows more about these two genera of wonderful labrids. He has been most generous to share his observations and some of his photos with me.

My colleagues in marine fishkeeping circles have also provided a constant source of new information and insights on the species of interest to aquarists. My sincere thanks to Chip Boyle, Steve Bunz, Mitch Carl, J. Charles Delbeek, Tom Frakes, Kevin Gaines, Jim Gryczanowski, Jay Hemdal, Larry Jackson, Kelly Jedlicki, Martin A. Moe, Jr., Bronson Nagareda, Tony Nahacky, Alf Jacob Nilsen, Vince Rado, Orlando Suarez, the late Gregory Schiemer, Frank Schneidewind, Mike Schied, Terry Siegel, Julian Sprung, Tony Vargas, and Sanjay Yoshi.

I am especially appreciative of years of support from many fine friends and acquaintances in the aquarium trade, including Bill Addison (C-Quest), Chris Buerner and Bob Pascua (Quality Marine),Millie, Ted, and Edwin Chua (All Seas Marine), Eric Cohen and Carl Coloian (Sea Dwelling Creatures), Mark Haeffner (Fish Store Inc.), Kevin Kohen (Live Aquaria), Betsey Moore (CaribSea), Dave Palmer (Pacific Aqua Farms), Joe Russo (Russo's Reef), Wayne Sugiyama (Wayne's Ocean World), Leng Sy (Ecosystem Aquarium), Jeffrey Turner (Reef Aquaria Design), Jeff Voet (Tropical Fish World), Jim Walters (Old Town Aquarium), and Forrest Young and Angus Barnhart (Dynasty Marine). Fenton Walsh sent me some rare and unusual Australian fishes, as well as some beautiful photos for this volume. My friend and expert fishfinder Dennis Reynolds (Aqua Marines) deserves special recognition for all the unusual fishes and years of reliable information.

Many individuals, companies, and resorts have also assisted me in traveling to exotic locations to photograph the fishes contained within these volumes. They include Karen Gowlett-Holmes, Avi Klapfer (Undersea Hunter, Coco Island), Carol Palmer (Ambon Dive Centre), the late Larry Smith, and Martin and Lori Sutton (Fisheye, Grand Cayman). Several dive operators deserve special recognition: Rob Vanderloos (Chertan, Papua New Guinea), one of the nicest people in the dive travel industry, has provided great diving opportunities for me in Milne Bay, and Mark Ecenbarger (Kungkungan Bay Resort, Sulawesi) has been incredibly helpful in enabling Janine, Roger Steene,

Large *Scarus rubroviolaceus*, Ember Parrotfish, appears to grin at the camera as it settles in for the night on a Maldivian Reef in the Indian Ocean.

and me to study and photograph the amazing marine life of Lembeh Strait. Toshikazu and Junco Kozawa (Anthis Corp.) were incredibly gracious hosts during our dive travels to Japan, and Takamasa and Miki Tonozuka (Dive and Dives) provided wonderful photo opportunities in Bali.

I would never have been able to assemble a comprehensive collection of species photographs without the help of some of the best fish photographers in the world. I thank Dr. Gerald R. Allen, Fred Bavendam, Ned DeLoach, Tomonori Hirata, John P. Hoover, Paul Humann, Keisuke Imai, Larry Jackson, Rudie H. Kuiter, Tomoshibi Mizutani, Robert F. Myers, Hiroshi Nagano, Alf Jacob Nilsen (Bioquatic), Yasuhiro Morita Ogasawara, G. Ogawa, Dr. John E. Randall, Andre Seale, Roger Steene, Keoki Stender, Hiroshi Takeuchi, Hiroyuki Tanaka, Takamasa Tonozuka, Toshio Tsubota, Fenton Walsh, and Kiyoshi Yanagiba, who have helped to fill the gaps with their own magnificent photographs.

I can't fail to recognize my diving companions over the years. This list includes Mary Findlay, John Greenamyer, Joe and Melisa Hancock, Richard Harker, Larry Jackson, Phyllis Randall, David Salmanowitz, Ron and Midge Silver, Cameron Snow, and George Willoughby. I need to give special recognition to one of my favorite travel companions, Roger Steene. Not only has his company been good for lots of laughter and informative fish talk, my photographic skills have been honed as a result of his tutelage. I also want to extend a big thanks to my dive buddies and Coral Realm business partners, Terry Majewski and Terri Parson, for their support.

I am extremely appreciative of the work of my publishing team at Microcosm, especially my editor James Lawrence, as well as designer Linda Provost, and copy editors Emily Stetson and Louise Watson for the many months they have invested in this volume and their dedication to book publishing excellence. Thanks also to the folks at T.F.H. Publications, Inc., especially Glen Axelrod, for helping this effort come to fruition.

On a more personal level, I want to express sincere thanks to my family, especially my wonderful parents, Donna and Duane Michael, for encouraging my interest in the ocean's inhabitants and saltwater aquarium keeping. Thanks also to my New Zealand mum, Margaret, and to the late William Cairns for providing a friendly way station during our South Pacific expeditions, and for letting me use their compost pile as a post dissection repository for Carpet Shark remains. My sister Sandy Michael took me to my scuba classes before I was able to drive and my sister Suzie McDaniel and her husband Tommy provided a lab in their garage during my summer trips to the Gulf of Mexico.

My wife, Janine, has been a continuous inspiration throughout 28 years of nuptial bliss. She has not only encouraged me to travel to reef-fish-infested waters when we could not afford for both of us to go, she has also escorted me on many a trip (which sometimes meant living in very primitive conditions) and has contributed greatly to our marine life photo library. Thank you Janine for three decades of an amazing friendship!

I would also wish to express thanks to our Creator for the marvelous planet on which we dwell, and for the extraordinary creatures and natural wonders we marvel at and which demand our responsible stewardship.

Finally, along with ichthyophiles everywhere, I am forever indebted to Jack Randall and Gerald Allen for dedicating their lives to the study of coral reef fishes. Through their astonishing volume of scientific papers and books, they have both been been a constant inspiration over the many years that I was writing this text. Without their enormous contribution to the science of ichthyology, our knowledge about the taxonomy and ecology of this wonderful guild of fishes would be sorely lacking.

—*Scott W. Michael, Lincoln, Nebraska*

Larabicus quadrilineatus, Red Sea Cleaner Wrasse, one of a guild of labrids that picks parasites off compliant hosts, in this case a *Naso vlamingi*.

The Fishes

A SEA OF CHOICES AVAILABLE
TO MARINE AQUARISTS: SELECTING SPECIES WISELY
AND HOW TO USE THIS GUIDE

"Nothing is rich but the inexhaustible wealth of nature. She shows us only surfaces, but she is a million fathoms deep."
—Ralph Waldo Emerson

A CORAL REEF OR A MARINE AQUARIUM WITHOUT FISHES HAS BEEN likened to a garden without birds or butterflies—beautiful but lacking the flashing colors, the dynamics of movement, and the captivating behaviors that truly complete the scene.

While the gardener must rely on nature to provide the desirable avian and insect life, an aquarist has almost divine control over the fish species that populate his or her created piece of ocean. Given the astonishing diversity of choices available, with fishes from the far reaches of the tropical world, the aquarium keeper today can assemble groupings of marine species that provide endless hours of pleasure—or unhappy scenes of strife, territoriality, and unwanted predation.

Matching species in a marine aquarium is both science and art. Doing it well may take years of experimentation and reading, and it is far from uncommon for inexperienced or bewildered aquarists to select fishes that are inappropriate for one reason or another. The accounts that follow are intended to provide the aquarium keeper with a tool to better understand the groups and species available, to choose intelligently among them, and, once the choices have been made, to keep the fishes alive and well.

Cirrhilabrus lubbocki, Lubbock's Fairy Wrasse, exhibiting noctural coloration.

Cheilinus chlorourus, Floral Wrasse: large male displaying the canine-like teeth that are a prominent trait of the labridae and an anatomical advantage in being able to catch and crush mollusk and crustacean prey.

In these pages and the companion volumes in this series, the aquarist will find information about, and photographs of, the majority of coral reef fishes that can be encountered in the trade by aquarists and by divers exploring reefs around the world. This is not to say that all of these fishes are readily or constantly available. Some of the species covered rarely enter the ornamental marine fish trade, but they are included because they would make desirable aquarium specimens—or are of general interest to fishkeepers.

Others, as will be clear from the descriptions, are not suitable for home aquariums, even though they may frequently be offered for sale to marine hobbyists. While even experienced fishkeepers sometimes fall prey to the "must have" or "love at first sight" syndrome when encountering a new species that turns up in the local aquarium shop, uninformed purchases very often have unhappy endings.

The simple rule of thumb is to examine the care requirements of each species very carefully before seeking out or purchasing a particular fish. I have made every attempt to discourage aquarists from purchasing those species that do not fare well in captivity. Although things are improving, it is still possible to see innocent hobbyists heading home with fishes that have, for decades, defied the best efforts of experts—even professional public aquarists—to keep them alive. If you observe such species in your local aquarium store, please point them out to the management. It is critical that we police our own hobby.

An overview of the systematics, biology, behavioral ecology, and captive care of the group—whether it is a family, subfamily, or genus—is provided in each section. The reader is urged to examine these overviews before moving into the species accounts, as there is often important general information covering a family group that is not repeated for each and every species. In order to make information more readily available to the hobbyist or diver, the species accounts are broken down into the following divisions.

Scientific Name

This is the most current Latin name applied to the fish by the scientific community. The name is in the form of a binomial. The first name indicates the genus to which the fish belongs, while the second name is the species name. At first mention of a scientific name, the "author" is listed after it. This is the ichthyologist or naturalist who formally described the fish. If the name is in parentheses, it indicates that the species was originally placed in a different genus. For example, the Hispid Frogfish (*Antennarius hispidus*) (Bloch & Schneider, 1801) was originally placed in the genus *Lophius* by its describers, but has since been moved to the genus *Antennarius*.

Common Name

One or more common names are listed for each species. The first name provided is the name most frequently used in the authoritative checklists and field guides written by ichthyologists. It is the name we will use in this series. In many cases, the names used in the aquarium trade are not given as the preferred name. This is often because the trade name(s) are confusing and lend little insight into the systematics or relatedness of various species. For example, in the aquarium trade, the name "scooter blenny" is applied to members of the family Pinguipedidae and the family Callionymidae. Members of these two families are referred to as sand perches and dragonets by ichthyologists, while blennies belong to the family Blenniidae. In assigning the preferred common name to each species, I have attempted to steer away from such misnomers and toward names that will minimize confusion and bring science and hobby closer together. For example, the names used in ichthyological circles often incorporate the scientific name into the common name. For instance, *Dendrochirus biocellatus* is called the Twinspot Lionfish—*biocellatus* means "two ocelli" or "two spots"—hence the name Twinspot.

I believe that by using a common name that is derived from the scientific name, amateur aquarists, divers, and marine scientists can better communicate with one another. However, to make the book more user-friendly, I have tried to include most of the common names used in the aquarium hobby in the list of common names and in the index.

"In many cases, the names used in the aquarium trade are not given as the preferred name. This is often because the trade name(s) are confusing and lend little insight into the systematics or relatedness of various species. In assigning the preferred common name to each species, I have attempted to steer away from such misnomers and toward names that will minimize confusion and bring science and hobby closer together."

Bodianus rufus, Spanish Hogfish: in the process of ingesting a spiny mouthful of *Diadema* sea urchin. Many of the larger wrasses are fascinating aquarium subjects and will not touch live corals. Other invertebrates, however, are fair game, including mollusks (clams, mussels, snails), crustaceans (shrimps, lobsters, crabs), and echinoderms (sea urchins, brittle stars, sea stars).

Thalassoma rueppellii, Klunzinger's Wrasse (terminal male shown), is a colorful reef fish that, like others in the genus, can be very aggressive toward fish tankmates and make short work of motile invertebrate neighbors.

Maximum Length

This refers to the greatest length that an individual of that particular species can attain—or the longest ever reported—measuring from the end of the snout to the tip of the tail. In most cases, the length of a specimen will fall short of this measure, but the aquarist should always assume that his or her fish will reach a maximum length near to that presented. In some cases, the standard length (SL)—which is measured from the tip of the snout to the base of the caudal (tail) fin—may be given.

Range

The distribution of a fish is presented from its eastern, western, northern, and southern geographical limits. This information is of great value to those aquarists who want to set up a tank that represents a fish community from a specific geographical location. It may also provide clues to the environmental conditions to which a species is subjected (e.g., fishes from Easter Island will tolerate cooler water temperatures than species limited to coral reefs around the Philippines).

Biology

In this section, information is provided on the natural history of the fish. This includes details on the habitats and reef zones occupied by the fish, its depth range, food habits, feeding behavior, reproductive behavior, social organization, and any known relationships with other species. The information was compiled from scientific papers, fish guides, and personal observations.

Captive Care

This section includes specific husbandry requirements, food preferences, color fastness, how aggressive a species is toward conspecifics and heterospecifics, unusual habits, suitability of the species for the invertebrate aquarium, and captive breeding information, if available.

Aquarium Size

This is the minimum suitable aquarium size for an adult individual of the species. Of course, juveniles and adolescents can be housed in smaller tanks. Activity levels and behavior patterns of a particular species have been accounted for whenever possible. As this is the minimum suitable size, please note that providing as much room as possible will allow any fish to acclimate better and display less aggression toward its tankmates.

Temperature

This is the temperature range most suitable for the species. The data is based on captive observation and/or examination of the geographical distribution

Labroides dimidiatus, Bluestreak Cleaner Wrasse, preens a tailstanding parrotfish, whose pose signals that it is ready and willing to be approached and cleaned by the wrasse.

of the species. For example, a species that is found around Pitcairn Island can withstand lower water temperatures than a fish that is limited in its distribution to Micronesia. In many cases, the fish would survive at higher and lower water temperatures than recommended.

Aquarium Suitability Index

I have provided a number from 1 to 5 to give the reader some indication of the durability, hardiness, and/or adaptability of each species. Factors such as readiness to feed, dietary breadth, competitiveness, tolerance of sudden changes, and deteriorating conditions were taken into account when applying a captive suitability rating. A species typically loses one rating point on my scale if live food is usually required. The origin of an individual also influences its likelihood of survival in captivity. In some regions, the fishes being collected are handled with less care or are captured using chemicals. This makes them stressed and less likely to acclimate. Although fishes from the Philippines and Indonesia are most often considered "handicapped" because of the stress they are exposed to before being shipped, I have seen collectors and wholesalers in Florida who housed and handled fish with little regard for their long-term health. The following is a breakdown of the rating system:

1 These species are almost impossible to keep and should be left on the reef. These fishes may rarely feed, may be prone to disease, may be incurably shy, and, for one or more of these reasons, will almost always waste away and die in the home aquarium.

2 Most individuals of these species do not acclimate to the home aquarium, often refusing to feed and wasting away in captivity. However, the occasional individual may adapt if kept in optimal water conditions and housed on its own or with noncompetitive tankmates. These species are best left in the wild or ordered only by the experienced aquarist with the aptitude and willingness to devote the time and energy to maintaining them.

3 These species can be successfully kept, but special care may need to be provided if they are to thrive. This may include offering live food to induce a feeding response, keeping them with less competitive (and less aggressive) tankmates, and providing aquarium conditions that resemble those of their natural habitats. For some of these species, a lush growth of filamentous algae may also provide a natural source of food and increase the chances of their successful maintenance.

4 These species are durable, with most individuals acclimating to the home aquarium. Even so, they should not be exposed to dramatic changes in

Choerodon fasciatus, Harlequin Tuskfish: despite the prominent canine teeth, used to crush hardshelled invertebrate prey, this is a personable fish that fits well in communities of large, self-assured fishes.

environment or to poor water conditions. They will accept a wide range of commercially available foods. In the case of some fish or crustacean feeders, live food may either be required to induce feeding or may be the only type of food accepted. These fishes could be kept by aquarists with limited experience (e.g., 6 months).

5 These species are very hardy with almost all individuals readily acclimating to aquarium confines. They are undemanding and are more likely to withstand some neglect and deteriorating conditions. They will accept a wide range of commercially available fish foods and will not require live food to survive. These fish are great for the beginning hobbyist.

While these rankings are arbitrary, they are based on the collected experiences of hundreds of amateur and professional aquarists, marine biologists, aquarium trade importers, distributors, retailers, and others. (Readers with additional information—or contrary opinions—are invited to contact the author or publisher.)

Remarks

If sexual dimorphism and sexual dichromatism exist for the species, details are provided in this section. In addition, information on salient identifying characteristics and color variation is included. In some cases, morphological and chromatic differences between similar species and incorrect or obsolete scientific names often used in the aquarium literature are given—as well as interesting anecdotes about the species.

Wherever possible, at least one photograph is provided for each of the species accounts. In some cases, two or more photographs of the same fish are provided to show color differences between males and females or between adults and juveniles. Multiple photos may also be used to demonstrate the chromatic variability within a species. A complete listing of salient distinguishing characteristics and detailed descriptions of the color pattern is not included, but can be found in more technical reference works listed in the bibliography. Instead, photographs are provided to enable the hobbyist to make a correct identification.

Bodianus paraleucosticticus, Fivestripe Hogfish, with mouth agape, displaying to threaten a rival.

Scarus frenatus, Bridled Parrotfish: beautiful Red Sea specimen of a species best observed in the wild.

Cirrhilabrus roseafascia, Redstripe Fairy Wrasse, large male: a colorful threat display, with all fins erect and intense colors flashing.

One additional note: while the organization of these books follows standard taxonomic order, the reef-dwelling cartilaginous fishes, or elasmobranchs, are covered in *Aquarium Sharks & Rays* and the forthcoming *Reef Fishes Encyclopedia.*

Finally, I hope that this series will help the aquarist target the species that he or she finds most appealing and that are appropriate for his or her intended aquarium and tankmates. Just using one's buying power to bring home a fish without foresight and planning is something the thoughtful aquarist will want to avoid.

In the words of John Berry, "The bird of paradise alights only upon the hand that does not grasp." Simply acquiring fishes without studying their natural histories and biological requirements too often leads to problems for the animals and expensive and unhappy experiences for their owners—there are better ways of approaching and enjoying these wonderful works of nature.

GENERALIZED BONY FISH ANATOMY

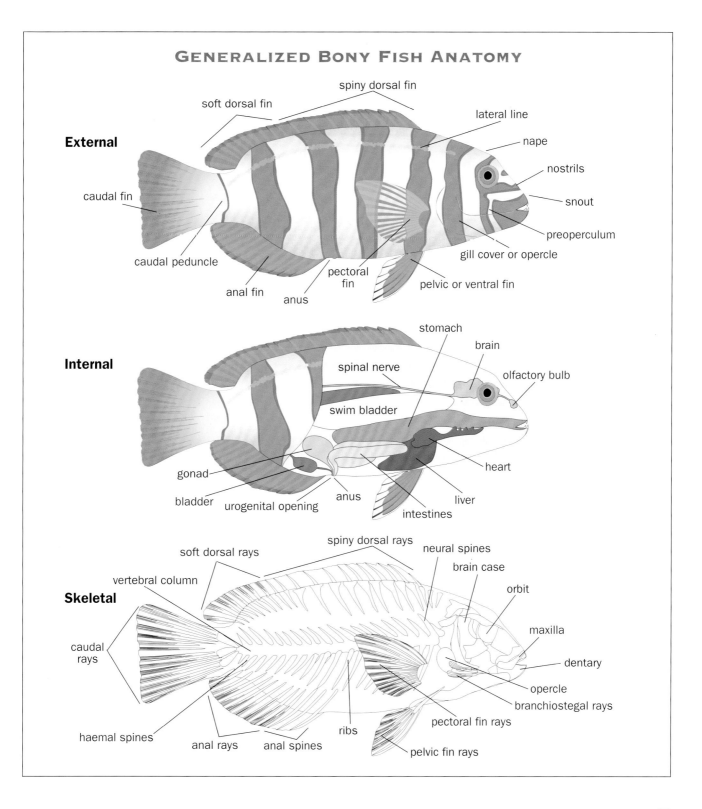

External

soft dorsal fin
spiny dorsal fin
lateral line
nape
nostrils
snout
preoperculum
gill cover or opercle
caudal fin
caudal peduncle
anal fin
anus
pectoral fin
pelvic or ventral fin

Internal

stomach
brain
spinal nerve
olfactory bulb
swim bladder
gonad
bladder
urogenital opening
anus
intestines
liver
heart

Skeletal

soft dorsal rays
spiny dorsal rays
neural spines
brain case
orbit
vertebral column
maxilla
caudal rays
dentary
opercle
branchiostegal rays
pectoral fin rays
haemal spines
anal rays
anal spines
ribs
pelvic fin rays

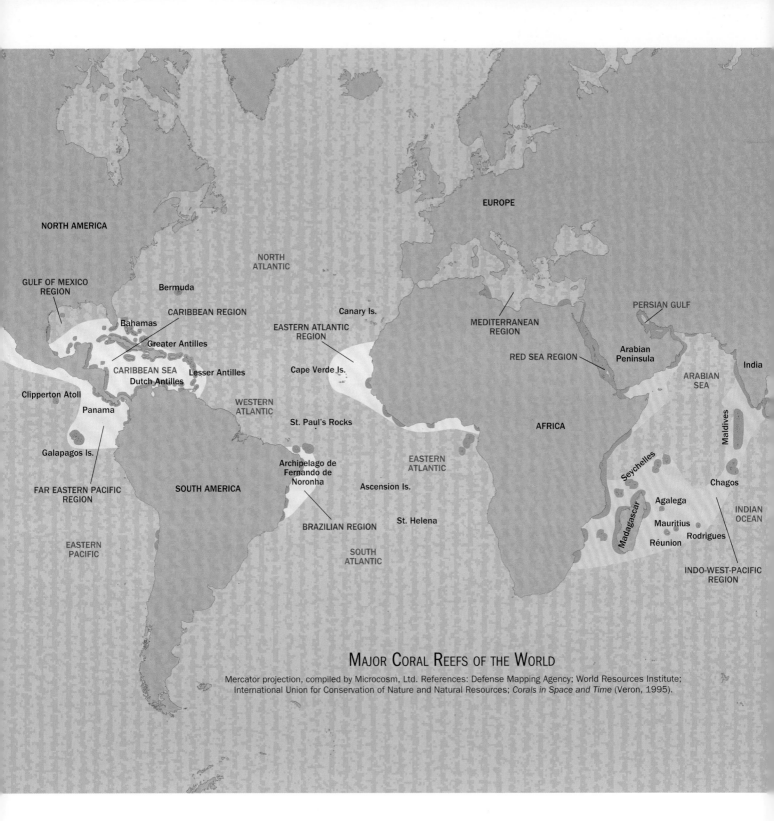

NORTH AMERICA

EUROPE

NORTH
ATLANTIC

GULF OF MEXICO
REGION

Bermuda

CARIBBEAN REGION

Canary Is.

PERSIAN GULF

Bahamas

MEDITERRANEAN
REGION

Greater Antilles

EASTERN ATLANTIC
REGION

RED SEA REGION

Arabian
Peninsula

India

CARIBBEAN SEA

Lesser Antilles

Cape Verde Is.

ARABIAN
SEA

Dutch Antilles

Clipperton Atoll

WESTERN
ATLANTIC

AFRICA

Maldives

Panama

St. Paul's Rocks

Galapagos Is.

Seychelles

Chagos

Archipelago de
Fernando de
Noronha

EASTERN
ATLANTIC

Agalega

INDIAN
OCEAN

FAR EASTERN PACIFIC
REGION

SOUTH AMERICA

Ascension Is.

Mauritius

Madagascar

Rodrigues

Réunion

EASTERN
PACIFIC

BRAZILIAN REGION

St. Helena

INDO-WEST-PACIFIC
REGION

SOUTH
ATLANTIC

MAJOR CORAL REEFS OF THE WORLD

Mercator projection, compiled by Microcosm, Ltd. References: Defense Mapping Agency; World Resources Institute;
International Union for Conservation of Nature and Natural Resources; *Corals in Space and Time* (Veron, 1995).

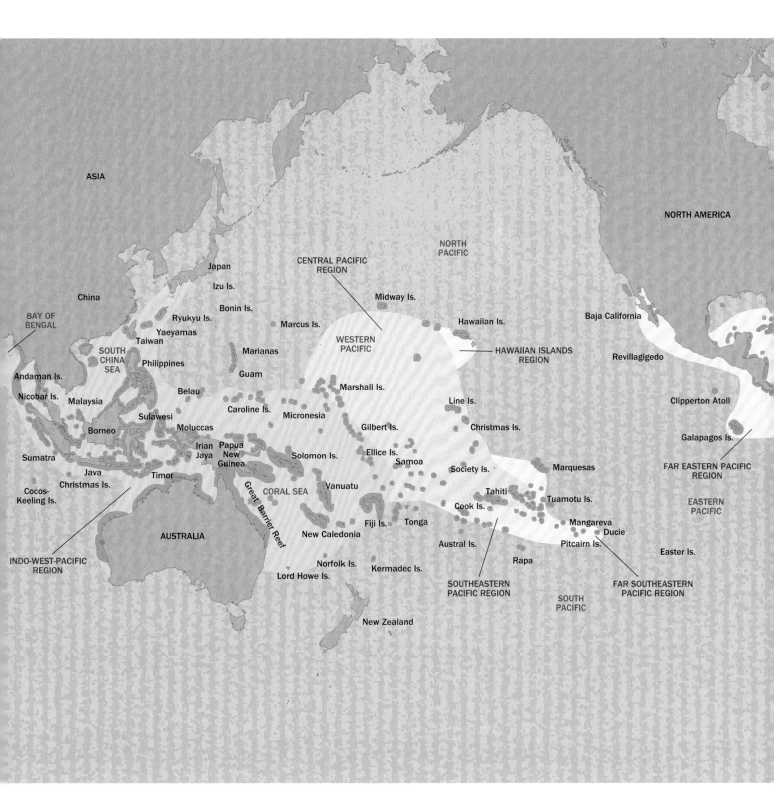

ASIA

NORTH AMERICA

NORTH
PACIFIC

CENTRAL PACIFIC
REGION

Japan

Izu Is.

Midway Is.

Hawaiian Is.

Baja California

China

Bonin Is.

BAY OF
BENGAL

Ryukyu Is.

Marcus Is.

WESTERN
PACIFIC

HAWAIIAN ISLANDS
REGION

Yaeyamas

Taiwan

SOUTH
CHINA
SEA

Philippines

Marianas

Revillagigedo

Andaman Is.

Belau

Guam

Line Is.

Clipperton Atoll

Nicobar Is.

Malaysia

Caroline Is.

Marshall Is.

Christmas Is.

Sulawesi

Micronesia

Galapagos Is.

Borneo

Moluccas

Gilbert Is.

Sumatra

Irian
Jaya

Papua
New
Guinea

Solomon Is.

Ellice Is.

Samoa

Society Is.

Marquesas

FAR EASTERN PACIFIC
REGION

Java

Christmas Is.

Timor

Vanuatu

Tahiti

Tuamotu Is.

EASTERN
PACIFIC

Cocos-
Keeling Is.

CORAL SEA

Cook Is.

Fiji Is.

Tonga

Mangareva
Ducie

AUSTRALIA

New Caledonia

Austral Is.

Pitcairn Is.

Easter Is.

Great Barrier Reef

Rapa

INDO-WEST-PACIFIC
REGION

Norfolk Is.

Kermadec Is.

SOUTHEASTERN
PACIFIC REGION

FAR SOUTHEASTERN
PACIFIC REGION

Lord Howe Is.

SOUTH
PACIFIC

New Zealand

THE FISHES COLLECTIVELY KNOWN AS LABRIDS ARE AN ASTON-ishing and diverse lot—they comprise the third largest family of marine fishes in the world, consisting of 68 genera and about 470 species, and are eclipsed only by the gobies (Gobiidae) and the sea basses (Serranidae). Consider that the Labridae range in size from the tiny Minute Wrasse (*Minilabrus striatus*, maximum length 6 cm [2.4 in.]) to the labrid behemoth, the Humphead Wrasse (*Cheilinus undulatus*, maximum length 229 cm [7.5 ft.]). The attributes that make these fishes attractive to aquarists and underwater naturalists alike are their brilliant colors, swimming styles, and piscine intelligence.

Many species can undergo remarkable color changes. Some do so to enhance crypsis or their ability to go undetected by predators. Others, such as members of the often flamboyant genera *Cirrhilabrus* and *Paracheilinus*, exhibit spectacular nuptial colors. Many wrasses exhibit dramatic color differences between females and males. Some have a particularly extraordinary "super male" (terminal) phase. Juveniles can also differ in color from the adults. The wrasses vary in shape from elongated to deep-bodied. Some are snub-nosed, others have very elongated snouts, and there are many species between these extremes. Most labrids have prominent canine teeth, giving some a buck-toothed appearance. Some have truncate caudal fins; in others the tail is lunate.

Wrasses are found in tropical, subtropical, and temperate seas, but most occur in tropical ecosystems. Over 80% of the species in the family are found in Indo-Pacific, with Australia boosting the greatest number of species (over 33% of the species and 70% of the genera are found in the warm to temperate waters of Australia). Most of the wrasses occur on shallow coral or rocky reefs. However, some genera, such as *Bodianus*, *Cirrhilabrus*, *Polylepion*, and *Decodon*, include members that frequent deep reef habitats (greater than 200 m [650 ft.]). Most species are found in tropical seas, although they are also well represented in

some subtropical and warm-temperate fish communities.

While some of the true reef beauties are wrasses, it is their behavior, not just their appearance, that have always attracted my attention as a diver and an aquarist.

Swimming Behavior

The wrasses engage in a swimming mode referred to as "labriform locomotion." Rather than using the caudal fin for forward locomotion, these fishes most often use their pectoral fins. (They may employ the caudal fin when they require a quick burst of speed.) In some species, the pectoral fins stroke in a rowing motion—forward and backward. In others, the fins are flapped up and down as if the fish were flying. The pectoral fin shape has been shown to be linked to the swimming mode and lifestyle of the labrid in question. Wainright et al. (2002) measured the aspect ratio (that is the ratio of the longer dimension to its shorter dimension) of the pectoral fins of 143 different wrasses on the Great Barrier Reef and found they ranged from 1.12 to 4.48. A high aspect pectoral fin tends to be long and tapered at the ends and is characteristic of wrasses that are very active and fast swimmers. This makes sense as this fin shape produces less drag. Wrasses that have pectoral fins with a high aspect ratio include many of the banana wrasses (*Thalassoma* spp.), which are often found in surge-prone reef zones, and the Creole Wrasse (*Clepticus parrae*), which feeds high in the water column and requires speed to evade piscivores. These species also tend to flap the pectoral fins when they swim, which also increases thrust and speed.

Those wrasses that employ more of a rowing motion when they swim (e.g., Slingjaw Wrasse [*Epibulus insidiator*] and the lined wrasses [*Pseudocheilinus* spp.]), are not as "fleet-of-fin." Instead, they tend to exhibit greater maneuverability and are better at accelerating from rest. The pectoral fins of these labrids tend to have a lower aspect ratio; that is, they are more broad and rounded. They also tend to spend more time near the substrate and feed on benthic prey. For example, the tubelip wrasses (*Labropsis* spp.) have large, more rounded pectoral fins, which enable these fish to perform subtle movements as they pluck polyps from stony coral colonies or clean ectoparasites from other fishes (which they do as juveniles). While there are labrid examples from both ends of the continuum, many wrasses employ a combination of the two types of pectoral fin swimming motions, depending on their cir-

Pteragogus enneacanthus, Cockerel Wrasse: one of almost 500 known species in the family Labridae, this is an unusual and fascinating aquarium fish that often associates with soft corals, such as the *Xenia* shown here, in the wild. As with most wrasses, it is entirely safe with sea anemones and captive corals of all types, making a good candidate for the reef aquarium. Like many wrasses, it will target various motile invertebrates that constitute its natural diet: crustaceans, mollusks, and various worms.

Cirrhilabrus rubrimarginatus, Redmargined Fairy Wrasse, male: all wrasses use their pectoral fins as a primary source of propulsion, but the *Cirrhilabrus* species also undulate the rear edge of the dorsal fin.

cumstances, and have pectoral fins that exhibit pectoral fin aspect ratios that fall somewhere between the two extremes.

Food Habits and Feeding Behavior

The wrasses are important components of coral reef communities. There are labrids that feed on almost every type of reef organism. Most labrids are opportunistic carnivores, feeding on a wide range of invertebrate prey items, but some are highly specialized, like the parasite-picking genera (e.g., *Labroides*) or those species that eat only stony coral polyps (e.g., *Labrichthys*, *Labropsis*, and *Diprocta-canthus*). A number of genera have enlarged molariform teeth in the upper and lower pharynxes (referred to as the "pharyngeal jaws") that are used to crush hard-shelled invertebrates. The leop-

ard wrasses (genus *Macropharyngodon*) use their oversized pharyngeal dentition to crush small snails. There are also labrids that make their living by snatching zooplankton from the water column (e.g., *Cirrhilabrus*, *Paracheilinus*, and *Pseudocoris*). Several genera include specialized piscivores that feed heavily on smaller fishes. Species in the genus *Hologymnosus* and *Cheilio* are arrow-like in form and can initiate fast swimming bursts to pick off unsuspecting piscine prey. Some tropical labrids do ingest plant material, but most do so incidentally—they do not target plant material like their cousins the parrotfishes (family Scaridae).

Labrids employ a variety of different hunting strategies. When it comes to food, wrasses seem to learn very quickly. Some labrids have learned to engage in what has even been described as

TABLE I

SUBORDER LABROIDEI Bleeker, 1859
Family LABRIDAE Cuvier, 1816 (68 genera: ~ 470 species)

Genus *Acantholabrus* (1 species)
Genus *Achoerodus* (2 species)
Genus *Ammolabrus* (1 species)
Genus *Anampses* (13 species)
Genus *Anchichoerops* (1 species)
Genus *Austrolabrus* (1 species)
Genus *Bodianus* (39 species)
Genus *Centrolabras* (3 species)
Genus *Cheilinus* (8 species)
Genus *Cheilio* (1 species)
Genus *Choerodon* (25 species)
Genus *Cirrhilabrus* (44 species)
Genus *Clepticus* (3 species)
Genus *Conniella* (1 species)
Genus *Coris* (26 or 27 species)
Genus *Ctenolabrus* (1 species)
Genus *Cymolutes* (3 species)
Genus *Decodon* (4 species)
Genus *Diproctacanthus* (1 species)
Genus *Doratonotus* (1 species)
Genus *Dotalabrus* (2 species)
Genus *Epibulus* (2 species)
Genus *Eupetrichthys* (1 species)
Genus *Frontilabrus* (1 species)
Genus *Gomphosus* (2 species)
Genus *Halichoeres* (~ 75 species)
Genus *Hemigymnus* (3 species)
Genus *Hologymnosus* (4 species)
Genus *Iniistius* (7 species)
Genus *Labrichthys* (1 species)
Genus *Labroides* (5 species)
Genus *Labropsis* (6 species)
Genus *Labrus* (5 species)
Genus *Lachnolaimus* (1 species)
Genus *Lappanella* (2 species)
Genus *Larabicus* (1 species)
Genus *Leptojulis* (5 species)
Genus *Macropharyngodon* (10 species)
Genus *Malapterus* (1 species)
Genus *Minilabrus* (1 species)
Genus *Nelabrichthys* (1 species)

Genus *Notolabrus* (7 species)
Genus *Novaculichthys* (6 species)
Genus *Ophthalmolepis* (1 species)
Genus *Oxycheilinus* (12 species)
Genus *Oxyjulis* (1 species)
Genus *Paracheilinus* (13 species)
Genus *Parajulis* (1 species)
Genus *Pictilabrus* (3 species)
Genus *Polylepion* (2 species)
Genus *Pseudocheilinops* (1 species)
Genus *Pseudocheilinus* (7 species)
Genus *Pseudocoris* (6 species)
Genus *Pseudodax* (1 species)
Genus *Pseudojuloides* (13 species)
Genus *Pseudolabrus* (11 species)
Genus *Pteragogus* (8 species)
Genus *Semicossyphus* (3 species)
Genus *Stethojulis* (10 species)
Genus *Suezichthys* (11 species)
Genus *Symphodus* (10 species)
Genus *Tautoga* (1 species)
Genus *Tautogolabrus* (1 species)
Genus *Terelabrus* (1 species)
Genus *Thalassoma* (28 species)
Genus *Wetmorella* (3 species)
Genus *Xenojulis* (1 species)
Genus *Xiphocheilus* (1 species)
Genus *Xyrichtys* (25 species)

A note on the taxonomy of the labrids in this book: There are likely to be a number of changes in wrasse taxonomy in the future, especially in the larger genera (e.g., *Coris*, *Halichoeres*). For example, molecular studies indicate that the genus *Halichoeres* should be broken down into several different genera. As more and more DNA studies of reef fishes are done, established taxonomic groups are certain to go through a period of upheaval, but what is shown here is the best we know at this point in time.

Leptojulis chrysotaenia, Ochreband Wrasse: juveniles often associate with sea anemones.

Epibulus insidiator, Slingjaw Wrasse: protrusible jaws allow specialized feeding behaviors.

Paracheilinus filamentosus, Filamented Flasher Wrasse: flamboyant displays for rivals and mates.

Bodianus bimaculatus, Twinspot Hogfish, juvenile: this and other hogfishes may serve as facultative cleaners of other fishes on the reef and in the aquarium.

Oxycheilinus diagrammus, Cheeklined Maori Wrasse, male: facial markings are suggestive of the traditional tattoos of New Zealand's Maori people.

tool use. These species will grab food items that are too large to swallow whole (e.g., scallops, crabs, sea urchins) and use a piece of hard substrate as an anvil to bash the prey into bite-sized morsels. Some labrids will follow octopuses and fish species that disturb the substrate when feeding. These hunting fishes, referred to as "nuclear species," often flush out potential prey, which the labrids then pounce upon. It has been demonstrated that when wrasses follow substrate-disturbers, they tend to enjoy greater rates of prey capture than they do when they hunt on their own. Some wrasses will even defend a nuclear species from conspecifics or displace fishes following them. For example, large Mexican Hogfish (*Bodianus diplotaenia*) will chase smaller individuals away from nuclear species and take their place.

A few of the wrasses engage in the fascinating foraging behavior known as "hunting by riding." This includes the Cigar Wrasse (*Cheilio inermis*) and the Bandcheek Maori Wrasse (*Oxycheilinus diagrammus*). These species will use feeding herbivores as moving blinds so they can more readily get into striking range. The Slingjaw Wrasse (*Epibulus insidiator*) will also swim with schooling fish in order to catch unwary prey. The Bandcheek Maori and Slingjaw Wrasses may also be aggressive mimics, resembling omnivores or herbivores in order to dupe would-be prey. Some wrasses cooperate with other fish species, especially goatfishes, when hunting. The Slingjaw Wrasse, certain Maori wrasses (*Oxycheilinus* spp.) and the Indian Bird Wrasse (*Gomphosus caeruleus*) regularly hunt with the Yellowsaddle Goatfish (*Parupeneus cyclostomus*). The goatfish will hang just under the wrasse's belly as they swim along. When they come to good hunting grounds they begin probing crevices for food, perhaps going in opposite directions around a coral head to flush prey into each other's paths.

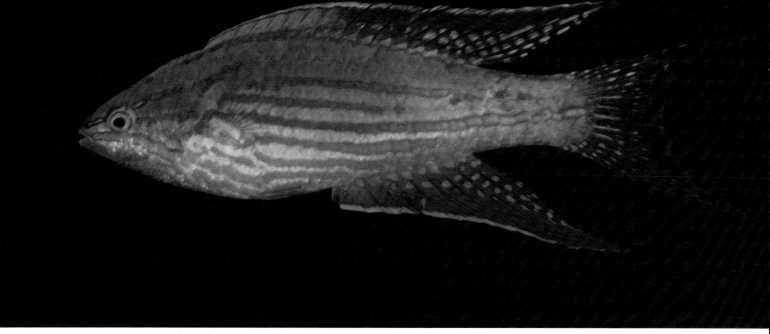

Paracheilinus angulatus, Sharpfinned Flasher Wrasse, male: many of the smaller planktivore wrasses are ideal, reef-safe aquarium species.

Antipredation Strategies

The wrasses employ a variety of different strategies to avoid being eaten. Some species exhibit effective camouflage; some of these live in seagrass beds and are bright green in color so that they resemble the plant material. The razorfishes dive, head first, underneath the sand or mud and can even "swim" from one location to another while buried. Many wrasse species bury under the sand at night, while others take refuge in reef crevices. Some of these species (e.g., *Cirrhilabrus* spp.) exude a mucus envelope, which may serve to trap stimuli that could attract nocturnal predators. When feeding in the water column, certain zooplankton-feeding wrasses form groups for protection.

The anemonefishes are well known for their habit of living among the tentacles of certain sea anemones. But there are also some wrasses that associate with sea anemones, possibly exploiting them as a protective harbor. These wrasses may hang over a sea anemone, rarely if ever making contact with the cnidarians' stinging tentacles. There are, however, some labrids that will actually rub against or hide among the tentacles. Labrids have been observed contacting the tentacles of *Condylactis gigantea*, *Entacmaea quadricolor*, *Heteractis magnifica*, and *Macrodactyla doreensis*.

The Bluehead Wrasse (*Thalassoma bifasciatum*), a ubiquitous member of tropical Western Atlantic reef fish communities, often refuges among the tentacles of the Giant Anemone. It carefully maneuvers between the tentacles or lies on the nematocyst (stinging cell) free oral disc. This is particularly true of the juveniles and initial phase individuals. There are also a number of Indo-Pacific wrasses that deftly move among and over the tentacles of sea anemones.

While the sea anemone may serve as a source of protection

Thalassoma amylycephalum juvenile with Heteractis magnifica.

Some wrasses known to associate with sea anemones in the wild.

Species	Life Stage	Sea Anemone
Twinspot Maori Wrasse (*Cheilinus bimaculatus*)	J, A	2
Pastel Green Wrasse (*Halichoeres chloropterus*)	J, IP	4
Checkerboard Wrasse (*Halichoeres hortulanus*)	J	3
Yellowhead Wrasse (*Halichoeres garnoti*)	J	5
Hartzfeld's Wrasse (*Halichoeres hartzfeldii*)	J	4
Green Razorfish (*Xyrichtys splendens*)	J	5
Pearly Razorfish (*Xyrichtys novacula*)	J	5
Sixline Wrasse (*Pseudocheilinus hexataenia*)	J, A	2
Flasher Wrasse (*Paracheilinus* sp.)	J	4
Blunthead Wrasse (juvenile above) (*Thalassoma amblycephalum*)	IP	1, 3
Bluehead Wrasse (*Thalassoma bifasciatum*)	IP	5
Moon Wrasse (*Thalassoma lunare*)	J, IP	3

Life Stage: J = juveniles; A = adults; IP = initial phase

Key to Sea Anemones:
1. Bubbletip Sea Anemone (*Entacmaea quadricolor*)
2. Leathery or Sebae Sea Anemone (*Heteractis crispa*)
3. Magnificent Sea Anemone (*Heteractis magnifica*)
4. Corkscrew Tentacle Sea Anemone (*Macrodactyla doreensis*)
5. Giant, Pinktipped or Condylactis Sea Anemone (*Condylactis gigantea*)

for these labrids, there may be other reasons that wrasses associate with anemones. According to a study conducted by Arvedlund et al. (2005), the Blunthead Wrasse (*Thalassoma amblycephalum*) actually utilizes the sea anemone as a food source rather than a refuge. Individual *T. amblycephalum*, ranging in size from 1.5 to 3.0 cm (in.) and in groups of 3 to 10 individuals, were recorded by these researchers in both *E. quadricolor* and *H. magnifica* off of southern Japan. These wrasses shared their sea anemones with anemonefish (i.e., Tomato Anemonefish [*Amphiprion frenatus*] and Ocellaris Clownfish [*A. ocellaris*]). Arveduland et al. found that when threatened, these wrasses would take refuge in nearby coral thickets, not in the sea anemone. They watched the fish pick at the tips of the anemone's tentacles and concluded that they were actually feeding on mucus and necrotic tissue. They may also pick zooplankton from the sea anemone's mucus. These researchers found that *T. amblycephalum* is protected from the stinging cells of *E. quadricolor*, but not the other sea anemones.

There are many wrasses that exhibit color patterns that may serve to confuse potential predators. A number of labrids have ocelli, or eyespots, on their fins or bodies. These consist of a dark spot that may or may not be trimmed with white. These eyespots apparently serve an antipredation function. For example, in some species the ocelli may serve to dupe would-be predators into attacking less vulnerable portions of the body. In order to incapacitate their prey, most predators strike the head of their quarry, cueing in on the prey species eyes. Many of the eyespot-bearing species have this chromatic ornamentation near the rear edge of the dorsal fin or on or near the tail, while the eye itself is disguised by obliterative eye markings (e.g., *Anampses neoguinaicus*, *A. meleagrides*, *Pseudocheilinus ocellatus*, *Wetmorella* spp.). There is a greater interorbital distance between the eyes of a piscivore—a characteristic fishes use to distinguish a fish-eater from sessile invertebrate predator or herbivore. A number of fishes appear to take advantage of this. These species have two ocelli on each side of the body that are separated by a distance similar to the interorbital distance observed in many piscivores. When these fishes are observed from the side, the position of the eyespots resembles the "head-on" perspective of a larger predator. This may act to deter predators thinking about eating the ocelli-laden fish.

There are many wrasses that have cryptic attire that helps them blend with their surroundings. Some of these species can rapidly change their color based on the hue of their habitat or their mood. Some species show those chromatic shift to avoid being seen by predators (e.g., *Pteragogus*); others do it to remain concealed from potential prey (e.g., *Oxycheilinus*). Still others change color to make themselves more conspicuous to females (e.g., *Paracheilinus*).

Pseudocheilinus ocellatus, Whitebarred Wrasse: one of a number of deep-water wrasses only recently described by ichthyologists, and prized by aquarists.

Pseudocheilinus hexataenia, Sixline Wrasse, like a number of labrids, occasionally picks parasites, slime, and scales from willing neighbors.

Reproduction

All are the labrids are protogynous hermaphrodites—that is, they change sex from female to male. Many exhibit diandric development, where there are two types of males: the initial (primary) phase (IP) and terminal (secondary) phase (TP). Initial phase individuals are either females or males; individuals that hatch and develop as males are referred to as primary males. Terminal phase fish are males that result from female sex change (secondary males) or, more often, from the transformation of an IP male. There are also species that are monandric—that is, only secondary males are present. Examples of monandric species include the *Labroides*, some of the *Halichoeres* spp., and at least some *Xyrichtys* spp. Sex change, in at least some species, is socially controlled, with dominant males suppressing sexual transformation. At least some species (e.g., *Cirrhilabrus* spp.) are capable of bi-directional ("both-ways") sex change. That is, a female that has transformed into a male can change back into a female in certain social situa-tions. All the tropical wrasses produce pelagic eggs that are shed and drift freely in the water column, sometimes for long distances. There are a few temperate-water species that are demersal spawners, creating nests on the substrate.

As far as wrasse mating systems are concerned, some are promiscuous and nonharemic. Some of these species spawn in groups. In other species, a male defends a large territory that includes the smaller territories of the females in its harem. These wrasses typically spawn in pairs. Other wrasse species exhibit no territorial defense, even during the spawning period.

Captive Care

Because they exhibit so much diversity in their sizes and biological strategies, the husbandry of the labrids varies greatly from one genus to another. Detailed care information for the genera discussed will be found in the following pages. I have limited my coverage to the genera found in tropical oceans, as the temperate

Wrasses to Avoid: Species to Keep Away from Your Reef

While many wrasses are well suited to a fish-only home aquarium, some are not appropriate for all reef aquarium venues. The "bad reef wrasses" have one or more of the following characteristics: they are difficult to keep alive, they are large and active, they are debris-flippers, or they have catholic diets that include many of the ornamental invertebrates that reef keepers consider desirable.

At right is a chart listing some wrasse genera that are best avoided by reef aquarists. There are always exceptions to the rule, and if an aquarist is willing to make allowances or aquarium modifications for some of these species, there are a number that can be kept with sessile invertebrates.

A. These species are more difficult to keep alive in the home aquarium. They are often poor shippers that don't bounce back after spending many hours or days in a shipping bag. Some survive the rigors of shipping but have a difficult time switching to normal aquarium foods. Many do better in reef tanks because of the presence of natural fare (shelled protozoa, minute worms, and crustaceans) associated with the live rock and sand. Even in a reef tank, these wrasses have poor track records.

B. These wrasses are too large and active for most reef aquariums, which are usually filled with live rock and corals that limit the unobstructed swimming space needed by fishes that "pace" or constantly swim around the tank. Some reefkeepers have huge tanks with plenty of swimming space for these species, but most home aquarists' tanks are smaller than 200 gallons. Unless you have an extra-large tank or design one specifically for active species, you should avoid the larger, more active wrasses.

C. These wrasses will take pieces of rubble, rock, or debris in their mouths, lift them up, and flip them over to expose hidden prey. Others will simply push these items over with the side of the head. This is fascinating to watch, but it can cause problems because unattached corals may get knocked over or flipped, resulting in mechanical damage to the polyps. If you plan to add a known coral-flipping wrasse, make sure you first firmly affix stony corals to the reef structure using an underwater epoxy or putty. Also, avoid keeping bottom-dwelling, solitary polyps like slipper and plate corals, as these wrasses are likely to flip them over. Smaller pieces of live rock, placed near the top of the aquascaping, can be problematic too: the wrasse may move these pieces and send them tumbling down on the corals below. Keep in mind that the larger the wrasse, the larger the pieces of coral or rock it can effectively overturn.

D. These wrasses are a threat to a wide range of ornamental invertebrates. While few labrids prey upon stony or soft coral polyps, many eat a variety of noncoralline inverts. For these species, the reef tank can be a veritable smorgasbord. Some, especially those that attain larger sizes, will consume almost any motile invertebrates (e.g., snails, worms, sea stars, brittle stars, sea urchins), and some will even eat tridacnid clams. Even smaller species may make short work of ornamental crustaceans.

CAUTION: Be wary of these Wrasses

GENUS	HUSBANDRY CONCERN
Tamarin Wrasses (Genus *Anampses*)	A
Hogfishes (Genus *Bodianus*)	B, D
Maori Wrasses (Genus *Cheilinus* and *Oxycheilinus*)	B, D
Tuskfishes (Genus *Choerodon*)	B, C, D
Coris Wrasses (Genus *Coris*)	B, C, D
Razor Wrasses (Genus *Cymolutes* and *Iniistius*)	B, D
Slingjaw Wrasses (Genus *Epibulus*)	B, D
Bird Wrasses (Genus *Gomphosus*)	D
Thicklip Wrasses (Genus *Hemigymnus*)	B, D
Ring Wrasses (Genus *Hologymnosus*)	B, D
Cleaner Wrasses (Genus *Labroides*)	A
Tubelip Wrasses (Genus *Labropsis*)	A
Leopard Wrasses (Genus *Macropharyngodon*)	A
Rockmover Wrasses (Genus *Novaculichthys*)	B, C, D
Pencil Wrasses (Genus *Pseudojuloides*)	A
Belted Wrasses (Genus *Stethojulis*)	A
Banana Wrasses (Genus *Thalassoma*)	B, D

Juvenile Vermiculate Leopard Wrasse, *Macropharyngodon bipartitus*.

Wrasse Compatibility

KEY: ● = Low risk ■ = Moderate risk ▼ = High risk **F** = Facultative cleaner, usually as juvenile **O** = Obligatory cleaner

WRASSE GENERA	Stony Corals	Soft Corals	Clams	Snails	Tube Worms	Shrimps	Crabs	Sea Cucumbers	Sea Urchins	Serpent Stars	Sea Stars	Small Fish	Parasite Picker?
Tamarin Wrasse (*Anampses*)	●	●	●	■	■	■	■	●	●	●	●	●	
Hogfishes (*Bodianus*)	●	●	■	■	■	▼	▼	■	■	■	■	■	✔ F
Maori Wrasse (*Cheilinus*)	●	●	■	■	■	▼	▼	■	■	■	■	■	
Pencil Wrasse (*Cheilio*)	●	●	●	●	●	▼	▼	●	●	●	●	▼	
Tuskfishes (*Choerodon*) ✳	■	■	■	■	■	▼	▼	■	■	■	■	■	
Fairy Wrasses (*Cirrhilabrus*)	●	●	●	●	●	●	●	●	●	●	●	●	
Creole Wrasses (*Clepticus*)	●	●	●	●	●	●	●	●	●	●	●	●	
Coris Wrasses (*Coris*) ✳	■	■	■	■	▼	▼	▼	■	■	■	■	■	✔ F
Knifefish (*Cymolutes*)	●	●	●	■	■	▼	▼	●	●	●	●	●	
Slingjaw Wrasses (*Epibulus*)	●	●	●	●	●	●	▼	●	●	●	●	▼	
Bird Wrasse (*Gomphosus*)	●	●	■	●	■	▼	▼	●	●	●	●	●	
Halichoeres Wrasses (*Halichoeres*)	●	●	■	■	■	■	■	■	■	■	■	■	✔ F
Thicklip Wrasses (*Hemigymnus*)	●	●	■	●	■	■	■	■	■	■	■	■	
Ring Wrasses (*Hologymnosus*) ✳	■	■	■	■	■	▼	▼	●	●	●	●	▼	
Razorfishes (*Iniistius*)	●	●	●	●	●	●	●	■	●	●	●	●	
Cleaner Wrasses (*Labroides*)	●	●	■	●	●	●	●	●	●	●	●	●	✔ O
Tubelip Wrasses (*Labropsis*)	▼	●	■	●	●	●	●	●	●	●	●	●	✔ F
Red Sea Cleaner Wrasse (*Larabicus*)	▼	●	■	●	●	●	●	●	●	●	●	●	✔ F
Leopard Wrasses (*Macropharyngodon*)	●	●	●	●	●	■	■	●	●	●	●	●	
Rockmover Wrasses (*Novaculichthys*) ✳	■	■	■	■	■	▼	▼	■	■	■	■	▼	
Slender Maori Wrasse (*Oxycheilinus*)	●	●	●	●	●	▼	▼	●	●	●	●	▼	
Flasher Wrasses (*Paracheilinus*)	●	●	●	●	●	●	●	●	●	●	●	●	
Lined Wrasses (*Pseudocheilinus*)	●	●	●	●	●	■	■	●	●	●	●	●	✔ F
False Corises (*Pseudocoris*)	●	●	●	●	●	■	●	●	●	●	●	●	
Chiseltooth Wrasse (*Pseudodax*)	●	●	●	●	●	●	●	●	●	●	■	●	✔ F
Pencil Wrasse (*Pseudojuloides*)	●	●	●	●	■	■	●	●	●	●	●	●	
Secretive Wrasse (*Pteragogus*)	●	●	●	●	■	▼	●	●	●	●	●	▼	
Ribbon Wrasses (*Stethojulis*)	●	●	●	●	■	■	■	●	●	●	●	●	
Banana Wrasses (*Thalassoma*)	●	●	■	■	■	▼	▼	■	■	●	■	▼	✔ F
Razorfishes (*Xyrichtys*)	●	●	●	■	■	▼	■	●	●	■	■	■	
Possum Wrasse (*Wetmorella*)	●	●	●	●	●	■	●	●	●	●	●	●	

✳ These wrasses may turn over or topple corals as they search for food

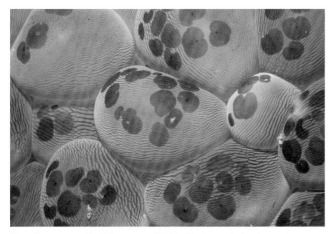

Planaria sp., parasitic flatworms on Bubble Coral: can decimate corals.

Halichoeres marginatus, Dusky Wrasse: known predator of flatworms.

Pyramidellid snails: notorious parasites that attack Tridacnid clams.

Pseudocheilinus hexataenia, Sixline Wrasse: will eat pyramidellid snails.

Aeolid nudibranch that can invade reef aquariums, attacking corals.

Thalassoma duperrey, Saddle Wrasse: will hunt *Montipora*-eating nudibranchs.

Bodianus loxozonus, Blackfin Hogfish, feeding on brittle star: larger wrasses, including many of *Bodianus* spp., cannot be trusted with motile invertebrates.

water species are rarely, if ever, seen in the aquarium trade. Because this family is so diverse, I strongly urge you do your research before purchasing a wrasse. Some get very large, have specialized diets, or can be quite aggressive and/or predatory. Many others are among the very best of aquarium fishes. Select carefully. I have included a sidebar with information on those genera that are not well suited to the reef aquarium, as well as a quick reference chart that deals with the compatibility of the more popular labrid genera and various invertebrate groups.

Feeding Wrasses

As mentioned above, all of the wrasses are carnivorous (some incidentally ingest algae), and most are fairly generalized in their dietary preferences. Most feed on a variety of motile invertebrates. Some could be classified as microcarnivores, while others feed on relatively large prey. What a wrasse eats is only constrained by the size of its jaws, both the mandible/maxilla and pharyngeal jaws (at least in those species that possess a set of pharyngeal teeth), and the crushing power of the latter.

All this is good news for the potential wrasse-keeper and potentially bad news for the aquarist who wants to house his or her wrasse with invertebrates. Labrids will usually eat the aquarium foods most of us have ready access to. Microcarnivores will readily accept meaty frozen foods, like brine shrimp, mysid shrimp, minced table shrimp, and frozen preparations for either carnivores or herbivores. Smaller zooplankton-feeding wrasses will even eat frozen *Cyclops*. Those wrasses that fall into the macrocarnivore category will suck down pieces of fresh or frozen seafood,

frozen preparations, and live crustaceans (e.g., fiddler crabs, ghost shrimp) or feeder fish.

It is important to include color enhancers in the diet of all wrasses, as there colors may fade somewhat if the diet breadth is limited. Smaller wrasses may ingest pigment-laced flake foods and frozen *Cyclops*, while larger labrids may eat pieces of salmon and carotenoid-rich crustacean exoskeletons and flesh. While they are not herbivores, wrasses will sometimes browse on freeze-dried algae sheets attached to the side of the aquarium. I have even seen fairy wrasses consume large quantities of this plant material. It is hard to know how many nutrients they extract from these algae sheets, as they do not have an alimentary tract that is adapted to a herbivorous diet.

Wrasses are often described as "active" fishes. That equates to a higher metabolic needs, which means they need to be fed often. Most wrasses should be fed at least twice a day. There are some less active species, that I would define as "lurkers," like the *Cheilinus*, *Oxycheilinus*, *Pteragogus*, and *Wetmorella*, that can be fed less frequently. There are some species that are hyperactive that should be fed at least three times a day. Many of these are zooplankton-feeders (e.g., *Cirrhilabrus*, *Paracheilinus*, *Pseudocoris*) that swim about in the water column or actively move over a large home range or territory looking for prey or following other fish that disturb the substrate and flush out potential food (e.g., *Halichoeres*, *Thalassoma*). If the aquarium contains some natural fodder, food additions will not need to be made as often. Of course, if you are feeding frequently, it is a good idea to have a efficacious protein skimmer to help maintain good water quality.

There have been suggestions made that a wrasse that feeds on microcrustaceans and worms may be detrimental to the tank—that by decimating populations of these invertebrates, labrids will encourage algae growth. But there are plenty of macro-herbivores (larger snails, hermit crabs, conchs) and detritivores that are not threatened by smaller wrasses that can help control algae growth. If you are keeping dragonets (Mandarin Dragonet [*Synchiropus splendidus*]) or other fishes that need a healthy population of small crustaceans to feed on to remain healthy, do not add a wrasse to the tank as they will out compete and possibly reduce natural prey levels to a point where these fishes will not get enough to eat. Larger wrasses are prone to decimate worm, crustacean, and even mollusk populations.

Utility Wrasses

While there are some labrids that are best left out of the reef aquarium (see sidebar on page 41 and the table on page 42), there are others that can perform a valuable function in the invertebrate aquarium. Tridacnid clams are cherished reef aquarium inhabitants that are occasionally parasitized by small snails of the family Pyramidellidae. This tiny gastropod (it rarely exceeds 10 mm in length) thrusts its elongate proboscis into the clam's mantle and feeds on its body fluids. It readily reproduces in captivity and can become a serious problem in a reef tank very quickly. Symptoms of pyramidellid infestation include mantle bleaching, gaping behavior (where the clam extends the valves too far open), mantle not fully extended or retracted, and death. These snails can be manually removed or they can be controlled by biological means. Some of the best snail exterminators are wrasses. The Six-line Wrasse (*Pseudocheilinus hexataenia*) and the Fourline Wrasse (*P. tetrataenia*) feed on these snails, as do many members of the genus *Halichoeres* (e.g., Golden Wrasse, *H. chrysus*, Tailspot Wrasse, *H. melanurus*), juvenile *Hologymnosus* spp., and adult leopard wrasses (*Macropharyngodon* spp.). There are no doubt others that will eat these small snails, too. Unfortunately, these snails usually hide during the day and come out to feed at night. Because of their nocturnal habits, they often avoid predatory wrasses. Therefore, manual removal, as well as help from wrasses, may be necessary to control their numbers.

Flatworms are another potential pest that labrids can help control. Flatworms can be innocuous, causing no harm to corals, while others are parasitic. The Acoel flatworms, which are regularly seen on mushroom anemones, soft corals, and large-polyped stony corals, are reported to graze on minute crustaceans, algae, and detritus that adheres to the mucus of these cnidarians. When in small numbers, they do not appear to harm their host, but severe infestations can interfere with the photosynthetic activity of the corals they infest. Wrasses that are known to feed on flatworms include Tamarin wrasses (*Anampses*), Halichoeres wrasses

Halichoeres garnoti, Yellowhead Wrasse, juvenile eating unidentified crustacean: many of the labrids will consume both desirable and undesirable invertebrates.

Cheilinus rhodochrous, Thickstripe Maori Wrasse: certain wrasses are more streamlined and better equipped to pursue fast-moving prey, like small fishes.

(*Halichoeres* spp.), leopard wrasses (*Macropharyngodon* spp.), and lined wrasses (*Pseudocheilinus* spp.). Do not expect any of these fishes to decimate a major flatworm infestation. It is best to place them in the tank before flatworms become a problem.

While not as effective as some of the larger goby species, there are a number of wrasses that disturb the substrate when they feed or refuge. Their behavior disturbs the substrate and puts accumulated detritus in suspension. Free-floating particles of feces, uneaten food, and associated bacteria can then by removed from the tank by external, mechanical filters. When feeding, some wrasses displace sediment to expose infaunal prey. For example, there are tuskfishes that employ a series of interesting behaviors

to dig up infaunal worms, mollusks, and crustaceans. They will flip over large pieces of coral rubble and then lay flat on its side where the rubble had been. They then vigorously fan the substrate with their pectoral fins to uncover buried prey. Other wrasses excavate infaunal prey by blowing jets of water out of their mouths at the sand. This behavior is called "hydraulic jetting." While the feeding activities of these species may help put detritus into suspension, they are typically not as well utilized by reef aquarists because many feed on small fishes and motile invertebrates (e.g., crustaceans). Those wrasses that bury at night (e.g., *Anampses*, *Halichoeres*) or when threatened may also help the upper layer of a sand bed from becoming impacted.

Coris atlantica, West African Rainbow Coris Wrasse: juvenile.

Coris atlantica, West African Rainbow Coris Wrasse, adult.

Bodianus speciosus, Blackbar Hogfish: found along Africa's West Coast.

Thalassoma newtoni, Newton's Wrasse: collected in the Gulf of Guinea.

The Wrasses Are Running!
East Atlantic Wrasses

In the last few years, an export conduit has been established that enabled aquarists to gain access to some labrids from the East Atlantic. (Most of the collecting occurs around São Tomé Island—an island nation in the Gulf of Guinea.) Many of these labrids are not only beautiful, but are also hardy aquarium residents.

One of the most spectacular is the **West African Rainbow Coris (*Coris atlantica*) Günther 1862**. This multicolored fish readily adapts to aquarium life, although it may remain hidden under the substrate for several days before making an appearance. It reaches a length of at least 20 cm (7.9 in.) in length (and possibly up to 25 cm [9.8 in.]), so it will need to be housed in a larger tank and it will need a sand bed in which to refuge. Like others in the genus, adults are a threat to an array of motile invertebrates. It is a very capable leaper, so make sure your tank is covered.

Another vivid labrid that is commonly exported is the **Newton's Wrasse (*Thalassoma newtoni*) (Osório, 1891)**. This species is somewhat similar in husbandry and behavior to the Moon Wrasse (*Thalassoma lunare*). It is very active and a potential threat to small fish and a wide variety of motile invertebrates. Information on its maximum size is hard to find, but it probably reaches around 14 cm (5.5 in.) in total length.

Finally, although not as colorful, the **Blackbar Hogfish (*Bodianus speciosus*) (Bowdich, 1825)** is a handsome and hardy species. The juveniles are part-time cleaners, that will regularly engage in this behavior in the aquarium. While juveniles are fairly well behaved, as they grow they become a threat to worms, mollusks, crustaceans, and echinoderms. This fish gets rather larger—50 cm (19.7 in.) long. Keep that in mind before adding one to your tank. In the wild, it inhabits algae-rich, rocky reefs and seagrass meadows. It is known to occur at Madeira, the Canary Islands, and Cape Verde to Angola.

GENUS ANAMPSES (TAMARIN WRASSES)

The genus *Anampses* includes some of the most striking members of the wrasse family. Only one of the 13 species that make up this genus would be classified as "chromatically challenged"; the rest are brightly colored and/or have sharply contrasting body markings. Some of the anatomical characteristics shared by all the *Anampses* spp. include a single pair of broad, projecting incisiform teeth in the front of the jaws, no scales on the head, a complete lateral line, and a smooth preopercle margin.

Two of the *Anampses* wrasses have restricted distributions and rarely, if ever, make it into the aquarium trade. Lennard's Tamarin Wrasse (*Anampses lennardi*) is known only from Western Australia, and the Green Tamarin Wrasse (*A. viridis*) is found around the island of Mauritius. Two other *Anampses* spp., the Pearl Tamarin Wrasse (*A. cuvier*) and the Redtail Tamarin Wrasse (*A. chrysocephalus*), are also limited in their distribution, but, unlike the previous species, they occur in an area where there is extensive collecting for the aquarium trade. Another species that has a broader, but spotty, geographical range and is rare in aquarium stores is the Feminine Tamarin Wrasse (*A. femininus*).

Biology

The *Anampses* spp. are residents of rocky and coral reef environments. They typically occur in sheltered lagoons, often near the back of the barrier reef or on fore-reef terraces where there is sand and rubble substrate. Several of these wrasses are also commonly found in the turbulent waters of the surge zone.

The Tamarin wrasses hunt during the day and hide under the sand at night. They also bury when stressed or threatened. Smaller individuals feed primarily on minute crustaceans and polychaete worms, but as they grow larger they eat more hefty crustaceans and mollusks, as well as polychaetes. Even large individuals feed on relatively small prey items. For example, Hobson (1974) reports that most of the prey items consumed by Cuvier's wrasses as long as 23 cm (9 in.) were shorter than 3 mm (.12 in.). In contrast, similar-sized members of other wrasse genera, like the hogfishes or Maori wrasses, feed on much larger prey items, including echinoids and mollusks. The forward-projecting flattened teeth of the *Anampses* spp. are adapted for plucking small invertebrates from the algal mat. Rather than being crushed up by the pharyngeal teeth, these small prey items are swallowed intact.

Anampses chrysocephalus, Redtail Tamarin Wrasse, male: one of a genus of peaceful, reef-safe fishes needing expert aquarium care and feeding.

The *Anampses* spp. are sexually dichromatic. In fact, in five of the 13 species, males and females were recognized as separate species until a revision of the genus was made in 1972. Juveniles and females display the initial phase coloration; terminal phase individuals are adult males, which result from female sex change. In most cases terminal phase specimens are more colorful than initial phase specimens. The exception is *A. femininus*. In this species, females are more striking than their terminal phase counterparts, sporting a bright orange body and fluorescent blue longitudinal stripes. Although the social organization of the *Anampses* spp. has never been studied, field observations suggest that males guard a harem of females, which forage and move about together over expansive home ranges.

The reproductive strategy of these wrasses is somewhat of an enigma. De Bernado (1975) reports having observed the Pearl Tamarin Wrasse (*Anampses cuvier*) digging a "nest" and laying its eggs on the substrate in the aquarium. Eckert (1987) observed two other species (*A. neoguinaicus* and *A. geographicus*) spawning on the Great Barrier Reef, where these two species spawn daily during the summer months. Terminal males will seek out a prominent point on the reef some 7 to 32 minutes before spawning begins. One terminal phase male of a species will be present at each site and will spawn with up to four different females. Females move up to 100 m (330 ft.) from their home range to the spawning site.

In Eckert's study (1987), males exhibited several courtship behaviors. They swam rapidly in wide circles just over the seafloor; they engaged in "looping," rapidly swimming toward the surface and then returning to the substrate; and they hung in the water column and fluttered their pectoral fins and vibrated their bodies and fins (this is referred to as a "fluttering" display). Spawning occurred between 9:20 A.M. and 5:37 P.M., always

Anampses chrysocephalus, Redtail Tamarin Wrasse, females graze over reef in search of worms, small crustaceans, and other benthic prey.

within 15 minutes of high tide. Based on these observations, it is likely that benthic spawning by *A. cuvier* was an artifact of being kept in captivity.

Captive Care

Many of the *Anampses* spp. are a challenge to maintain in the home aquarium, and, therefore, are only recommended for the advanced aquarist. These wrasses tend to ship poorly and usually refuse food when first introduced to the tank. Live black worms and live brine shrimp may induce a feeding response in a finicky individual, while live rock, or a tank with a healthy amphipod population, can also help to maintain their weight while they adjust to the more popular aquarium foods. In time some individuals will accept frozen mysid shrimp, frozen brine shrimp, or finely chopped fresh or frozen table shrimp, while others will eat only live food. Once a Tamarin wrasse has acclimated to its new environment and begins to feed, it is important that you ensure there is enough food to sustain it. Juveniles have high metabolic demands and will need to be fed several times a day—more if there is little natural fodder available in the tank. A productive refugium is one way to provide a more consistent supply of natural prey items for your *Anampses* spp.

The Tamarin wrasses should be kept with nonaggressive tankmates like grammas, reef basslets, sand tilefishes, butterflyfishes, chromis, flasher wrasses, fairy wrasses, gobies, rabbitfishes, and boxfishes. Juvenile and female Tamarin wrasses often fare better in captivity if kept in pairs or small groups, but putting two males in the same tank could result in fighting and dead fish. If you are going to keep a male and female in the same tank it is best to add them to the tank simultaneously or introduce the female first. Although Tamarin wrasses are typically very peaceful fishes that ignore unrelated species, larger males occasionally harass small conspecifics or congeners, especially in small tanks.

Because these wrasses bury in the sand at night or when threatened, their aquarium home should have at least 5 cm (2 in.) of fine sand on the bottom. Avoid using larger-grained bottom materials, many of which are abrasive and can cause damage to the fish's mouth and fins. These injuries provide a site for secondary bacterial and viral infections. When initially introduced to the aquarium, these wrasses will often hide under the sand for a day or two before emerging and investigating their new environment. If you are keeping this fish in a reef tank, make sure there is plenty of sandy bottom space available for burying and feeding.

Tamarin wrasses often pick at live rock, which can result in clouds of sediment and debris being temporarily suspended in the water column. The advantage of this is that detritus can be removed by an external, mechanical filter while it is in suspension. However, if there is insufficient water flow and mechanical filtration, floating particles may take away from the beauty of your aquarium.

Anampses caeruleopunctatus, Bluespotted Tamarin Wrasse, male.

When selecting a Tamarin wrasse, closely inspect its mouth and make sure that the skin is intact. These wrasses will often rub up against the bag during shipping and damage the mouth area. These fish are also prone to jumping out of open aquariums. It is also prudent to make sure the *Anampses* sp. is eating before you take it home. Your chances of successfully acclimating a Tamarin wrasse are increased if you choose a medium-sized specimen. Adult fish tend to ship poorly and have a more difficult time adjusting to a new environment, while very young fish have greater metabolic demands to sustain their health and for growth. Therefore, an adolescent individual is most likely to acclimate to aquarium life.

Tamarin Wrasses Species

Anampses caeruleopunctatus Rüppell, 1829
Common Names: Bluespotted Tamarin Wrasse, Bluespotted Wrasse.
Maximum Length: 42 cm (16.5 in.).
Distribution: Red Sea to Easter Island, north to southern Japan, and south to Lord Howe Island.
Biology: The Bluespotted Tamarin Wrasse is most common in shallow surgy conditions on the fore-reef crest, but it has been reported from depths of at least 18 m (60 ft.). It is most often found over coral rubble or sand substrates. According to Gushima (1981), small specimens, between 9 and 15 cm (3.5 to 5.9

Anampses caeruleopunctatus, Bluespotted Tamarin Wrasse, older juvenile: this age fish is ideal to begin acclimation to life in a reef aquarium.

Anampses cuvier, Pearl Tamarin Wrasse, female: sexes are dichromatic and easy to distinguish. (Compare to male, below.)

Anampses cuvier, Pearl Tamarin Wrasse, male: relatively durable species.

in.), feed mainly on small crustaceans (amphipods, harpacticoid copepods, and tanaids) and polychaete worms, while larger individuals, over 16 cm (6.2 in.), consume larger quantities of decapod crustaceans, bivalves, and polychaete worms. They also eat chitons. Females may forage in pairs or join loose aggregations of *Stethojulis* wrasses.

Captive Care: After it has been in the aquarium for several days, the Bluespotted Wrasse will usually accept foods like mysid shrimp, brine shrimp, or finely shredded table shrimp. Females can be kept in the same tank together, or one or more females can be housed with a single male. However, male specimens are rarely seen in the aquarium trade. If you acquire a female, it may transform into a male. Although females can be kept in a reef aquarium, large males may feed on delicate, ornamental crustaceans and pick at small tridacnid clams. Fan worms are a potential prey for both females and males.

Aquarium Size: 180 gal. **Temperature:** 23° to 28°C (74° to 82°F).

Aquarium Suitability Index: 3.

Remarks: Females are brown on the back, shading to reddish brown on the ventrum, with bright blue spots on each scale and blue lines on the head. Males are olive brown or green overall, with blue vertical lines on each scale, a blue-green bar near the pectoral fin, blue bands between the eyes, and blue markings on the dorsal, anal, and caudal fins. Adult females measure from about 18 to 28 cm (7 to 11 in.) in total length, while males usually measure between 19 and 42 cm (7.4 and 16.5 in.). However, in some locations (e.g., Chagos), adult males as small as 13 cm (5.1 in.) in total length have been reported. The male color phase of this fish was once known as *Anampses diadematus*.

Anampses cuvier Quoy & Gaimard, 1824

Common Names: Pearl Tamarin Wrasse, Pearl Wrasse, Cuvier's Wrasse.

Maximum Length: 31 cm (12 in.).

Distribution: Hawaiian Islands.

Biology: The Pearl Tamarin Wrasse is most common around large basalt boulders, often in areas exposed to surge. It occurs at water depths of less than 1 to at least 24 m (3 to 80 ft.) and is occasionally observed in large tidepools. Cuvier's Wrasse is a solitary species that moves close to the substrate, scanning the bottom for the small invertebrates on which it feeds. Its diet is composed primarily of amphipods, isopods, copepods, ostracods, shrimp, brachyuran crabs, and prosobranch gastropods, but it also consumes polychaete worms, peanut worms, chitons, xanthid crabs, demersal fish eggs, urchins, serpent star arms, foraminifers, and tunicates. Excluding elongate invertebrates like polychaete worms, this species rarely ingests any prey organism that exceeds

Anampses chrysocephalus, Redtail Tamarin Wrasse, adult female.

Anampses chrysocephalus: female transforming to male.

Anampses chrysocephalus, Psychedelic Tamarin Wrasse, adult male.

4 mm in size. It will often pluck its prey from the algal mat and incidentally ingests a considerable amount of sand and debris. I have seen this species follow the Orangespine Unicornfish (*Naso lituratus*) and move up alongside this herbivore as it feeds, watching for flushed prey items. Aquarium observations suggest that this is a demersal spawner that lays its eggs in a nest excavated in the substrate. However, these observations may represent an aquarium artifact, not normal reproductive behavior.

Captive Care: The Pearl Wrasse is one of the more durable members of the genus. It will accept live black worms, finely chopped shrimp, mysid shrimp, and brine shrimp; occasional specimens will even eat flake food. Females can be kept together, or a male

and a female can be housed in the same tank. They are rarely pugnacious towards their tankmates and should not be housed with overly aggressive fish species. Small specimens will not harm the desirable invertebrates in the reef aquarium if it has a thick sand substrate. However, larger specimens may nip at small, delicate shrimp species (e.g., *Periclimenes*) and tube worms.

Aquarium Size: 135 gal. **Temperature:** 22° to 28°C (72° to 82°F).
Aquarium Suitability Index: 3
Remarks: Males of this species usually measure more than 13 cm (5.1 in.) in standard length.

Anampses chrysocephalus Randall, 1958
Common Names: Redtail Tamarin Wrasse (female), Redtail Wrasse, Psychedelic Tamarin Wrasse (male), Psychedelic Wrasse, Psych-head Wrasse.
Maximum Length: 17 cm (6.7 in.).
Distribution: Hawaiian and Midway Islands.
Biology: The Redtail Tamarin Wrasse has been reported at depths from 10 to 139 m (33 to 459 ft.). It is found on fore reef slopes over a variety of different types of substrate. Hoover (1993) reports that females are often seen in small aggregations, while males are either solitary or accompany groups of females.
Captive Care: The Redtail Wrasse is a difficult species to keep, especially male specimens. Live food is often needed to induce these fish to feed. Females should be kept in pairs or small groups, while a single male should be housed with one or more females. This is a nervous fish that will often pace from one end of the tank to the other.
Aquarium Size: 75 gal. **Temperature:** 22° to 28°C (72° to 82°F).

Anampses femininus, Feminine Tamarin Wrasse, female.

Anampses geographicus, Geographic Tamarin Wrasse, male.

Anampses geographicus, Geographic Tamarin Wrasse, female.

Aquarium Suitability Index: 2.

Remarks: The female Redtail Tamarin Wrasse is dark brown overall with a white spot on each scale and a bright red tail with a white band at the base. Males are brown overall, with blue spots on each scale and a bright orange head with bright blue spots. The male color phase of the Redtail Wrasse was once considered to be a distinct species referred to as *Anampses rubrocaudatus*.

Anampses femininus Randall, 1972
Common Names: Feminine Tamarin Wrasse, Feminine Wrasse, Bluestriped Orange Tamarin Wrasse.
Maximum Length: 24 cm (9.4 in.).
Distribution: Southern Great Barrier Reef and New South Wales, Australia, New Caledonia, Lord Howe, Rapa, Pitcairn, and Easter Islands.

Biology: This species is found on rocky and coral reefs at depths of 10 to 40 m (33 to 132 ft.). It is often found in small groups. The juveniles are more secretive than adults. They will hide among macroalgae or bury in the sand.
Captive Care: The Feminine Tamarin Wrasse is a beautiful species that rarely appears in the aquarium trade and commands a high price. It is a sensitive fish that often has difficulty acclimating to captive life. Like all members of the genus, it should be provided with fine sand to bury in and live foods to initiate a feeding response. Initial phase individuals are more likely to acclimate. These fish should be kept at lower water temperatures.
Aquarium Size: 100 gal. **Temperature:** 20° to 25°C (68° to 77°F).
Aquarium Suitability Index: 2–3.
Remarks: The initial phase individuals are orange with a bright blue tail and blue lines on the head and body. The terminal phase male has a darker head with blue lines and blue flecks on the orangish brown body, and the median fins are dark with blue highlights. Young fish have ocelli on the rear of the dorsal and anal fins.

Anampses geographicus Valenciennes, 1840
Common Names: Geographic Tamarin Wrasse, Geographic Wrasse.
Maximum Length: 31 cm (12 in.).
Distribution: Mauritius to Fiji, north to the Ryukus, and south to southwest Australia and Lord Howe Island.
Biology: The dominant prey items in the diet of this wrasse are small crustaceans (e.g., amphipods and harpacticoid copepods), while sedentary polychaete worms, chitons, crabs, isopods, sea spiders, snail eggs, and snails are minor parts of the bill of fare.

Anampses lineatus, Whitedashed Tamarin Wrasse, female.

Anampses lineatus, Whitedashed Tamarin Wrasse, male.

Captive Care: Although the Geographic Wrasse is not highly sought after because of its muted coloration, this species occasionally enters the aquarium trade and is often sold as an "assorted wrasse." Although I would still consider this species unsuitable for beginners, it tends to adapt more readily to captivity than many of its relatives. Live food may be required to stimulate this fish to feed.

Aquarium Size: 135 gal. **Temperature:** 22° to 28°C (72° to 82°F).

Aquarium Suitability Index: 3.

Anampses lineatus Randall, 1972

Common Names: Whitedashed Tamarin Wrasse, Whitedashed Wrasse.

Maximum Length: 12 cm (4.7 in.).

Distribution: Red Sea, south to Natal and east to Bali.

Biology: The Whitedashed Tamarin Wrasse is a resident of coastal reef slopes and dropoffs, where it occurs at a depth range of 10 to 42 m (33 to 139 ft.). However, it is usually found at depths greater than 20 m (66 ft.). This wrasse typically occurs in aggregations that consist of one male and several females.

Captive Care: This fish is typical of the *Anampses* wrasses, requiring special care and feeding as described for the genus previously.

Aquarium Size: 55 gal. **Temperature:** 23° to 28°C (74° to 82°F).

Aquarium Suitability Index: 3.

Remarks: This wrasse was once considered to be a subspecies of *Anampses melanurus.* The females have a yellow tail with a wide black distal margin. Males do not have a yellow tail, but instead have blue lines on the tail and a fine blue margin. Males also have a patch of yellow behind the pectoral fin axil.

Anampses melanurus, Whitespotted Tamarin Wrasse, juvenile.

Anampses melanurus, Whitespotted Tamarin Wrasse, female.

Anampses meleagrides, Yellowtail Tamarin Wrasse, female: a regular in the aquarium trade, but often a victim of shipping stresses and anorexia.

Anampses melanurus Bleeker, 1857

Common Names: Whitespotted Tamarin Wrasse, Whitespotted Wrasse.

Maximum Length: 12 cm (4.7 in.).

Distribution: Red Sea to Easter Island, north to the Ryukus, and south to Lord Howe Island.

Biology: The Whitespotted Wrasse is reported at a depth range of 5 to 30 m (17 to 99 ft.), but is more common at depths in excess of 15 m (50 ft.). This fish is usually found over sandy bottoms near the edges of coral reefs. It occurs singly or in pairs.

Captive Care: This is a smaller member of the genus that should be housed in a relatively peaceful tank with a layer of fine sand on the aquarium bottom. *Anampses melanurus* tends to be more durable than some members of the group, possibly because it attains a smaller size and often ships better than adults of larger species.

Aquarium Size: 75 gal. **Temperature:** 70° to 82°F (21° to 28°C).

Aquarium Suitability Index: 3.

Remarks: The female Whitespotted Wrasse has a uniformly yellow tail. The Yellowtail Wrasse is a similar species, but the female *A. melanurus* lacks the eyespots on the dorsal and anal fins that are present in *A. meleagrides*.

Anampses meleagrides Valenciennes, 1840

Common Names: Yellowtail Tamarin Wrasse, Yellowtail Wrasse.

Maximum Length: 22 cm (8.7 in.).

Distribution: Red Sea to the Tuamotus, north to southern Japan, and south to northwest Australia and Lord Howe Island.

Biology: The Yellowtail Tamarin Wrasse is found on fore-reef slopes in areas of mixed hard coral, rubble, consolidated limestone, and sand. It occurs at a depth range of 4 to 60 m (13 to 198 ft.). Juveniles of this species usually occur singly, while adults are found in pairs or loose aggregations. I once saw a large Forster's Hawkfish (*Paracirrhites forsteri*) eat a female Yellowtail Wrasse.

Captive Care: This is one of the most commonly encountered *Anampses* in the aquarium trade. Like many members of the genus, it is a poor shipper and the aquarist may have trouble getting it to eat. Live food is usually a must, at least to induce an initial feeding response. Smaller specimens have a better chance of acclimating to aquarium confines than larger individuals.

Aquarium Size: 100 gal. **Temperature:** 22° to 28°C (72° to 82°F).

Aquarium Suitability Index: 2–3.

Remarks: Females of this species are brown overall with white spots and a yellow tail. The male is brown with short blue lines on the body and a maze of blue markings on the head. In males, most of the tail is brown with blue spots, and there is a transparent, V-shaped section with a blue cast in the middle, which gives the impression that the tail fin is deeply notched.

Anampses neoguinaicus Bleeker, 1878

Common Names: New Guinea Tamarin Wrasse, Blackbacked Wrasse.

Maximum Length: 15 cm (5.9 in.).

Distribution: Taiwan to Fiji, north to the Izu Islands, and south the Great Barrier Reef and New Caledonia.

Biology: The New Guinea Tamarin Wrasse is found on fore-reef and back barrier reef slopes and on outer reef crests and reef faces at depths from 4 to 25 m (13 to 83 ft.). It usually frequents areas with mixed sand and rubble or habitats with rich stony coral growth (e.g., plating *Acropora* spp.). Terminal males usually occur singly, occasionally visiting loose groups of females.

Captive Care: The New Guinea Wrasse is a delicate species that often succumbs to shipping stress. It should be housed in a tank with other peaceful fishes, with plenty of swimming room and an expansive sand bottom in which to take shelter at night or when threatened. When this fish is first added to the aquarium it will usually ignore frozen or prepared foods. Live foods, like brine shrimp, black worms, or amphipods living on live rock, are often required to initiate feeding.

Aquarium Size: 75 gal. **Temperature:** 74° to 82°F (23° to 28°C).

Aquarium Suitability Index: 2.

Anampses twistii Bleeker, 1856

Common Names: Yellowbreasted Tamarin Wrasse, Yellowbreasted Wrasse, Twister Wrasse.

Maximum Length: 18 cm (7 in.).

Distribution: Red Sea to the Tuamotus, north to the Ryukus, and south to Mauritius and Rapa.

Anampses meleagrides, Yellowtail Tamarin Wrasse, male.

Anampses neoguinaicus, New Guinea Tamarin Wrasse, male.

Anampses neoguinaicus, New Guinea Tamarin Wrasse, male.

Anampses neoguinaicus, New Guinea Tamarin Wrasse, male variant.

Anampses twistii, Yellowbreasted Tamarin Wrasse, juvenile.

Anampses twistii, Yellowbreasted Tamarin Wrasse, adult.

Biology: The Yellowbreasted Tamarin Wrasse is found in the shallow surge zone down to 30 m (98 ft.), in clear lagoons and on back reefs, reef faces, and fore-reef slopes. In some areas, it prefers protected patch reefs. It is usually a solitary species that is most common over mixed hard coral, rubble, and sand. Juveniles sometimes swim in a head-down posture, exposing the ocelli on the rear of the dorsal and anal fins. This may serve to dissuade attacks by potential predators.

Captive Care: The Yellowbreasted Wrasse is a difficult species to keep. Even if these fish begin to feed in captivity, they often waste away for no known reason. Keeping them in a tank with live rock and providing a varied diet may increase your chances of success with this species. It is prudent to house only one male per tank. Initial phase individuals can be kept together in a larger tank.

Aquarium Size: 75 gal. **Temperature:** 22° to 28°C (72° to 82°F).

Aquarium Suitability Index: 2.

Remarks: Some suggest that the Red Sea population represents a distinct species, or at least a subspecies. Individuals from this area have blue spots on the body as juveniles and adults, while the head of the adult remains mostly yellow.

SUBFAMILY BODIANINAE (HOGFISHES)

What's in a name? Hmmm. A hawkfish swoops out from its calcareous perch to snatch its prey, a parrotfish has fused teeth that resemble the beak of its avian counterpart, and the coral catfish has barbels around its mouth that look like the whiskers of its furry namesake. But hogfish? What characteristic does a hogfish share, either behaviorally or anatomically, with the filthy glutton of the barnyard? These fish do not look like any hog I've ever seen (I am from Nebraska, so I have seen plenty of swine), but they do act like hogs on occasion. For example, while diving in the Sea of Cortez, I watched a Mexican hogfish (*Bodianus diplotaenia*) follow a foraging Mexican goatfish (*Mulloidichys dentatus*). As the goatfish flipped rocks with its barbels to locate hidden prey, its greedy attendant would rush forward to snap up any exposed morsels before the goatfish could.

Although we may never know if greed earned the hogfish its common name, we do know that all of the members of the genus *Bodianus* possess the following characteristics: they have 11 to 14 dorsal spines and 6 to 11 dorsal rays, 3 anal spines and 8 to 13 anal rays, 15 to 21 pectoral rays, a continuous lateral line, at least one pair of canines in the front of each jaw, and a finely serrated edge on the preopercle. There are at least 43 described species in

Bodianus sepiacaudus, Crescenttail Hogfish: one of a number of very appealing red-and-white *Bodianus* species found in deep reef habitats.

the genus *Bodianus*, which, unknown to many aquarists, are members of the wrasse family Labridae.

Biology

The majority of hogfishes are found on coral reefs and are most common in shallow to moderate depths (less than 40 m [130 ft.]). However, some species reside on rocky reefs in subtropical and warm temperate waters. For example, the Harlequin Wrasses (*Bodianus eclancheri*), which are often Koi-like in color, are only known from rocky reefs off the coast of Peru and Chile (including the Galapagos Islands). A few species are restricted to deep water. *Bodianus tanyokidus*, for instance, has only been taken at depths greater than 100 m (325 ft.)

All the hogfishes are active predators whose diets consist mainly of benthic invertebrates, including mollusks, worms, and crustaceans. The adults of several hogfish species commonly associate with fish that feed by grubbing in the substrate (e.g., goatfishes), thereby accessing prey unavailable to most hogfishes. A number of *Bodianus* spp. act as facultative (part-time) parasitepickers while they're juveniles.

All the hogfishes studied thus far are protogynous hermaphrodites, and all males result from female sex change. According to Hoffman (1985), the members of this genus display a surprising variety of social and mating systems. Some species, like the Spanish Hogfish (*Bodianus rufus*), are haremic, with males defending a territory containing a number of females throughout the day. The male visits and spawns with each female in his defended area. In these species the males are the largest, most dom-

inant members of the harem, and if a male is removed the largest female will change sex and take his place. Mexican Hogfish (*B. diplotaenia*) males do not defend areas during the day, but larger males set up temporary territories just before sunset. Females visit the mating territories and each spawns once with a single male. In contrast, certain males may mate with dozens of females in a single evening. In this species the females transform into males as they grow larger, and the sex ratio of males to females is 1:2. Finally, in the Harlequin Hogfish (*B. eclancheri*), sex change occurs in half of the immature females just before maturity, so that the sex ratio is about 1:1. Individuals occupy overlapping home ranges during the day, but before spawning males aggregate at a specific mating site on the edge of the reef. Females swim into the spawning area and mate with numerous males. In this species, spawning is not initiated just before the sun goes down, but occurs during the day, usually 30 minutes before the highest tide.

Captive Care

The hogfishes are some of the hardiest members of the wrasse family. As a whole, they are durable aquarium fish that readily accept most aquarium fare. This includes chopped, fresh, or frozen sea food, frozen preparations for carnivores, frozen or live brine shrimp, live black worms, cleaned earthworms, flake food, live ghost shrimp, and even small feeder fish. Although they might not accept all food offered from the onset, they will typically eat any food available after they are fully acclimated to their new home.

The size of the aquarium needed to harbor a hogfish will depend on the species you are interested in keeping. Most small to medium-sized members of the family (i.e., those species that attain a maximum length of less than 10 in.) can be kept in tanks ranging from 75 to 100 gallons, while the more massive species will need a tank of 180 gallons or larger once they reach adult size. Although a hogfish's home should have plenty of hiding, it is also important to provide a lot of swimming room for these active fishes. Unlike some other wrasse species, the hogfishes do not bury under the substrate, so the type of bottom material you use in your tank is of little concern. However, several of these fish will hunt buried prey items by blowing jets of water at the finer substrate, which is very interesting to observe. This behavior can also help to aerate the upper layers of the substrate.

Many hogfishes will not tolerate the presence of members of their own kind in the same tank, but there are exceptions, which

Bodianus dictynna, Redfin Hogfish: newly settled juvenile sheltering in a sea fan, typical behavior for the young of some *Bodianus* species.

Bodianus anthioides, Lyretail Hogfish, juvenile: a facultative cleaner.

Bodianus anthioides, Lyretail Hogfish, adult: needs rugged tankmates.

large-sized hogfishes should be kept with fish species that can hold their own, like lionfishes, squirrelfishes, soldierfishes, small groupers, goatfishes, angelfishes, hawkfishes, medium-sized damselfishes, sand perch, less aggressive triggerfish species, pufferfishes, and porcupinefishes. However, adding a hogfish to an established community of aggressive fishes can cause a hogfish to remain hidden most of the time and never acclimate. Of course, large frogfishes, scorpionfishes, and groupers will eat any hogfish that they can swallow whole.

Most of the hogfish species can be kept in reef aquariums as juveniles, but as they grow they will eat worms, snails, small clams, crustaceans, and echinoderms.

Genus *Bodianus* (Hogfishes)

Bodianus anthioides (Bennett, 1832)
Common Name: Lyretail Hogfish.
Maximum Length: 21 cm (8.2 in.).
Distribution: Red Sea to the Line and Tuamotu Islands, north to southern Japan, and south to New Caledonia and Tonga.
Biology: The Lyretail Hogfish is found in areas with rich coral growth on coastal reefs, fore-reef slopes, dropoffs, and the backs of barrier reefs. This species is reported from a depth range of 6 to 60 m (20 to 198 ft.). In the Red Sea, adults are often found in shallow, sandy areas on the back reef, while small juveniles occur in deeper water and commonly associate with the sea fan, *Subgorgia hicksoni*, feeding on the small organisms that get trapped in the fan's latticelike structure. Juveniles are also facultative cleaners, setting up cleaning stations near sea fans or other prominent features on the reef. When feeding, large Lyretail Hogfish often blow jets of water out of their mouths at the sand surface to uncover buried prey (this is known as "hydraulic jetting"). Adults also associate with goatfishes to consume prey items these fish flush out or expose with their chin barbels. Although the Lyretail Hogfish is usually observed singly, it is probably a haremic species. I have witnessed the spawning behavior of this species in the Red Sea. At dusk, a male courted two females near the top of a large coral head. The male was larger than the females and differed in color. He was much darker toward the front of the body than the females, his head was rusty brown rather than the orangish brown of the female's head, and his "cheek" area had changed to gray. The male swam around the females with his fins erect until one of them joined him. The pair then swam side by side into the water column and shed their gametes.
Captive Care: Although this species generally does well in the home aquarium, small juveniles can be more sensitive to transport stress and may have a more difficult time adjusting to captivity

will be discussed in the species accounts that follow. Most hogfishes can be kept with other members of their genus, but you should avoid placing two similarly colored species in the same tank. When hogfishes fight they will usually face off and simultaneously open their mouths toward one another. Often this is the extent of an aggressive encounter. However, if aggression escalates, these fish may lock jaws and tug and jerk one another to and fro, which can cause damage to the flesh around the mouth. The more dominant combatant may also chase and bite its rival, before or after jaw-locking occurs. If aggression reaches this level, the two fish should be separated.

Hogfishes can be belligerent toward smaller unrelated fishes, more docile species, or those fish introduced after the hogfish has become an established resident of the tank. The moderate- to than large juveniles or subadults. In order to increase their chances of survival, smaller *B. anthioides* should be housed with docile fish species and provided with plenty of hiding places. Adolescents and small adults will readily adapt to aquarium life, but are quite active and need plenty of open swimming space. Although juveniles are usually quite peace-loving, once a larger Lyretail Hogfish is established in its captive home it may behave aggressively toward smaller or more docile tankmates. Moderately aggressive tankmates like groupers, hawkfishes, angelfishes, and some of the more placid triggerfishes can be introduced into a tank containing an acclimated, adult Lyretail Hogfish. Juveniles will often clean other fish in the confines of the aquarium—this can be fascinating to watch. Small *B. anthioides* can be kept in either a shallow or deep water reef aquarium. However, as it grows this fish will become a threat to worms, small clams, and crustaceans. The hydraulic jetting performed by adolescent and adult individuals can help to stir the upper layers of soft aquarium substrate.

Aquarium Size: 100 gal. **Temperature:** 22° to 28°C (72° to 82°F).

Aquarium Suitability Index: 3.

Remarks: This species is easily recognized by its deeply incised to emarginate tail and its bold color pattern: the head and anterior part of the body are orangish brown, and the rest of the body is white with black spots. The juveniles and adults of this species do not differ radically in their color patterns, but adults may display temporary, and possibly permanent, sexual dichromatism and appear to be sexually dimorphic, with males attaining a larger size than females.

Bodianus axillaris (Bennett, 1832)

Common Name: Axilspot Hogfish.

Maximum Length: 20 cm (7.8 in.).

Distribution: Red Sea to the Marquesas and Pitcairn Islands, north to southern Japan, and south to Lord Howe Island. (It is apparently excluded from the coasts of India, Sri Lanka, most of Indonesia, and the Philippines.)

Biology: The Axilspot Hogfish is found around patch reefs in clear lagoons and on fore-reef slopes and dropoffs at depths ranging from 2 to 40 m (7 to 132 ft.). Adults are common at depths of 1 to 8 m (3.3 to 26 ft.). Juveniles often live in deeper water (14 to 26 m [46 to 85 ft.]) under ledges or in caves, while adults, which occur singly, move about the reef, often in areas with rich coral growth. Juvenile *B. axillaris* are facultative cleaners that will inspect and pick parasites off the bodies and fins of groupers, parrotfishes, unicornfishes, and other species that visit their cleaning stations. Adults occur singly.

Captive Care: This is a durable hogfish species that can be housed with moderately aggressive tankmates. Large *B. axillaris* are more

Bodianus axillaris, Axilspot Hogfish, juvenile: will clean other fishes.

Bodianus axillaris, Axilspot Hogfish, adult: often found in caves.

Bodianus neilli, Neill's Hogfish: Indian Ocean species similar to *B. axillaris*.

durable than small individuals. Juveniles will do best if they are housed with peaceful species, but adolescent and adult specimens should not be kept with smaller, more passive fishes. Juveniles will often clean other fish in the confines of the aquarium. Although small Axilspot Hogfish are suitable for the shallow or deep-water reef aquarium, adult specimens will feed on worms, clams, snails, and crustaceans.

Aquarium Size: 75 gal. **Temperature:** 22° to 28°C (72° to 82°F).
Aquarium Suitability Index: 4.

Remarks: The juveniles and initial phase individuals are dark brown to black with nine white spots, while terminal males are reddish brown on the back and head and whitish on the posterior part of the body. Sex change can occur in about one week in this species. The caudal fin is emarginate in adults and deeply incised, or forked, in juveniles. **Neill's Hogfish (*Bodianus neilli*) (Day, 1867)** is a closely related form from India, Sri Lanka, the Maldives (where those in the trade usually come from), and the Andaman Sea. It is reported from depths of 5 to 18 m (16 to 59 ft.). The juveniles are similar to those of *B. axillaris*, though they differ in subtle details (in *B. axillaris* there is a pale spot that covers the entire tip of the snout), while the color of the adults is quite distinct.

Deep-water Hogfishes (*Terelabrus* spp.)

In recent years, more and more reef fishes from deep reef habitats have been making their way into the aquarium trade. One such group of fishes are the members of the genus *Terelabrus*. The first and only species in this interesting genus described to date, the **Redlined Deepwater Hogfish (*Terelabrus rubrovittatus*)**, was given its name in 1998. This species attains a maximum length of at least 10 cm (3.9 in.) and is known to occur around New Caledonia, Papua New Guinea, Indonesia, Palau, and Japan. A second species occurs in the tropical Indian Ocean (e.g., Maldives) and differs in having more slender red lines down the body with yellow edges and a shorter snout (based on photos). There may be others in the genus, as this group is restricted to deep reef habitats where relatively limited collecting has occurred. *Terelabrus rubrovittatus* is found at depths to at least 100 m (325 ft.), although on rare occasions they are found at safe diving depths. Little else is known about its biology. I speculate it probably feeds on small fish and crustaceans, like other labrids that exhibit a similar elongated body plan.

There are two color forms of *T. rubrovittatus* (or possibly two distinct species) that have been reported in the aquarium trade. One is white and red, the other is yellow and red.

The white "form" has a distinct spot on the gill cover and orange markings under the eye and below the operculum spot. Both are very attractive fish.

The *Terelabrus* make wonderful aquarium pets. Unfortunately, because of their deep-dwelling habits, they will never be common in the hobby. When first added to the tank, they may be a bit skittish, but it does not take long for them to acclimatize to their new surroundings, as long as they are not being harassed by dottybacks, damsels, other wrasses, or surgeonfishes. Initially, they will exhibit more boldness if the tank is dimly lit, but they will also adapt to high light conditions with time. Their propensity for less luminous deep reef habitats might explain why they move about the tank just before and after the lights of the aquarium go on or off or when only the actinics are on. The *Terelabrus* tend to be quite amiable toward other fishes. A larger specimen might attempt to eat fishes it can swallow whole or more delicate shrimps. Two *Terelabrus* can be kept together, but try to get two smaller fish or a pair that differ in size appreciably; this will increase the chances you will acquire a male and female. This hogfish skulks about the tank, examining rocky surfaces and interstices for potential prey. It is shaped like an arrow and gives the impression that it may be a jumper, although I have yet to have one leap out of a tank. If you are lucky enough to run across one of these beauties, I recommend you snap it up quickly!

Terelabrus rubrovittatus, Redlined Deepwater Hogfish: rare but a great aquarium species.

Bodianus bilunulatus (Lacepède, 1801)

Common Name: Saddleback Hogfish.
Maximum Length: 55 cm (22 in.).
Distribution: East Africa east to Japan, the Philippines and New Caledonia.
Biology: The Saddleback Hogfish is a resident of coastal sand and rubble slopes, clear lagoon reefs, and fore-reef slopes and dropoffs at depths from 8 to 108 m (26 to 356 ft.). Terminal phase individuals are usually found in deeper water (over 15 m [50 ft.]). Juveniles are reported to be most common on rubble ridges with profuse soft coral and sponge growth. The Saddleback Hogfish is usually found in areas with rich, hard coral growth. This solitary wrasse feeds

Bodianus bilunulatus, Saddleback Hogfish, juvenile.

Bodianus bilunulatus, Saddleback Hogfish, larger juvenile.

Bodianus albotaeniatus, Hawaiian Hogfish, juvenile color form.

Bodianus albotaeniatus, Hawaiian Hogfish, adult: handsome, hardy species.

during the day on mollusks, both bivalves and snails, as well as sea urchins, hermit crabs, and crabs, which it crushes with its well-developed pharyngeal teeth. It also takes serpent stars and small fishes on occasion, and I once saw an adult individual swim past with a Multicolored Sea Star (*Linckia multifora*) hanging out of its mouth.

Captive Care: This is a durable aquarium species that should be provided with plenty of swimming room and several suitable hiding places. Although juveniles are rarely aggressive, adolescent and adult individuals may pester smaller, more docile fish species. As with other large hogfishes, it is risky to add them to the reef aquarium. They will eat a large variety of motile invertebrates and may displace corals with their mouths when hunting.

Aquarium Size: 180 gal. **Temperature:** 22° to 28°C (72° to 82°F).

Bodianus albotaeniatus, Hawaiian Hogfish, large adult.

Bodianus bimaculatus, Twinspot Hogfish, adult: small, deep slope species.

Bodianus bimaculatus, Twinspot Hogfish, adult color variant.

Bodianus sanguineus, Bloody Hogfish: nice, small Hawaiian endemic species.

Aquarium Suitability Index: 4.

Remarks: The Hawaiian Hogfish (*Bodianus albotaeniatus*) (Valenciennes, 1839) was once considered a subspecies but has been elevated to species status by Gomon (2006). Young *B. albotaeniatus* differ from *B. bilunulatus* in having a broad black band on the rear of the body with an indistinct front margin and a distinct rear edge. Initial phase individuals of this species differ from the Saddleback Hogfish in several ways: they have a moderately small saddle on the caudal peduncle that never extends below the lateral line, and their background color is yellow (initial phase *B. bilunulatus* have a pink background color). The color of the terminal phase *B. albotaeniatus* are mottled rather than uniformly dusky. It is limited to the Hawaiian Islands and Johnston Island and has been reported at depths of 8 to 110 m (26 to 358 ft.). The **Large Saddle Hogfish (*Bodianus busellatus*) (Gomon, 2006)** is a saddled hogfish that is known only from the Marquesas Islands, Henderson Island, and Ducie Atoll in the Pitcairn Group. This species has a larger peduncle spot than that of its close relatives, and the spot is retained even by the terminal phase individuals. It has a pink background color, rather than the yellow seen in *B. bilunulatus*.

Bodianus bimaculatus Allen, 1973

Common Names: Twinspot Hogfish, Twospot Slender Hogfish, Yellow Hogfish.

Maximum Length: 10 cm (3.9 in.).

Distribution: Mauritius and the Maldives to Papua New Guinea, north to southern Japan, and south to the Poor Knight Islands, New Zealand.

Biology: The Twinspot Hogfish is a resident of sand slopes with scattered boulders, fore-reef slopes, and vertical dropoffs. It occurs at depths from 20 to 60 m (66 to 198 ft.), but is most common in water deeper than 40 m (132 ft.). This species is usually found in small aggregations and sometimes mixes with the Golden Wrasse (*Halichoeres chrysus*).

Captive Care: This is a great aquarium fish. It will readily acclimate to life in captivity, and its diminutive size and preference for small prey items make it the best hogfish for a small tank. Although juveniles do best if housed with non-aggressive tankmates, as this species grows it will become more boisterous and may bully smaller, more docile fish tankmates. It can be especially intolerant of other yellow, elongated fishes, like the Golden Wrasse (a species it commonly associates with in the wild). The Twinspot Hogfish is most likely to assert its dominance over newly introduced fishes, especially in small tanks. When this hogfish behaves aggressively, it will often perform a frontal display where it spreads its gill covers forward so that the spots on

Bodianus masudai, Masuda's Hogfish: a deepwater rarity, similar to the Twinspot Hogfish, but found only in Japanese waters and New Caledonia.

the operculum are visible to its approaching rival. This probably serves to increase its apparent size. Only one Twinspot Hogfish should be housed per tank, unless your tank is large (e.g., 180 gallons or larger), and then you should introduce all individuals at the same time. It does not feed on most desirable invertebrates, but large specimens may harass delicate shrimp or even large shrimp species just after they have molted. Although it prefers deep-water habitats, the Twinspot Hogfish will readily acclimate to the more intense illumination present in a shallow-water reef aquarium.

Aquarium Size: 55 gal. **Temperature:** 23° to 28°C (74° to 82°F).

Aquarium Suitability Index: 4.

Remarks: There are two color forms. One is has red lines on the flanks, and the other is neon yellow overall. Pyle (in Gomon, 2006) reports that on a deep reef of Papua New Guinea, at a depth of 60 m (195 ft.), the red form was found near ledges and under overhangs on dropoffs, while the neon yellow form was more common on isolated rocks on muddy slopes. This is the smallest of the hogfishes, with females attaining sexual maturity at a standard length of 4 cm (1.6 in.). It belongs to the subgenus *Trochocopus*, which includes seven other small, slender-bodied hogfishes: the Redstriped Hogfish (*B. opercularis*); the **Bloody Hogfish** (**B. sanguineus**) (**Jordan & Evermann, 1903**); the Striped Hogfish (*B. izuensis*); **Masuda's Hogfish** (**B. masudai**) **Araga & Yoshino, 1975**; the Pacific Redstriped Hogfish (*B. neopercularis*); the Crescenttail Hogfish (*B. sepiacaudus*); and the **Tanyokidus Hogfish** (**B. tanyokidus**) **Gomon & Madden, 1981**. The Bloody Hogfish is only found in the Hawaiian Islands (67 to 238 m [218 to 774 ft.]); Masuda's Hogfish is known from Japan, New Caledonia (30 to 113 m [98 to 367 ft.]); the Tanyokidus Hogfish has been reported from the Comoro Islands, Mauritius, Japan. Of these three species, the only one that

Bodianus diana, Diana's Hogfish, large juvenile: grows increasingly predatory.

Bodianus diana, Diana's Hogfish, adult: Indian Ocean species.

Bodianus dictynna, Redfin Hogfish, juvenile: facultative cleaner.

has entered the hobby, and then only very rarely, is *B. sanguineus*. The Bloody Hogfish is common at depths in excess of 100 m (325 ft.), where they are often found in pairs; one individual in the pair is typically larger than the other (Pyle in Gomon, 2006). It has also been reported at depths of 67 to 238 m (217 to 774 ft.). The other three species listed above are covered elsewhere in the text.

Bodianus diana (Lacepède, 1801)

Common Name: Diana's Hogfish.
Maximum Length: 25 cm (9.8 in.).
Distribution: Red Sea and East Africa to the Andaman Sea and Christmas Island.
Biology: Diana's hogfish is found on fore-reef slopes and dropoffs, usually in areas with profuse soft coral growth, at depths from 6 to 40 m (20 to 132 ft.). Juveniles are often found near the entrances of caves or under ledges, at depths of 20 to 30 m (65 to 100 ft.), and often associate with black coral or gorgonians. Juvenile Diana's Hogfish often occur in aggregations and are facultative cleaners, with more than one individual often cleaning a single host. They sometimes join the Bluestreak Cleaner Wrasse (*Labroides dimidiatus*) as they pick parasites from other fishes. I have also seen an adult Diana's Hogfish picking at the carapace and flippers of a feeding hawksbill turtle as the reptile fed on sponges.
Captive Care: Like its relatives, *B. diana* readily acclimates to captive life. It is, however, one of the least sociable members of the genus, often behaving aggressively toward newly introduced fishes or more docile tankmates. I have even seen adults of this species persistently nip at juvenile morays. They will also eat any smaller fish that can be ingested whole. *B. diana* can be housed in a shal-

low- or deep-water reef aquarium as a juvenile, but will prey upon small bivalves, clams, worms, and crustaceans as it grows.
Aquarium Size: 100 gal. **Temperature:** 23° to 28°C (74° to 82°F).
Aquarium Suitability Index: 4.
Remarks: The **Redfin Hogfish** (*Bodianus dictynna*) (**Gomon, 2006**) was once considered to be the same species as *B. diana*. Adults of *B. dictynna* retain the spots on the pelvic and anal fins, while Diana's Hogfish has a splash of red in that area. The juveniles of *B. diana* also have more elaborate white spots on the body than *B. dictynna*. *Bodianus dictynna* is known from the Indo-Malaysian Archipelago to Japan, Palau, western Micronesia, Samoa, Tonga, and southeastern Australia. The biology and size of the Pacific form is very similar to that of *B. diana*. The Redfin Hogfish is more common in the aquarium trade than the

Bodianus dictynna, Redfin Hogfish, adult: very similar to *Bodianus diana*.

Bodianus diplotaenia, Mexican Hogfish, adult female: Eastern Pacific species.

Indian Ocean species. Juvenile *B. dictynna* often associate with gorgonians and black coral. This species occurs at depths of 9 to 30 m (29 to 98 ft.) and reaches a length of 25 cm (9.8 in.).

Bodianus diplotaenia (Gill, 1862)

Common Names: Mexican Hogfish, Cortez Hogfish, Streamer Hogfish.
Maximum Length: 76 cm (29.9 in.).
Distribution: Central Gulf of California to Chile, and Coco, Malepalo, Revillagigedo, and the Galapagos Islands.
Biology: This species occurs on rocky reefs, often amid large macroalgae stands, mixed areas of rock-rubble and sand, and large boulders, at depths from 1 to 76 m (3.3 to 251 ft.). However, it is most common at depths of less than 18 m (60 ft.). Juveniles of this species often form small aggregations and clean parasites from other fish species. On several occasions, I have observed aggregations of small juveniles picking at the skin of White-tip Reef Sharks (*Trizeneodon obesus*) as they lay on the substrate. Adults are solitary or form small aggregations. The Mexican Hogfish feeds on mollusks, crustaceans, urchins, and small fishes. I have seen adult individuals attempt to capture grapsid crabs at the edge of the tidal flat as the crustaceans moved near the edge of the water. I have also seen them crush and eat urchins, spines and all. They often follow other fish that disturb the substrate as they feed, including the Mexican Goatfish (*Mulloidichthys dentatus*). This species will also swim near a parrotfish's head and inspect the substrate around its jaws as the parrotfish scrapes the substrate with its beaklike teeth. The Mexican Hogfish is not territorial during the daytime, but as night closes in the largest males form temporary reproductive territories, which the females visit. Females mate once per evening, while a male may mate

Bodianus diplotaenia, Mexican Hogfish, adult male: note streaming fins.

with as many as 100 females in one spawning period. Females mature at about 14 cm SL (5.5 in.), while males mature at between 27 and 30 cm SL (11 to 12 in.). In one population studied, the sex ratio of males to females was 1:2.
Captive Care: *Bodianus diplotaenia* is a hardy aquarium species. Adolescent and adult specimens can be aggressive toward peaceful tankmates or fish introduced after they have become well established in the aquarium. This problem will be amplified if space is limited. The Mexican Hogfish can be housed in a shallow- or deep-water reef aquarium as a juvenile, but it will prey upon a wide range of invertebrates as it grows.
Aquarium Size: 240 gal. **Temperature:** 20° to 28°C (68° to 82°F).
Aquarium Suitability Index: 4.
Remarks: Juveniles under 2.5 cm (1 in.) are bright yellow, without

Bodianus eclancheri, Galapagos Hogfish: an insular, koi-like species.

Bodianus izuensis, Izu Hogfish: attractive species with spotty distribution.

Bodianus loxozonus, Blackfin Hogfish: attractive, but adults are large, voracious.

markings. Initial phase individuals are dusky yellow to reddish pink overall with a yellow caudal fin and yellow on the posterior portions of the dorsal and anal fins and two dark stripes running from the eye to the caudal fin origin. Terminal phase males are green to blue-green overall with a fleshy hump on the forehead, a more rounded snout, and long filaments extending from the ends of all the fins except the pectorals. Younger terminal phase individuals often have a yellow bar in the middle of the body, lack the hump on the head, and have a more pointed snout. Adults from deeper reef areas are often more red overall. The **Harlequin** or **Galapagos Hogfish** (*Bodianus eclancheri*) (**Valenciennes, 1846**) is another member of the genus found only in the eastern Pacific. It occurs from Ecuador to Chile, and is common around some of the Galapagos Islands. This species has a unique color pattern reminiscent of that seen in Koi or Japanese Carp. The predominant colors are orange, black, and white, and no two individuals sport the exact same pattern. All Harlequin Hogfish have a black spot at the base of the pectoral fins. Unfortunately, this unusual hogfish species does not enter the aquarium trade.

Bodianus izuensis Araga & Yoshino, 1975

Common Names: Izu Hogfish, Striped Hogfish.
Maximum Length: 10 cm (3.9 in.).
Distribution: Shizuoka Prefecture, Japan; New South Wales, Australia; New Caledonia. It no doubt occurs in intermediate locations—in the aquarium trade, some of these specimens are apparently originating from the Philippines.
Biology: Very little is known about the biology of this hogfish. It is reported at depths of at 20 to at least 50 m (66 to 165 ft.). It exhibits tropical submergence—in tropical climes, it is found in much deeper water. This fish is a resident of rocky reef slopes and dropoffs. Kuiter (1993) states that very small individuals (around 15 mm [0.6 in.]) are often found over open sand bottoms.
Captive Care: This is a small, hardy hogfish that will do well in the home aquarium. It can even be kept in the reef tank, although it will eat small, shelled mollusks and ornamental crustaceans. The Izu Hogfish may respond aggressively to the introduction of new fish to its home aquarium and will fight with members of its own kind and similar congeners unless the tank is large. Try habituating close relatives to the tank before releasing them into a tank that contains *B. izuensis*. This species will jump from an open aquarium.
Aquarium Size: 75 gal. **Temperature:** 15° to 27°C (59° to 80°F).
Aquarium Suitability Index: 4.
Remarks: Juveniles have three dark stripes with narrow reddish brown edges. It differs from its closest relative, *Bodianus bimaculatus*, in having black stripes on the body.

Bodianus mesothorax, Coral Hogfish: juveniles are cleaners, while adults feed on a wide array of motile invertebrates.

Bodianus loxozonus (Snyder, 1908)

Common Name: Blackfin Hogfish.

Maximum Length: 47 cm (18.5 in.).

Distribution: Vietnam east to French Polynesia and the Line Islands, north to the Ryukus and Bonin Islands.

Biology: The Blackfin Hogfish is a resident of clear lagoons and fore-reef slopes, where it is found at depths ranging from 3 to over 40 m (10 to 132 ft.).

Captive Care: The Blackfin Hogfish is a good aquarium fish, but because of its large size it will require ample space to move about. Large individuals are also a threat to small fish. Although juveniles are a threat to relatively few desirable invertebrates housed in the reef aquarium, adults will cause problems as they get bigger, eating mollusks, worms, and crustaceans. Once they have been in a tank for a while, the adults can also become aggressive, pestering newly introduced species, especially those that have a similar shape (e.g., other hogfishes and wrasses).

Aquarium Size: 180 gal. **Temperature:** 22° to 28°C (72° to 82°F).

Aquarium Suitability Index: 4.

Remarks: There are two subspecies, *B. loxozonus loxozonus* and *B. loxozonus totteri*, which differ slightly in color. This species is often misidentified as the **Mauritius Hogfish** (*Bodianus macrourus*) (**Lacepède, 1802**), which is known only from Mauritius and Reunion Islands. In the Mauritius hogfish, the black totally encircles the caudal peduncle and extends onto the posterior portion of the dorsal fin, there is no black on the anterior part of the dorsal fin, and the entire anal fin is black. It is found on coral reefs at depths of 13 to 40 m (42 to 130 ft.).

Bodianus mesothorax (Bloch & Schneider, 1801)

Common Names: Coral Hogfish, Mesothorax Hogfish.

Maximum Length: 19 cm (7.5 in.).

Distribution: Christmas Island, Malaysia, Andaman Sea in the Indian Ocean, to Papua New Guinea, north to southern Japan, and

Bodianus mesothorax, Coral Hogfish, small juvenile.

Bodianus opercularis, Redstriped Hogfish: a coveted deep-water species.

south to New South Wales, Australia in the Pacific.

Biology: This species lives on steep fore-reef slopes, often in areas of rich coral growth, at depths from 1 to 40 m (3.3 to 132 ft.). Adult *B. mesothorax* are most often seen in caves and under overhangs, where they often swim upside down. Adults occur singly.

Captive Care: This is a hardy aquarium species that will quickly settle in to captive life. It should not be kept with small, docile fish species. However, it can be kept with larger, less aggressive tankmates. Although it can be housed with other hogfish species, avoid keeping two individuals together or keeping this species with the very similar Axilspot Hogfish. Juveniles can be housed in a reef tank, but adults are destructive, feeding on mollusks, worms, and crustaceans.

Aquarium Size: 75 gal. **Temperature:** 23° to 28°C (74° to 82°F).
Aquarium Suitability Index: 4.

Remarks: This species is very similar to the Axilspot Hogfish. Juveniles of this species have yellow, rather than white, spots. Adults have a black diagonal line that runs from the base of the pectoral fin to the beginning of the soft portion of dorsal fin, and lack spots on the dorsal and anal fins.

Bodianus opercularis (Guichenot, 1847)

Common Name: Redstriped Hogfish.
Maximum Length: 18 cm (7.1 in.).
Distribution: Red Sea to Madagascar and Mauritius, east to Christmas Island, Indian Ocean.
Biology: The Redstriped Hogfish occurs on steep outer reef slopes, at depths from 35 to 70 m (116 to 231 ft.). Little is known about its biology. Field observations indicate that it is a solitary species that moves very close to the substrate. It probably feeds on crustaceans, but may also dart after more elusive prey, like small

fishes. Its streamlined form suggests it would be capable of making quick strikes on fast quarry.

Captive Care: Unfortunately, this beautiful fish is rare in the aquarium trade because of its geographical range and its predilection for deep water. It is a great display animal that readily adjusts to life in a captive environment. *Bodianus opercularis* will spend much of its time in the open, always staying near the aquarium decor in case it has to quickly seek shelter. It is also one of the best hogfishes for the reef aquarium, and although it will acclimate to the higher levels of illumination in a shallow-water reef tank, it is likely to initially spend more time in the open if placed in a tank with less intense lighting. It is also possible that larger *B. opercularis* may eat small bivalves and crustaceans, including ornamental shrimp.

Aquarium Size: 75 gal. **Temperature:** 23° to 28°C (74° to 82°F).
Aquarium Suitability Index: 4.

Remarks: The **Pacific Redstriped Hogfish** (*Bodianus neopercularis*) **Gomon, 2006** differs in having a deeper, less pointed head and in its color. Gomon (2006) states the following: "in *B. neopercularis*, pale spaces between red horizontal stripes are narrower and red stripes slightly broader in specimens of equivalent size, the dorsal-most stripe impinges little if at all onto the base of the dorsal fin, the ventral-most stripe covers virtually all of the pectoral-fin base, the black opercular spot is smaller and diminishes in size with growth, the dorsal fin has a black mark between the anterior spines, the red on the anal fin is more expansive covering all but a narrow white distal margin, the red on the pelvic fin encompasses all but the white narrow anterior and broader antero-distal edges, and the broad transparent or whitish corners of the caudal fin become suffused with red in larger specimens." (Do not confuse *B. neopercularis* with *B. sepiacaudus*—I have used the term Pacific Redstriped Hogfish to refer to the latter species in other books I have written, but the common name Crescenttail Hogfish is better suited to the this species.) *Bodianus neopercularis* is known only from Kwajalein Atoll, in the Marshall Islands, but no doubt occurs elsewhere in this region. It has been collected in 50 m (163 ft.) of water.

Bodianus paraleucosticticus Gomon, 2006

Common Name: Fivestripe Hogfish.

Maximum Length: 20 cm (7.9 in.).

Distribution: Papua New Guinea, Bali, Palau, New Caledonia, Vanuatu, Rarotonga (this deep-water species is probably widely distributed in the South Pacific).

Biology: The Fivestripe Hogfish occurs on deep reef slopes, from at least 50 to 115 m (ft.). It is reported from dropoffs with numerous ledges and caves.

Captive Care: Very few of these fish have been imported for the aquarium trade. I have kept a single specimen, and it proved to be fairly hardy. It was quite frenetic when first added to the tank, dashing back and forth until it was so worn out it would stop, lie on its side for several minutes, and pant. It was not too aggressive and quickly learned to feed on frozen mysid shrimp. It was quite shy for some time, retreating to a cave or behind the rocks when there was activity near the tank. With time, it became more brazen. This *B. paraleucosticticus* would also display at and attack its reflection in the aquarium glass.

Aquarium Size: 75 gal. **Temperature:** 22° to 27° (72° to 80°F).

Aquarium Suitability Index: 4.

Remarks: The Fivestripe Hogfish is a member of a group that includes a number of species that Gomon (2006) places in the subgenus *Peneverreo*. This includes three other species that tend to occur in deep water (usually at depths of 50 m [163 ft.] or more) and have very scattered geographic distributions. The species in this subgenus all have narrow red or orange stripes along the body; juveniles and females have a black spot on the base of the pectoral fin.

Bodianus perditio (Quoy & Gaimard, 1834)

Common Names: Goldspot Hogfish, Goldsaddle Hogfish, Yellow Hogfish.

Maximum Length: 80 cm (31.5 in.).

Distribution: This species has a spotty, antitropical distribution: North Mozambique to southern Africa, east to Mauritius; southern Japan and Taiwan; northwest and eastern Australia to New Caledonia and Lord Howe Island; Tuamotus and Rapa to Pitcairn Islands.

Biology: The adult Goldspot Hogfish are most often found on

Bodianus paraleucosticticus, Fivestripe Hogfish: newly described species.

Bodianus perditio, Goldspot Hogfish, initial phase: prefers cooler water.

Bodianus perditio, Goldspot Hogfish, large adult: too big for most aquaria.

Bodianus prognathus, Longnose Hogfish: similar to *B. dictynna*.

Bodianus pulchellus, Cuban Hogfish: juvenile: a facultative cleaner.

Bodianus pulchellus, Cuban Hogfish, adult: a deep-water beauty.

deep offshore reefs (from 10 to 40 m [33 to 132 ft.]. The juveniles occur on coastal reefs as shallow as 9 m (29 ft.). In New South Wales the juveniles of this species are sometimes found in estuaries. Little else is reported on the biology of this species. It is sometimes taken in trawl nets and is reported to represent 12 percent of the fishes taken on a hook and line off New Caledonia. There are anecdotal reports of their feeding on sea urchins, crabs, and gastropods.

Captive Care: This species is infrequently encountered in aquarium stores. Those individuals that are available are the bright yellow juvenile specimens. They are quite hardy, but will require a large tank as they grow. They can be kept with aggressive tankmates and should not be housed with small, docile fish species. As they get larger they will eat small fishes and crustaceans. Only the smallest specimens are suitable for the reef aquarium, and even they will quickly wear out their welcome when they begin feeding on desirable invertebrates, like worms, bivalves, snails, crustaceans, and echinoderms.

Aquarium Size: 240 gal. **Temperature:** 20° to 25°C (68° to 76°F).
Aquarium Suitability Index: 4.

Remarks: The juvenile of this species is yellow and has a black saddle with a white bar at the anterior edge on its back. Larger individuals are mainly red with small yellow spots on the head, and a diffuse black saddle below and on the dorsal fin with a pale yellow bar preceding it. The Indian Ocean population differs slightly in color from the Pacific form.

Bodianus prognathus Lobel, 1981
Common Name: Longnose Hogfish.
Maximum Length: 18 cm (7.1 in.).

Distribution: Line Islands and Phoenix Group, Central Pacific.
Biology: The Longnose Hogfish occurs on fore-reef slopes and has been collected at depths of 7 to 20 m (23 to 65 ft.). The elongate snout of this species allows it to take advantage of prey hiding in reef crevices and between coral branches that are out of the reach of other *Bodianus* spp.

Captive Care: This is a great aquarium fish that readily acclimates to captivity. It is a peaceful species and can be kept with other, less belligerent fishes. It will eat small bivalves, worms, and crustaceans. Not many fish are collected in the area where these interesting fish live, so few aquarists will ever have the opportunity to keep one of them.

Aquarium Size: 75 gal. **Temperature:** 23° to 27°C (74° to 80°F).
Aquarium Suitability Index: 4.

Remarks: The juveniles of this species are black overall with six

Bodianus rufus, Spanish Hogfish, juvenile: common Caribbean species.

Bodianus rufus, Spanish Hogfish, large male: toothy maw belies invert diet.

large white spots on each side of the body. In overall form and color, the Longnose Hogfish is very similar to Diana's Hogfish (*Bodianus diana*), but its elongate snout sets it apart; the head profile is more like that of the bird wrasses (*Gomphosus* spp.) than other hogfishes.

Bodianus pulchellus (Poey, 1860)

Common Names: Cuban Hogfish, Spotfin Hogfish.
Maximum Length: 15 cm (5.9 in.).
Distribution: South Florida and Gulf of Mexico to Brazil.
Biology: The Cuban Hogfish is a resident of deep rocky and coral reef slopes. This species is most common at depths greater than 30 m (98 ft.), and has been reported as deep as 106 m (345 ft.). However, during the spawning season, juveniles are often found under ledges at depths as shallow as 7.5 m (25 ft.). The juveniles of this species, like many hogfishes, are facultative cleaners.
Captive Care: This is a very hardy, colorful aquarium fish that will thrive if kept in a well-maintained aquarium with plenty of swimming room and adequate hiding places. It will accept a variety of foods, including chopped seafood, frozen preparations, and flake foods. It can be kept with an assortment of tankmates, although an occasional adult may pick on smaller fishes, especially if they are all housed in a small tank. More than one of these hogfish can be kept in the same tank, or it can be housed with other hogfish species. If you want to keep more than one individual in the same tank, it is prudent to add them to the tank simultaneously. Unfortunately, the intense red color often fades in captivity. This might be able to prevent this if you feed the fish a varied diet and keep more than one individual in the same tank. Juveniles frequently clean their tankmates.

Aquarium Size: 55 gal. **Temperature:** 12.5° to 25°C (55° to 78°F).
Aquarium Suitability Index: 4.
Remarks: Juveniles of this species, under about 6 cm (2.5 in.), are lemon yellow overall, with a black spot on the anterior part of the dorsal fin. They usually assume the adult color phase within weeks after being placed in the aquarium. *Bodianus pulchellus* has been reported to cross-breed with the Spanish Hogfish.

Bodianus rufus (Linnaeus, 1758)

Common Name: Spanish Hogfish.
Maximum Length: 40 cm (15.7 in.).
Distribution: South Florida and Bermuda to southern Brazil.
Biology: This is a resident of rocky and coral reefs. It is found on reef flats, sand and rubble slopes, and fore-reef slopes at depths from 1 to 60 m (3 to 198 ft.). The Spanish Hogfish feeds primarily on crabs, serpent stars, and urchins, but it will also eat snails, bivalves, shrimp, hermit crabs, mantis shrimp, isopods, chitons, and polychaete worms. Adults commonly follow fishes that disturb the substrate when they feed, like snake eels and goatfishes. Juveniles are also facultative cleaners, removing crustacean parasites from the bodies and fins of their clients. They will set up cleaning stations that are frequently visited by groupers and Creole Wrasses (*Clepticus parrae*). They will often clean with other parasite-pickers, like the gobies in the genus *Gobiosoma*.

This hogfish lives in harems consisting of one male and up to 12 females. The females live within the territory of the male, which covers an area of about 400 to 600 m² (4,304 to 6,456 ft.²). During the day, males spend most of their time patrolling their territory, while females forage. About an hour before sunset, the male begins visiting, and spawning with, every female in his

Bodianus sepiacaudus, Crescenttail Hogfish: hardy, but prone to jumping.

Bodianus sepiacaudus, Crescenttail Hogfish: darker color morph.

harem. If something happens to the male, the most dominant female will undergo a sex change and become a fully functional male within 7 to 10 days. A female's position in the dominance hierarchy is a function of size, with smaller fish being subservient to larger individuals.

Captive Care: This species can be shy and retiring when first introduced to the aquarium, but within a day or two it will become bold and boisterous. Adolescent and adult individuals should not be kept with docile fish species, as they are likely to bully them. The Spanish Hogfish is an active species, and the large specimens require plenty of swimming room. Juveniles will often clean other fishes in captivity, although they are not as dependent on parasites or fish slime for survival as some of the obligatory cleaners.

Aquarium Size: 180 gal. **Temperature:** 72° to 80°C (22° to 27°F).
Aquarium Suitability Index: 4.
Remarks: The coloration of this species varies. The dorsal coloration may be reddish brown, deep purple, or blue, while the ventrum, the paired fins, and most of the anal fin are yellow. Specimens from greater depths may be bluish black overall.

Bodianus sepiacaudus Gomon, 2006

Common Names: Crescenttail Hogfish, Inktail Hogfish, Pacific Redstriped Hogfish.
Maximum Length: 10 cm (3.9 in.).
Distribution: Sulawesi, Flores and Bali, Indonesia, Fijian Islands, and Kiritimati Atoll and Line Islands in the central Pacific.
Biology: Rudie Kuiter reports seeing this species at depths be-

tween 20 and 50 m (66 to 165 ft.) off Sulawesi, while off Christmas Island it is reported from depths greater than 60 m (200 ft.). Kuiter reports observing a loose group of six individuals moving along a wall with ledges and enormous sponges. He observed young fish at greater depths (50 m [165 ft.]). This hogfish occurred in the same habitat with Burgess' Butterflyfish (*Chaetodon burgessi*).

Captive Care: I have found the Crescenttail Hogfish to be a great display animal that readily adjusts to captive life. The individual I kept was relatively nonaggressive, ignoring butterflies, pygmy angels, cardinalfishes, large gobies, and a fairy wrasse kept with it. While I have never kept two together, I have seen it behave aggressively toward its reflection in a mirror I placed in the tank, indicating that placing two individuals in the same aquarium may be risky. Larger individuals may eat small bivalves and crustaceans, including ornamental shrimp. I have seen this fish target similarly shaped wrasses and chase them incessantly. For example, an individual in a 105-gallon tank (a prior resident) harassed a Whitebarred Wrasse (*Pseudocheilinus ocellatus*) until it jumped into the overflow box. I put the wrasse back into the tank, and the chasing began again. This hogfish moves just over the substrate, inspecting cracks, crevices, and polyps for potential food. I never saw it turning pieces of rubble or disturbing the aquarium substrate in any way. It is fairly bold, spending most of its time moving in the open. It is a voracious feeder that will accept a wide array of aquarium foods, including chopped table shrimp, frozen mysid shrimp, frozen preparations, and flake foods. I have kept it with a variety of cleaner shrimp species and with pistol

Lachnolaimus maximus, Rooster Hogfish, adult: note long dorsal filaments.

Lachnolaimus maximus, Rooster Hogfish, juvenile: cute but bound to grow.

shrimps that were living with shrimpgobies and never observed it attacking these crustaceans. I did keep a larger individual with a Banded Coral Shrimp (*Stenopus hispidus*), which it ignored until the shrimp molted, at which time the hogfish nipped all of its legs off. However, I have only seen this hogfish attack shrimp on this one occasion. The Crescenttail Hogfish will become a great pet, swimming to the front of the tank when it sees the aquarist coming toward the aquarium. In fact, it spends most of its time swimming about in the open. This fish will jump out of an open aquarium.

Aquarium Size: 55 gal. **Temperature:** 72° to 82°C (22° to 28°F).

Aquarium Suitability Index: 4.

Remarks: The Crescenttail Hogfish has a yellowish caudal fin with a red margin, and the lines running down the body turn from red to black where they meet on the caudal peduncle.

Genus *Lachnolaimus* (Hogfish)

Lachnolaimus maximus (Walbaum, 1792)

Common Names: Rooster Hogfish, Hogfish, Common Hogfish, Hog Snapper.

Maximum Length: 91 cm (35.8 in.).

Distribution: North Carolina, Bermuda, Gulf of Mexico, throughout the Caribbean, south to Brazil.

Biology: The Rooster Hogfish is most abundant in sandy areas with large stands of gorgonians, although it is also observed on fore reef slopes and near patch reefs on occasion. It is reported from depths of 3 to 30 m (10 to 98 ft.). It feeds mainly on ben-thic invertebrates, including bivalves, snails, crabs, hermit crabs, and sea urchins. It shoves its large jaws into the substrate and takes in a mouthful of sand, then sorts the edible infaunal organisms from the inedible sediment. It tends to be a solitary species. This hogfish spawns in the summer.

Captive Care: Most Rooster Hogfish that enter the aquarium trade are juveniles, but aquarists, beware. This species attains immense proportions and will outgrow all but the largest home aquarium. It is a durable aquarium fish that should be provided with plenty of open sandy bottom. Larger individuals will eat small fishes, and most sizes of this species will eat ornamental crustaceans. Although juveniles can be housed together in the same tank, adolescent and adult individuals are likely to fight. Larger specimens are very effective at stirring up the aquarium substrate.

Aquarium Size: 240 gal. **Temperature:** 20° to 29°C (68° to 82°F).

Aquarium Suitability Index: 4.

Remarks: This species has three elongate dorsal spines that resemble the comb of a rooster, hence the common name. The coloration of this species is variable. Juveniles and subadults are usually brown, reddish brown, or greenish, with darker mottling and a black spot on the rear margin of the dorsal fin. Large males are pearl white overall with a dark maroon area from the tip of the snout, running under the eye, to the origin of the dorsal fin. They have black on the pelvic fins and all the median fins. This species is not only sexually dichromatic; large males also have a longer snout with a concave, rather than straight, head profile and a larger mouth. The mouth is very protrusible.

The first time I met a cheeklined Maori wrasse (*Cheilinus diagrammus*) I was not in my local aquarium store but on a coral reef in Fiji. I recognized the fish, having had seen its photo in books before, but I was not aware that it was a fish with such "personality." I was moving along the edge of the reef, occasionally resting on the sand. I noticed that this wrasse was following me and that every time I would put my fin on the soft substrate, it would dash in to see if I had displaced some poor, sheltering worm or crustacean. I soon became intrigued by my piscine companion and began flipping bits of rubble and digging in the sand, as my "pet" *C. diagrammus* followed along and pounced on anything I succeeded in flushing out. From that encounter on, I have been in love with Maori wrasses.

Unfortunately, not all Maori wrasses are ideal aquarium inhabitants. But if you have a large enough tank, and are prepared to make some sacrifices when it comes to selecting tankmates, the Maori wrasses can make a delightful addition to the large home aquarium.

Biology

The Maori wrasses belong to the labrid tribe Cheilinini and the subfamily Cheilininae, which also includes the fairy wrasses (*Cirrhilabrus*), slingjaw wrasses (*Epibulus*), flasher wrasses (*Paracheilinus*), lined wrasses (*Pseudocheilinus*), the pinkstreaked wrasse (*Pseudocheilinops ataenia*), sneaky wrasses (*Pteragogus*), and possum wrasses (*Wetmorella*).

There are 16 described species in the two Maori wrasse genera, *Cheilinus* and *Oxycheilinus* (Kuiter [2000] suggests that the latter is a subgenus). They get their name from their facial markings, which are reminiscent of the tattoos that the indigenous people of New Zealand adorn themselves with. The Maori wrasses, on the whole, are different from many of the other genera in this subfamily.

First of all, consider the maximum lengths of the Maori wrasse species. They range in size from the Twinspot Maori Wrasse (*Oxycheilinus bimaculatus*), which reaches 15 cm (5.9 in.) in total length, to the leviathan of the reef fish world, the Humphead Maori Wrasse (*Cheilinus lunulatus*), which attains a span of

Cheilinus lunulatus, Broomtail Wrasse: a big, dramatic species from the Western Indian Ocean and Red Sea. Small specimens come into the aquarium trade, but note the full adult size of 50 cm (19.6 inches).

Cheilinus fasciatus, Redbreasted Maori Wrasse: a wily predator, the wrasse (top) shadows a hunting *Parupeneus* goatfish, ready to snatch any prey it disturbs.

229 cm (90 inches). Most of the members of the genera *Oxycheilinus* are smaller than those in the genus *Cheilinus* (most are under 20 cm [7.9 in.] in total length).

Because most of the Maori wrasses attain greater proportions, they are able to handle a wider range of prey items. All of the *Cheilinus* and *Oxycheilinus* spp. are voracious predators that feed on a variety of invertebrates and fishes. They have strong jaws and large canine teeth that are effective at grasping active prey species as well as breaking up larger food items, and pharyngeal teeth to crush up invertebrate hard parts (see image on the facing page of a *Cheilinus fasciatus* crunching up a mollusk). They stalk or ambush their prey and some employ unusual hunting techniques.

For example, many Maori wrasses (e.g., Floral Maori Wrasse, *Cheilinus chlororus*) associate with goatfishes, triggerfishes, and stingrays (i.e., species that disturb bottom materials) and capture prey that these fish flush from the substrate. Likewise, a diver can attract them very easily underwater by lifting and turning over pieces of rubble or wafting the sand with his or her hand.

At least one species, the Cheeklined Maori Wrasse (*Oxycheilinus diagrammus*), will also use herbivores as a moving blind to approach its prey. Food habit studies suggest that they typically consume one large prey item and then don't feed again for possibly two or three days. At least one species (i.e., *Oxycheilinus unifasciatus*) hunts most frequently early and late in the day and all Maori wrasses sleep in reef crevices at night.

These wrasses are thought to be protogynous hermaphrodites and are sexually dichromatic and/or dimorphic. In most cases the morphological differences between the sexes involves the shape of the tail (e.g., males have one or more long filamentous rays). Males are generally larger than females. No information exists on the social structure of the Maori wrasses, but they are usually observed as solitary individuals.

Oxycheilinus dragrammus, Cheeklined Maori Wrasse: eating a dragonet.

Cheilinus undulatus, Humphead or Napoleon Wrasse: urchin spines in "lips," signs of an urchin dinner.

Captive Care

Their large size, strong dentition, and predatory nature makes the Maori Wrasses a greater threat in the aquarium than other members of the subfamily Cheilininae. But when first placed in the aquarium, they are often shy, lying behind reef structures—sometimes for days—before making an appearance. Although they can be aggressive fishes once they acclimate, they are very sensitive to being picked on during the initial adjustment period. If they are intimidated or attacked by larger angelfishes, surgeonfishes, triggerfishes, or porcupinefishes they will not adapt and die. Therefore, they should be introduced into the aquarium first if housed with these types of fishes. If they are going to be kept with less aggressive species (e.g., butterflyfishes, sweetlips, goatfishes) they should be added to the aquarium after them.

It is also important that the aquarist not bother them during acclimation. As they become more accustomed to the aquarium they will do less lurking and explore more exposed areas of the tank. They may display combative tendencies, occasionally nipping other fishes or chasing new introductions. Beware, they can and will eat smaller fishes. No more than one Maori wrasse of the same species should be kept per aquarium, since fighting is likely to occur in aquarium confines. If you want to keep two *Cheilinus* or *Oxycheilinus* spp. in the same aquarium introduce them simultaneously and provide plenty of hiding places. Species that are different in shape and color (e.g., *C. chlorourus* and *O. unifasciatus*) will be more likely to get along than similar forms (e.g., *O. diagrammus* and *O. unifasciatus*). Some Maori wrasses may also display aggression toward similarly shaped wrasses.

Maori wrasses are usually not particular about what they eat. They will feed on larger pieces of fresh seafood, cubes of frozen prepared foods (that have been thawed), and live feeder fish or

Cheilinus fasciatus, Redbreasted Maori Wrasse: attempts to ingest clam.

shrimp. If you have a specimen that is reluctant to feed, try adding some small live bearers (e.g., guppies or mollies) to the aquarium. I have yet to see a Maori wrasse refuse such an offering. It is important to switch them over to a more natural food source once they have been induced to feed. These fishes will also eat snails, tubeworms, ornamental shrimps, small crabs, brittle stars, sea stars, and even urchins. I would not recommend them for the reef aquarium. They eat mantis shrimps, so if you can house one with your live rock and remove it before adding your desirable invertebrates it may help decrease stomatopod numbers. I have also had larger specimens consume fireworms.

Cheilinus abudjubbe, Abudjubbe's Maori Wrasse, female.

Cheilinus abudjubbe, Abudjubbe's Maori Wrasse, male.

Cheilinus chlorourus, Floral Maori Wrasse, juvenile.

Cheilinus chlorourus, Floral Maori Wrasse, adult male, note tail filaments.

Genus *Cheilinus*

Cheilinus abudjubbe Rüppell, 1835
Common Name: Abudjubee's Maori Wrasse.
Maximum Length: 40 cm (15.7 in.).
Distribution: Red Sea.
Biology: This species is found on protected back reefs and sheltered bays in areas with rich stony and soft coral growth. It is found at depths from 3 to 15 m (10 to 49 ft.). Males are often seen in the open, while juveniles and females are more secretive.
Captive Care: Abudjubee's Maori Wrasse does well in the aquarium if carefully acclimated. Provide plenty of hiding places and avoid introducing it into an aquarium with aggressive fishes, like large damselfishes, large hawkfishes, angelfishes, and triggerfishes. Despite its potential size, it is easily bullied at first. Once acclimated it may behave aggressively toward fishes introduced after it, especially conspecifics and related forms. This species will eat smaller fishes, ornamental shrimps, bivalves, and snails.
Aquarium Size: 135 gal. **Temperature:** 22° to 28°C (72° to 82°F).
Aquarium Suitability Index: 4.
Remarks: This species is closely related to the Floral Maori Wrasse (*Cheilinus chlorurus*) and the Tripletail Maori Wrasse (*C. trilobatus*).

Cheilinus chlorourus (Bloch, 1791)
Common Names: Floral Maori Wrasse, Whitedotted Maori Wrasse.
Maximum Length: 45 cm (17.7 in.).
Distribution: East Africa to the Marquesas and Tuamotus, north to the Ryukyus, and south to New Caledonia and Rapa.

Cheilinus chlorourus, Floral Maori Wrasse, female. Adults are sometimes found in repose among sponges and corals during the day, in rocky crevices at night.

Biology: The Floral Maori Wrasse is most common in lagoons and along fringing coastal reef faces. It is usually observed searching for prey among coral rubble or following goatfishes feeding in the sand. The Floral Maori Wrasse is found at depths from 2 to 30 m (7 to 98 ft.). It feeds primarily on small snails, which it ingests whole or masticates into smaller pieces, but also consumes crustaceans, polychaete worms, and sea urchins. One individual was reported to have eaten beetles.

Captive Care: In captivity, juvenile *C. chlorourus* tend to be quite secretive. When initially introduced to the aquarium they will lay against the decor and assume a mottled color pattern. It will not be long, however, before they start making short forays into the open to catch passing food items. This wrasse is one of the least aggressive members of the genus and can be kept with fishes as small as half its total length if they are introduced before it. It is interesting to house it with goatfishes or other predators that grub in the substrate. This wrasse is larger and will make short work of many motile invertebrates.

Aquarium Size: 135 gal. **Temperature:** 22° to 27°C (72° to 80°F).

Aquarium Suitability Index: 4.

Remarks: The Floral Maori Wrasse is occasionally sold in aquarium stores, but because it is not extremely colorful it is not highly sought after. It is typically brown or greenish brown overall with lines of white dots on its body and pink dots on its face. It has a black spot on the front of the dorsal fin base. Adult males differ from females in having filaments extending from the top and bottom of the tail fin.

Cheilinus fasciatus (Bloch, 1791)

Common Names: Redbreasted Maori Wrasse, Redband Maori Wrasse.

Maximum Length: 38 cm (14.9 in.).

Distribution: Red Sea to Samoa, north to the Ryukyus, and south to New Caledonia.

Biology: The Redbreasted Maori Wrasse is most often found near lagoon patch reefs, where the bottom consists of patches of live coral, sand and coral rubble. It if found at depths of 4 to at least 40 m (13 to 130 ft.). The Redbreasted Maori Wrasse will take

Cheilinus fasciatus, Redbreasted Maori Wrasse, juvenile.

Cheilinus fasciatus, Redbreasted Maori Wrasse, female, Red Sea.

Cheilinus fasciatus, Redbreasted Maori Wrasse, male.

Cheilinus quinquecinctus, Fivebanded Maori Wrasse, male, Red Sea.

Cheilinus quinquecinctus, Fivebanded Maori Wrasse, male.

pieces of rubble in its mouth and lift them to one side to expose prey hidden beneath. It often associates with species that disturb bottom sediments when they feed. It is a voracious, opportunistic predator that often follows grubbing goatfishes. Donaldson (1995) reported on the spawning in this species. He observed a male patrolling in the water column above a coral promontory in the afternoon (i.e., 3:00 p.m.). Soon, females began rising from surrounding *Acropora* beds and aggregated in the center of this coral structure. The male then approached one of the seven females and circled her. The pair rose into the water column, engaging in circling and head bobbing as courtship escalated. The pair then swam parallel to one another and began to rise in the water column. About 2 m (7 ft.) above the starting point, gametes were released. The female swam back to the seafloor while

Cheilinus lunulatus, Broomtail Maori Wrasse, a popular specimen at Denmark's Copenhagen Public Aquarium. Note stout canines.

Cheilinus lunulatus, Broomtail Maori Wrasse: adult male over reef.

Cheilinus oxycephalus, Snooty Maori Wrasse: brown variant.

the male moved on to the next female. Courtship and spawning occurred with all seven females in a 5-minute time span.

Captive Care: This attractive species is suitable for some large fish aquariums. Its larger size, both length and girth, means that it is potentially dangerous to smaller fishes. However, juveniles are usually well behaved.

Aquarium Size: 135 gal. **Temperature:** 22° to 27°C (72° to 80°F).

Aquarium Suitability Index: 4.

Remarks: The body is brown overall with white bars. Juveniles and females have a yellow-orange area near the pectoral fin, while in large males there is a large bright orange area behind the head. Males also have a truncate tail with elongate rays at the top and bottom. The **Fivebanded Maori Wrasse (*Cheilinus quinquecinctus*) Rüppell, 1835** is a similar species that is endemic to the Red Sea. *Cheilinus quinquecinctus* has a ragged tail margin and differs in color. This wrasse is found on back reefs, reef faces, and reef slopes at depths of 7 to 25 m (23 to 83 ft.). This species is sometimes the victim of scale-eating blennies (*Plagiotremus* spp.), possibly because of the excessive amounts of slime it produces and its large scales. I have seen them chase these blennies for 1 or 2 m (3 to 7 ft.) before the little fish even had a chance to bite them, and observed one specimen getting nipped several times by different blennies as it swam a meter or more above the reef. The wrasse would abruptly stop, lean to one side, and curve its body, anticipating the next blennioid assault. *Cheilinus quinquecinctus* attains a length of 40 cm (15.7 in.).

Cheilinus lunulatus (Forsskål, 1775)

Common Name: Broomtail Maori Wrasse.

Maximum Length: 50 cm (19.7 in.).

Distribution: Red Sea and Gulf of Oman.

Biology: The Broomtail Maori Wrasse most often occurs on the reef flat and near the edge of steep reef slopes but is also found in deep water on the fore reef. It is reported at depths from the surface to at least 30 m (98 ft.). I had the opportunity to see this species spawn on Jackson reef in the Straits of Tiran about an hour before sunset. Females aggregated near the reef edge as one large male patrolled the area and displayed its magnificent finnage and coloration. As the male approached, a female rose from the bottom to swim just beneath him. The male placed his lower jaw against the female's upper flank and begin pushing her through the water. At the same time she swam slightly upward so the two fish maintained contact as they moved forward. The male's back often broke the water's surface as the two swam together. Suddenly, the male rapidly pushed the female down, gametes were released, and the female rushed back to the bottom. The male then chased nearby fishes, like snappers hanging in the water column, or began to patrol again. The male spawned with three females and was still patrolling when I had to abort the dive.

Captive Care: This Maori wrasse requires a large aquarium with plenty of swimming room, as well as several suitable hiding places, to thrive in captivity. It can be fed chunks of seafood and frozen preparations, as well as freshwater crayfish, cleaned earth-

Cheilinus oxycephalus, Snooty Maori Wrasse: beautiful red variant of a commonly available species that tends to be somewhat shy and secretive.

worms, and fiddler crabs. *Cheilinus lunulatus* will eat a wide variety of aquarium invertebrates and fishes that it can swallow whole. It is prudent not to house this fish with other Maori wrasses, including members of its own kind.

Aquarium Size: 240 gal. **Temperature:** 22° to 28°C (72° to 82°F).

Aquarium Suitability Index: 4.

Remarks: The Redbreasted Maori Wrasse (*C. fasciatus*) is often sold as *C. lunulatus*, but they are easily differentiated by the yellow markings on the operculum edge which are present on both male and female Broomtail Maori Wrasses. The male Broomtail has extremely long filaments on the edge of its caudal fin (hence the name), has a flatter profile, longer pelvic fins, and is more colorful than the female. Males are also much larger.

Cheilinus oxycephalus Bleeker, 1853

Common Name: Snooty Maori Wrasse.

Maximum Length: 17 cm (6.7 in.).

Distribution: East Africa to the Marquesas and Society Islands, north to Taiwan, and south to the Great Barrier Reef.

Biology: The Snooty Maori Wrasse is typically found in areas with heavy coral growth and rarely ventures far from its hiding places. In certain parts of Fiji it is commonly seen swimming among large stands of the soft coral *Sinularia flexibilis* and will disappear under these cnidarians if threatened. *Cheilinus oxycephalus* occurs at depths from 1 to 40 m (3 to 130 ft.). Its diet consists of alpheid shrimp, crabs, amphipods, and small snails. This species will also follow feeding goatfishes.

Captive Care: The Snooty Maori Wrasse is a secretive species that is regularly seen in the North American trade. It is a more sensitive species due to its more reclusive nature; therefore, good hiding places and less aggressive tankmates are a prerequisite for successful acclimation. If it acclimates it will thrive. It tends to be less aggressive than its congeners as well, so it can be kept with less pugnacious species. But it is still an unacceptable addition to an aquarium with small passive fishes.

Aquarium Size: 75 gal. **Temperature:** 22° to 27°C (72° to 80°F).

Aquarium Suitability Index: 4.

Remarks: This species has a longer, pointed snout, a concave head profile, and the tail is rounded. The body is brownish red to bright red with small white spots.

Cheilinus trilobatus, Tripletail Maori Wrasse, female.

Cheilinus trilobatus, Tripletail Maori Wrasse, large male.

Cheilinus trilobatus Lacepède, 1801

Common Name: Tripletail Maori Wrasse.
Maximum Length: 45 cm (17.7 in.).
Distribution: East Africa to the Tuamotus, north to the Ryukyus, and south to New Caledonia and Austral Island.
Biology: This Maori wrasse occurs at depths from 1 to over 30 m (3 to 98 ft.), inhabiting coral-rich areas of the lagoon and fore reef, especially where there are numerous crevices and holes. Around the Marshall Islands, *C. trilobatus* feeds mainly on fishes and crustaceans (including crabs, hermit crabs, and shrimps), and it will occasionally consume mollusks. Off the Kenyan coast it is an important urchin predator. Large individuals will take urchins and break them into manageable pieces by bashing them against the reef. Smaller urchins are simply crushed in the powerful jaws. Urchin predation is more common in terminal phase

males; this is because they are larger and better equipped to handle these spiny invertebrates.
Captive Care: This is a large, showy species that is not common in the aquarium trade. It is quite shy, spending most of its time lurking in crevices in the wild and in the aquarium. Like all Maori wrasses, *C. trilobatus* can be trained to come out to feed, becoming bolder once they start associating the aquarist with food. The Tripletail Maori Wrasse is hazardous to small fishes, small *Tridacna* clams, and many other invertebrates.
Aquarium Size: 200 gal. **Temperature:** 22° to 28°C (72° to 82°F).
Aquarium Suitability Index: 4.
Remarks: The body color is olive to brown with a pink and pale blue-green line on each scale, and pink dots and lines on the head and thorax. Juveniles, which are most common in the hobby, have three dark spots running down the middle of each side. The caudal fin is rounded in juveniles and females, but in large males the tail has three distinct lobes.

Cheilinus undulatus Rüppell, 1835

Common Names: Humphead Maori Wrasse, Napoleon Wrasse.
Maximum Length: 229 cm (90 in.). A specimen of this length weighed 191 kg (419 lb.).
Distribution: Red Sea to the Tuamotus, north to the Ryukyus, and south to New Caledonia.
Biology: The Humphead Maori Wrasse occurs at depths from 1 to 60 m (3 to 195 ft.). Juveniles are most common in shallow lagoons, where they refuge among branching corals, while adults are found on steep outer-reef slopes and in reef channels. This species is usually solitary or occurs in small aggregations consisting of one male and several females. Large *C. undulatus* are home ranging and usually sleep in the same cave every night. This wrasse is an eating machine. It feeds primarily on bivalves (including *Tridacna* clams), as well as fishes (including eels, fairy wrasses, and sleeper gobies), crustaceans, sea urchins, brittle stars, and sea stars. It is not uncommon to see larger specimens with broken urchin spines sticking out of their lips (see photo on page 81). The Humphead will even feed on toxic species, like the coral-eating Crown-of-Thorns Sea Stars, trunkfishes, and sea hares. The Humphead Maori Wrasse has very protrusible jaws that can be used to extract prey out of reef crevices. I observed a large female *C. undulatus* extract a moray eel corpse out of a reef interstice by shooting its extensible jaws into the hollow. Several larger groupers tried to get at this morsel but were unsuccessful.

Cheilinus undulatus, Humphead Maori Wrasse or Napoleon Wrasse: a magnificent fish, but threatened by overfishing to supply Asian food markets, where it is considered a gourmet treasure and fetches large sums of money.

Cheilinus undulatus, Humphead Maori Wrasse: large male yawning. Listed as endangered, and one of the few predatory biocontrols for Crown-of-Thorns Starfish.

Cheilinus undulatus, Humphead Wrasse, juvenile: sold as "assorted wrasses."

It also uses its extensible jaws to pluck nocturnal mollusks from the reef during the day. This species gets concealed prey items by biting off coral branches, by blowing water out its mouth toward the sand, and by overturning rocks by lifting them in its powerful jaws. Jacks will sometimes associate with this species, using the larger wrasses as moving blinds to approach prey or hanging around them when they excavate prey buried in the sand. I have also seen adolescent Humphead Maori Wrasses associating with large aggregations of Yellowsaddle Goatfish (*Parupeneus cyclostomus*). This wrasse's body is compressed and surprisingly supple, which allows it to enter narrow fissures in the reef and swim under low ledges to find prey. Adult Humphead Maori Wrasses usually occur singly, but are sometimes observed in pairs or small aggregations. Groups consisting of an adult male and up to five females have been observed swimming in single file along the reef edge near sunset. Juveniles also aggregate on occasion, with as many as 12 young *C. undulatus* having been reported mixing with a school of adult rabbitfish. This species exhibits diandric protogyny—that is, males are derived from female sex change and from small juveniles.

Captive Care: Believe it or not, this behemoth does make its way to aquarium stores from time to time. Due to their huge maximum size, these fish should be avoided unless you have an extra-large aquarium.

Aquarium Suitability Index: Not suitable. Should be reserved for public aquaria or left in the wild.

Remarks: Juveniles look nothing like the adults; they are light brown to pale green with elongate black spots on each scale, and two black lines extending from the back of the eye, two from the top of the eye, and two from the front of the eye downward onto the snout. Juvenile *C. undulatus* also lack the hump on the head, which is especially pronounced in adult males.

Genus *Oxycheilinus*

Oxycheilinus arenatus (Valenciennes, 1840)

Common Names: Arenate Maori Wrasse, Thinline Maori Wrasse.
Maximum Length: 19 cm (7.4 in.).
Distribution: Red Sea to Samoa and north to the Philippines.
Biology: The Arenate Maori Wrasse is most common on steep fore-reef slopes and is often found in caves or moving among soft corals. It occurs at depths of 25 to over 50 m (83 to 165 ft.).
Captive Care: The Arenate Maori Wrasse is a hardy aquarium fish that should be housed with moderately aggressive tankmates. I have seen this species retaliate toward fishes that behaved aggressively toward it. For example, when a sandperch nipped my Arenate Maori Wrasse, the wrasse turned and bit it back and began chasing it around the tank. It is often reclusive when first introduced to the aquarium, but will become bolder with time. It is easily startled. I have had one jump out of the tank when I was cleaning the aquarium glass. This fish will eat most aquarium fare, but live ghost shrimp and guppies are favorite foods. This wrasse can be kept in a shallow- or deep-water reef aquarium; however, it will eat ornamental crustaceans (including *Stenopus* shrimps) and small fishes.

Aquarium Size: 100 gal. **Temperature:** 22° to 27°C (72° to 80°F).
Aquarium Suitability Index: 5.
Remarks: This species can change its color in an instant, changing from totally red to pinkish white with a red stripe down its side. *Oxycheilinus arenatus* has a stripe down the middle of the body and a bluish blotch on the front of the dorsal fin. It is often sold in the aquarium trade as a "Longjaw" Wrasse. The **Mental Maori Wrasse** (*Oxycheilinus mentalis*) (**Rüppell, 1828**) is thought to be endemic to the Red Sea (although some suggest it also occurs in the western Indian Ocean). It attains a length of 20 cm (7.8 in.) and is most common on fringing reefs and on shallow fore-reef slopes, at depths from 1 to 20 m (3 to 66 ft.). Kuiter (2000)

Oxycheilinus celebicus, Sulawesi Maori Wrasse: one of many Maori wrasses that hunt cooperatively with goatfishes, such as this Yellowsaddle Goatfish.

Oxycheilinus arenatus, Arenate Maori Wrasse: deep-water species.

Oxycheilinus bimaculatus, Twinspot Maori Wrasse: color variable.

Oxycheilinus nigromarginatus, Blackmargined Maori Wrasse.

Oxycheilinus orientalis, Oriental Maori Wrasse: one of several similar species.

distinguishes it from similar species by a black spot that occurs above the pectoral base of male individuals. Juveniles have a small ocellus in the middle of the caudal peduncle. The **Oriental Maori Wrasse (*Oxycheilinus orientalis*) (Günther, 1862)** is a very similar species that is found from northern Indonesia to the Ryukyus. It attains a maximum length of 12 cm (4.7 in.). The Oriental Maori Wrasse is most common in lagoons, in areas of rich coral or dense algae growth, at depths from 18 to 70 m (60 to 231 ft.). Juveniles are often found living among crinoids. *Oxycheilinus orientalis* is often found foraging on mixed rubble and algae slopes with conspecifics and other wrasse species. This species usually has a spot at the base of the tail and one further forward on the body. Kuiter (2000) reports they also have a black blotch on the side between the dorsal fin and the lateral line. The **Blackmargined Maori Wrasse (*Oxycheilinus nigromarginatus*) Randall, Westneat & Gomon, 2003** is a small species (14 cm [5.5 in.] from East Australia, New Caledonia, and Tonga.

Oxycheilinus bimaculatus (Valenciennes, 1840)
Common Name: Twinspot Maori Wrasse.
Maximum Length: 15 cm (5.9 in.).
Distribution: East Africa to the Hawaiian Islands, north to southern Japan, and south to Vanuatu.
Biology: The Twinspot Maori Wrasse is typically found in lagoon seagrass meadows, over coral rubble bottoms, and among macroalgae and sponge on coastal reefs. It also occurs in estuaries and harbors. Young individuals are often found living among macroalgae. It has been reported at depths of 2 to 110 m (7 to 358 ft.). I have observed this species following an Indian Goatfish (*Parupeneus indicus*) as it fed and joint-hunting with a juvenile Yellowsaddle Goatfish (*P. cyclostomus*). Males often engage in vio-

Oxycheilinus bimaculatus, Twinspot Maori Wrasse: colorful male in typical wild habitat, over coral rubble bottoms. Often sold as the "Longjaw Wrasse."

lent combat. They display at each other, at which time their color intensifies and they erect all their fins. If aggression escalates, they lock jaws, twisting and pulling, sometimes resulting in torn flesh around the jaws. I have seen a pair remain with jaws locked for over 10 seconds. They then separated and began the whole process over again until they were once again engaged in "jaw-to-jaw" combat. Finally, the loser swam off.

Captive Care: This is the most common member of the genus in the U.S. aquarium trade and is usually sold as the red "Longjaw" Wrasse. It is also the smallest *Cheilinus* spp. and is attractively marked. It is a fairly durable fish that will quickly acclimate to captive life. Although it becomes quite aggressive once it has fully adjusted to its new home, if introduced to a tank that contains pugnacious species it may have difficulty acclimating. This fish will eat almost anything: small fishes, ornamental crustaceans, and many other motile invertebrates (including snails and serpent stars); bristle worms and small mantis shrimps; flake and pelletized foods, fresh and frozen seafood, and frozen preparations.

Aquarium Size: 75 gal. **Temperature:** 22° to 28°C (72° to 82°F).

Aquarium Suitability Index: 5.

Remarks: The color is variable, but it is typically reddish brown overall with white flecks and blotches and a dark blotch behind the pectoral fin. It has orange lines radiating from the eye with a small green spot behind. Males differ from females in having a rhomboid caudal fin with a single elongate filament extending from the top (females have round tails with no filament).

Oxycheilinus bimaculatus, Twinspot Maori Wrasse: fighting males frequently engage in jaw-locking behavior. The loser eventually will flee the territory.

Oxycheilinus celebicus, Sulawesi Maori Wrasse, juvenile.

Oxycheilinus celebicus, Sulawesi Maori Wrasse, female.

Oxycheilinus celebicus, Sulawesi Maori Wrasse, male.

Oxycheilinus celebicus (Bleeker, 1853)

Common Names: Sulawesi Maori Wrasse, Celebes Maori Wrasse.

Maximum Length: 24 cm (9.4 in.).

Distribution: Indonesia to the Marshall Islands, north to Japan, and south as far as Rowley Shoals, near northwestern Australia.

Biology: The Sulawesi Maori Wrasse occurs at depths from 3 to 30 m (10 to 98 ft.) on sheltered reefs with rich coral growth. I have also seen numerous juveniles of this species on turbid, low-profile coastal reefs composed primarily of algae, sponge, and large-polyped stony corals. Adults are also seen on fore-reef slopes over coral rubble. The Sulawesi Maori Wrasse often moves or hovers among soft corals. Though this is a solitary species, I have seen it cooperatively hunting with the Multibarred Goatfish (*Parupeneus multifasciatus*).

Captive Care: The husbandry of this species is similar to that of the Cheeklined Maori Wrasse (*Oxycheilinus diagrammus*). It is slightly smaller than this species, but is still a threat to many different types of motile invertebrates and small fishes. It will jump out of open aquariums.

Aquarium Size: 100 gal. **Temperature:** 22° to 28°C (72° to 82°F).

Aquarium Suitability Index: 4.

Remarks: This species differs from the Cheeklined Maori Wrasse in its coloration; although it has pink lines radiating from its eyes, it does not have diagonal reddish stripes running under the eye to the edge of the operculum as *O. diagrammus* does. It is typically light brown to white overall with a central darker line that can be obscured by darker scribbling and short, dark bars. Kuiter (2000) recognizes a very similar species: the **Eared Maori Wrasse** (*Oxycheilinus oxyrhynchus*) (Bleeker, 1862). This species is found from the Andaman Sea east to the northern Moluccas, south to northeastern Australia, and north to southern Japan. It differs from *O. celebicus* in having lines under the eye and scribbling on the upper flanks. Males also have a white spot near the upper edge of the operculum (this marking is faint in females). In his book, Kuiter also includes an apparently undescribed species that he calls the **Longnose Maori Wrasse**. This species is found in Papua New Guinea and Indonesia. It is recognized by its extremely long snout and a black spot at the base of the tail. This species is found on rubble slopes with mixed macroalgae and ramose coral colonies.

Oxycheilinus diagrammus (Lacepède, 1801)

Common Names: Cheeklined Maori Wrasse, Bandcheek Maori Wrasse.

Maximum Length: 35 cm (13.8 in.).

Distribution: Red Sea to Samoa, north to the Ryukyus, and south to New Caledonia.

Oxycheilinus diagrammus, Cheeklined Maori Wrasse: one of the truly sporty models in this genus, with vivid facial pinstripes (adult variant).

Biology: *Oxycheilinus diagrammus* is found in coral-rich areas on sheltered reef faces and fore reefs or in lagoons. It is found at depths from less than 1 to 38 m (3 to 124 ft.). Although there is no data available on the food habits of *C. diagrammus,* a closely related species (*C. unifasciatus*) is known to feed on fishes, crabs, shrimps, brittle stars, heart urchins, and sea urchins. This species will stalk or ambush its prey and sometimes employs more ingenious hunting techniques. For example, it will associate with goatfishes, triggerfishes, and stingrays (species that disturb bottom materials) and capture prey that these fishes flush from the substrate. In the Red Sea, the Cheeklined Maori Wrasse will adopt the color pattern of the Longbarbel Goatfish (*Parupeneus macronema*), which is pale with a dark lateral stripe. It will associate with shoals of feeding *P. macronema* and pounce on prey items that the goatfish scares out during its feeding activities. It will also associate with and mimic the coloration of several dark-colored damselfishes. This behavior, where a predator mimics a species that is not a threat to its prey, is known as aggressive mimicry. The Cheeklined Maori Wrasse will employ an even more sophisticated strategy to capture its prey. It will use other fishes as a moving blind to approach its unsuspecting quarry. Studies on this species in the Red Sea demonstrated that it swims alongside larger herbivores (e.g., Sohal Surgeonfish, *Acanthurus sohal,* and Striated Bristletooth, *Ctenochaetus striatus*). In order to be even less conspicuous, this wrasse adopts a color similar to the species it is riding. This feeding tactic is known as "hunting by riding." These wrasses are solitary fish and are apparently territorial. I have seen hunting specimens chase away conspecifics as they approached an area where the substrate was being disturbed by feeding goatfish.

Captive Care: This species' interesting behavioral repertoire alone makes it a worthy addition to a fish-only aquarium. It is an extremely personable fish and can provide hours of interesting observation. The Cheeklined Maori Wrasse has strong dentition

Oxycheilinus diagrammus, Cheeklined Maori Wrasse: mottled pattern.

O. diagrammus: seconds later, same fish displays a dramatic color change.

Oxycheilinus diagrammus, Cheeklined Maori Wrasse: young specimen.

and a highly predatory nature, which makes it a greater threat to potential fish and invertebrate tankmates. *Cheilinus diagrammus* will eat any fish it can swallow. If it is able to capture a larger fish, it may attempt to break it into bite sized pieces by smacking it against hard substrate. My friend, Larry Jackson, has a wonderful photo showing a Cheeklined Maori Wrasse swimming with a large dragonet sticking out of its mouth (see page 81). *Cheilinus diagrammus* is also a threat to a variety of invertebrates. They will eat snails, tubeworms, ornamental shrimps, small crabs, brittle stars, sea stars, and even urchins. Therefore, I would not recommend them for an invertebrate aquarium. They do eat mantis shrimps. To help decrease the mantis shrimp population in your tank, house this wrasse with your live rock and remove it before adding your desirable invertebrates. I have also seen larger specimens consume fireworms. However, they will also eat pistol shrimps and tubeworms growing on or in the rock. Once they acclimate, Cheeklined Maori Wrasses may display combative tendencies, occasionally nipping or chasing newly introduced fish tankmates. No more than one *O. diagrammus* of the same species should be kept per aquarium, since fighting is likely to occur in captivity. If you want to keep two *Cheilinus* spp. in the same aquarium, introduce them simultaneously and provide a lot of hiding places. Species that are different in shape and color will be more likely to get along than similar forms. The Cheeklined Maori Wrasse may also display aggression toward similarly shaped wrasses.

Aquarium Size: 135 gal. **Temperature:** 23° to 28°C (74° to 82°F).
Aquarium Suitability Index: 4.
Remarks: This is one of the "sports models" of the genus. It is sleek in form, complete with pink or maroon pinstripes on the face and gill covers. Its body color is variable, and as noted above, it can change in an instant, allowing it to blend in better with its surroundings or a fish that it is following. The most common body color is olive to gray brown with an orange bar on each scale, but it can range from pale gray to deep purple. The **Thickstripe Maori Wrasse (*Oxycheilinus rhodochrous*) (Günther, 1867)** is often misidentified as *O. diagrammus*. The juveniles of this species have a row of black ocelli along the midline of the body. Larger individuals have a wide stripe running along each flank and lines on the lower portion of the opercula. This species is thought to be widespread in the Indo-West Pacific and reaches 20 cm (7.8 in.) in length.

Oxycheilinus unifasciatus, RIngtail Maori Wrasse: a dominant male such as this may have several females in his harem, spawning with each in quick succession.

Oxycheilinus unifasciatus (Streets, 1877)

Common Name: Ringtail Maori Wrasse.

Maximum Length: 46 cm (18 in.). A specimen of this size may weigh 1.4 kg (3 lbs.).

Distribution: Christmas Island to the Hawaiian Islands, Marquesas and Tuamotus, north to the Ryukyus, and south to New Caledonia and Rapa.

Biology: The Ringtail Maori Wrasse occurs in coral-rich areas of lagoon and coastal reefs at depths of 9 to 162 m (30 to 528 ft.). It will hang, head down, one meter or less above the substrate, ready to strike unwary prey. In Hawaii, it feeds primarily on relatively large fishes (including damsels, surgeonfishes, and filefishes), but also consumes crabs, shrimps (e.g., Saron shrimp, *Saron marmoratus*), brittle stars, heart urchins, and sea urchins to a lesser degree. This species will often swim up in the water column as it moves over the reef (males have been seen patrolling their home range 10 to 13 m [33 to 43 ft.] over the reef). This species is haremic. Donaldson (1995) reports on the spawning of a male and the three females in his harem. Spawning occurred late in the morning during a falling tide. Courtship commences when the females rise in the water column where the male typically engages in patrolling. He briefly visits and circles each female before moving on to the next. As spawning approaches, the frequency of female visits increases. When it is time to spawn, the male circles the fe-

male, with his head pointed slightly downward, and the female begins to slowly rise in the water column. The pair engage in mutual circling and the male then poses for the female, hovering in the water column with all his fins contracted except the caudal fin, which is spread wide. The pair, in parallel orientation, then rise up in the water column and release their gametes. The spawning *O. unifasciatus* rise as high as 7 m (23 ft.) from the spot where the pair began the ascent. In this harem, the male spawned with all three females within five minutes of the start of spawning. This species shows temporary sexual dichromatism during courtship and spawning. The male becomes dark gray on the back and white on the ventrum and develops a distinct, pale eye bar. The females become pale overall at this time.

Captive Care: The husbandry of this species is similar to that of *O. diagrammus.*

Aquarium Size: 200 gal. **Temperature:** 22° to 27°C (72° to 80°F).

Aquarium Suitability Index: 4.

Remarks: Distinguished from *O. diagrammus* by the presence of a red bordered bar with no lines within it, running from the back of the eye to the pectoral fin base. This bar may be the same color as the rest of the body or white. Usually there is also a white ring just in front of the tail, a characteristic sometimes shared with *O. diagrammus.* Adult *O. unifasciatus* have distinct black blotches on the dorsal and anal fins that are lacking in smaller specimens.

Choerodon anchorago, Yellowcheek or Anchor Tuskfish: leans on its side and wafts sand with its pectoral fin to expose buried prey.

GENUS *CHOERODON* (TUSKFISHES)

There are around 25 species in this genus. While some live on coral reefs, more species are found on rocky reefs and in seagrass beds in subtropical to warm temperate waters. Most of the tuskfishes have relatively deep bodies and steep head profiles. Their common name is from the enlarged teeth that protrude from the mouth like tusks. The members of the genus range in size from about 17 to 90 cm (6.7 to 35.4 in.). Some species are important food fishes and have been subject to overexploitation in certain areas; in some places, the populations of certain tuskfish species have declined radically, apparently due to overfishing. For example, off Hong Kong it has been proposed that sea urchin populations are out of control due to a lack of their predators, namely the Blackspot Tuskfish (*Choerodon schoenleinii*), which has been an important human food in this region.

The tuskfishes hunt over sand and rubble bottoms adjacent to reefs, feeding on mollusks, crustaceans, worms, echinoderms, and small fishes. They have well-developed pharyngeal teeth that they use to crush hard-shelled prey. Some species will also lie on their side and use the pectoral fin nearest the substrate to excavate holes in the sand. They rapidly beat the pectoral fin to expose infaunal invertebrates. They do not bury themselves in the sand, like some other wrasses, but hide in reef crevices at night and often simply rely on speed to dash off when threatened.

The tuskfishes are protogynous hermaphrodites and exhibit either monoandric or diandric sexuality. For example, the Graphic Tuskfish (*Choerodon graphicus*) and the Blackspot Tuskfish (*C. schoenleinii*) are monoandric, while the Blue Tuskfish (*C. cyanodus*) is diandric. At least some tuskfishes exhibit both sexual dichromatism and dimorphism. For example, the female Blackspot Tuskfish matures at a length of about 24 cm (9.4 in.) and changes to a male between 40 and 64 cm (15.7 to 25.2 in.). There is also a greenish yellow to blue color change associated with sexual transformation.

A study on the tuskfishes of Shark Bay, Western Australia, gives us some interesting insight into the life history strategies and social organization of these fishes. In the four tuskfishes investigated in this study (*Choerodon cauteroma*, *C. cyanodus*, *C. rubescens*, and *C. schoenleinii*), all changed sex within a certain age range, which varied from 4 to about 12 years of age. Sexual maturity is reached at an age of 1.5 to 3 years in these four species. The ratio of females to males in these four species studied at this location varied from 1:1 in *C. cyanodus* to 85:1 in *C. schoenleinii*. Those species with a highly skewed ratio exhibit a haremic mating system. Those in whom the ratio is not so disparate exhibit facultative monogamy. A large female of one of the larger tuskfish species may produce up to 128,000 eggs per spawn.

At least some tuskfishes exhibit species-distinct reproductive periods, especially those from subtropical seas. For example, in Japan, *C. schoenleinii* spawns from February to May. During the peak of the reproductive season (March and April) they spawn daily. In this species, those individuals of the appropriate age will change sex between spawning periods. Tuskfishes can be either daytime or dusk spawners. For example, the Blackspot Tuskfish is a daytime spawner, while the Harlequin Tuskfish (*Choerodon fasciatus*) spawns near sunset.

The growth rate of juvenile Blackspot Tuskfish is reported to be approximately 0.5 mm/day in the wild and probably greater in many aquariums. Their potential lifespan is 12 to 16 years.

Captive Care

The few species that are regularly encountered in the aquarium trade are relatively durable aquarium residents. They are active fishes that will need lots of swimming space. While most should be kept in larger aquariums (135 gallons or larger), the smaller species can be housed in a medium-sized tank (75 gallons). The tuskfish may take several days to fully acclimate to captivity. Once fully adjusted, they begin recognizing their caretaker as a source of food, swimming to the front glass to greet the aquarist. The *Choerodon* spp. eats a wide variety of foods, including frozen mysid shrimp, fresh or frozen chopped seafood, freeze-dried krill, and pelletized foods. They should be fed twice per day. An occasional individual will suddenly begin to fast after having been in a tank for a while. Try different foods (including live, gut-packed ghost shrimp) and make sure the temperature is at the higher end of their preference range. One peculiar habit these fishes sometimes practice is spitting water at the surface of the tank. It is not known why they do this, but a larger individual could easily shoot a jet of water onto a nearby power supply, so plan accordingly.

The large teeth of the tuskfishes is partly responsible for their acquired reputation as a poor community labrid. However, if care is taken in tankmate selection, less aggressive species are

Choerodon fasciatus, Harlequin Tuskfish, Philippine specimen: a great species for a large community aquarium with other self-reliant, bigger fishes.

Choerodon azurio, Scarbreast Tuskfish: beautiful Japanese species.

Choerodon schoenleinii, Blackspot Tuskfish, large male. Note teeth.

Choerodon anchorago, Yellowcheek Tuskfish: may attack *Tridacna* clams.

added before the tuskfish, and the aquarium is large enough, *Choerodon* spp. tend to be fairly well behaved in a community tank. They will often try to prey on smaller fishes added to a tank in which they are residents. That said, if you add small, nimble species (e.g., damsels, gobies) before adding a tuskfish, these more vulnerable tankmates can usually avoid the tuskfish if there are many hiding places. You should avoid keeping more than one tuskfish in the same tank. They have been known to quarrel with other wrasses if crowded. Space is the key to a copacetic community tank when it comes to tuskfishes, so if it is in ample supply, behavioral problems are much less likely.

Tuskfish feeding behavior can be very interesting to watch in the home aquarium, but these fishes are prone to rearrange their living quarters when hunting. For this reason, larger species are not as well suited to reef aquariums. While they don't eat coral, they may move coral colonies when looking for hidden prey. The smaller species, including the ever-popular Harlequin Tuskfish (*Choerodon fasciatus*), do well in the reef aquarium, as they are less prone to this kind of behavior. The more diminutive species are a potential threat to small snails, ornamental shrimps, and brittle and serpent stars, and the bill of fare of the large species also includes urchins and sea stars. Like many of the larger wrasses, all the tuskfishes are much less destructive as juveniles than they are as adults.

Tuskfish Species

Choerodon anchorago (Bloch, 1791)†††
Common Names: Yellowcheek Tuskfish, Anchor Tuskfish, Orange-dotted Tuskfish.
Maximum Length: 38 cm (14.9 in.).
Distribution: Sri Lanka eastward to French Polynesia, north to the Ryukyus, and south to New Caledonia.
Biology: This attractive tuskfish is most often seen on fringing coastal reefs and in lagoons at depths of 1.5 to 20 m (5 to 66 ft.). It often occurs over sand and rubble substrates and refuges in crevices at night. It is sometimes observed in seagrass beds, especially juveniles. While it normally occurs on its own, often with associating opportunistic labrids, it is occasionally found in small groups. It preys upon gastropods, isopods, amphipods, cumaceans, and sea urchins. This species often uses its teeth to displace shells, rubble, and debris when hunting. It will take these items in its mouth and throw them to the side. When hunting infaunal prey, it will also place its side along the substrate and use its pectoral fin to excavate a depression in the sand.
Captive Care: This species is regularly encountered where fishes are collected for the aquarium trade, but it is not common in

Choerodon cyanodus, Blue Tuskfish: usually changes sex at 4 years of age.

Choerodon fasciatus, Harlequin Tuskfish, juvenile: note ocelli (eyespots).

local fish stores. It is a handsome species and will adapt to a larger aquarium. Young fish (around 5 to 8 cm [2 or 3 in.]) are the best choice for the home aquarium, as adults do not ship well and may have difficulty adjusting to captivity. Hiding places are essential to make them feel at home, as is plenty of open sand and rubble on the bottom. Although shy initially, they will become brazen aquarium inhabitants with time. Feed them twice a day or even more often if you are keeping them with potential invertebrate prey. They love infaunal worms and mollusks (large adults may even attempt to eat snails and smaller Tridacnid clams).

Aquarium Size: 135 gal. **Temperature:** 23° to 28°C (74° to 82°F).

Aquarium Suitability Index: 4.

Remarks: The color of the juvenile *C. anchorago* does not vary much from that of the adult species. Juveniles that live in seagrass may have a more greenish hue.

Choerodon cyanodus (Richardson, 1843)

Common Name: Blue Tuskfish.

Maximum Length: 70 cm (27.6 in.), but usually less than 40 cm (15.7 in.).

Distribution: Sri Lanka to Papua New Guinea, north to southern Japan, and south to Western and Queensland Australia and New Caledonia.

Biology: *Choerodon cyanodus* is found in lagoons, on reef flats, back reefs, reef faces, and reef slopes. It is found over sand and rubble at depths of 1 to 35 m (3.3 to 116 ft.). It is a solitary species. It feeds on a variety of invertebrates, including worms, mollusks, and crustaceans. The Blue Tuskfish is an industrious predator that will grasp relatively large slabs of coral rubble in its jaws and flip them over, then inspect the exposed area for prey. It will also lean on its side and wave the pectoral fin forward to dig

in the sand and expose buried prey. It seems to be dominant over the Graphic Tuskfish (*Choerodon graphicus*). I have seen the latter species leave an excavation it was hunting in to give way to *C. cyanodus*. This species spawns in the summer off the Queensland coast and in Shark Bay, Western Australia. It has been reported to be a monoandric protogynous hermaphrodite. This species reaches sexual maturity at 1.5 years and usually changes sex at an age of around 4 years. The ratio of males to females is 1:1 in the population in Shark Bay.

Captive Care: The Blue Tuskfish is not readily available in the aquarium trade. It is a large species that requires a large tank with plenty of swimming room. Otherwise its husbandry requirements are similar to those of other larger members of the genus (see the Captive Care section for the genus). Its large size means it is a threat to a wider range of tankmates and is capable of displacing larger pieces of rubble and coral.

Aquarium Size: 240 gal. **Temperature:** 21° to 28°C (70° to 82°F).

Aquarium Suitability Index: 4.

Remarks: The Blue Tuskfish has a white spot on the dorsum and often exhibits four or five faint bars.

Choerodon fasciatus (Günther, 1867)

Common Name: Harlequin Tuskfish.

Maximum Length: 30 cm (11.2 in.). Reports in the aquarium literature that this fish attains 61 cm (24 in.) are erroneous.

Distribution: Taiwan, the Ryukyus, Vanuatu, Great Barrier Reef, New Caledonia, and Lord Howe Island. It is most common on the Great Barrier Reef.

Biology: Coastal reefs, outer lagoons, and along outer-reef faces. When they hunt, they inspect reef crevices, ledges, and coral rubble. Juveniles are solitary along reef channel walls. In most

cases, single *C. fasciatus* are observed swimming just over the substrate, often along the reef face. Kuiter and Tonozuka (2001) state that this species is found in small, loose aggregations in caves, under overhangs, or on rubble slopes. During the reproductive period (which includes November and December on the Great Barrier Reef), heterosexual pairs may be observed swimming together along the reef edge and foraging together, ranging as far as 100 m (330 ft.) along the reef face. Pair members will separate for several minutes, but then reunite. When this species spawns, the pair will swim side by side or the female will swim just in front of the male until they are about 5 m (17 ft.) above the seafloor. The pair will begin circling in a head-to-tail orientation and then rush another 2 m (7 ft.) into the water column before releasing their gametes. Spawning occurs near sunset. This species is thought to exhibit facultative monogamy—at lower densities it may be monogamous, while at higher densities it is thought to be haremic.

Captive Care: This fish should be housed in a tank with plenty of hiding places. It tends to slink around the aquarium decor, especially when young or when initially added to the tank. It may even hide much of the time when first added. With time, adults will become more bold and spend much of their time cruising the tank length in full view. Make sure to provide these fish with suitable shelter sites, as they do not bury under the substrate at night or when threatened, but hide within the reef. This species has a reputation for being rather pugnacious. However, I think some of this reputation is based more on its fearsome grin than on a true desire to inflict harm. It has been my experience that this fish is usually not overly aggressive toward similar-sized or larger fish tankmates. You can even keep it with small fishes in a large tank with plenty of nooks and crannies where diminutive tankmates can seek shelter if threatened. In a small tank, a Harlequin Tuskfish may prey on fish tankmates small enough to subdue. They are also a greater threat to their aquarium tankmates as they get larger, and occasional individuals may be more ill-tempered than other members of their species. These tuskfishes (especially juveniles) may be bullied by large dottybacks (e.g., *Ogilbynia*), more aggressive damsels, large angels, larger and/or more pugnacious wrasses (e.g., *Cheilinus* spp.), surgeonfishes, and certain triggers. This is more likely if *Choerodon fasciatus* is added to a tank with resident bullies. If harassed or uncomfortable in its surroundings, this tuskfish will hide or may swim incessantly at the front of the aquarium.

In most cases, these fish are not picky about what they consume. However, it is not unusual for a new tuskfish to refuse food for several days after it is introduced to a tank. Once acclimated it will eat with gusto. Feed a varied diet (e.g., fresh seafood, pre-

Choerodon fasciatus, Harlequin Tuskfish, variant. Opposite page: colorful adults have blue teeth. Australian-collected specimens are especially prized.

pared foods for carnivores) and make sure to include foods with added pigments to facilitate color fidelity. Not overly susceptible to problems, these fish occasionally become infested with common parasites and maladies like *Cryptocaryon*, *Amyloodinium*, flukes, bacterial infections, pop-eye, and occasionally head and lateral line erosion (HLLE).

In the wild, the Harlequin Tuskfish is known to prey on a variety of invertebrates (e.g., mollusks, crustaceans, worms, and echinoderms). However, they do not eat coral and they rarely bother other ornamental invertebrates if well fed. These fish are more likely to prey on shrimps introduced after them. Adults are more destructive than juveniles. Do not place more than one in the same tank. Paying more for Australian individuals is worth it. Not only are they more attractive, they have better long-term survival rates than those from the Philippines. It is best to buy individuals that are 8 to 13 cm (3 to 5 in.) long. Small juveniles (5 cm or less) are often difficult to keep because of their higher metabolic demands, and larger adults often suffer greater stress during shipping.

Aquarium Size: 75 gal. **Temperature:** 22° to 28°C (72° to 82°F).
Aquarium Suitability Index: 4.
Remarks: The Harlequin Tuskfish is white overall, with five to nine bars on the head and body. In juveniles, the bars are coppery orange or brown and there are two eyespots on the dorsal fin and one on the anal fin. As the fish ages, the head and body bars become brighter orange with blue trim, and the ocelli on the fins disappear. The rear portion of the body becomes darker and in some individuals the posterior body bars become paler. In adults,

Choerodon graphicus, Graphic Tuskfish: large Australian species.

Choerodon jordani, Blackwedge Tuskfish: nice, small-size tuskfish.

Choerodon zamboangae, Purple Eyebrowed Tuskfish: deep-water species.

the dorsal, anal, and pelvic fins are also red, while the tail is pale (often with a red edge toward the rear). There is no sexual dichromatism, but in pairs observed spawning, the males were larger than the females. The teeth are sky blue, and this dental pigment typically becomes more intense as the fish gets larger. There are apparently two distinct populations of Harlequin Tuskfish in the Western Pacific. There is a northern population, which ranges from southern Japan to Taiwan (including the Philippines and Micronesia). Many of the individuals in the aquarium trade come from the Philippines. There is also a more strikingly colored southern population, which ranges from Vanuatu and New Caledonia to Queensland, Australia.

Choerodon graphicus (De Vis, 1885)

Common Name: Graphic Tuskfish.
Maximum Length: 46 cm (18.1 in.).
Distribution: Queensland, Australia to New Caledonia.
Biology: This species is found in lagoons, on coastal reefs, and on seaward reef faces or slopes. It is found over sand and rubble substrates at depths of 2 to 30 m (7 to 98 ft.). The Graphic Tuskfish feeds on worms, hard-shelled mollusks, crustaceans, and sea urchins. It employs some interesting hunting techniques to locate and feed on infaunal prey. I have observed a Graphic Tuskfish flipping over large pieces of coral rubble and then lying flat on its side where the rubble had been. With its nose up against a piece of coral, the tuskfish vigorously fanned the substrate with its pectoral fin. This caused a sediment cloud to rise into the water, which attracted other opportunistic wrasses in the area. After it disturbed the substrate, the Graphic Tuskfish righted itself and examined the newly made depression. It then took mouthfuls of sand, spit the sediment to the side, and looked for prey items again. Occasionally the wrasse took a quick bite at the substrate and began to chew. During one such five-minute feeding episode, I observed a Graphic Tuskfish fan the substrate 13 times. I have also seen this species tear chunks of algae off the substrate and then spit it out, likely to flush out hidden prey.
Captive Care: This is a large tuskfish that rarely makes it into the aquarium trade. Its husbandry requirements are similar to those of other large members of the genus.
Aquarium Size: 200 gal. **Temperature:** 22° to 28°C (72° to 82°F).
Aquarium Suitability Index: 4.

Choerodon jordani (Snyder, 1908)

Common Names: Blackwedge Tuskfish, Jordan's Tuskfish.
Maximum Length: 17 cm (6.7 in.).
Distribution: Ryukyus Islands south to Western Australia and the Great Barrier Reefs, and east to Samoa and Tonga.

Choerodon zosterophorus, Darkstripe Tuskfish, juvenile: ideal small tuskfish.

Choerodon zosterophorus, Darkstripe Tuskfish, adult.

Biology: This species is found on coastal reef slopes, in reef channels, and on outer reef slopes at depths of 10 to 40 m (33 to 132 ft.). It is found over sand and rubble substrates. Solitary individuals are usually seen moving over the ocean bottom with their heads down inspecting the bottom for prey. On rare occasions, *C. jordani* can be found in small, loose groups.

Captive Care: This is one of the better home aquarium tuskfishes because of its small size. It can be kept in a reef tank, but make sure to provide plenty of open sand substrate so it can engage in natural foraging behavior.

Aquarium Size: 75 gal. **Temperature:** 23° to 28°C (74° to 82°F).

Aquarium Suitability Index: 4.

Remarks: *Choerodon jordani* is possibly sexually dichromatic, with the black wedge extending onto the caudal fin in females and ending at the white spot in males. This species is similar to the Darkstripe Tuskfish (*Choerodon zosterophorus*), which has a white band that runs from the base of the posterior dorsal fin to the base of the pectoral fin. *Choerodon jordani* is gray overall with a black wedge along the flank.

Choerodon zamboangae (Seale & Bean, 1907)

Common Name: Purple Eyebrowed Tuskfish.

Maximum Length: 45 cm (17.7 in.).

Distribution: Philippines south to Indonesia and northwestern Australia.

Biology: This is a deep-water tuskfish that is found on sand slopes and rubble with scattered patch reefs. In some cases, it occurs in habitats with rich macroalgae growth. Occurs singly.

Captive Care: This is very rare in the aquarium trade. See Captive Care notes for the genus.

Aquarium Size: 180 gal. **Temperature:** 23° to 28°C (74° to 82°F).

Aquarium Suitability Index: 4.

Remarks: This attractive fish has blue markings around the eye. The body is suffused with pink and there is a yellow slash from the caudal peduncle onto the side. Some species are bicolored, with a yellow line between the darker dorsal coloration and the white ventrum. The chin can also be blue.

Choerodon zosterophorus (Bleeker, 1868)

Common Name: Darkstripe Tuskfish.

Maximum Length: 18 cm (7.1 in.). Some sources list 25 cm (9.8 in.) as the maximum size.

Distribution: Malaysian Peninsula, Indonesia, and the Philippines.

Biology: The Darkstripe Tuskfish is found near coastal fringing reefs, near lagoon patch reefs, in deep channels, and on fore-reef slopes. It is usually found over sand and rubble substrates, often in current-prone habitats. It is reported at depths of 10 to 40 m (33 to 132 ft.). While it is usually a solitary species, they are occasionally seen in small, loose groups.

Captive Care: This is another ideal aquarium tuskfish because of its small size. It should be housed in a tank with plenty of open sand/rubble substrate. It is not an overly aggressive species, but it has been known to harass newly introduced smaller fish species (e.g., demoiselles, gobies) and it will eat ornamental crustaceans. It may jump from an open tank if harassed by aggressive tankmates or startled.

Aquarium Size: 75 gal. **Temperature:** 23° to 28°C (74° to 82°F).

Aquarium Suitability Index: 4.

Remarks: *Choerodon zosterophorus* has a white band that runs from the base of the posterior dorsal fin to the base of the pectoral fin.

GENUS *CIRRHILABRUS* (FAIRY WRASSES)

Coral reefs are home to a wide variety of incredibly colorful fishes. The angelfishes, butterflyfishes, and surgeonfishes are all well known for their brilliant chromatic attire. But there are few fish, including these beauties, that can compare with the fairy wrasses (genus *Cirrhilabrus*). These members of the family Labridae are "clad" with some of the most amazing color patterns seen in the animal kingdom. Fortunately, a number of fairy wrasses are available to the marine aquarist—and many of them are relatively easy to keep.

Classification and Biology

The fairy wrasses belong to the subfamily Cheilininae, along with the genera *Paracheilinus*, *Pseudocheilinus*, *Pseudocheilinops*, and *Pteragogus*. All these genera have a double pupil, an adaptation that aids in locating small prey items. The fairy wrasses are so closely related to another spectacular genus, the *Paracheilinus*, that at least one ichthyologist has suggested the latter should be a subgenus of the former. One subtle difference is that *Cirrhilabrus* have nine dorsal rays, while *Paracheilinus* have eleven. The fairy wrasses differ from many other members of the family in the way they swim. Not only do they use their pectoral fins and tail to propel themselves forward in a characteristic wrasse fashion, but they also undulate the posterior portion of the dorsal fin.

The genus *Cirrhilabrus* is the second largest genus in the wrasse family—and may soon be the largest, if the genus *Halichoeres* is split into multiple genera. More than 44 species of fairy wrasse are currently recognized, and at least three other species are awaiting formal description. There has been some debate as to whether some of the known species comprise more than one valid form. The controversy is due to the fact that some *Cirrhilabrus* spp. are highly variable in their chromatic characteristics. Certain fish taxonomists (often referred to as "splitters") separate some of these color variants into valid fairy wrasse species; others (the "lumpers") argue that differences in color simply represent geographical variations. For example, the colors of the Pacific and Indian Ocean versions of the Exquisite Fairy Wrasse (*Cirrhilabrus exquisitus*) differ. Some fish taxonomists now consider these distinct populations to represent two disparate species, not one broadly distributed form. (The Indian Ocean form would be called *C. exquisitus*, while the Pacific form has yet to be given a scientific name.) One "species" that has caused even more taxonomic headaches is the Bluehead Fairy Wrasse (*C. cyanopleura*). It was once thought that this was simply a highly variable species

that ranged from the Andaman Sea along the Asian mainland to southern Japan. But at least two *C. cyanopleura* variations are now considered to be valid species. These are the Orangeback Fairy Wrasse (*Cirrhilabrus aurantidorsalis*) and the Redeyed or Redheaded Fairy Wrasse (*C. solorensis*). The Yellowflanked Fairy Wrasse (*C. lyukyuensis*) is considered by most to be a synonym of *C. cyanopleura*, although at least one prominent fish expert lists it as a distinct species. Unlike the Exquisite Fairy Wrasse populations, *C. cyanopleura* overlaps in distribution with some of these closely related forms, and they may even hybridize on occasion.

On the reef, fairy wrasses form feeding shoals in which females typically outnumber males. Individuals swim up in the water column (sometimes up to 7 m [23 ft.]) and feed on zooplankton swept past by ocean currents. They often join with groups of other zooplankton-feeding fishes, like flasher wrasses (*Paracheilinus*), and plankton-feeding damselfishes. Some fairy wrasses aggregate with congeners and may hybridize on occasion. The majority of *Cirrhilabrus* spp. prefer coastal reef habitats and are often found over coral rubble substrate, mixed sponge-macroalgae beds, or coastal reefs mainly made up of large-polyped stony corals. They often hang over small coral mounds, soft corals, or stands of macroalgae, in which they retreat if danger threatens. Some fairy wrasses are found on clean oceanic reefs, where they live on rubble slopes.

While some of the fairy wrasses are found on shallow reefs at depths of less than 1 m (3.3 ft.), many species prefer moderate to great depths. For example, the Rhomboid Fairy Wrasse (*Cirrhilabrus rhomboidalis*) is usually found on fore-reef slopes and walls at depths in excess of 38 m (124 ft.). In their investigations of deep reef communities off Enewetak, Thresher and Colin (1986) reported seeing two apparently undescribed species of fairy wrasse at depths of 75 and 90 m (244 and 293 ft.).

Most fairy wrasses are sexually dimorphic and dichromatic. The males display more vibrant colors, attain greater size, and have more elongate pelvic fins. Some large males may also have a slightly humped back, which makes it look as though they have curvature of the spine. In a number of species, the color of the juveniles is different from that of the adults. These wrasses are also protogynous, monandric hermaphrodites. That is, all individuals start out as females and then change into males. Young fish (just under 2.5 cm [1 in.] in one species) are asexual, and as they grow the ovaries begin to form. Most individuals develop functional ovaries, reproduce, and then begin transforming into males, but a small number of fish will never reproduce as females; instead, they immediately begin changing sex. Aquarium observations indicate that males can reverse their sex. For example, I have seen the coloration and finnage of a submissive male Long-

Cirrhilabrus jordani, Jordan's Fairy Wrasse: large male. This genus exhibits some of the most glorious pigmentation in the animal kingdom.

Prime *Cirrhilabrus* fairy wrasse habitat: coral rubble with a profusion of nooks, crannies, and caves offers protective cover when predators approach.

finned Fairy Wrasse (*Cirrhilabrus rubriventralis*) change back to that of the female phase. I was told by advanced aquarist Tony Vargas about a captive male that changed back to a female and even spawned with another male.

Most of what we know about the social organization and mating systems of these wrasses is based on studies conducted on the Bluestripe Fairy Wrasse (*Cirrhilabrus temminckii*) (Bell, 1982; Moyer and Shepard, 1975). During the breeding season, most of the large male *C. temminckii* form territories and attack intruding males, while groups of females move over a large home range that encompasses more than one male territory. Males perform loop displays and flash their colors to attract females and ward off rivals. The male's color can vary depending on the intensity of the aggressive or courting interaction. During courtship, the male moves through groups of females and displays his brilliant colors. As this increases in frequency, the male will veer toward a female and rush at her. Just prior to spawning, the male performs a loop up into the water column. The pair then executes a loop together, releasing their gametes at the top of the ascent. Males will spawn from one to 26 times a day. Those males that do not set up territories employ other mating strategies. For example, some engage in "sneak" spawning: a male hangs around the ter-

ritory of a larger male and entices approaching females to spawn with him. Others employ "streaking," where a male joins a territorial male and female as they make their spawning ascent and releases his gametes along with theirs.

The fairy wrasses often take on a blotchy color pattern at night or when stressed, and like their relatives, the parrotfishes, they exude excessive slime and form cocoons around themselves when they sleep. Studies conducted on parrotfish have demonstrated that by enveloping their bodies in slime they may prevent olfactory stimuli from reaching nocturnal predators hunting nearby. However, it has also been suggested that the mucous covering has no adaptive function but is just the result of the buildup of copious slime that is normally shed into the water when they are swimming.

Captive Care

The fairy wrasses are good additions to the passive community tank, and some species can be kept with moderately aggressive fishes. They are ideally suited to the reef aquarium. With the possible exception of small, delicate shrimp species (e.g., *Periclimenes* spp.), these wrasses usually do not harm invertebrates. Some fairy wrasses are initially shy when introduced to the aquarium and hide for several days. But if a peaceful acclimation period is provided, these species will become quite brazen, even to the point of nipping or lying against the aquarist's hand or forearm as he or she cleans the aquarium. There are other species that tend to be more brazen, even when new to the tank. The main key to successful acclimation is to place them in an aquarium with nonaggressive species. If a fairy wrasse is introduced to a tank with belligerent fish, it will typically stay hidden and end up starving to death or succumbing to disease. It is also important that there is limited human activity inside and outside of the aquarium during this acclimation period. Dither fishes (e.g., *Chromis* spp.) can be helpful in drawing shy or acclimating fairy wrasses from their refuges.

While the smaller fairy wrasses are a good choice for the both beginning and advanced hobbyists, larger individuals often have great difficulty adjusting to captivity and more frequently succumb to the rigors of capture and shipping stress. This is especially true of those species that reach great sizes: the Lined (*Cirrhilabrus lineatus*), Laboute's (*C. laboutei*), Yellowstreaked (*C. luteovittatus*), Redmargin (*C. rubrimarginatus*), Bluestriped (*C. temminckii*), and Finespotted (*C. punctatus*) Fairy Wrasses. That said, fishmongers are now shipping them in larger bags and the mortality rate of larger individuals appears to have declined. Still, juveniles, females, and smaller males tend to suffer less during the rigorous transport process.

Large males are often much more colorful than juveniles or females and make a more tempting prosp.ect for the aquarist. If you decide to try a large individual from your local fish store, do not purchase it until it is feeding and behaving normally (e.g., swimming about the aquarium). Look at the tip of its snout to make sure that the skin was not abraded during transport. Some individuals, in their vigorous attempts to break out of the shipping bag, will rub their snouts raw. This is a potential site for viral and bacterial infections.

In the wild, males of some species form breeding territories and will display at, and even fight with, intruding males. Fights can consist of lateral displays, chasing, head-to-tail circling, biting, and jaw-locking. Males also chase females on occasion, apparently to suppress female sex change, but aggressive behavior between females is rare. They do not typically defend a defined territory when not reproducing, but males may defend a group of females.

In the aquarium, male fairy wrasses will fight each other and may display some, but rarely lethal, aggression toward other fish introduced after them. Aggression is more likely if they are closely related (e.g., other fairy and flasher wrasses) or are small, docile species. If you are going to keep fairy wrasses with *Paracheilinus*

Cirrhilabrus solorensis, male: hanging in tentacles of *Heliofungia* stony coral.

Cirrhilabrus cf. *temminckii*: young fish sheltering among *Diadema* sea urchins.

spp., always add the latter first. Flasher wrasses tend to be less aggressive, smaller than many *Cirrhilabrus*, and more sensitive to bullying. As is the case with many coral reef fishes, fairy wrasses are more likely to attack species that have similar color, form, or behavior. For example, I had a male Redfinned Fairy Wrasse (*Cirrhilabrus rubripinnis*) that persistently chased several red cardinalfishes and a soldierfish, even though they were all introduced to the tank before the *Cirrhilabrus*. In the aquarium, fairy wrasse

Cirrhilabrus scottorum, Scott's Fairy Wrasse, male, Cook Islands: relaxed posture. This popular species has many color forms, and these vary with mood.

aggression usually consists of chasing and charging, but these fish will occasionally nip at an opponent and may injure it.

If you are keeping male fairy wrasses with more passive zooplanktivores (e.g., small anthias, certain cardinalfishes, chromis, flasher wrasses, dart gobies), the *Cirrhilabrus* should be the last fish introduced. On the other hand, if they are being kept with potentially pugnacious tankmates (e.g., pygmy angelfishes, small hawkfishes, large damselfishes, sand perch) they should be the first fish in the aquarium. I would avoid keeping these wrasses with groupers, large dottybacks, large angelfishes, or aggressive wrasses like *Coris* spp., large *Pseudocheilinus* spp., and *Thalassoma* spp., pugnacious surgeonfishes (e.g., the Sohal Surgeonfish [*Acanthurus sohal*], the Purple Tang [*Zebrasoma xanthurum*]), most triggerfishes, and large puffers). If you have a very large tank, however, it is possible to successfully keep these wrasses with potentially aggressive tankmates. While some of the smaller, more docile hogfishes, such as the Crescenttail Hogfish (*Bodianus sepiacaudus*), can make great aquarium neighbors for a fairy wrasse, larger species may be aggressive toward confamilials. Also, large, aggressive anthias, like the male Lyretail Anthias (*Pseudanthias squamipinnis*) and the Redbelted Anthias (*P. rubrizonatus*), may behave aggressively toward smaller fairy wrasses, especially in small aquariums.

The fairy wrasses are also a potential meal for frogfishes and scorpionfishes. Because the *Cirrhilabrus* spp. are elongated in shape, these predators can swallow wrasses that are relatively large. The carpet sea anemones (*Stichodactyla* spp.), Adhesive Sea Anemone (*Cryptodendrum adhaesivum*), and tube anemones (Cerianthidae) are also potential threats to fairy wrasses. These invertebrates have been known to capture wrasses at night.

If you want to keep more than one fairy wrasse, try maintaining a harem consisting of one male and several females. To avoid fighting among harem members, it is important to introduce them simultaneously or to add the females first. After the females have adjusted to the tank, add the more aggressive male. You are much more likely to have success keeping groups of fairy wrasses if you place them in a large aquarium; in small tanks, even females may not get along and males may pester females to death. Males of the larger species of fairy wrasses should never be housed together in the same tank, but those representing smaller species can be if the aquarium holds at least 180 gallons. If a submissive male can avoid being beaten up and killed by an aggressive consexual, it may reverse sex and become a functional female.

If different species of *Cirrhilabrus* can be housed together in the same tank, the largest male will typically be dominant over congeners. For example, I had an aquarium with a pair of Redstripe (*C. roseafascia*), a Pyle's (*C. pylei*) and a Deep-sea Fairy

Cirrhilabrus scottorum, Scott's Fairy Wrasse: displaying. Note that dorsal and ventral fins are erect, tail fin spread to its maximum, and colors are very bright.

Wrasse (*C. bathyphilus*). I introduced all four fish to the tank at the same time. Initially, the *C. pylei*, the second largest fish of the quad, established itself as the boss. But within the week, the more reclusive male *C. roseafascia*, which was the largest of the fairy wrasses, had taken over the top rung of the social ladder. Then all the *Cirrhilabrus* gave way to him as he patrolled the tank. The smallest fish, the female *C. bathyphilus*, was the target of more chases and more nipping than any other of its congeners.

It is not uncommon for two male fairy wrasses (especially those of similar size) to fight for a short time until they work out their rank in the pecking order. In other cases, they may battle until one individual jumps out of the tank (if it can) or it begins to hide all the time. It is not uncommon for subordinate *Cirrhilabrus* to have missing scales and torn fins, which is unsightly and can lead to lethal infections. You will have a greater chance of success keeping fairy wrasse males of varying size and avoid species that look similar (e.g., have the same general coloration). There is also more and more anecdotal evidence that feeding rates can impact aggressiveness. Fishes, including fairy wrasses, that are hungry tend to be more competitive and pugnacious with one another. Make sure you are very cautious when keeping fairy wrasses together in smaller tanks (less than 100 gallons). It can be done, but to avoid fish death and aquarist headaches,

choose species/individuals carefully. In larger tanks, subordinates will be better able to avoid higher-ranking congeners and squabbles are likely to be fewer and more brief.

When introducing a new fairy wrasse to a existing population of conspecifics, it is also a good idea to use a transparent container to allow the resident fish to become habituated to the newcomer before it is added to the tank. One way to do this is with an acrylic divider. If your tank is small enough and you can section off a portion of the tank for the new fish, this will work well. Make sure the divider is perforated so that oxygenated seawater readily moves between the sectioned-off portion of the tank and the main aquarium. Of course, it is also important that the divider is see-through. An easier method you can employ is to place the new fish in a plastic basket or a transparent specimen cup/breeding trap that hangs on the side of the tank or floats on the water's surface. In the case of the basket, the holes should not be large enough for the acclimating fish to escape but must be large enough so visual contact can occur between the "greenhorn" and the "veterans." If you use an aquarium specimen container/breeder trap, make sure it has holes in it that allow water flow.

Even though fairy wrasses form shoals or groups in nature, individuals will do fine on their own in the aquarium. But there is one potential drawback to keeping some male *Cirrhilabrus* (e.g., Exquisite [*Cirrhilabrus exquisitus*], Scott's [*C. scottorum*], Solar [*C. solorensis*], Temminck's Fairy Wrasse [*C. temminckii*]) on their own. While color loss in many reef fishes can be attributed to an improper diet, in male fairy wrasses chromatic changes are more often the result of a lack of social interactions with conspecifics. If these fishes are not kept together, the males color (and possibly his gender) will begin to revert back to that of the female. For example, it is not uncommon for male Scott's Fairy Wrasse (*C. scottorum*) to lose the bright red blotch on its sides (a chromatic feature of the male) if it is not housed with members of its own kind. One way you might be able to prevent this from happening is to place a mirror on the front or side of the tank for short periods of time (e.g., every other day for several hours). In this way, the resident male *Cirrhilabrus* may be duped into thinking there are other males in the area. If you leave the mirror up all the time, the resident fish may become habituated to it or, even worse, it may damage the skin around the jaws as it attempts to get at the consexual in the mirror's reflection. If your fairy wrasse exhibits such damage, stop using the mirror.

Fairy wrasses appreciate good water movement, numerous hiding places and plenty of room to swim. In the case of larger specimens (over 10 cm [4 in.]) I would recommend a tank no smaller than a standard 55 gallon. The shallow-water species will have no problems adjusting to the high light levels characteristic of shallow-water reef aquariums, while those deep-water species adapt more quickly if placed in tanks with less intense illumination. (*Note:* the deep-water forms can be kept successfully in high light conditions, but may take longer to acclimate and some may exhibit a blanching of their bright colors or be more reclusive.)

The fairy wrasses are very good jumpers. Therefore, you will need to be careful when working in the tank or when extinguishing the lights. Ambient light levels should be reduced gradually so that you do not frighten your fairy wrasse. One way to prevent them from becoming startled when the aquarium lights are turned off is to mount a nightlight (e.g., a 15-watt incandescent bulb) over the aquarium. If you want to keep the aquarium open, make a PVC frame to fit on top of your aquarium and attach fiberglass screen to it or make a cover out of egg-crate material. Even when you're in the process of working on the tank, do not leave it uncovered any longer than you have to. I know of several instances where a fairy wrasse jumped out of an uncovered tank when the aquarist's back was turned. They can jump with such force, in fact, that they have been known to break metal halide bulbs. Fairy wrasses are also prone to going over overflow boxes (these should also be covered). When stressed (e.g., picked on by tankmates), a fairy wrasse may continuously swim near and bob at the water's surface. If you can catch the fish, it should be removed and placed in a hospital tank for observation and a respite from other fishes.

One other interesting note about jumping *Cirrhilabrus*: male fairy wrasses are more prone to engaging in this undesirable behavior than females. This appears to be related to their behavioral repertoire, which in males includes lots of extravagant displays. These displays often consist of rapid, vertical swims into the water column. This is not a problem when the fish does this in 20 m (66 ft.) of water. But in an aquarium 61 cm (24 in.) deep, this often means the wrasse is going to break the water's surface and may be even leap out of the aquarium.

Fortunately, the fairy wrasses are very disease-resistant. Occasionally they will suffer from ich (*Cryptocaryon irritans*) or other parasites, but they are usually one of the last fish to contract it. It is important to feed these wrasses at least twice a day (three times a day is even better) to ensure they do not become emaciated and subsequently perish. A productive refugium will also help meet their nutritional needs. Most foods will be accepted, but a variety of finely chopped fresh seafood (e.g., shrimp, marine fish flesh), frozen mysid shrimp, and a good frozen prepared food will help to maintain their colors and good health. Regularly feeding them food soaked in Selco is also a good idea. Although in nature they feed primarily from the water column, fairy wrasses will pick food off aquarium substrate as well. While algae does not form part of their natural diet, these wrasses will readily ingest freeze-dried algae (nori). If you feed your *Cirrhilabrus* frequently (which I certainly recommend),

Cirrhilabrus bathyphilus, Deep-sea Fairy Wrasse: hooded Vanuatu male of a small species occasionally available to rare-fish collectors.

you will need an effective protein skimmer to keep the aquarium water in top shape.

One sign of inadequate nutrition is atrophying dorsal musculature. When this occurs, the head seems to enlarge as the adjoining muscle tissue shrinks in mass. I have seen this condition frequently in individuals housed in reef aquariums that were fed infrequently. If you are not willing to feed your fish in your reef tank at least once a day, do not purchase a fairy wrasse. If you need to remove a fairy wrasse from a reef tank, just get a good fish trap. In my estimation after years of keeping countless fairy wrasses, these fish do not seem to be especially bright. I have had numerous individuals enter an Ultralife fish trap that contained food, at the same time, even after some of these fish had had a "bad experience" (i.e., been caught and removed) with such a trap in the recent past. (Many fish learn to avoid these traps, including other labrids, after a single capture attempt.)

Fairy Wrasse Species

Cirrhilabrus adornatus Randall & Kunzmann, 1998
Common Names: Decorated Fairy Wrasse, Adorned Fairy Wrasse.
Maximum Length: 6.5 cm (2.6 in.) (unverifiable reports to 10 cm [3.9 in.])
Distribution: Southwest coast of Sumatra and the Mentawai Islands, Indonesia.
Biology: It lives on rubble slopes at depths of 10 to 30 m (33 to 99 ft.). It is usually in loose groups; in some cases small groups of males aggregate, at least for short periods of time. It is said to swim in an unusual manner, with its head down, in the wild, but exhibits normal *Cirrhilabrus* swimming in captivity.
Captive Care: The Decorated Fairy Wrasse is showing up in the aquarium trade sporadically. Its small size means that it can be housed in a smaller tank (e.g., 30 gallons). You should feed this wrasse at least once a day (two or three times a day is even better) to ensure it does not become emaciated and subsequently perish. Most foods will be accepted, but a variety of finely chopped fresh seafood (e.g., shrimp, marine fish flesh), frozen mysid shrimp, and a good frozen prepared food will help to maintain its color and good health. Keep only one male per tank, as more will fight. Males may also pick on females if crowded in a small tank. Right now, females are not readily collected as the males are much more attractive and command a higher price.
Aquarium Size: 30 gal. **Temperature:** 23° to 28°C (74° to 82°F).
Aquarium Suitability Index: 4.
Remarks: This species appears to be closely related to the Yellowfin Fairy Wrasse (*Cirrhilabrus flavidorsalis*). In fact, the females of the two species are virtually indistinguishable. The male *C. ador-*

Cirrhilabrus adornatus, Decorated Fairy Wrasse, female: small adult size.

Cirrhilabrus adornatus, Decorated Fairy Wrasse, male: displaying fish.

natus is white to pale pink overall with a pair of bright red blotches on the back (the blotches sometimes merge or the rear blotch maybe absent) and a red border on the dorsal fin. When stressed, the red blotches may fade. There is some variability in color, with some males exhibiting a orangish yellow base body color, rather than the more common white.

Cirrhilabrus aurantidorsalis Allen & Kuiter, 1999
Common Names: Goldback Fairy Wrasse, Orangeback Fairy Wrasse.
Maximum Length: 12 cm (4.7 in.).
Distribution: Northern and East-central Sulawesi, Indonesia.

Cirrhilabrus aurantidorsalis, Goldback Fairy Wrasse: young male specimen.

Cirrhilabrus aurantidorsalis, Goldback Fairy Wrasse: typical male coloration.

Cirrhilabrus aurantidorsalis, Goldback Fairy Wrasse: male in spawning colors.

Biology: *Cirrhilabrus aurantidorsalis* occurs on coastal coral reefs and rubble slopes at depths of 7 to at least 25 m (23 to 83 ft.). I have seen it mixing with the Redhead Fairy Wrasse (*Cirrhilabrus solorensis*) in Lembeh Strait, although it is much less common than this species. It tends to live in small, loose groups.

Captive Care: This is a good aquarium fish that readily acclimates. Smaller *C. aurantidorsalis* may do so a bit more easily than large adults, although large males are more common in the trade due to their bright colors. The Goldback Fairy Wrasse can be aggressive toward conspecifics or congeners (adult males are especially prone to aggression). Keep only one male per tank unless the aquarium is extra-large and add conspecifics to the tank at the same time.

Aquarium Size: 55 gal. **Temperature:** 23° to 28°C (74° to 82°F).

Aquarium Suitability Index: 4.

Remarks: The male Goldback Fairy Wrasse has an orange or yellow back. There is a thick purple line down the flank and the belly can be white, blue, or pinkish purple. The females are almost indistinguishable from female *C. solorensis*.

Cirrhilabrus bathyphilus Randall & Nagareda, 2002

Common Name: Deep-sea Fairy Wrasse, Coral Sea Fairy Wrasse, Hooded Fairy Wrasse, Rosy-fin Fairy Wrasse.

Maximum Length: 9 cm (3.5 in.) (possibly greater than 10 cm [3.9 in.]).

Distribution: Coral Sea (Holmes and Flora Reefs), Chesterfield Bank (near New Caledonia), Vanuatu (Efate and Tanna Islands).

Biology: The Deep-sea Fairy Wrasse is usually found in deep water. Most have been collected at depths of 60 to 217 m (198 to 716 ft.). However, Fenton Walsh reports having observed this fish as shallow as 8 m (26 ft.). In Vanuatu, *C. bathyphilus* is usually collected at depths of 28 to 43 m (91 to 140 ft), where water temperature is around 23°C (74°F). It is usually found over rubble substrates or aggregating around patch reefs on fore-reef slopes. The sex ratio of *C. bathyphilus* groups is usually around three females to every one male. They tend to co-occur with the Longfinned Anthias (*Pseudanthias ventralis*) (K. Kohen, personal communication).

Captive Care: Although *C. bathyphilus* is currently not uncommon in the North American aquarium trade, it is still quite an expensive fish. However, it is usually a good investment as it tends to be a hardy aquarium resident. It is initially a shy fish that will peek out from cover until it feels secure in its new home. Therefore, it is best to add this fish to relatively peaceful surroundings, although once it has acclimated, large males can usually fend for themselves with moderately aggressive tankmates

Cirrhilabrus bathyphilus, Deep-sea Fairy Wrasse, female: rare but hardy fish.

Cirrhilabrus bathyphilus, Deep-sea Fairy Wrasse, "hooded" male, Efate.

Cirrhilabrus bathyphilus, Deep-sea Fairy Wrasse, male, Coral Sea.

Cirrhilabrus bathyphilus, Deep-sea Fairy Wrasse, male variant, Tanna Island.

(e.g., pygmy angelfishes, smaller dottybacks, small damsels). It can be aggressive toward other fairy wrasses, especially members of its own kind or similarly colored species. Randall and Nagareda (2002) report that a captive individual displayed at and chased other *Cirrhilabrus* kept with it. I have also seen it picked on by individual fairy wrasses (e.g., *C. pylei*, *C. punctatus*) that were larger than it was. This species tends not to lose its amazing colors, even when conspecifics are not present.

Aquarium Size: 30 gal. **Temperature:** 23° to 28°C (74° to 82°F).
Aquarium Suitability Index: 4.

Remarks: *Cirrhilabrus bathyphilus* exhibits geographical differences in coloration. Males from the Coral Sea have red on the head that extends down the dorsum all the way to the caudal fin. In males from Efate Island, Vanuatu, the red forms a hood on the head that ends near the middle of the body (the name Hooded

Fairy Wrasse has been coined for these specimens). Tanaka (2007) states that males from Tanna Island, Vanuatu, differ from those from Efate in having an orangish red streak down the side of the body. When *C. bathyphilus* displays, the red coloration (especially on the caudal fin) becomes more intense, red may develop on the side of the body, and the blue trim on the fins becomes more conspicuous. It has a large eye, an apparent adaptation to its deep-dwelling habits. It is most similar to Lyretail Fairy Wrasse (*Cirrhilabrus lunatus*). Another deep-water beauty (found at depths of 37 to 62 m [120 to 202 ft.]) has been collected in Fiji, Tonga, and Vanuatu that has been dubbed the "Tongan Flame Wrasse." In the future, the common name **Nahacky's Fairy Wrasse** will be applied to this species. It is a beautiful fish, with males being orange on the anterior half of the body and yellow on the back half with a red caudal fin and black margin on the

Cirrhilabrus sp., Nahacky's Fairy Wrasse: undescribed new species, also known as the Tongan Flame Wrasse. A fish to quicken the pulse of reef aquarists.

tail and dorsal fins. (There seems to be some geographical color variation.) The male also has an elongated, slightly hooked first dorsal spine (in some individuals there are purple highlights on the anterior dorsal fin). Kevin Kohen (personal communication) reports that this wrasse is found on steep slopes composed of coarse rocky rubble. The water temperature in this habitat is around 23°C (74°F). Nahacky's Fairy Wrasse occur in groups that consist of approximately one male to every five females. The harem of the females tends to be a function of male size (the larger the male, the larger the harem). Although very different in color, **Marjorie's Fairy Wrasse (*Cirrhilabrus marjorie*) Allen, Randall & Carlson, 2003** is similar to *C. bathyphilus* in morphology. It has only be found off Vanua Levu, Fiji. It is found at depths of 20 to 50 m (66 to 165 ft.) over rubble substrates. It is

reported to sometimes mix with the ubiquitous *C. punctatus*. Ten pairs were sent to the U.S. and Japan for the aquarium trade in 2007 and commanded a very healthy price (more than $1,200 a pair in the U.S.). It is a durable aquarium species, although it may be a bit more shy than some other forms. The females of this species are red with a black spot on the caudal peduncle. The male has a strongly lunate caudal fin.

Cirrhilabrus condei Allen & Randall, 1996
Common Name: Conde's Fairy Wrasse.
Maximum Length: 8 cm (3.1 in.) (possibly to 10 cm [3.9 in.]).
Distribution: Eastern Indonesia, Papua New Guinea, Solomon Islands, and Vanuatu.
Biology: Conde's Fairy Wrasse is usually found on sheltered rock

Cirrhilabrus sp., Nahacky's Fairy Wrasse, female.

Cirrhilabrus sp., Nahacky's Fairy Wrasse, male displaying.

Cirrhilabrus marjorie, Marjorie's Fairy Wrasse: rare find from Vanua Levu, Fiji.

Cirrhilabrus condei, Conde's Fairy Wrasse, female.

and algae flats and slopes. I have also seen it near small patch reefs on mixed sand and rubble slopes. It typically occurs at a depth range of 3 to 23 m (10 to 76 ft.), although it has been reported to depths of 70 m (231 ft.). It often occurs in loose groups. I observed a group that consisted of several males, females and juveniles. The males would display toward each other and toward consexuals. Members of this group stayed close to the substrate, refuging among waterlogged branches, *Halimeda* algae, a few soft corals, and rubble. One of the males moved around the group and displayed to the local females. When the male displays, the anterior of the dorsal fin is erected like a sail (only the anterior two-thirds of the fin is erected) and the overall coloration changes (it takes on a whitish blue coloration).

Captive Care: *Cirrhilabrus condei* is a hardy aquarium fish that is well suited to the smaller reef tank (e.g., 55 gallons). Because of its small size, it tends to suffer less during shipping than some of its larger cousins. Keep only one male per tank, unless your aquarium is extra-large (180 gallons or more). A male can be kept with a group of females, but all members of the group should be added simultaneously. The males of this species are likely to quarrel with males of the similar *Cirrhilabrus* spp. (e.g., Redfinned Fairy Wrasse [*C. rubripinnis*] and the Longfinned Fairy Wrasse [*C. rubriventralis*]). It does not tend to lose its color, even when conspecifics are not present.

Aquarium Size: 30 gal. **Temperature:** 22° to 28°C (72° to 82°F).
Aquarium Suitability Index: 4.
Remarks: The males of this species are unique in having a black margin along the edge of the dorsal fin and a bluish white line

Cirrhilabrus condei, Conde's Fairy Wrasse, male, Papua New Guinea.

Cirrhilabrus condei, Conde's Fairy Wrasse, male displaying.

Cirrhilabrus condei, Conde's Fairy Wrasse, male variant displaying.

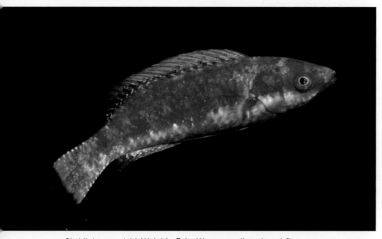

Cirrhilabrus walshi, Walsh's Fairy Wrasse: yellow dorsal fin.

along the base (the amount of black on the fin can vary between populations). The dorsal fin is also sail-like (it is curved). When it "flashes," a region on the mid to posterior portion of the body turns yellow (at least in Vanuatu specimens), while individuals from the Solomon Islands may display yellow along the entire back and a blue mid-body line. **Walsh's Fairy Wrasse (*Cirrhilabrus walshi*) Randall & Pyle, 2001** is a similar species that reaches a maximum length of 7.5 cm (3.0 in.). It is known from the Coral Sea to American Samoa (it was originally collected by fish expert Fenton Walsh). This wrasse is a deep-water species, having been reported from depths of 37 to 46 m (122 to 152 ft.). This species differs from similar forms in having a yellow dorsal fin.

Cirrhilabrus cyanopleura (Bleeker, 1851)

Common Names: Bluehead Fairy Wrasse, Bluesided Fairy Wrasse, Bluescaled Fairy Wrasse, Yellow-flanked Fairy Wrasse.

Maximum Length: 13 cm (5.1 in.).

Distribution: Eastern Malaysia to Palau, north to southern Japan, south to Rowley Shoals.

Biology: *Cirrhilabrus cyanopleura* occurs at depths of 1 to 35 m (3.3 to 116 ft.) over low-profile patch reefs composed of coral or sponge and macroalgae, coral rubble, and seagrass beds. It feeds in small to very large, loose aggregations. Individuals in these aggregations will swim up to 4.5 m (15 ft.) over the substrate and will often pause to near the substrate to be cleaned by cleaner wrasses. Large groups are often joined by related species, like Lubbock's Fairy Wrasse (*C. lubbocki*), Pink Flasher Wrasse (*Paracheilinus carpenteri*), and the Filamented Flasher Wrasse (*Paracheilinus filamentosus*), and nonrelated zooplankton feeders, like sergeants (*Abudefduf* spp.). Females outnumber males in ag-

Cirrhilabrus cyanopleura, Bluehead Fairy Wrasse, male. This species is commonly available and is seen in many color forms and variations.

gregations, but males are often quite common. It will hide among macroalgae or coral rubble when threatened. When spawning, this species often aggregates near coral promontories. Males will dash about over milling groups of females. Males will approach females and intensify in color ("flash"). When the female is ready to spawn, she will join a male that rushes at her and the pair will ascend a short distance (about 1 to 1.8 m [3.3. to 5 ft.]) into the water column and release their gametes. Males will spawn with multiple females during a single afternoon (spawning has been observed during the mid- to late afternoon). In the Philippines, I found this species on coastal slopes where they group in rock-filled channels that run perpendicular to the beach or in rocky areas with profuse macroalgae growth. In these locations they mix with several flasher wrasses (*Paracheilinus* spp.) and the Red-finned Fairy Wrasse (*Cirrhilabrus rubripinnis*). In the Philippines, they spawn in the late afternoon, at which time the head of the male lightens and they dash through mixed groups of fairy and flasher wrasses. In Japan, this species mixes with Temminck's

Cirrhilabrus cyanopleura, Bluehead Fairy Wrasse: odd female color form, photographed in West Papua.

Cirrhilabrus cyanopleura, Bluehead Fairy Wrasse, female, Banda Sea.

Cirrhilabrus cyanopleura, Bluehead Fairy Wrasse, male, Banda Sea.

Cirrhilabrus cyanopleura, Bluehead Fairy Wrasse, pastel variant, Sulawesi.

Cirrhilabrus cyanopleura, Bluehead Fairy Wrasse, male, Philippines.

Cirrhilabrus cyanopleura, Bluehead Fairy Wrasse, male, West Papua.

Fairy Wrasse (*Cirrhilabrus temminckii*).

Captive Care: The Bluehead Fairy Wrasse does well in captivity if properly acclimated. This species sometimes ships poorly, therefore, it is prudent not be to hasty about taking a newly acquired individual home from the pet store. Achterkamp (1987) reported that this wrasse is best kept in a small groups, composed of one male and up to four females. I have also had solitary specimens thrive in aquariums. You can keep more than one male in an extra-large aquarium (e.g., 180 gallons or larger), but they should be introduced simultaneously. If you do have an individual that is a finicky eater, try live brine shrimp or black worms to induce feeding. However, most individuals will accept a wide range of captive fare. The Bluehead Fairy Wrasse should not be introduced into a tank with aggressive tankmates and should always have access to numerous hiding places. Larger individuals may behave

Cirrhilabrus earlei, Earl's Fairy Wrasse, male: Micronesian beauty.

Cirrhilabrus earlei, Earl's Fairy Wrasse, female.

agonistically toward other fairy wrasses and zooplankton feeders once they have become established, especially when they are housed in smaller aquariums. Males tend to lose color if females are not present.

Aquarium Size: 55 gal. **Temperature:** 23° to 28°C (74° to 82°F).
Aquarium Suitability Index: 4.

Remarks: There has been much confusion about the status of this fish in ichthyology circles. One color form of the Bluehead Fairy Wrasse has been referred to as the **Yellowflanked Fairy Wrasse** (*Cirrhilabrus lyukyuensis*) **Ishigawa, 1904** (sometimes incorrectly called *C. ryukyuensis*) (see Michael 2006). Some suggest this species is valid and differs in that the males are dark blue over the anterior third of the body, have purple flanks and a white or yellow ventrum. They often have a yellow path on the side just behind the pectoral fin. The proponents of recognizing this species state it is found from Bali to southern Japan. I now am following Tanaka (2007) and consider the two synonymous.

Cirrhilabrus earlei Randall & Pyle, 2001

Common Names: Earl's Fairy Wrasse, Orangestriped Fairy Wrasse.
Maximum Length: 8.5 cm (3.3 in.) (possibly to 10 cm [3.9 in.]).
Distribution: Palau, Kwajalein, Yap Islands.
Biology: This is a deep-water fairy wrasse having been reported from depths of 60 to over 100 m (198 to 325 ft.). It is reported from the base of outer reef dropoffs, where it lives over mixed sand and rubble slopes. Females as small as 4.5 cm (1.8 in.) in standard length are sexually mature.
Captive Care: Although not common in the trade, some have been collected and shipped to North America in recent years. It is reported to be a fairy hardy aquarium resident, although, be aware of individuals with buoyancy problems. It often comes

from great depths and may be damaged if improperly decompressed. Do not add it to a tank of aggressive tankmates. It commands a high price.

Aquarium Size: 30 gal. **Temperature:** 23° to 28°C (74° to 82°F).
Aquarium Suitability Index: 4.

Remarks: Small adult *C. earlei* have a pointed (lanceolate) caudal fin which becomes more truncate in larger males. It sports a lovely color that is different from all other *Cirrhilabrus* spp. The males are pink overall with six magenta lines running down the body and a yellow patch behind the eye. The caudal fin is purple or red. When it "flashes," the body becomes more reddish and metallic purple appears over the eyes and along the back. Females are similar to males but have less yellow behind the eye and are less intense in overall coloration.

Cirrhilabrus exquisitus Smith, 1957

Common Name: Exquisite Fairy Wrasse
Maximum Length: 12 cm (4.7 in.).
Distribution: Indian Ocean form from East Africa to Sumatra. Pacific form from Christmas Islands, Western Australia, Indonesia east to the Tuamotus, north to the Izu Peninsula, Japan south to the Great Barrier Reef.
Biology: *Cirrhilabrus exquisitus* is one of the most common members of the genus over much of its range. It is found at depths of 2 to 32 m (7 to 106 ft.); however, it usually lives in less than 10 m (33 ft.) of water. It occurs on reef faces, fore-reef slopes and lagoon habitats, over rubble or mixed rubble and sand bottoms. It typically is found in current-prone areas. The Exquisite Fairy Wrasse is usually found in small to large aggregations. The male displays intense metallic blue markings when courting females or challenging rival males.

Cirrhilabrus exquisitus, Exquisite Fairy Wrasse, adult male, Fiji: a large, commonly seen species with a profusion of color forms from different regions.

Captive Care: Care requirements are similar to other large fairy wrasse species. Females and small males usually display little interspecific aggression; I have successfully kept them in small groups, consisting of only females, along with several flasher wrasses. Large males may behave aggressively toward other fairy wrasses and zooplankton feeders in small tanks. This species will accept most aquarium foods. The coloration of males may fade if conspecific females are not present.

Aquarium Size: 55 gal. **Temperature:** 23° to 28°C (74° to 82°F).

Aquarium Suitability Index: 4.

Remarks: There is considerable color variation between Pacific and Indian Ocean forms (there is also variation within these two populations). Populations from the South Pacific are all similar—they all have a red distal margin on the dorsal fin. Specimens from Vanuatu differ slightly in often having red behind the head that extends onto the flank. In the Indian Ocean, males from Christmas Island are similar to those from the Pacific. In other regions of the Indian Ocean, they do not have the red fin markings but exhibit red areas on the head and near the base of the pectoral fin. Both forms exhibit bright blue markings when they "flash." Some ichthyologists are proposing that the two populations actually represent different species. If this is true, the Indian Ocean form would retain the name *C. exquisitus*. The juveniles of this species have a white spot on the nose.

Cirrhilabrus exquisitus, Exquisite Fairy Wrasse: female, Papua New Guinea.

Cirrhilabrus exquisitus, Exquisite Fairy Wrasse: male variant, Vanuatu.

Cirrhilabrus exquisitus, Exquisite Fairy Wrasse, male displaying, Pacific form.

Cirrhilabrus exquisitus, Exquisite Fairy Wrasse, juvenile, Indian Ocean.

Cirrhilabrus exquisitus, Exquisite Fairy Wrasse, young male, Indian Ocean.

Cirrhilabrus exquisitus, Exquisite Fairy Wrasse: male, Indian Ocean.

Cirrhilabrus filamentosus, Filamented Fairy Wrasse, male. Small, hardy fish.

Cirrhilabrus filamentosus, Filamented Fairy Wrasse, displaying male.

Cirrhilabrus filamentosus (Klausewitz, 1976)

Common Names: Filamented Fairy Wrasse, Whipfin Fairy Wrasse, Threadfin Fairy Wrasse.

Maximum Length: 8 cm (3.1 in.).

Distribution: Java Sea to the Lesser Sunda Islands, Timor Seas.

Biology: The Whipfin Fairy Wrasse is not abundant in the wild. It inhabits deep coastal reef slopes, usually deeper than 14 m (46 ft.), but as shallow as 6 m (20 ft.). It also lives in more turbid estuaries. When displaying toward a rival or potential mates, the male will erect all of its fins, its color will intensify, and it will dart forward for about 20 cm (8 in.) using its pectoral fins for propulsion. It will usually perform this display several times in succession. It is found in aggregations, consisting mainly of juveniles and females, and sometimes mixes with other *Cirrhilabrus* and *Paracheilinus* wrasses.

Captive Care: This small fairy wrasse will thrive in a peaceful community tank. It will quickly adapt to its new home and will feed on any food placed in the tank. This species will do best if kept with shrimp gobies, dart gobies, worm gobies, flasher wrasses, and other smaller fairy wrasse. Females can be kept in small groups, but only one male should be kept per aquarium, unless you have a larger tank (e.g., 135 gallons). Because of its small size it is more likely to be picked on by larger fairy wrasse species.

Aquarium Size: 30 gal. **Temperature:** 23° to 28°C (74° to 82°F).

Aquarium Suitability Index: 4.

Remarks: This fish is red above and white below. The females have fine blue lines along the body and may have a black spot at the tail base. Male *C. filamentosus* have yellow median fins and some have a bright blue tail, while others do not (in some species the blue extends from the tail, along the ventrum, almost to the pelvic fin bases). All mature males have very long pelvic fins that

Cirrhilabrus tonozukai, Tono's Wrasse, female. Sulawesi, Indonesian species.

Cirrhilabrus tonozukai, Tono's Wrasse, male in full display.

Cirrhilabrus sp., Sailfin Fairy Wrasse, male displaying: undescribed species very similar to both Cirrhilabrus filamentosus and Cirrhilabrus tonozukai.

extend back to about the middle of the anal fin. **Tono's Fairy Wrasse** (*Cirrhilabrus tonozukai*) **Allen & Kuiter, 1999** is a very similar species. In fact, for many years it was thought to be *C. filamentosus*. The males of the later species has a yellow dorsal fin, while the dorsal of *C. tonozukai* is multicolored. Tono's Fairy Wrasse is only known from eastern Sulawesi to West Papua. It occurs at depths of 10 to 40 m (33 to 132 ft.) in Lembeh Strait. It is usually found in mixed rubble-sponge-algae beds with mixed large-polyped stony corals and soft corals. This species forms small to large groups (that are comprised mainly of females and juveniles), often mixing with other zooplanktivores (including flasher wrasses). In the late afternoon, adult males are often observed dashing about displaying toward one another and to females. This species is sometimes available in the aquarium trade. It husbandry requirements are similar to those of *C. filamentosus*. There is also an undescribed species that is similar to *C. filamentosus* and *C. tonozukai*. This species, the **Sailfin Fairy Wrasse** (*Cirrhilabrus* **sp.**) is known from Malaysia (Kapalai Island,

Mabul, and Sipadan), possibly Java, and southern Sulawesi. This species is red above with a white ventrum. The male has blue on

Cirrhilabrus sp., Sailfin Fairy Wrasse, female.

Cirrhilabrus flavidorsalis, Yellowfin Fairy Wrasse, male, not displaying.

Cirrhilabrus flavidorsalis, Yellowfin Fairy Wrasse, male displaying.

the throat. When it "flashes," there is a magenta pink on the dorsal fin, the flank, and the anal fin (at least in some populations). Some also have yellowish orange on the cheeks and ventrum. The caudal fin has a dark blue to black band on the rear margin. Tanaka (2006) reports that photographer Ryoichi Sato observed this species in water as shallow as 10 m (33 ft.). It attains a maximum length of at least 7 cm (2.8 in.).

Cirrhilabrus flavidorsalis Randall & Carpenter, 1980

Common Name: Yellowfin Fairy Wrasse.
Maximum Length: 9 cm (3.5 in.).
Distribution: Indonesia, Palau, Philippines, possibly Malaysia.
Biology: The Yellowfin Fairy Wrasse is found on fore-reef slopes, over rubble and soft coral substrate, or protected bays with rich hard and soft coral growth. It occurs at a depth range of 6 to 40

m (20 to 132 ft.). When feeding, this species rarely strays more than 1 m (3.3 ft.) above the bottom. In the Philippines, this species sometimes intermingles with larger aggregations of Lubbock's Fairy Wrasse (*Cirrhilabrus lubbocki*), while in West Papua it mixes with large groups of *C. cyanopleura* and the Blue Flasher Wrasse (*Paracheilinus cyaneus*). It may even hybridize with *C. lubbocki* (Tanaka, 2007). I have seen this species spawn in West Papua. The *C. flavidorsalis* group consisted of dozens of females and six males. The females form scattered, cohesive groups that stay near the substrate. The males are very active, they swim over considerable distances, and they often rise high in the water column (several meters). As dusk approached, the two males displayed toward one another and chasing often occurred. On one occasion, I watched the more dominant male chase its advisory for over 20 m (66 ft.). Both of these fish ended up back with the group of females after this long, vigorous sprint. The males display to females by swooping down past them and then back up in the water column—they do this in quick succession. On other occasions, they will swoop down and then rapidly circle the female two or three times with all the fins spread. When females were ready to spawn, the pair would dash up 60 cm (24 in.) or so into the water column to release their gametes. These males exhibited the banded color phase all the time.

Aquarium Care: This small fairy wrasse will thrive in the aquarium if proper care is given. It can be quite shy, racing for cover when the aquarist nears the tank. It can also become very aggressive toward conspecifics and other small wrasses. This is especially true once it has been in a tank on its own for a while. For example, I had an individual that vigorously attacked flasher wrasses that were introduced after it had become well established. This same individual exhibited some aggression toward newly added Rainford's Goby (*Amblygobius rainfordi*). When behaving in an agonistic manner, its color will intensify (especially the banding on the body) and it will dash toward the intruder and turn abruptly when it gets very close or attempt to nip it. It exhibits strong color fidelity. I have found *C. flavidorsalis* to be very disease resistant. One individual that I kept became covered with ich in a reef aquarium. After suffering from a severe infection for several weeks, it eventually recovered without treatment.

Aquarium Size: 30 gal. **Temperature:** 23° to 28°C (74° to 82°F).
Aquarium Suitability Index: 4.

Cirrhilabrus joanallenae Allen, 2000

Common Names: Blackfin Fairy Wrasse, Pulauweh Fairy Wrasse.
Maximum Length: 7 cm (2.8 in.).
Distribution: Weh Island, Northern Sumatra and Phuket, Thailand.

Cirrhilabrus joanallenae, Blackfin Fairy Wrasse, male with black pelvic fins.

Cirrhilabrus joanallenae, Blackfin Fairy Wrasse, male: interesting variant.

Biology: The Blackfin Fairy Wrasse occurs on rubble flats at the base of the reef slope at depths of 12 to 40 m (40 to 132 ft.). It occurs in groups of 10 to 15 individuals. Courting occurs in this species in the late afternoon. Males chase females and engage in impressive displays where they extend all their fins.

Captive Care: The Blackfin Fairy Wrasse is a hardy aquarium species that occasionally shows up in marine fish trade. It can be kept singly or in small groups if you have a larger aquarium (i.e., 100 gallons or more). It is best to house one male per aquarium. If two or more males are kept in the same tank, the coloration of subordinate individuals will begin to revert back to that of a female. This species will accept a variety of fresh and frozen foods. It can be kept in a shallow- or deep-water reef aquarium.

Aquarium Size: 30 gal. **Temperature:** 23° to 28°C (74° to 82°F).

Aquarium Suitability Index: 4.

Remarks: This recently described species is very similar to *C. rubriventralis*. The males are similar in overall coloration but have dark blue or black pelvic fins (in *C. rubriventralis* they are red and black). Some males also have a broad, bright yellow stripe running down each side or on the back. Males that lack the yellow markings often have black suffused on the red area near the tail. This species also differs from *C. rubriventralis* in that the males lack the blue dots on their sides and they have no, or few, blue spots on their tails and median fins.

Cirrhilabrus jordani Snyder, 1904

Common Names: Jordan's Fairy Wrasse, Hawaiian Flame Wrasse, Flame Wrasse.

Maximum Length: 10 cm (3.9 in.).

Distribution: Hawaiian and Johnston Islands, Midway Atoll.

Biology: Jordan's Fairy Wrasse occurs on fore-reef slopes and walls

Cirrhilabrus jordani, Jordan's Fairy Wrasse, displaying male: note color change.

in water deeper than 19 m (63 ft.). It is most abundant at depths greater than 28 m (92 ft.). It has been reported as deep as 91 m (296 ft.). It often occurs on reef ledges that are covered with coral rubble. Males are very territorial and defend a harem that can consist of a few to over 100 females. They display at rivals by raising their median fins and sometimes hang in the water with their head up and tail down. "Tail standing" is also employed by males to attract potential mates. During courtship the male has two white stripes, located under the lateral line, that run the full length of the body and converge at the tail. Males often race through the group of females displaying this brilliant coloration.

Captive Care: Jordan's Fairy Wrasse is a hardy introduction to the fish or invertebrate aquarium, where it will accept most foods, including flake food. Only one male should be kept per aquarium, unless you have a very large tank (e.g., 300 gallon), but

Cirrhilabrus jordani, Jordan's Fairy Wrasse, female.

Cirrhilabrus jordani, Jordan's Fairy Wrasse, male.

Cirrhilabrus katherinae, Katherine's Fairy Wrasse, female.

Cirrhilabrus katherinae, Katherine's Fairy Wrasse, male.

several females can be housed with a male if they are introduced simultaneously. Although they may display at other fish species, they rarely "come to blows" with their tankmates, with the exception of congeners: in some instances large males may bully smaller fairy wrasses. This species exhibits a high degree of color fidelity, even when conspecifics are not present. During some years they are more abundant in shallower depths, where they are easy to collect (R. Pyle, personal communication). It is during these times when they are readily available in the trade.

Aquarium Size: 55 gal. **Temperature:** 22° to 27°C (72° to 80°F). **Aquarium Suitability Index:** 4.

Remarks: Females are orangish pink, with yellow under the head and onto the fins. In males the yellow spreads onto the flanks, the ventrum is vivid yellow, the dorsal and caudal fins are red, and there are red lines from tip of the snout down back and also under the eye from the lower jaw to the pectoral fin base. **Claire's Fairy Wrasse (*Cirrhilabrus claire*) Randall & Pyle, 2001** is another deep-water member of the genus that is similar in color to *C. jordani*. This species is known only from the Cook Islands, where it has been collected at depths of 55 to 100 m (182 to 330 ft.). It may make it into the aquarium trade on rare occasions but will command very high prices.

Cirrhilabrus katherinae Randall, 1992

Common Name: Katherine's Fairy Wrasse.
Maximum Length: 11 cm (4.3 in.).
Distribution: Izu and Ogasawara Islands of Japan south to the Marianas, Carolines, and Palau.

Biology: *Cirrhilabrus katherinae* is found at a depth range of 10 to 40 m (33 to 132 ft.) in harbors, around lagoon patch reefs, and on outer reef faces and slopes. It is found in small aggregations. This fish has been observed to spawn during midafternoon (e.g., 3:30 to 4:00 P.M.). Donaldson (1995) observed a group of 40 females and several males moving 3 to 5 m (10 to 17 ft.) above the sea floor. The males moved over and around the females and occasionally circled them while head-bobbing. When displaying toward females, the males erect their fins and exhibit dramatic color change, including the presence of blue bands on the dorsal and anal fins. Just prior to spawning, the male will exhibit nuptial colors, erect its fins, and begin rapidly circling the female. The pair will assume a parallel position and make a short spawning ascent. The female will return to the group and the male will begin courting another female.

Captive Care: This species is not common in the aquarium trade. Its husbandry is probably similar to that of *C. temminckii.*

Aquarium Size: 55 gal. **Temperature:** 23° to 28°C (74° to 82°F).

Aquarium Suitability Index: 4.

Remarks: This species is similar to *C. balteatus* and *C. temminckii* (some have suggested it is a subspecies of the latter). The **Belted** or **Girdled Fairy Wrasse (*Cirrhilabrus balteatus*) Randall, 1988** is also known from the Marshall Islands, as well as Yap. The color of the male *C. balteatus* is very distinct. It is greenish brown above, white below, with a large yellowish patch on the side behind the pectoral fin base. Both the male and female of the closely related *C. katherinae* have a black spot at the pectoral fin base. The pelvic fin rays are also very long and it reaches a length of 14 cm (5.5 in.). The Girdled Fairy Wrasse is found in lagoons and fore-reef slopes, over rubble, patch reefs, and algae beds composed of *Halimeda* and *Dictyota*. This wrasse is found at depths of 7 to 22 m (23 to 73 ft.). It forms feeding groups that move up to 2 m (7 ft.) off the substrate. While not common in the aquarium trade, it does show up from time to time. Males have been reported to be aggressive when space is limited.

Cirrhilabrus katoi Senou & Hirata, 2000

Common Name: Kato's Fairy Wrasse.

Maximum Length: 10 cm (3.9 in.).

Distribution: Izu Peninsula south to Kashiwajima and Okinawa.

Biology: Kato's Fairy Wrasse occurs on rocky reefs at depths of 20 to 40 m (65 to 130 ft.). It forms aggregations that usually consist of one or two males and several females. It is also occurs singly or in pairs. *Cirrhilabrus katoi* is often found mixing with other fairy wrasses, including the Yellowflanked (*C. lyukyuensis*), Lyretail (*C. lunatus*), Redmargin (*C. rubrimarginatus*) and Temminck's Fairy Wrasse (*C. temminckii*).

C. balteaus, Belted Fairy Wrasse, female: note black patch on pectoral base.

Cirrhilabrus balteaus, Belted Fairy Wrasse, male: note salmon-colored band.

Cirrhilabrus katoi, Kato's Fairy Wrasse, displaying male, Kochi, Japan.

Cirrhilabrus laboutei, Laboute's Fairy Wrasse, male: a stunning species.

Cirrhilabrus laboutei, Laboute's Fairy Wrasse, female, Coral Sea.

Cirrhilabrus laboutei, Laboute's Fairy Wrasse, male variant.

Captive Care: This beautiful fairy wrasse is not readily available to North American aquarists. Its husbandry requirements are probably similar to that of other fairy wrasses. The only possible difference would be water temperature preferences.

Aquarium Size: 30 gal. **Temperature:** 19° to 23°C (66° to 74°F).

Aquarium Suitability Index: 4.

Remarks: This species has a larger anal fin than others in the genus. *Cirrhilabrus jordani* is most similar.

Cirrhilabrus laboutei Randall & Lubbock, 1982

Common Name: Laboute's Fairy Wrasse.

Maximum Length: 12 cm (4.7 in.).

Distribution: Vanuatu, New Caledonia to the Loyalty Islands and the Great Barrier Reef.

Biology: This glorious fish is usually encountered on the reef face, reef slopes, or channels at depths of 8 to 55 m (26 to 182 ft.). It is typically found over rubble bottoms. It occurs in small to large groups which consist mainly of females. *Cirrhilabrus laboutei* sometimes forms mixed feeding aggregations with *C. lineatus* and *C. scottorum*. Anthias (e.g., Purple Queen Anthias, *Pseudanthias pascalus*) and juvenile surgeonfishes sometimes join these groups as well.

Captive Care: Subadults and females acclimate more readily than large males; in fact, young individuals are extremely durable aquarium fish. Larger specimens need lots of swimming room (at least a 30-gallon aquarium), as well as adequate places to hide when threatened. Females are rarely aggressive toward other species; for example, I have kept them with other fairy wrasses and flasher wrasses without incident. Once they have become established in a tank, they may behave aggressively toward other small planktivores and smaller congeners. *Cirrhilabrus laboutei* exhibits strong color fidelity, even when members of its own kind are not present. This species will spawn in a large home aquarium. Eggs and larvae are pelagic and challenging to culture.

Aquarium Size: 55 gal. **Temperature:** 22° to 28°C (72° to 82°F).

Aquarium Suitability Index: 3.

Remarks: In females of this species the top of the head and body are yellowish brown with three magenta stripes and the ventrum is lavender and white. Subadult females have red stripes and a black spot at base of tail. The color pattern of males is similar to females, but there are two distinct magenta stripes with yellow edging, a deep lavender-pink ventrum, and the first two anal fin spines are prolonged.

Cirrhilabrus lineatus, Lined Fairy Wrasse, displaying male: coveted, eye-catching species most abundant at depths of 100 ft. (30 m); shy in the reef aquarium.

Cirrhilabrus lineatus Randall & Lubbock, 1982
Common Name: Lined Fairy Wrasse.
Maximum Length: 12 cm (4.7 in.).
Distribution: New Caledonia to the Loyalty Islands, the Great Barrier Reef, and the Coral Sea.
Biology: *Cirrhilabrus lineatus* occurs at a depth range of 15 to 55 m (50 to 182 ft.). It is most abundant at depths greater than 30 m (99 ft.). This labrid is found on reef faces, fore-reef slopes, and around dropoffs. The Lined Fairy Wrasse often forms large shoals, but it occasionally lives in smaller groups as well. It will form mixed feeding aggregations with other fairy wrasses (e.g., *C. laboutei*, *C. scottorum*) and anthias (including the Painted Anthias, *Pseudanthias pictilus*, and the Squareblock Anthias, *P. pleurotaenia*).

Captive Care: Small specimens (under 7 cm [3 in.]) make great aquarium inhabitants, while larger individuals can be difficult to acclimate. I added an individual to a small reef aquarium with other fairy and flasher wrasses and it had no problem adjusting and did not behave aggressively toward its tankmates, even though it was slightly larger. In fact, this individual accepted food the same day it was shipped. Sometime latter, I introduced this specimen to a larger aquarium containing some Azure Demoiselle (*Chrysiptera hemicyanea*) and a male Oblique-lined Dottyback (*Cypho purpurascens*) and it had a difficult time acclimating to this more hostile environment. It fed, but spent most of its time hiding in the corners of the aquarium. Larger individuals tend to be quite shy when first introduced, but if they are placed in peaceful environs, they usually come around. Keep only one

Cirrhilabrus lineatus, Lined Fairy Wrasse, displaying male variant.

Cirrhilabrus lineatus, Lined Fairy Wrasse, female.

male per tank. This species does not lose its color in the absence of conspecifics like some *Cirrhilabrus.*

Aquarium Size: 55 gal. **Temperature**: 22° to 28°C (72° to 82°F).
Aquarium Suitability Index: 3–4.

Cirrhilabrus lubbocki Randall & Carpenter, 1980
Common Name: Lubbock's Fairy Wrasse.
Maximum Length: 8 cm (3.1 in.).
Distribution: Flores, Sulawesi, Flores, the Philippines, Palau and Okinawa.
Biology: *Cirrhilabrus lubbocki* occurs at depths between less than 1 to 45 m (3.3 to 149 ft.) but is most often deeper than 5 m (16 ft.). It most commonly occurs over rubble bottoms or heads of branching corals, on coastal fringing reefs, rocky channels, fore-reef slopes, and vertical dropoffs. This species usually stays close to the bottom when feeding and sometimes forms mixed schools with the Yellowfin Fairy Wrasse (*C. flavidorsalis*). In the Philippines, this species is found mixing in rocky channels with the Bluehead (*C. cyanopleura*), the Redfinned (*C. rubripinnis*), and the Philippine Bluestripe Fairy Wrasse (*C.* cf. *temminckii*), as well as several *Paracheilinus* spp. This species stays near the substrate when feeding and courting. When male *C. lubbocki* court, they dash up into the water column (up to approximately 40 cm [16 in.] above the bottom) and then dash back toward the seafloor. They "turn on" a metallic light blue coloration when they engage in this behavior.
Captive Care: *Cirrhilabrus lubbocki* is a sturdy aquarium fish. Keep one male per tank unless your tank is quite large (minimum of 135 gallons). Females can be kept together in smaller aquariums. This species' requirements are similar to other small fairy wrasses. It tends not to fade in color.
Aquarium Size: 30 gal. **Temperature:** 23° to 28°C (74° to 82°F).
Aquarium Suitability Index: 4.
Remarks: The coloration of males in this species can vary considerably from one geographical area to another. Philippine males have a disjunct purple stripe down the side, the top of head and back are orangish yellow, and the rest of the head and body are red with small blue flecks. Indonesia males have more yellow on the head, back, dorsal, anal, and pelvic fins and some individuals lack the purple lateral stripe.

Cirrhilabrus lunatus Randall & Masuda,1991
Common Names: Lyretail Fairy Wrasse, Crescent-tail Fairy Wrasse.
Maximum Length: 11.8 cm (4.6 in.).
Distribution: South Japan, Ogasawara Islands, Okinawa, Indonesia (Sulawesi and Bali).
Biology: Off Okinawa the Lyretail Fairy Wrasse has been observed over rubble and dead coral at a depth of 32 m (106 ft.). Additional individuals have been collected off the Ogasawara Islands, over a sloping rubble bottom, at depths between 35 and 45 m (116 to 149 ft.). What is possibly this species has been observed by Rudie Kuiter off the island of Sulawesi, Indonesia, at a depth of 55 m (180 ft.). This species is found in small groups that consist mainly of juveniles and females.
Captive Care: I have only encountered one specimen of this beautiful fairy wrasse in the U.S. aquarium trade. Like many members of the genus, this species appears to adapt well to captivity. It hid for several days in a tank that contained active fish species but came out almost immediately when I moved it to a smaller tank of its own. It accepted frozen brine shrimp and and other frozen foods.

Cirrhilabrus lubbocki, Lubbock's Fairy Wrasse, female, Philippines.

Cirrhilabrus lubbocki, Lubbock's Fairy Wrasse, transforming female, Flores.

Cirrhilabrus lubbocki, Lubbock's Fairy Wrasse, male, West Papua.

Cirrhilabrus lubbocki, Lubbock's Fairy Wrasse, male, Lembeh, Indonesia.

Cirrhilabrus lubbocki, Lubbock's Fairy Wrasse, male, Philippines.

Cirrhilabrus lubbocki, Lubbock's Fairy Wrasse, nuptial coloration.

Cirrhilabrus lunatus, Lyretail Fairy Wrasse, juvenile, Japan.

Cirrhilabrus lunatus, Lyretail Fairy Wrasse, male, Japan.

Cirrhilabrus lunatus, Lyretail Fairy Wrasse, male, Philippines.

Aquarium Size: 55 gal. **Temperature:** 22° to 27°C (72° to 80°F). **Aquarium Suitability Index:** 4.

Remarks: This is the only fairy wrasse in which males have a lunate, or half-moon shaped, tail. The **Dark Fairy Wrasse (*Cirrhilabrus brunneus*) Allen, 2006** is a similar species from the western Philippines (Kalimantan), where it was collected from a dropoff at a depth of 40 m (130 ft.). The males of this species are brown overall with a purple hue. There is a patch of brown on the breast and belly region. The caudal fin is very similar to that of *Cirrhilabrus lunatus*.

Cirrhilabrus luteovittatus Randall, 1988

Common Names: Yellowstreaked Fairy Wrasse, Yellowbanded Fairy Wrasse.

Maximum Length: 12 cm (4.7 in.).

Distribution: Johnston Atoll, Marshall Islands, Chuk, Pohnpei and the Philippines.

Biology: This species occurs in lagoons, channels, and reef slopes at depths of 8 to 40 m (26 to 128 ft.), being most abundant at depths greater than 15 m (48 ft.). It is often found in small aggregations over coral rubble and macroalgae or patch reefs.

Captive Care: Although more attractive than the females, large male *C. luteovittatus* can be more difficult to acclimate to the aquarium. However, once adjusted they are equally hardy. Provide this active species with plenty of swimming space and do not place two males in the same aquarium. It may fade in color somewhat if conspecifics are not present. This fish may acclimate more readily in a dimly lit aquarium but can be housed in a brightly lit reef tank. It is a great jumper.

Aquarium Size: 55 gal. **Temperature:** 23° to 28°C (74° to 82°F). **Aquarium Suitability Index:** 3.

Remarks: Female Yellowstreaked Fairy Wrasses are olive and purplish blue overall, with two rows of red spots from pectoral fin base to the caudal fin, a light orange dorsal fin, a dark spot at the base of the pectoral fin, and a black spot on the upper part of caudal peduncle. Females are typically no longer than 7.5 cm (2.9 in.). Males of this species are maroon overall, with a dark bar at the base of the pectoral fin, a bright yellow streak on the flank, and blue stripes on the dorsal and anal fins, which intensify during courtship. Juveniles have a yellowish white spot on the tip of the snout. The Yellowstreaked Fairy Wrasse is similar to **Randall's Fairy Wrasse (*Cirrhilabrus randalli*) Allen, 1995** from coral reefs off northwest Australia (i.e., Rowley Shoals, Scott and Hibernia Reefs). Randall's Fairy Wrasse differs in having a larger dark patch at the axil of the pectoral fin base (i.e., it extends from below the pectoral fin to its upper edge), the yellow steak on the side is

Cirrhilabrus luteovittatus, Yellowstreaked Fairy Wrasse, female.

Cirrhilabrus luteovittatus, Yellowstreaked Fairy Wrasse, transforming male.

Cirrhilabrus luteovittatus, Yellowstreaked Fairy Wrasse, fully developed male.

Cirrhilabrus randalli, Randall's Fairy Wrasse: a rarity from northwestern Australia.

broader, and the head is often dark. Randall's Fairy Wrasse is found in lagoons, reef faces, and slopes at depths down to 40 m (132 ft.). This species and *C. luteovittatus* are members of the *C. cyanopleura* complex.

Cirrhilabrus punctatus Randall & Kuiter, 1989
Common Names: Finespotted Fairy Wrasse, Dotted Wrasse, Port Villa Fairy Wrasse.
Maximum Length: 13 cm (5.1 in.).
Distribution: Papua New Guinea to Great Barrier Reef and New South Wales, east to Lord Howe Island, New Caledonia, and Tonga.
Biology: This is a shallow-water species, occurring at depths of 2 to 32 m (7 to 106 ft.). In the Fijian islands I have regularly seen this fish in less than 13 m (43 ft.) of water, while at Heron Island, Great Barrier Reef, it is abundant at a depth of around 11 m (36 ft.). It occurs in a variety of habitats, from calm lagoons to the outer fore-reef slopes, but is most common in more protected areas. Often found over rubble substrate. In Fiji, it forms loose aggregations and often associates with the Redspot Wrasse (*Pseudocoris yamashiroi*). During courtship the male exhibits considerable color change.
Captive Care: This handsome fish is a hardy aquarium inhabitant. As with others in the genus, juveniles or smaller adults have an easier time acclimating than larger individuals. I kept one in a smaller reef aquarium with a Lined Fairy Wrasse (*C. lineatus*) and a number of flasher wrasses, and it acclimated quickly and was always well behaved. However, I have also kept individuals that bullied smaller fairy wrasses. A larger female I once kept even fought with a much larger male. While size typically determines which *Cirrhilabrus* is boss of a tank, I believe that this species may

Cirrhilabrus punctatus, Finespotted Fairy Wrasse, female, Great Barrier Reef.

Cirrhilabrus punctatus, Finespotted Fairy Wrasse, juvenile, Fiji.

Cirrhilabrus punctatus, Finespotted Fairy Wrasse, male displaying, Fiji.

Cirrhilabrus beauperryi, male: newly described species.

C. beauperryi, male, Papua New Guinea.

C. beauperryi: same male as at left, displaying, with associated color change.

Cirrhilabrus punctatus, Finespotted Fairy Wrasse, female, Fiji: This highly variable fish has many color forms, all sporting a distinctive pattern of tiny spots.

have more aggressive tendencies. Of course, tank size will also determine if it causes a problem with resident zooplanktivores.

Aquarium Size: 55 gal. **Temperature:** 23° to 28°C (74° to 82°F).

Aquarium Suitability Index: 4.

Remarks: This is a highly variable species. There may be more than one species (or at least subspecies) "lumped" under this binomial. In general, both males and females have numerous small blue dots on the head and body, thus the species name *punctatus*, which is Latin for "dot." Individuals from New Caledonia and Vanuatu are unique in possessing a yellowish green streak along the flank, while Tongan specimens have a white, vertical line on the caudal fin. Juveniles can be red with a pink ventrum or greenish brown with a white ventrum, but both color forms have small blue dots, a white spot on the nose, a black bar at the base of the pectoral fins, and a black spot at the base of the tail. The Finespotted Fairy Wrasse is similar in morphology to *C. temminckii*. Beware, there are other fairy wrasses that sport small spots as juveniles.

Cirrhilabrus punctatus, Finespotted Fairy Wrasse, female, Vanuatu.

Cirrhilabrus punctatus, Finespotted Fairy Wrasse, male variant, Vanuatu.

Cirrhilabrus pylei, Pyle's Fairy Wrasse, transforming female, Philippines.

Cirrhilabrus pylei, Pyle's Fairy Wrasse, small male, Philippines.

Cirrhilabrus pylei, Pyle's Fairy Wrasse, large male, Phillipines.

Cirrhilabrus pylei, Pyle's Fairy Wrasse, male, Vanuatu.

Cirrhilabrus pylei, Pyle's Fairy Wrasse, displaying male, Vanuatu: a wonderful deepwater species that usually proves hardy when kept with passive tankmates.

Cirrhilabrus pylei Allen & Randall, 1996

Common Name: Pyle's Fairy Wrasse.

Maximum Length: 10 cm (3.9 in.).

Distribution: Indonesia (Bali, Sulawesi), Papua New Guinea, Vanuatu, and the Philippines.

Biology: This species occurs near rocky outcroppings on sand slopes or on rubble slopes at depths of 75 to 85 m deep (244 to 276 ft.).

Captive Care: Pyle's Fairy Wrasse is a hardy aquarium species that should be housed with passive tankmates, like flasher wrasses, dart gobies, firefishes, razor gobies, and shrimp gobies. Most individuals I have kept ate within hours after being placed in a quarantine tank. I did have one larger individual that did not eat for days and spent most of its time hiding. That said, I have found this species to be less flighty when initially introduced to the tank than some other larger *Cirrhilabrus*. Stressed individuals will hang in the water column in a heads-up position. They will not hesitate to come out and feed if they are not harassed by bellicose tankmates. Pyle's Fairy Wrasse is now being exported regularly from Vanuatu. The color of the male may fade some if females are not present or if kept in a brightly lit, shallow-water reef tank.

Aquarium Size: 55 gal. **Temperature:** 23° to 28°C (74° to 82°F).

Aquarium Suitability Index: 3.

Remarks: This species exhibits some degree of geographical variation. The males of this species have incredibly long pelvic fins, the tips extend back to about the middle of the anal fin base. Males from Vanuatu tend to turn yellow when displaying, while individuals from Bali are pink. Most males have a blue rim along the posterior caudal fin margin.

Cirrhilabrus rhomboidalis, Rhomboid Fairy Wrasse, male: a deep-water species that may hide incessantly and lose its color in a brightly-lit aquarium.

Cirrhilabrus rhomboidalis Randall, 1988
Common Name: Rhomboid Fairy Wrasse.
Maximum Length: 15 cm (5.9 in.), most less than 12 cm (4.7 in.).
Distribution: Marshall Islands (Kwajalein), Palau, and Yap.
Biology: The Rhomboid Fairy Wrasse occurs on steep outer reef slopes, over sand and dead coral, where it has been reported to occur at depths from 38 to 40 m (125 to 132 ft.). It stays closer to the substrate than most of the other fairy wrasses from the Marshall Islands. It is also more secretive than other *Cirrhilabrus*. Like other species in the genus, the male's color intensifies during courtship. In this species, the head and body turn yellow and an intense blue appearing on the anterior portion of the dorsal fin. Just prior to spawning, the abdomen of the female fairy wrasse will also swell with hydrated eggs.
Captive Care: The Rhomboid Fairy Wrasse was once a very difficult fish to obtain, due to its limited distribution. While not common, it is now more readily available. Larger specimens sometimes ship poorly and are best shipped in large shipping bags with ample amounts of water. If you obtain a healthy individual, you should have no problem getting this fish to eat. The Rhomboid Fairy Wrasse is typically considered to be one of the less aggressive members of the genus. It is likely to be picked on by more pugnacious forms, like Scott's Fairy Wrasse (*C. scottorum*). However, it has been known to pick on other, smaller fairy wrasses, especially if they are introduced after it is well established and tank space is limited. If you are going to keep a *C. rhomboidalis* with more bellicose species, be sure it is added to the tank first. A male can be housed with one or more females, but do not keep two males together. Males tend to be shyer than females and will hide more, and may lose color in a brightly lit reef tank. The females will often scull about the tank, paying little notice to the human observers. A male, in contrast, may be reluctant to spend much time in the open if there is activity near the tank. Instead, he will slink from one crevice to another. Make sure the tank is always covered. It is not uncommon for these fish to engage in dramatic displays along the front or sides of the tank when the room is dark. Apparently, they see their reflection in the glass, which releases these aggressive displays. You can encourage this behavior by attaching black black acrylic to the exterior of the tank. This enhances the reflective qualities of the glass.
Aquarium Size: 55 gal. **Temperature:** 23° to 28°C (74° to 82°F).
Aquarium Suitability Index: 3–4.
Remarks: This species is very similar to the Lined Fairy Wrasse (*C. lineatus*). However, *C. lineatus* has larger eyes, and a rounder

Cirrhilabrus rhomboidalis, Rhomboid Fairy Wrasse, male: note long pelvic fins.

Cirrhilabrus rhomboidalis, Rhomboid Fairy Wrasse, female.

and shorter caudal fin, and the lines on its body are straighter and narrower than the interspaces between them. The coloration is also different.

Cirrhilabrus roseafascia Randall & Lubbock, 1982

Common Names: Redstripe Fairy Wrasse, Roseband Fairy Wrasse, Pink-banded Fairy Wrasse.

Maximum Length: 20 cm (7.9 in.).

Distribution: New Caledonia, Vanuatu, Tonga, Fiji, Samoa, Palau, and the Philippines.

Biology: This large, beautiful fairy wrasse is found on deep reef slopes and dropoffs. It has been reported from 30 to 113 m (98 to 367 ft.), although juveniles may occur at lesser depths. Little is reported on its behavior.

Captive Care: *Cirrhilabrus roseafascia* is a spectacular display animal. It tends to acclimate readily, but may adjust more quickly if housed in a deep-water reef or dimly lit aquarium. It is not particularly aggressive, but because it tends to be larger than most congeners, it is usually the dominant fairy wrasse in the tank. It is a good jumper. Mostly females and small to medium-sized males found in the trade. The large males are ostentatious! (See page 26.)

Aquarium Size: 75 gal. **Temperature:** 22° to 28°C (72° to 82°F).

Aquarium Suitability Index: 3–4.

Remarks: The male Redstripe Fairy Wrasse is pink overall with an orange line along the back, often with a yellow dorsal and anal fin. It is distinguished by close relatives by the pelvic fins, with have a blue and or black and blue patch. In the aquarium trade, this species was often confused with the **Longtail Fairy Wrasse** (*Cirrhilabrus lanceolatus*) **Randall & Masuda, 1991.** The Longtail is known from the Izu region to the Ryukus (there is a report of this species from Palau, but it is rare here). It has been reported at depths of 42 to 60 m (139 to 198 ft.) on steep, outer rocky reefs. Male *C. lanceolatus* is a salmon pink or greenish tan with a red, pink, or light blue line from the snout to the caudal fin. The tail is a rhomboid shape. Females are red with white lines on the body. Juveniles have a black spot on the caudal peduncle. It reaches a maximum length of 15 cm (5.9 in.). The **Splendid** or **Pintail Fairy Wrasse** (*Cirrhilabrus* sp.) is another amazing member of the genus that has the lanceolate caudal fin. This species is also known from the Izu and Ryuku Islands, Taiwan, and the Philippines and reaches a maximum length of 12 cm (4.7 in.). It has been reported from deep water (32 to 40 m [104 to 130 ft.]). While it has been referred to as *C. lanceolatus* in the past, it is no doubt a distinct species. It makes it into the aquarium trade on rare occasions and does well in captivity. The **Purple Bone Fairy Wrasse** (*Cirrhilabrus blatteus*) **Springer & Randall, 1974** is another species in which large males have a lanceolate caudal fin. This species is only known from the Gulf of Aqaba, Red Sea, where it has been reported from water depths of 43 to 46 m (142 to 152 ft.). It lives in small groups.

Cirrhilabrus rubrimarginatus Randall, 1992

Common Names: Redmargined Fairy Wrasse, Pinkmargined Fairy Wrasse.

Maximum Size: 14 cm (5.5 in.).

Distribution: Vanuatu to Fiji and Tonga, north to southern Japan.

Biology: This is a deep-water species, having been reported at

Cirrhilabrus roseafascia, Redstripe Fairy Wrasse, female.

Cirrhilabrus roseafascia, Redstripe Fairy Wrasse, variant male.

Cirrhilabrus roseafascia, Redstripe Fairy Wrasse, male.

Cirrhilabrus lanceolatus, Longtail Fairy Wrasse, male: similar to *C. roseafascia.*

Cirrhilabrus sp., Splendid or Pintail Fairy Wrasse, male: note lanceolate tail fin.

Cirrhilabrus blatteus, Purple Bone Fairy Wrasse, male, Red Sea.

Cirrhilabrus rubrimarginatus, Redmargined Fairy Wrasse, male, Fiji.

Cirrhilabrus rubrimarginatus, Redmargined Fairy Wrasse, female, Fiji.

Cirrhilabrus rubrimarginatus, male, Kochi, Japan: nuptial coloration.

depths of 25 to 52 m (83 to 172 ft.). It is typically found over sand and rubble bottoms near low-profile patch reefs, among rocks, soft corals, and macroalgae. It is found on fore-reef slopes or dropoffs. I observed a group of several males and 10 females aggregating with a large number of Finespotted Fairy Wrasses (*C. punctatus*) off Savu Savu, Fiji. This group was in 22 m (66 ft.) of water, over a steep rubble slope with the occasional head of staghorn coral (*Acropora* sp.) offering them shelter when threatened. **Captive Care:** Large males of this species make spectacular display animals. Unfortunately, like others in the group, larger specimens tend to suffer more during the shipping process. Juveniles and females do tend to ship better, but they pale in color to large males. Like other *Cirrhilabrus*, it is an amazing jumper. Make sure the top is covered as well as any holes in the top and overflow box. The beautiful males will lose their color somewhat if a female is not present or if not given a pigment-rich diet. While not overly aggressive, this species is more likely to squabble with similar fairy wrasses (e.g., Lined, Pyle's, Rhomboid Fairy Wrasse).

Aquarium Size: 55 gal. **Temperature:** 23° to 28°C (74° to 82°F).
Aquarium Suitability Index: 3–4.
Remarks: Female Redmargined Fairy Wrasse are dusky orange dorsally, with four pairs of small, faint white spots on the back. The paired fins are pale and there is a red margin on the dorsal and caudal fins. Males are pink dorsally, with a lavender to bright blue belly, irregular lines of orange dots on the sides, a blue head with pink on gill cover, a bright blue dorsal margin, and a broad, vivid red band on the dorsal fin and tail, and the pelvic fins are orangish with bright blue and black streaks. Juveniles of this species are pink with a yellow stripe on the head and back and a black spot near the base of the tail. This species is most closely related to *C. temminckii* and *C. lineatus*.

Cirrhilabrus rubripinnis Randall & Carpenter, 1980
Common Names: Redfin Fairy Wrasse, Red Fairy Wrasse.
Maximum Length: 8 cm (3.1 in.).
Distribution: Philippines and northern Indonesia.
Biology: Randall and Carpenter (1980) report that the Redfin Fairy Wrasse occurs on reef slopes among coral rubble, disc corals (*Fungia* spp.), and soft corals. They found it at depths of 10 to 30 m (33 to 98 ft.) associating with Lubbock's Fairy Wrasse (*C. lubbocki*), flasher wrasses (*Paracheilinus* spp.), pencil wrasses

Cirrhilabrus rubripinnis, Redfin Fairy Wrasse, female, Philippines.

Cirrhilabrus rubripinnis, Redfin Fairy Wrasse, young male, Philippines.

Cirrhilabrus rubripinnis, Redfin Fairy Wrasse, large male, Philippines.

Cirrhilabrus rubripinnis, Redfin Fairy Wrasse, male, Philippines: nuptial colors.

(*Pseudojuloides* spp.), and perchlets (*Plectranthias*)—all small species that refuge among coral rubble. I have encountered many of these fish off the coast of Batangas, Philippines. It is most common on coastal sand slopes, where they aggregate in channels that are filled with rocks, macroalgae, debris, and *Diadema* sea urchins, sharing this habitat with several other fairy and flasher wrasses. Male *C. rubripinnis* engage in spectacular displays. They extend their fins and the color intensifies (the dorsal becomes crimson red, there is metallic blue on the tail, the head lightens or takes on a yellowish hue, and, during the most intense displays, a white patch appears on the side). The males will cover a large area of over 300 m² (3,229 ft.²), displaying at rivals and rapidly circling groups of females, lowering their pelvic fins and swooping down when displaying. The males move at an incredible pace when they engage in this behavior.

Captive Care: The Redfin Fairy Wrasse is a durable aquarium fish. When first introduced to your aquarium, this species may spend much of its time hiding. If it is not kept with aggressive tankmates it will overcome this shyness and become a highly conspicuous member of your fish community. Some male individuals may become quite pugnacious, chasing smaller fish around the aquarium. For example, I once had an individual chase other fairy wrasses, cardinalfish, chromis, anemonefish, and even a soldierfish. Males are likely to behave aggressively

Cirrhilabrus rubrisquamis, Redscaled Fairy Wrasse, male displaying.

toward similar-looking *Cirrhilabrus* (e.g., *C. condei, C. filamentosus, C. tonozukai*). It is not uncommon for adult males to ship poorly: therefore, it is prudent to purchase them only after they are swimming about the aquarium and feeding. This is a great fish for both shallow- and deep-water reef aquariums.

Aquarium Size: 30 gal. **Temperature:** 23° to 28°C (74° to 82°F).
Aquarium Suitability Index: 4.

Cirrhilabrus rubrisquamis Randall & Emery, 1983

Common Name: Redscaled Fairy Wrasse.
Distribution: Chagos, Mauritius, Maldives Islands, and Sri Lanka.
Maximum Length: 8.5 cm (3.3 in.).
Biology: *Cirrhilabrus rubrisquamis* occurs on deep fore-reef slopes and walls. I observed this species swimming at the openings of large caves and overhangs at a depth of 39 m (130 ft.), along with the Diadem Anthias (*P. parvirostris*) and the Resplendent Anthias (*P. pulcherrimus*). It is found at depths to at least 50 m (165 ft.). This wrasse stays near the bottom, swimming along reef crevices, at the base of gorgonians and black coral trees. It usually occurs in small groups. During courtship, the sides of the male's body turn white.
Captive Care: The Redscaled Fairy Wrasse acclimates quickly to captivity, readily accepts most foods, and spends most of its time swimming about the aquarium. Adult males will behave aggressively toward other fairy wrasses and small schooling planktivores. If you keep two males together in a small- to medium-sized aquarium, one specimen will dominate the other and prevent it from feeding and spending time in the open. You can successfully maintain more than one male in a larger system (minimum of 180-gallon aquarium). It can be kept in a shallow or deep-water reef aquarium, although it is best to slowly acclimate it to the brighter conditions in an aquarium with intense lighting.
Aquarium Size: 30 gal. **Temperature:** 23° to 28°C (74° to 82°F).
Aquarium Suitability Index: 4.
Remarks: This species is unmistakable. The **Bloody Fairy Wrasse** (***Cirrhilabrus sanguineus***) **Cornic, 1987** is a similar species that is only known from Mauritius. It reaches a length of 6.5 cm (2.6 in.). The male has a large red patch on the side of its body. This resident of rubble slopes occurs at depths of 40 to 60 m (132 to 198 ft.), forming small groups. Little information exists on the captive care of this seldom-collected fairy wrasse. Its husbandry requirements are probably similar to those of other small members of the genus. Because of its predilection for deep water, it is probably a good idea to at least start it out in a dimly lit aquarium.

Cirrhilabrus rubrisquamis, Redscaled Fairy Wrasse, female.

Cirrhilabrus sanguineus, Bloody Fairy Wrasse, male: displaying.

Cirrhilabrus rubriventralis, Longfinned Fairy Wrasse, female, Red Sea.

Cirrhilabrus rubriventralis, Longfinned Fairy Wrasse, male, Sri Lanka.

Cirrhilabrus rubriventralis Springer & Randall, 1974
Common Names: Longfinned Fairy Wrasse, Social Wrasse.
Maximum Length: 7.5 cm (2.9 in.).
Distribution: Red Sea, Oman, and Sri Lanka.
Biology: In the northern Red Sea this species occurs at depths from 3 to 42 m (10 to 138 ft.), but females are more common at shallow depths. It occurs on the fore reef, usually over coral rubble and sand, and will refuge among the branches of soft corals like *Sinularia*, rubble, and the spines of *Diadema* sea urchins. *Cirrhilabrus rubriventralis* forms loose groups, which typically consist of one male and eight to ten females. When males display

at females and rivals, the blue spots on their bodies and fins intensify, they erect the dorsal fin, lower the brilliant red pelvic fins, and undulate the tail. An occasional male may develop a yellow patch under the lower jaw.

Captive Care: This is a common species in the marine aquarium trade, and for good reason. Individuals may become quite aggressive after living in a tank for a while, chasing and nipping other small wrasses (e.g., flasher wrasses, *Paracheilinus* spp.), nonaggressive anthias (e.g., Lori's Anthias, *Pseudanthias lori*), and tobies (genus *Canthigaster*). If you are going to keep more than one individual it is best to keep one male and several females. However, it is possible to place two males in the same aquarium if the tank is large (e.g., 180 gallons) with lots of hiding places. I have seen a male change back to a female after being harassed by a consexual.

Aquarium Size: 30 gal. **Temperature:** 22° to 28°C (72° to 82°F).

Aquarium Suitability Index: 5.

Remarks: The female Longfinned Fairy Wrasse is orangish red with fine blue lines along the body and a dark spot on the caudal peduncle. *Cirrhilabrus rubriventralis* from the Red Sea and Oman have mostly red pelvic fins, while in individuals from Sri Lanka these fins are black and red. **Morrison's Fairy Wrasse (*Cirrhilabrus morrisoni*) Allen, 1999** is a similar species known only from Hibernia Reed in the Timor Sea. It is unlikely to make it into aquarium stores. It is reported over flat bottoms covered with dense *Halimeda* cover. It occurs at depths 23 to 35 m (76 to 116 ft.) and forms mixed groups with a flasher wrasse.

Cirrhilabrus scottorum Randall & Pyle, 1989

Common Name: Scott's Fairy Wrass.

Maximum Length: 13 cm (5.1 in.).

Distribution: Coral Sea, Fiji, Samoa, Society and Tuamotus Islands and the Pitcairn group.

Biology: *Cirrhilabrus scottorum* is most common on the fore reef in water ranging from 3 to 40 m (10 to 132 ft.). This species is typically found in small groups, consisting mainly of females and juveniles, which feed just above the bottom. The larger males will swim up to 3 m (10 ft.) over the bottom and display to females and rival males by erecting the dorsal and anal fins. I have also seen solitary individuals associating with shoals of Finespotted Fairy Wrasses (*C. punctatus*) in Fiji. Species pairs spawn by swimming up to 50 cm (20 in.) above the bottom before shedding their gametes.

Captive Care: This is one of the most popular of the *Cirrhilabrus* in the aquarium trade. Large males are most frequently available to aquarists due to their extraordinary coloration and tendency to be hardier than some other large fairy wrasse species. They should be placed in a tank with plenty of hiding places and may hide for a day or so before they venture out to investigate their new home. Once acclimated they can be quite boisterous and will feed aggressively on most foods. Two male Scott's Fairy Wrasses should not be housed in the same aquarium, unless it is extremely large (e.g., 240 gallons), and females should always be introduced before, or at least at the same time as, the male. I have found this to be one of the more aggressive members of the genus. Large males will often behave aggressively toward other fairy wrasses introduced after them, chasing them about the tank incessantly. This wrasse is a great addition to a shallow or deep-water reef aquarium, but beware: it is notorious for jumping out of open aquariums. This species is prone to color change in captivity, especially if female conspecifics are not present. It is not uncommon for the body to become more bluish and the red blotch on the side of Cook Island specimens to fade or disappear after they have been kept in captivity for a while.

Cirrhilabrus scottorum, Scott's Fairy Wrasse: a large, hardy fairy wrasse, Cook Islands. Note pinnate tail.

Cirrhilabrus scottorum, Scott's Fairy Wrasse: colors vary significantly, Cook Islands. Red blotch may disappear if not kept with conspecifics.

Cirrhilabrus scottorum, Scott's Fairy Wrasse, male, Tongan variant: the color of this labrid is like a human fingerprint—every individual is different.

Aquarium Size: 55 gal. **Temperature:** 23° to 28°C (74° to 82°F).
Aquarium Suitability Index: 4.
Remarks: Female *C. scottorum* are olive green above, often with slight traces of green, blue, and purple; yellowish white below; a bright blue area on top of the head; a red tail; and a yellowish orange dorsal and anal fin. Males of this species exhibit considerable geographical variation in color. In general, they have a darker body than females, with blue and blue-green on the top of the head. Those individuals from the Cook Islands have a prominent red streak on the side, while in Australian individuals this characteristic is less pronounced. Juveniles are similar to the female but have a dark spot on caudal peduncle, and rows of pinkish white spots along the side. Scott's Fairy Wrasse has a spine well in front of the dorsal fin above the eye that is erected when the males perform lateral displays. The **Blackmargin Fairy Wrasse** (*C. melanomarginatus*) **Randall and Shen, 1978** is most similar to this species. It is known from the Philippines, Taiwan, and southern Japan. It differs from *C. scottorum* in having a slightly shorter snout and a more oblique angle to the mouth, and in lacking the anterior yellow color on the front of the head and red caudal fin. It gets its name from the black margin along the dorsal fin. The Blackmargin Fairy Wrasse is the largest species, attaining a maximum length of about 15 cm (5.9 in.). Unfortunately, it rarely enters the aquarium trade. It occurs to a depth of 5 to 40 m (16 to 132 ft.).

Cirrhilabrus solorensis Bleeker, 1853

Common Names: Redhead Fairy Wrasse, Solar Fairy Wrasse, Red-eyed Fairy Wrasse, Tricolor Fairy Wrasse.
Maximum Length: 13 cm (5.1 in.).
Distribution: Indonesia, from Bali, Sulawesi, and the Flores regions, south to Christmas Island, Indian Ocean.

Cirrhilabrus scottorum, Scott's Fairy Wrasse, Cook Islands: note pinnate tail.

Cirrhilabrus scottorum, Scott's Fairy Wrasse, male, Australia.

Cirrhilabrus melanomarginatus, Blackmargin Fairy Wrasse, male, Japan.

C. melanomarginatus, Blackmargin Fairy Wrasse, male, Japan: highly variable fish.

Biology: The Redhead Fairy Wrasse occurs in lagoons, on the reef face, and on fore-reef slopes of coastal reefs. It is found at depths from 3 to 20 m (10 to 66 ft.) over stony corals and rubble. It occurs in loose, small to large groups and occasionally mixes with other fairy wrasses, like the closely related Goldback (*Cirrhilabrus aurantidorsalis*), Bluehead (*C. cyanopleura*), Lubbock's (*C. lubbocki*), and Tono's Fairy Wrasse (*C. tonozukai*). These feeding aggregations can also be comprised of sergeants (*Abudefduf*) and adult Moon Wrasses (*Thalassoma lunare*). *Cirrhilabrus solorensis* usually occur near the bottom of these mixed-groups, but it is not uncommon to also see this species swimming up to 7 m (23 ft.) above the seafloor.

Captive Care: This is a hardy fish that is commonly seen in aquarium stores. It can be kept singly or in small groups, but if you do choose to keep more than one in your tank, it is best to house one male and four or more females. Although it usually ignores other

C. solorensis, Redhead Fairy Wrasse, male, Sulawesi, Indonesia.

Cirrhilabrus solorensis, Redhead Fairy Wrasse, male variant: a common, highly variable species that can be kept in groups of one male to four or more females.

fish species, larger *C. solorensis* may bully small planktivores and other fairy species. In fact, it tends to be one of the more aggressive members of the genus. This species can be kept in a shallow- or deep-water reef aquarium. Female Redhead Fairy Wrasses are more often seen in the aquarium trade than males.

Aquarium Size: 55 gal. **Temperature:** 23° to 28°C (74° to 82°F).
Aquarium Suitability Index: 4.

Remarks: This species was once considered to be a color variant of *C. cyanopleura*, the Bluehead Fairy Wrasse. *Cirrhilabrus solorensis* males generally, but not always, have a dark red head, a purple crescent-shaped mark along the edge of the gill cover and onto the throat, greenish flanks, and a white belly. Small females

are red with a small, black spot on upper caudal peduncle and a white ventrum and larger females have a reddish head, yellowish orange back, and purplish or blue ventrum. The color of this species can vary. It is thought that *C. cyanopleura* and this species may hybridize with odd or unusual color variants resulting.

Cirrhilabrus temminckii Bleeker, 1853

Common Names: Bluestripe Fairy Wrasse, Temminck's Fairy Wrasse, Peacock Wrasse.

Maximum Length: 10 cm (3.9 in.).

Distribution: Indonesia to Papua New Guinea, north to southern Japan, south to north western Australia. (More than one species

Cirrhilabrus solorensis, Redhead Fairy Wrasse, juvenile.

Cirrhilabrus solorensis, Redhead Fairy Wrasse, male: common variant.

Cirrhilabrus temminckii, Bluestripe Fairy Wrasse, male, Sulawesi, Indonesia.

Cirrhilabrus solorensis, Redhead Fairy Wrasse, male, nuptial coloration.

Cirrhilabrus temminckii, Bluestripe Fairy Wrasse, male, Japan.

Cirrhilabrus temminckii, Bluestripe Fairy Wrasse, male, Japan, nuptial colors.

Cirrhilabrus cf. *temminckii*, Bluestripe Fairy Wrasse, juvenile, Phillipines.

Cirrhilabrus cf. *temminckii*, Bluestripe Fairy Wrasse, female, Phillipines.

is probably represented.)

Biology: It is usually found at depths 5 to 30 m (17 to 109 ft.) on coastal reef slopes. In Japanese waters, it is often found over rock and boulder bottoms, which are overgrown with macroalgae, while in western Australia I observed it on deep, low profile reefs. The Bluestripe Fairy Wrasse swims from 50 cm to 2 m (20 in. to 7 ft.) above the bottom. During the breeding season, some large males form territories, attacking intruding males, while groups of females (numbering from 5 to 40) move over a large home range, which encompasses more than one male territory. These breeding territories can be from 36 to 169 m² (388 to 1,818 ft.²) in area. Males perform loop displays and flash their colors to attract females and ward off rivals. When the male "flashes," the turquoise stripe widens, becomes an iridescent blue, and then changes to a whitish green. The tail can be maroon, blue, or gold, while the dorsal fin and anal fins also become blue. The male's color can vary depending on the intensity of the aggressive or courting interaction. Males are easily distinguished from females not only by their color but by their elongate pelvic fins, which are about twice as long in the masculine sex. During courtship the male moves through groups of females and displays its brilliant colors. As this increases in frequency the male will veer toward a female and rush at her. Just prior to spawning the male will perform a loop up into the water column. The pair then execute a loop together, releasing their gametes at the top of the ascent. Males will spawn from 1 to 26 times a day (Bell 1982). Nonterritorial males will employ other mating strategies. For example, some will engage in "sneak" spawning: a male will hang around the territory of a large male and entice approaching females to spawn with him. Others employ "streaking": a male will join a territorial male and female as they make their spawning ascent and will release its gametes along with the pair's. Females often associate with other small wrasses and parrotfishes. Near Indonesia this species may form mixed aggregations with the Exquisite Fairy Wrasse (*C. exquisitus*), and may hybridizes with this species. In Japan it has been observed to cross-breed with the much rarer *C. cyanopleura*, and males chase this species from their breeding territories.

Captive Care: The Bluestripe Fairy Wrasse is a durable aquarium fish that is sometimes aggressive toward related or similarly colored species. For example, I had a large male that was aggressive towards a Redfinned Fairy Wrasse (*C. rubripinnis*) and a small Tomato Clownfish (*Amphiprion frenatus*). This same specimen was successfully kept with a Yellowstreaked Fairy Wrasse (*C. luteovittatus*) when both were introduced to a tank simultaneously. It is not uncommon for this species to jump out of an uncovered aquarium, and is similar to other large fairy wrasses in its general husbandry. Males of this species are prone to color fading if females are not present. The Bluestripe Fairy Wrasse can be kept in a shallow- or deep-water reef aquarium.

Aquarium Size: 55 gal. **Temperature:** 22° to 28°C (72° to 82°F). **Aquarium Suitability Index:** 4.

Remarks: *Cirrhilabrus temminckii* is occasionally seen in fish stores, and its scientific name is regularly seen misapplied to other species in fish identification guides. It is likely that there are several different species that are currently classified as *C. temminckii*. Kuiter (2002) suggests that the true *C. temminckii* is only found in southern Japan (which Kuiter dubs Temminck's Fairy Wrasse). There is a second species that is found in Indonesia and Malaysia (he calls this fish the Bluestripe Fairy Wrasse), and a third species that is only known from western Australia (he calls this the Peacock Fairy Wrasse). To confuse matters worse,

Cirrhilabrus cf. *temminckii*, Bluestripe Fairy Wrasse, male, Phillipines.

Cirrhilabrus cf. *temminckii*, Bluestripe Fairy Wrasse, male displaying.

Cirrhilabrus walindi, Walindi Fairy Wrasse, male, Papua New Guinea.

Cirrhilabrus cenderwashi, Cenderawasih Fairy Wrasse, male, West Papua.

there is a species of *Cirrhilabrus* that has been called *C. temminckii* in the past and appears to be a distinct species. The taxonomy of this apparent species complex needs to be studied further to determine just how many species there are.

Cirrhilabrus walindi Allen & Randall, 1996

Common Name: Walindi Fairy Wrasse.
Maximum Length: 8 cm (3.1 in.).
Distribution: New Guinea and Solomon Islands.
Biology: This fairy wrasse is found on rubble slopes, usually in areas with sessile invertebrate growth, at depths of 10 to 65 m (33 to 215 ft.). It usually occurs deeper than 20 m (66 ft.). *Cirrhilabrus walindi* forms loose groups, with males moving higher in the water column than females when feeding.

Captive Care: This fish is occasionally exported from the Solomon Islands. Like most of the smaller members of the genus, *C. walindi* readily acclimates to captivity. It is best to add it to a tank that contains docile fishes, although if the aquarium is large with plenty of hiding places it can usually avoid potential bullies. Males will fight in small tanks, while females typically get along. It is a good jumper (it will even jump out of relatively small openings in the aquarium top).
Aquarium Size: 30 gal. **Temperature:** 23° to 28°C (74° to 82°F).
Aquarium Suitability Index: 4.
Remarks: The overall shape of *C. walindi* are similar to *C. flavidorsalis* and *C. lubbocki*, but the color and caudal fin shape (lunate in *C. walindi*) of the male is very different. The only other species with a lunate caudal fin are *Cirrhilabrus johnsoni* and *C. lunatus*.

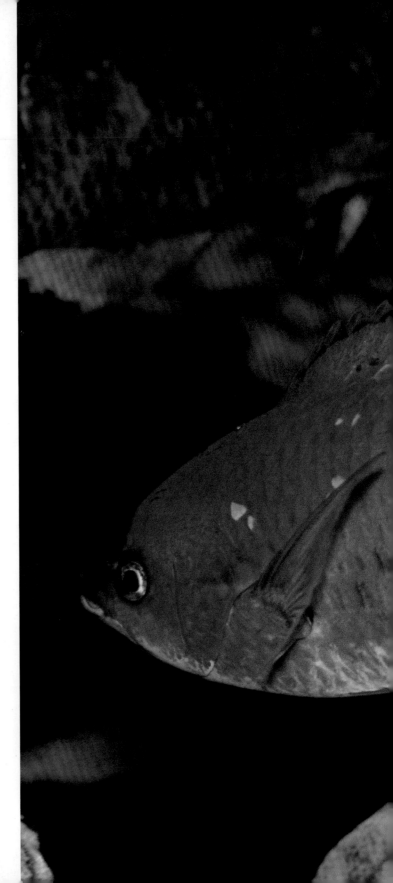

GENUS *CLEPTICUS* (CREOLE WRASSES)

Diurnal zooplanktivores from various coral reef fish families exhibit similar morphological characteristics that benefit them when they feed on minute animals in the water column. Many zooplanktivores have small, highly protrusible, upturned mouths, and teeth are small or lacking. The mouth size and its position near the end of the head allow the fish to see its small target with both eyes, thus providing better depth perception and greater feeding accuracy. Due to the minute size of their prey, precise targeting and mouth movements are necessary to ensure successful prey capture. Diurnal planktivores also tend to have more and larger gill-rakers that prevent small prey items from escaping through the gill openings.

When diurnal planktivores feed, they leave the shelter of the reef and maintain a position up in the water column in order to pick off passing plankton. As a result, these fishes are more vulnerable to the attacks of piscivorous predators like jacks and groupers, and the farther they stray from the reef, the greater the risk. Because of this selective pressure, some zooplanktivorous fishes possess body types that enable them to get back to the reef more quickly. For example, a lunate (moon-shaped) tail and a fusiform (torpedo-shaped) body are indicative of superior speed.

The Creole wrasses (*Clepticus* spp.) possess most of the characteristics described above. In many ways they are more similar in general appearance to anthias (*Pseudanthias*), chromis damsels (*Chromis*), or swallowtail angelfishes (*Genicanthus*) than they are to other labrids. All these fishes feed on zooplankton. The Creole wrasses are most similar to zooplankton-feeding wrasse genera from the Indo-Pacific, like the fairy wrasses (*Cirrhilabrus*), flasher wrasses (*Paracheilinus*), and false coris (*Pseudocoris*).

All of the *Clepticus* spp. are limited in distribution to the Atlantic Ocean. While these fishes spend little time near the reef, they do depend on it for protection from predators and shelter at night, as well as to access to the cleaning services of parasite-picking species. The young of one species (*Clepticus parrae*) occasionally make it into aquarium stores, but they are not highly sought after, as the young fish are not nearly as attractive as the adults. We will discuss the biology and captive care in more detail in the single species account below.

Clepticus parrae, Creole Wrasse: a colorful species less familiar to aquarists than to divers and snorkelers in the Caribbean, Bahamas, south Florida, and the Gulf of Mexico. These zooplanktivores bear strong similarities to anthias (*Pseudanthias*), *Chromis*, and swallowtail angelfishes (*Genicanthus*).

Clepticus parrae, Creole Wrasse, juvenile.

Clepticus parrae, female being cleaned by small Spanish Hogfish.

Creole Wrasse Species

Clepticus parrae (Bloch & Schneider, 1801)

Common Name: Creole Wrasse.

Maximum Length: 30.0 cm (11.8 in.).

Distribution: Bermuda and southern Florida and the Bahamas, south to northern South America.

Biology: Adult Creole Wrasses are found on reef faces and fore-reef slopes at depths of 1 to 40 m (3.3 to 130 ft.). Juveniles often "swarm" close to patch reefs in clear-water lagoons or near ledges on the reef face. In some cases, the young fish will refuge in tube sponges. Immature Creole Wrasses shoal with conspecifics of similar size. This wrasse uses its large pectoral fins to scull through the water column, employing its large tail as a rudder unless it

needs to rapidly accelerate back to the protection of the reef. It feeds primarily on minute crustaceans (namely copepods), siphonophores, and pteropods. It will also eat shrimp larvae, salps, crab larvae, fish eggs, ostracods, gastropod larvae, and stomatopod larvae, but to a lesser degree. The Creole Wrasse is usually found in large shoals (often numbering in the hundreds) that move high into the water column to feed. It sometimes forms mixed groups with other zooplankton feeders, including the Blue Chromis (*Chromis cyanea*) and Brown Chromis (*C. multilineata*). In some parts of the Caribbean, this species is a favorite of cleaner fishes. In a study conducted off St. Croix, U.S. Virgin Islands, in about 85% of all cleaning events engaged in by three different cleaner fishes (*Gobiosoma evelynae*, *Bodianus rufus*, and juvenile *Thalassoma bifasciatum*), *C. parrae* was the host. Smaller groups of Creole Wrasse will peel off from the main shoal and visit these cleaners. When they are being cleaned, they often crowd around the parasite-picker and usually adopt a head-down orientation. They will also rest on the top of a coral head as one or more cleaner gobies move over their bodies and even enter their mouths to remove parasites. I have observed Creole Wrasses following and posing for young and even large female Spanish Hogfish as they foraged along the reef face. When presented with a choice, the Sharknose Goby (*G. evelynae*) prefers to clean larger *C. parrae* rather than smaller individuals (large individuals probably harbor greater numbers of parasites). The Creole Wrasse is host to the caligid copepod, *Belizia brevicauda*. Creole Wrasse predators include morays, groupers, and jacks. This species spawns in the early to late afternoon and reproduction occurs all year round (although in some areas it may peak during the summer months). I have seen huge groups of *C. parrae* streaming past along the reef face as they move to traditional spawning areas. In one case, I watched as a river of these fish flowed past for over 40 minutes. This wrasse is a protogynous hermaphrodite; males result from female sex change. Spawning males adopt bicolor chromatic attire (black to dark purple anteriorly, yellow on the posterior portion of the body and fins), and have white lips and black pectoral fins. During courtship, the male chases a female and attempts to contact her dorsum with his belly. If she is in the mood, she slows down, and the male moves beneath her and pushes her up into the water column by beating his caudal fin. If totally receptive, she will go limp and allow the male to continue to move her into the water column, which he typically does by placing his snout against her flared gill covers, until they reach the apex of the ascent and release their gametes. After that, they slowly swim apart and the female moves toward the substrate while the male searches for another potential mate. If a female is not ready to spawn, the male and female may engage in rapid head-to-tail circling as the male attempts to take his position under the female, or she may attempt to get rid of her potential suitor by dashing and diving erratically. In some cases, amorous males may chase heterospecific neighbors and try to court with them. Courtship can last for hours; an individual male might chase a single female for as long as 15 minutes. Like other wrasses, they produce pelagic eggs. Males may fight over females, and some bear scars as a result of these battles. It is usually smaller males that get chased and chastised by larger consexuals. Juvenile Creole Wrasses are approximately 2 cm (0.8 in.) in length when they settle from the plankton. The newly settled fish are mainly translucent, with a purplish cast. Some areas see a large influx of young *C. parrae* (ranging in size from 3 to 5 cm [1.2 to 2.0 in.]) in the fall.

Captive Care: The Creole Wrasse can make a colorful addition to the large reef or fish-only aquarium. Because it feeds on zooplankton, it is less of a threat to sessile invertebrates. Larger individuals, however, may try to consume delicate shrimps and the like, especially if the crustaceans are added after the wrasse is established. *Clepticus parrae* needs to be fed frequently—at least a couple of times per day—with prepared foods for carnivores, shredded seafood, and/ or mysid shrimp. Juveniles will eat frozen *Cyclops*. The Creole Wrasse also gets rather large and will need to be housed in a tank of at least 135 gallons with plenty of open swimming space and hiding places. It spends most of its time swimming and bobbing about the water column and is a capable jumper, so a tank cover is a must. While the Creole Wrasse is unlikely to pester larger or more aggressive fishes, adults may bully smaller zooplanktivores (e.g., smaller fairy wrasses, flasher wrasses, dartfishes). Although juveniles can be kept in small groups, adult males may fight with each other.

Aquarium Size: 135 gal. **Temperature:** 22° to 27°C (72° to 82°F).
Aquarium Suitability Index: 4.
Remarks: Males are more colorful than females. Sex change typically occurs at a length of 15 to 18 cm (5.9 to 7.1 in.). The caudal fin of this species is emarginate in juveniles and lunate in adults. Two other species of *Clepticus* have been described in recent

Clepticus parrae, Creole Wrasse, large male in spawning colors: this species is a spectacular Caribbean fish well suited to a biotope display in a large aquarium. It may be kept in groups, but males will fight.

years. The **Brazilian Creole Wrasse (*Clepticus brasiliensis*) Heiser, Moura, & Robertson, 2000** is an attractive species known from the coast and offshore islands of Brazil south of the Amazon and also from St. Paul Rocks. The second species is the **African Creole Wrasse (*Clepticus africanus*) Heiser, Moura, & Robertson, 2000**, which is known from São Tomé Island in the Gulf of Guinea off the equatorial African coast. Both new species are distinguished from *C. parrae* by their color and the presence of greatly elongated fin rays extending from the tips of the upper and lower lobes of the forked caudal fin. In male *C. brasiliensis* these filaments can be as long as the body. The African Creole Wrasse has only one filament on each of the lobes, while *C. brasiliensis* has two or more filaments on each of the caudal lobes. The African species is also mostly black, while the Brazilian species is mainly mauve to purple. The behavior of these two species is apparently similar to that of *C. parrae*. The Brazilian Creole Wrasse is usually found near reef dropoffs and has been reported to visit the cleaning stations of the Spanish Hogfish (*Bodianus rufus*) near a shipwreck. While zooplankton is its primary food, it has also been reported to feed on the feces of Spinner Dolphins (*Stenella longirostris*).

Coris gaimard, Yellowtail Coris Wrasse: exhibiting rock-throwing behavior characteristic of this and several athletic wrasse genera.

GENUS *CORIS* (*CORIS* WRASSES)

The *Coris* spp. have compressed, moderately elongate bodies with small scales, a complete lateral line, no scales on the head (except just above the eyes), and a round to slightly rounded caudal fin. Some larger individuals have a truncate tail. Most are brightly colored; males and females exhibit disparate chromatic attire, and in some species the color of the juveniles is also distinct from that of the adults.

The genus contains approximately 20 species, all but one of which are found in the Indo-Pacific. Several of these, like the Twinspot Coris (*Coris aygula*) and the Yellowtail Coris (*Coris gaimard*), are wide-ranging forms. Others have very limited distributions. For example, the reefs around the Hawaiian islands boast four *Coris* spp., three of which are endemic; the Variegated

Coris (*Coris variegata*) is only known from the Red Sea; and the Blackbar Coris (*C. nigrotaenia*) is only known from the rocky shores of Oman. A number of species with very limited ranges have recently been described from the South Pacific, including the Kiribati Coris (*Coris centralis*), the Easter Island Coris (*C. debueni*), Hewett's Coris (*C. hewettii*), and the Marquesan Coris (*C. marquesensis*). There is also an endemic species from western Australia known as the Western King Coris (*Coris auricularis*), which is not likely to be seen in the aquarium trade. The young and females of this species set up cleaning stations and remove parasites from other fishes. The Eastern King Coris (*Coris sandeyeri*) is a resident of rocky reefs around subtropical Australia, Norfolk Island, and New Zealand. Two members of the genus are found in the Atlantic: the Mediterranean Rainbow Coris (*Coris julis*) is common in the Mediterranean and certain parts of the eastern Atlantic, and the Atlantic Coris (*C. atlantica*) is also found in the eastern Atlantic.

All of the *Coris* spp. bury under the sand at night, and younger individuals will dart under the substrate when threatened. They feed on a wide range of invertebrates, mainly motile forms, which they pluck from the seafloor with their protruding canines and masticate with their well-developed pharyngeal tooth plates. Studies on one species of *Coris* (*C. gaimard*) have documented that size does matter when it comes to diet. Juveniles feed more on small crustaceans like gammarideans, while larger individuals feed more on bivalves, snails, chitons, and crabs. The larger wrasses are better able to handle these heavily armored mollusks and crabs. The young fish feed more on the substrate surface, while individuals greater than 5 cm (2 in.) in total length also flip stones and rubble when they feed. As the *Coris* grows it can flip over larger pieces of benthic debris and expose a different set of potential prey items. (Aquarists take note: a small *Coris* may not do much damage in a reef tank, but a larger individual can wreak havoc.)

The *Coris* spp. are very opportunistic, often following other fishes that disturb the substrate like stingrays, goatfishes, triggerfishes, and large puffers. They will also join heterospecific feeding aggregations that move over sand or rubble substrates, pouncing on any small crustaceans flushed out by other fish species.

The *Coris* spp. are protogynous hermaphrodites, displaying female and male color phases. Some authors use the terms "initial" and "terminal" when referring to the color phases of these fishes, suggesting that they are diandric—that is, that males either arise from sex-changed females and or are "born" males. In diandric forms those individuals exhibiting the initial color pattern are usually, but not always, female, while all terminal phase specimens are male. Others treat these fishes as monandric—all males arise from female sex change and all displaying the initial color phase are females. In either case, in terminal phase males the first two dorsal spines are more elongate than those of initial phase specimens, and there is great color disparity between the two color phases.

Captive Care

Like most of the wrasses, the *Coris* spp. are durable fishes that do well in many captive venues. However, large individuals are more likely to ship poorly and often have greater difficulty acclimating than juveniles or subadults. Because tiny juveniles can also be difficult to keep because of their high caloric requirements, individuals greater than 5 cm (2 in.) are preferable.

The most important prerequisite for successful coris wrasse maintenance is a layer of fine sand, 5 to 10 cm (2 to 4 in.) deep, on the aquarium bottom. In deep sand beds, it is possible that a large, burrowing *Coris* could disturb anaerobic areas of the gravel bed, releasing hydrogen sulfide into the aquarium. When a *Coris* buries it will shove its head in the sand, turn on its side, and vigorously beat its tail. This behavior is effective at disturbing the substrate and will help put some detritus into suspension, where it can be removed by external filters or even provide food for certain suspension feeders. This digging activity will also prevent substrate from compacting, at least in exposed portions of the tank. These fish typically do better during shipping if a fine layer of sand that they can partially bury under is placed in the bottom of the shipping bag.

These wrasses will eat a wide variety of foods, including frozen mysid shrimp, brine shrimp, fresh or frozen minced seafood, clam on the half-shell, ghost shrimp, and even flake food. They will also decimate populations of small crustaceans and worms that come in on live rock or in live sand. The *Coris* spp. should be provided with as diverse a menu as you can provide. If fed appropriately, they will grow fast and retain their bright colors. Some of the *Coris* spp. grow quite large, so make sure you have an appropriately sized tank to adequately house an adult specimen before you take the plunge.

When *Coris* spp. Are first introduced to the aquarium, it is not uncommon for them to bury for one to several days before emerging from the substrate to check out their new home. Resist the temptation to dig up a buried coris to check on its condition or show your fish-geek buddies. By disturbing the wrasse, you are simply prolonging the acclimation process. Once accustomed to their new home, these fishes typically emerge from and bury under the sand at the same time every day.

Although they are not overly prone to contracting the common fish protozoan or dinoflagellate infections, *Coris* will get sick on occasion. If they are kept in tanks with coarse, abrasive substrates, they often come down with *Lymphocystis*, a viral infection that shows up at the site of an injury. The white, cauliflower-like growths indicative of this virus appear around the mouth or on the fins. *Coris* are less susceptible to *Amyloodinium* or *Cryptocaryon* than most other aquarium fishes, but if your fish are afflicted with these parasites, they can be treated with commonly used aquarium medications.

One bad habit these wrasses have is flipping over pieces of rubble or coral to expose concealed prey items. This can be especially problematic in a reef tank, as it can cause irreparable damage to the corals' polyps. Therefore, if you add one these wrasses to your reef aquarium, it is very important to firmly affix any corals to the substrate, using one of the epoxies or putties available in the aquarium trade. You should also avoid keeping any bottom-dwelling solitary polyps, like slipper (e.g., *Herpolitha* or *Polyphyllia*) and plate (e.g., *Fungia* or *Heliofungia*) corals, with

Coris aygula, Twinspot Coris, young juvenile: typical size offered to aquarists.

Coris aygula, Twinspot Coris: large juvenile.

Coris aygula, Twinspot Coris, initial phase adult.

Coris aygula, Twinspot Coris, male.

Coris spp., as they are likely to flip these over and damage them. Keep in mind that the larger the *Coris*, the larger the pieces of coral or rock it can effectively overturn. Subadult and adult *Coris* spp. also prey on snails, small clams, tube worms, ornamental crustaceans, sea stars, sea urchins, and sea cucumbers, so many hobbyists refrain from adding them to a reef aquarium. Large individuals may also attack smaller fishes, especially benthic forms (e.g., gobies).

Coris Wrasse Species

Coris aygula Lacepède, 1801
Common Names: Twinspot Coris, Clown Coris.
Maximum Length: 120 cm (47.2 in.) reported, although few exceed 55 cm (21.7 in.)
Distribution: Red Sea to Line and Ducie Islands, north to southern Japan, and south to Lord Howe and Rapa Islands.
Biology: The juveniles of the Twinspot Coris are often found in shallow lagoon habitats over sand bottoms with scattered rocks or boulders. The subadults and adults occur over rubble bottoms, or mixed rubble, sand, and live coral substrates, on the back reef and fore-reef slopes. The Twinspot has been reported at depths of 1 to at least 30 m (3.3 to 98 ft.). This opportunistic predator feeds mainly on gastropods and sand-dwelling bivalves, although it will also eat hermit crabs, crabs, chitons, shrimp, isopods, amphipods, and sea urchins. *Coris aygula* will take an echinoid in its mouth and bash it against the substrate to expose the tasty internal organs within the test. Like most of its congeners, it will flip over rocks and dig in the sand to expose hidden prey.
Captive Care: The Twinspot Coris is resistant to external parasites, often showing no ill effects from either *Amyloodinium* or *Crypto-*

Coris ballieui, Lined Coris, initial phase hardly resembles the adult male, left.

Coris ballieui, Lined Coris, male: displaying for mate.

caryon while other fishes in the tank suffer. Although juvenile Twinspot Coris are not usually belligerent toward their piscine tankmates, including other *Coris* spp., the adults can be aggressive toward other fishes. This fish gets very large and will require plenty of swimming room as well as open sand bottom in which it can bury. Large adults should be kept in tanks no smaller than 180 gallons. Larger individuals are also very adept at flipping over larger corals and live rock. This fish will eat almost any food introduced into the aquarium, including small fishes, ornamental shrimp and crabs, small clams, flake food, mysid shrimp, and frozen preparations. Because of the large size this fish can attain and its catholic diet, I would not recommend this species for the reef aquarium.

Aquarium Size: 300 gal. **Temperature:** 22° to 28°C (72° to 82°F).

Aquarium Suitability Index: 4.

Remarks: Juvenile *C. aygula* are white overall with black spots on the head and on the dorsal and anal fins, and two large eyespots on the dorsal fin with red blotches underneath them on the body. Females are greenish anteriorly with small reddish spots on the head; there is a pale bar on the body above the anus and the body is dark grayish green behind this bar. The median fins have reddish or black spots. Males are dark bluish green overall and have a pale bar above the anal fin. Large males have a fleshy hump on the forehead, and the first two dorsal fin spines are elongate. Males also have a ragged-looking caudal fin. This fish often changes from its juvenile to subadult colors at a larger size in captivity than it does in the wild. For example, it may retain a color pattern not much different from that of the juvenile for as long as two years and up to a length of over 13 cm (5 in.). The **Doubleheader (*Coris bulbifrons*) Randall & Kuiter, 1982** is another large *Coris* species that exhibits a large bump on the head in

its terminal male phase. This species has a very limited distribution, having been reported from the east coast of Australia, Lord Howe Island, Middleton Reef, and Norfolk Island. It attains 60 cm (23.6 in.) in length and is rather subdued in color—the initial phase is brown with white spots or mottling, while the terminal phase is gray overall. It often occurs in groups consisting of one large male and numerous initial phase individuals.

Coris ballieui Valliant & Sauvage, 1875

Common Name: Lined Coris.

Maximum Length: 33 cm (13.0 in.)

Distribution: Hawaiian Islands.

Biology: The Lined Coris is found on fore-reef slopes, usually deeper than 20 m (66 ft.), and as deep as 81 m (263 ft.). It is typically found over sand and rubble substrates.

Captive Care: *Coris ballieui* is less common in the aquarium trade than many other members of this genus. It will do well in captivity if provided with sandy substrate under which it can bury and has access to a varied diet. Like the other members of this genus, it typically accepts a wide range of aquarium foods. It is a medium-sized species that can be kept in tanks as small as 100 gallons.

Aquarium Size: 100 gal. **Temperature:** 22° to 28°C (72° to 82°F).

Aquarium Suitability Index: 4.

Remarks: Initial phase *C. ballieui* are yellowish orange overall with salmon-colored longitudinal lines along the body and yellow median fins with light blue bands. Terminal phase males are yellowish to olive with thin blue stripes on the body, blue markings on the head, and blue bars on the tail. The terminal phase *C. ballieui* have longer first and second dorsal spines than the initial phase specimens.

Coris batuensis, Batu Coris, juvenile: often sold as "assorted wrasse."

Coris batuensis, Batu Coris, adult: small species suited to aquarium life.

Coris caudimacula, Spottail Coris, female: buries itself in sand.

Coris batuensis (Bleeker, 1858)

Common Name: Batu Coris.

Maximum Length: 17 cm (6.7 in.).

Distribution: East Africa to Marshall Islands, north to southern Japan, and south to the southern Great Barrier Reef and Tonga.

Biology: *Coris batuensis* is found on turbid coastal reefs, in clear lagoons, and on reef faces and fore-reef slopes, at depths of less than 1 to over 15 m (3.3 to 50 ft.). This fish is most often found over sand or rubble substrates. It feeds on infaunal organisms and is often seen following fishes that stir up the substrate. It feeds most heavily on crabs and snails, but gammaridean amphipods, hermit crabs, chitons, and foraminifers are also important prey. They will also eat harpacticoid copepods, small bivalves, planktonic fish eggs, errant ploychaete worms, isopods, crab megalops, shrimp, demersal invertebrate eggs, sponges, sedentary poly-

chaetes, barnacles, sea cucumbers, urchins, fish larvae, and filamentous algae. They are usually observed singly.

Captive Care: This attractive little wrasse is typically sold as an "assorted wrasse." It doesn't get very big and is thus suited to a large range of home aquariums. Like all of its congeners, it should have a sand substrate under which it can bury, and it should not be introduced into a tank that contains aggressive fishes. Males will fight, but a male and a female can be housed in the same tank if it is large enough (100 gallons or larger). Always add both sexes simultaneously or introduce the female first.

Aquarium Size: 55 gal. **Temperature:** 22° to 28°C (72° to 82°F).

Aquarium Suitability Index: 4.

Remarks: This species is very similar to the **Variegated Coris** (*C. variegata*) (**Ruppell, 1835**) from the Red Sea—in fact, they were once considered to be the same species. The Variegated Coris is paler overall and has more widely scattered spots on the body and approximately six light bars on the back. The male and female Batu Coris differ in coloration. The females are greenish overall with brown mottling on the dorsum, narrow pale and blackish bars on the back, an ocellus on the dorsal fin, and pink bands on the head. The males are more green overall, have wider dark bars on the back, and often have an area of pink on the sides and a blackish area on the abdomen.

Coris caudimacula (Quoy & Gaimard, 1834)

Common Name: Spottail Coris.

Maximum Length: 20 cm (7.9 in.).

Distribution: Red Sea and South Africa east to northwest coast of Australia and eastern Indonesia.

Biology: The Spottail Coris is found in lagoons and on reef flats, reef faces, and fore-reef slopes at depths of 1 to 57 m (3.3 to 188 ft.). It occurs in sand, rubble, and seagrass habitats. *Coris caudimacula* feeds on amphipods, tanaids, pelecypods, brachyuran crabs, gastropods, and polychaetes. Females are found in loose groups, while males occur singly.

Captive Care: This colorful fish occasionally shows up in aquarium stores. It usually is sold as an "assorted wrasse." It is not as common as the *C. dorsomacula*. The Spottail Coris is a good aquarium fish that can be housed in medium-sized aquariums.

Aquarium Size: 75 gal. **Temperature:** 22° to 28°C (72° to 82°F).

Aquarium Suitability Index: 4.

Remarks: The Spottail Coris gets its name from the large, diffuse blackish spot at the base of the caudal fin of adult males. The western Australian population of this wrasse has a slightly different color than that of *C. caudimacula* in other locations in the Indian Ocean.

Coris cuvieri (Bennett, 1831)

Common Name: African Coris.

Maximum Length: 38 cm (15.0 in.).

Distribution: Red Sea to Andaman Sea, south to southern Africa.

Biology: The African Coris occurs in lagoons and on outer reef flats, the reef face, and fore-reef slopes at depths of 5 to 50 m (16 to 163 ft.). It usually occurs over mixed sand, rubble, and live coral substrates. *Coris cuvieri* feeds on mollusks, crabs, hermit crabs, and sea urchins. It will take small urchins in its mouth and bash them against hard substrate to break them into pieces. The juveniles and adults usually occur singly.

Captive Care: This fish is less common in the aquarium trade then the similar Yellowtail Coris (*Coris gaimard*). Like the latter species, it is a durable aquarium fish that should be kept in an aquarium with plenty of open, sandy substrate. It can attain a fairly large size and adults will need to be housed in a relatively large aquarium. Although these fish rarely bother corals, they will decimate populations of motile invertebrates and may harass clams in the reef tank. One benefit to adding these fish to a tank with live rock (as well as any other *Coris* spp.) is that they will help control fire worm populations.

Aquarium Size: 135 gal. **Temperature:** 22° to 28°C (72° to 82°F).

Aquarium Suitability Index: 4.

Remarks: This species is very similar to *C. gaimard* and *C. formosa*. Juveniles have more black on the fins and bordering the white body bars, and the adults lack the yellow tail. In this species, the first body bar does not extend all the way to the ventral surface of the abdomen as it does in *C. formosa*. Small juvenile *C. cuvieri* often have a black spot in the middle of the dorsal fin. The adults of this species tend to be less colorful than those of *C. gaimard*. Adult females are reddish brown overall with green

Coris cuvieri, African Coris, juvenile: will feed heavily on motile invertebrates.

Coris cuvieri, African Coris, adult: large species needing plenty of space.

bands on the head and green spots on the body, while males have a green bar above the origin of the anal fin. In adults, the first two dorsal spines are elongate. This species is synonymous with *Coris africana*.

Coris dorsomacula Fowler, 1908

Common Name: Spotfin Coris.

Maximum Length: 20 cm (7.9 in.).

Distribution: Indonesia east to Tonga, north to southern Japan, and south to Victoria, Australia, and New Caledonia.

Biology: This species is found on coastal reefs, reef flats, back reefs, reef faces, and fore-reef slopes at depths of 2 to 40 m (7 to 132 ft.). It occurs over sand, rubble, and algae substrates.

Captive Care: This colorful fish irregularly shows up in the aquarium hobby, and when it does it is usually sold as an "assorted

Coris dorsomacula, Spotfin Coris, initial phase: opportunistic species.

Coris dorsomacula, Spotfin Coris, male.

Coris flavovittata, Yellowstripe Coris, initial phase.

Coris flavovittata, Yellowstripe Coris, male.

wrasse." This fish can be kept in a smaller aquarium than many of its *Coris* cousins need.

Aquarium Size: 55 gal. **Temperature:** 22° to 28°C (72° to 82°F).

Aquarium Suitability Index: 4.

Remarks: The Spotfin Coris has a black spot on the operculum and a spot on the posterior base of the dorsal fin. The **Kiribati Coris (*Coris centralis*) Randall, 1999** is a light-colored coris with a central dark stripe down the body and orange markings on the head. It is only known from the Line Islands, where it is reported to be quite common off the island of Kiribati. The **Easter Island Coris (*Coris debueni*) Randall, 1999** is another member of the genus with a very limited distribution. It has only been reported from tide pools at Easter Island.

Coris flavovittata (Bennett, 1828)

Common Name: Yellowstripe Coris.

Maximum Length: 18 cm (7.1 in.)

Distribution: Hawaiian Islands (most common in the northwestern Hawaiian Islands).

Biology: The Yellowstripe Coris is found in sand and rubble habitats on the fore-reef slope. Adults of this species are known to feed principally on sea urchins, heart urchins, bivalves, snails, and brittle stars, but also feed on crabs, hermit crabs, and polychaete worms. This is usually a solitary species.

Captive Care: This species is fairly hardy. As for others in the genus, provide a fine sand bed for them to bury in. See the Captive Care section for the genus for more details on how to keep this species.

Aquarium Size: 75 gal. **Temperature:** 22° to 28°C (72° to 82°F).

Aquarium Suitability Index: 4.

Remarks: Juvenile *C. flavovittata* are black overall with white or yellow longitudinal stripes. Females are white and black with two narrow yellow stripes, while males are a light blue-green overall with yellowish brown mottling, a pale blue head with a number of reddish spots, and a blue and black spot on the opercular flap.

Coris formosa (Bennett, 1830)

Common Names: Queen Coris, Formosan Coris.
Maximum Length: 60 cm (23.6 in.).
Distribution: East Africa to the southern Red Sea, Maldives, and Sri Lanka, and south to southern Africa.
Biology: *Coris formosa* is found on shallow outer reef faces in areas with sand and rubble. Juveniles are often found among beds of staghorn coral (*Acropora* spp.). It occurs at depths of 2 to 30 m (7 to 98 ft.), usually singly. The Queen Coris probably feeds on benthic invertebrates, like other members of the genus. This species can be approached, but you need to move along the bottom and approach it slowly. Flipping pieces of rock or rubble, or stirring the sand with your hand, can sometimes attract these fish into close range.
Captive Care: The Queen Coris is very similar to the more common *Coris gaimard*. It is hardy if provided with the appropriate aquarium setting. Large individuals tend to suffer more from stress during the shipping process than juveniles or small adults. Provide it with ample open, sandy substrate—at least 5 to 8 cm (2 or 3 in.) of fine-grade sand. Although it does not eat corals, this species will decimate populations of motile invertebrates (ornamental shrimps, crabs, snails) and may harass clams in the reef tank. *Coris formosa* may throw loose coral colonies over when searching for prey. (*Note:* this is a large species and its size will enable it to flip larger coral colonies.) One benefit to adding these fish to a tank with live rock is that they will help control fire worm populations.
Aquarium Size: 180 gal. **Temperature:** 22° to 28°C (72° to 82°F).
Aquarium Suitability Index: 4.
Remarks: Juvenile *C. formosa* differ from *C. cuvieri* in having broader black margins on the white body bars and head spots; the first body bar extends to the ventral surface of the abdomen (it only reaches to about the base of the pectoral fin in *C. cuvieri*); and there is a black spot on the dorsal fin. Females have a brownish gray or green body with small black spots and a yellow head with two blue diagonal lines, and the base of the caudal fin is red while the rest of the tail is white. The body and tail of males are brown or light red overall, with light green spots all over the body and dark purplish bars. The head is reddish gray with narrow green lines and the tail is purplish gray with bright blue spots and a red posterior margin. This species is synonymous with *Coris frerei*.

Coris formosa, Queen Coris, juvenile: starting with a young fish is often best.

Coris formosa, Queen Coris, initial phase: may displace coral colonies.

Coris formosa, male: displaces *Coris gaimard* in the Indian Ocean.

Coris gaimard, Yellowtail Coris, subadult: a great fish for reasonably large aquariums and other large community fishes. It is highly predatory on invertebrates.

Coris gaimard (Quoy & Gaimard, 1824)

Common Names: Yellowtail Coris, Red Coris.

Maximum Length: 38 cm (15.0 in.).

Distribution: Christmas Island, Indian Ocean, and Indonesia, east to the Hawaiian Islands, Marquesas, and Tuamotus, north to southern Japan, and south to New Caledonia and the Austral Islands.

Biology: This fish is most often found in lagoons, on reef flats, the edge of the reef face or reef slopes, moving over areas of mixed coral, rubble, and sand or on sand patches. The juveniles are more common in protected areas (e.g., lagoons). *Coris gaimard* is reported from depths of 3 to 50 m (10 to 165 ft.). This fish feeds during the day and is primarily a mollusk, bivalve, crab, hermit crab, and echinoid predator. However, it will also ingest foraminifers, didemnid tunicates, and gammaridean amphipods. It often excavates these prey organisms by moving sand with side-

ways movements of the head and by lifting pieces of rubble and overturning stones with its mouth. There is a defined ontogenetic change in diet. According to Shibuno et al. (1994), individuals under 5 cm (2.0 in.) in total length feed almost entirely on small crustaceans (e.g., gammarideans, copepods, tanaids, ostracods, and isopods). Individuals in the 5.0 to 9.9 cm (2.0 to 3.9 in.) size class feed mostly on gammarideans, but also eat some bivalves and snails. (*Coris gaimard* under 10 cm [3.9 in.] tend to feed on items that they can swallow whole.) The 10 to 14.9 cm (3.9 to 5.9 in.) size class feed heavily on gammarideans as well, but mollusks are a much more important part of the diet and they also eat some crabs. In the 15 to 19.9 cm (5.9 to 7.8 in.) size class and larger, mollusks dominate the diet, but crabs are also important; small crustaceans decrease in importance. In individuals over 25 cm (9.8 in.), mollusks and crabs dominate the diet. The Yellowtail Coris will also blow water out of its mouth

Coris gaimard, Yellowtail Coris, juvenile: typical size available to aquarists.

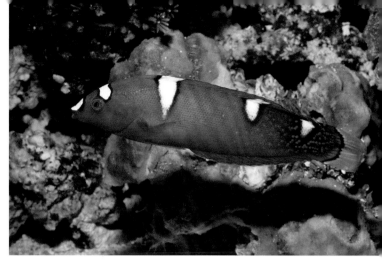

Coris gaimard, Yellowtail Coris, larger juvenile: note developing blue spots.

Coris gaimard, Yellowtail Coris, adult female.

Coris gaimard, Yellowtail Coris, male.

and flip gravel, stones, or rubble to expose buried prey. Shibuno et al. (1994) reported that larger *C. gaimard* forage by flipping benthic debris 35 percent of the time. Larger Yellowtail Coris flip stones 5.0 cm (2.0 in.) in diameter or larger. Smaller individuals do most of their feeding by picking prey off the substrate surface. Juveniles of this species are usually solitary, although they are occasionally observed in loose aggregations. Adults occur singly.

Captive Care: These wrasses will thrive in the home aquarium if the prerequisites discussed in the Captive Care section for the genus are met. *Coris gaimard* is typically not aggressive toward other fishes, although large individuals may harass smaller tankmates, especially those introduced after they are well established in an aquarium. The juveniles can be housed together but may fight as they become larger. Juvenile Yellowtail Coris will occasionally pick at the body surfaces of other fishes, apparently to remove parasites and dead tissue. As they grow larger, *C. gaimard* may

pick on more docile species like cardinalfishes, gobies, and dartfishes. Adults are also likely to quarrel with congeners. The juveniles of this species are sometimes added to reef aquariums, only to become terrors as they grow larger. Subadult and adult Yellowtail Coris will eat tubeworms, snails, hermit crabs, small urchins, and sea stars, and may even pick at tridacnid clams. They are also effective at decimating populations of small crustaceans and worms present in live sand, and will flip loose coral colonies.

Aquarium Size: 135 gal. **Temperature:** 22° to 28°C (72° to 82°F).

Aquarium Suitability Index: 4.

Remarks: Juveniles are spectacular fish, with a reddish orange body and head, three white body spots that are outlined in black, two white spots on the head, and a white tail. In the wild, individuals up to 7.5 cm (3 in.) in length exhibit the juvenile color phase. At a length between 6 and 10 cm (2.4 to 4 in.), a chromatic transformation takes place as these fish assume an interme-

Coris pictoides, Blackstripe Coris, male: young are parasite pickers.

Coris venusta, Elegant Coris, juvenile: excellent aquarium coris species.

Coris venusta, Elegant Coris, female.

Coris venusta, Elegant Coris, supermale.

diate color phase. The adult coloration is present when individuals reach a length of 8 to 21 cm (3.1 to 8.3 in.). Female *C. gaimard* have a reddish brown or brownish green body, with blue spots on the posterior portion. The tail is yellow and the head is reddish with distinct blue lines. The male color form of *C. gaimard* has more, smaller blue spots on the posterior portion of the body, the lines on the face are green, and a green bar develops on the side of the body. The **Marquesan Coris (*Coris marquesensis*) Randall, 1999** is similar to *C. gaimard*. The juveniles of both species are very similar (except that *C. marquesensis* has a black spot on the posterior portion of the dorsal fin), but the female *C. marquesensis* is orange with four stripes that consist of brilliant blue stripes along the sides of the body. As the fish grows, the spots increase in number but shrink in size. The adult male is apparently similar in color to *C. gaimard*. This fish is only known from the Marquesas Islands. It has been reported from depths to 30 m (98 ft.).

Coris pictoides Randall & Kuiter, 1982
Common Name: Blackstripe Coris.
Maximum Length: 15 cm (5.9 in.).
Distribution: Indonesia and the Philippines, and possibly Australia.
Biology: The Blackstripe Coris is found on coastal and offshore reefs. It occurs in estuaries and lagoons and on reef faces and fore-reef slopes at depths of 9 to 33 m (30 to 109 ft.). It is often found over sand or even mud substrates. *Coris pictoides* occurs in groups.
Captive Care: This wrasse is not common in the aquarium trade. It is a handsome species that does well in the home aquarium. It can be kept at lower water temperatures. Otherwise, its captive care is similar to that of others in the genus. The juveniles will

clean their tankmates.

Aquarium Size: 75 gal. **Temperature:** 20° to 27°C (68° to 80°F).

Aquarium Suitability Index: 4.

Remarks: This species is very similar to the **Australian Comb Wrasse** (*Coris picta*) (Bloch & Schneider, 1801) and the **Japanese Comb Wrasse** (*Coris musume*) (Jordan & Snyder, 1904). *Coris picta* is found on reefs off Australia (southern Queensland to northern Victoria, Lord Howe Island), Norfolk Island, the Kermadec Islands, and New Zealand, while *C. musume* is reported to occur off Taiwan and subtropical Japan. Both of these species attain a larger size than *C. pictoides*, reaching a size of around 25 cm (9.8 in.). Much is known about the biology of the Australian Comb Wrasse (see Ayling, 1982, for more information). This species spawns on New Zealand reefs from February to June. While the color of the adult male and female *C. picta* may look the same for much of the year, during the spawning period the males will "turn on" nuptial colors. The dark stripes on the back and dorsal portion of the body become a pale blue-gray, a yellowish band appears on the belly, and a portion of the pectoral fins becomes dark blue. These courtship colors can be switched off to reduce aggression between neighboring males (the males are more aggressive toward each other during this time of year). When spawning, the male moves over the female with his pelvic fins touching her dorsum, and they swim into the water column. The male then moves alongside the female when they spawn at the top of the ascent. *Coris picta* and its close relatives are cleaners. Groups of potential piscine clients often crowd around *C. picta* cleaning stations.

Coris venusta Vaillant & Sauvage, 1875

Common Name: Elegant Coris.

Maximum Length: 19 cm (7.4 in.).

Distribution: Hawaiian Islands.

Biology: The Elegant Coris is common along sandy beaches and shallow reef face habitats. It is found over both sand and rubble substrates. It has been reported at a depth range of 2 to 10 m (7 to 33 ft.). Adult Elegant Coris feed heavily on small bivalves and snails, but also eat crabs, urchins, heart urchins, hermit crabs, shrimp, polychaete worms, amphipods, isopods, chitons, and foraminifers.

Coris hewettii, Hewett's Coris, male, Marquesas Islands: unusual *Coris* species.

Captive Care: This is a great aquarium coris. It is both beautiful and small. It can be kept in a medium-sized tank that has at least a 5 cm (2 in.) bed of fine sand. While it will eat ornamental worms, snails, and crustaceans, because of its small size it is less of a threat to loose coral colonies.

Aquarium Size: 75 gal. **Temperature:** 22° to 28°C (72° to 82°F).

Aquarium Suitability Index: 4.

Remarks: Hewett's Coris (*Coris hewettii*) Randall, 1999 is a unique member of the genus that is limited in range to the Marquesas Islands. It attains a length of about 15 cm (5.9 in.) and is found at depths of 1 to 40 m (3.3 to 132 ft.) over rubble or mixed sand and rock substrates. According to Hawaiian fish expert John Hoover, this species usually lives in harems. He writes, "Males, ordinarily greenish and with dull brownish red stripes on head and body, displayed conspicuously to females by swimming well off the bottom, raising their large red dorsal fin, and quickly changing their reddish stripes to a light, bright, iridescent blue. The color change was quite amazing." This is apparently the only *Coris* sp. that uses this conspicuous courtship display. Hoover describes it as being very similar to the courtship displays seen in the *Cirrhilabrus* spp. The males have a very high dorsal fin. As is the case with many of the labrids, the female is rather dull when compared with the male.

Connie's, Mutant, or Candystripe Wrasse (*Conniella apterygia*)

Connie's, Mutant, or Candystripe Wrasse (*Conniella apterygia*) Allen, 1983

The only wrasse in this monotypic genus is very unique. Unlike any other species in the family, this species lacks pelvic fins and the supporting skeletal structure. For this reason, it is sometimes referred to as the Mutant Wrasse. Except for the fact it is missing these fins, it is otherwise very similar to a *Cirrhilabrus*. The coloration is superficially comparable to that of Earle's Fairy Wrasse (*Cirrhilabrus earlei*), a deep-water species known only from Palau. Although very attractive, *C. apterygia* is not a species that you are likely to see in the aquarium trade because of its very limited range. It is only found on offshore reefs (Rowley Shoals) off the coast of northwestern Australia. I am sure that if it ever does begin to show up in the aquarium trade, it will be as durable as most of the fairy wrasse species. Connie's Wrasse gets 10 cm (3.9 in.) in total length.

This species if usually found on relatively deep, steep outer reef slopes at depths of 25 to 50 m (83 to 165 ft.). However, Kuiter (2002) reports encountering them as shallow as 12 m (40 ft.) in a lagoon at Rowley Shoals. Connie's Wrasse is usually found over rubble bottoms with scattered coral heads. If threatened, these wrasses will disappear within the rubble interstices. Like its *Cirrhilabrus* cousins, it is usually found in small to large groups. Kuiter (2002) reports encountering small groups of large, adult males. In some locations, it joins groups of anthias as it feeds on zooplankton above the substrate.

GENUS GOMPHOSUS (BIRD WRASSES)

This genus only contains two species, which are easy to distinguish by their very long snouts. The snout of the juvenile *Gomphosus* spp. is a bit longer than that of the typical wrasse, but is certainly is not elephantine, as it is in their larger kin. The young Green Bird Wrasse (*Gomphosus varius*) is so different from the adult of the species that it was once placed in a different genus—it was called *Thalassoma stuckiae*. Interestingly enough, recent molecular studies (Bernardi et al., 2004) have suggested that *Gomphosus* should be included in the genus *Thalassoma*, referring to the two species in this genus as "specialized morphological variants." Other evidence to support this conclusion is that hybrids of *Gomphosus varius* and the Saddled Wrasse (*Thalassoma duperrey*) and the Moon Wrasse (*T. lunare*) have been reported.

So why the beaklike snout? It certainly comes in handy when hunting for secretive prey. These fishes will deftly pluck their quarry from their hiding places. The *Gomphosus* spp. are not microcarnivores like some of their labrid cousins. Their preferred prey are relatively large crustaceans (including xanthid, hermit crabs, decapod shrimps, and mantis shrimps), which they wrest from branching coral colonies. They are especially fond of the crabs of the genus *Trapezia*, which are obligate stony coral associates, and alpheid species (i.e., snapping or pistol shrimps) that lurk among coral branches. They will also eat small mollusks, brittle stars, and small fishes that live in coral colonies. The long snout hides the fact that the mouth is actually quite large, but if the prey item is too hefty to swallow whole, these wrasses will nimbly bash the oversized prey item against hard substrate to break it into bite-sized pieces.

Adults are very active and usually attempt to outswim predators rather than dive into the coral labyrinth. For locomotion, they flap their pectoral fins to propel them through the water. Of the wrasses studied, the *Gomphosus* "can achieve and maintain the highest pectoral fin–powered swimming speeds." (Walker and Westneat, 2002.) When a sudden burst of speed is required to avoid a predator or pursue a rival, they will use rapid lateral strokes of the caudal fin. The bird wrasses do not bury under the substrate at night, but rather rest in reef crevices. Some hobbyists report having seen them bury in fine substrate in the home aquarium, but this is the exception, not the rule; it may happen in the aquarium when an individual (including a newly introduced one) is very stressed.

These wrasses are protogynous hermaphrodites (males arise from female sex change). Spawning has been observed in both species. They concentrate on the reef edge, where the males set up temporary spawning territories. The males often select more prominent topographical features to form this lek. The females then arrive and the males vigorously court them. Spawning occurs from midafternoon to dusk.

Captive Care

These are two of the hardiest fish you can purchase for a marine aquarium. On a number of occasions, I have seen large Green Bird Wrasses (*Gomphosus varius*) survive otherwise total tank wipeouts. They sometimes succumb to common marine fish parasites, but tend to have a higher resistance. These fishes occasionally flash against the substrate. Keep a close eye on fish that do this and look for any other signs of parasitic infection (e.g., spots, heavy respiration, or constant hiding). As they get larger, it is not uncommon for male bird wrasses to develop large bumps on the snout. These protuberances, which may be fatty tumors, may be unattractive but they do not seem to interfere with the feeding and general health of the *Gomphosus*.

You can keep a male and female bird wrasse in the same tank. However, the two fish should be added simultaneously or the female should be introduced first, with the male following soon after. A solitary *Gomphosus* may transform into a male. In even the largest home aquarium, two male bird wrasses will typically fight until one is dead. Make sure a female that has been on her own for a while is not developing male secondary sexual characteristics (color) before you add a male. A female in the process of changing could revert back to a female if a male is added, but this situation is more risky than keeping a known female and male together.

The bird wrasses typically do quite well in the fish community tank. They will eat smaller fishes, like dottybacks, damsels, blennies, gobies, and dartfishes. While the *Gomphosus* are not likely to chase down and capture these smaller fishes, they are

Gomphosus varius, Green Bird Wrasse, male: an active species with swooping swimming patterns and a nearly bulletproof ability to survive in captivity.

Gomphosus varius, Green Bird Wrasse: mature male with fatty tissue growth on snout. This is a relatively common but not yet understood condition that is not considered a threat to the health of the fish.

well equipped to snatch them when they hide. They will definitely subdue stressed, newly introduced, or injured fishes. For example, I have seen them capture Firefish (*Nemateleotris magnifica*) that were too slow in finding a place to hide when added to a tank. But those firefish that successfully made it under coral slabs and came out the next day were fine as long as they dashed under cover when a wrasse approached. The bird wrasses may also fight with other wrasse species. The size of the tank—that is, the amount of living space—will play a major role in determining whether wrasses will get along in the home aquarium. If you crowd them, fighting is more likely.

The *Gomphosus* do present some problems when housed in the reef tank. They are very predatory, feeding on a wide range of invertebrates and even on small fishes. Their bill of fare can include small tridacnid clams and other bivalves, snails, feather duster worms, and a variety of crustaceans. They may attack clams through the byssal opening. The upside of bird wrasse ownership is that they will eat fireworms and mantis shrimps.

Bird Wrasse Species

Gomphosus caeruleus Lacepède, 1801
Common Names: Indian Bird Wrasse, Bird Wrasse, Elephant Wrasse.
Maximum Length: 28 cm (11.0 in.).
Distribution: East Africa and Red Sea, south to Natal, South Africa, and east to the Andaman Sea.
Biology: This labrid is found in coral-rich habitats in lagoons and on outer reef faces and slopes at depths of 1 to 30 m (3.3 to 98 ft.). It is often found on the turbulent reef crest and is also found on rocky reefs. The male *G. caeruleus* will cooperatively hunt with Yellowsaddle Goatfish (*Parupeneus cyclostomus*). The goatfish swims slightly above and behind the bird wrasse as they move from one hunting ground to the next. Once they find a coral head to inspect, they will part ways, often going opposite directions around the structure. The Indian Bird Wrasse will use its snout to probe holes and cracks, while the goatfish does the same

with its barbels. By taking opposite paths, the fish are more likely to flush potential prey into striking range of their hunting partners. Once they finish searching one coral head or rubble mound, they move to the next. Ormond (1981) reports that young and female *G. caeruleus* will also engage in cooperative hunting with the Red Sea Goatfish (*Parupeneus forsskali*). However, because this goatfish feeds more on infaunal organisms in soft substrate, it is more likely a case of following behavior. That is, the *Gomphosus* seeks feeding opportunities by following the goatfish, but the goatfish does not benefit from the relationship. Juveniles occur singly, while adult females are often seen in pairs or trios. Males are solitary, but regularly associate with female *G. caeruleus*. I have observed these fishes spawning in the Maldives. Males set up territories in the afternoon and begin courting females that visit the lek. Males will attempt to court females and, at the same time, drive off males that intrude into their spawning territories. Not only do they put a lot of energy into courtship and defending their potential mates, they also put their lives on the line. When they make their final spawning ascent into the water column, they are vulnerable to the large Napoleon Wrasses (*Cheilinus undulatus*) and groupers that mill around the mating arena. The spawning ascent takes the male and female 2 to 3 m (7 to 10 ft.) over the reef. After gametes are released, the fish dash back to the bottom. Fusiliers were observed hanging off the reef face feeding on the gametes of this species and those of surgeonfishes that were spawning at the same time.

Captive Care: This species is not as common in the aquarium trade as its Pacific cousin.
Aquarium Size: 75 gallons. **Temperature:** 23° to 28°C (74° to 82°F).
Aquarium Suitability Index: 5.
Remarks: The males of this species are very similar to *G. varius*, but the color differs slightly. Male *G. caeruleus* lack the lime green patch around the area of the pectoral fin and tend to be more blue green. The young and the females are brown dorsally and lighter on the ventrum. This species has been reported to hybridize with two species of *Halichoeres* wrasses.

Gomphosus varius Lacepède, 1801
Common Names: Green Bird Wrasse (male), Black Bird Wrasse (female).
Maximum Length: 28 cm (11.0 in.).
Distribution: Cocos-Keeling Island, Christmas Island, and Rowley Shoals in the eastern Indian Ocean east to the Hawaiian and Pitcairn Islands, north to southern Japan, and south to Lord Howe, New Caledonia, and Rapa Islands.
Biology: This species occurs in lagoons and on back reefs, reef faces, and fore reef slopes at depths of 1 to 30 m (3.3 to 98 ft.).

Gomphosus caeruleus, Indian Bird Wrasse, female: males resemble *G. varius*.

In at least some locations, it is more common around lagoon coral heads and patch reefs. In Hawaii, adults are typically found dashing to and fro in the high-energy surge zone and are often found in areas with greater *Pocillopora meandrina* coverage—the ideal hunting environment for this fish. The diet of this species includes small clams, crustaceans, brittle stars, and small fishes. Most of their prey are plucked from ramose coral heads. I have also seen these fishes almost lie on their sides as they probe under coral rubble and in reef crevices. Additionally, I have seen this species being followed by hunting goatfishes. For example, I observed a male *Gomphosus* being shadowed by a Multibarred Goatfish (*Parupeneus multifasciatus*) for over 5 minutes (the goatfish swam above and slightly behind the wrasse). During this observation period, the Green Bird Wrasse turned and tried to chase the goatfish away on two different occasions. Juveniles are solitary, often moving about ramose corals (e.g., *Pocillopora* and *Acropora*). At the slightest hint of danger, they disappear among the coral branches. Females occur singly, in pairs, or even in small, roving groups. I have seen females moving about together, maintaining close contact as they foraged. Males are solitary beasts, although they are usually not too far away from one or more females.

Captive Care: This species is very hardy. Extremely active, it needs plenty of open swimming room. The males tend to retain their bright colors, even when conspecifics are not present. It is important to keep only one male per tank. You can house a male and female together in a larger tank (135 gallons or larger), but they should be introduced together. Resident males can be especially

Gomphosus varius, Green Bird Wrasse, female: commonly sold as the "Black Bird Wrasse." They are very active and need multiple feedings each day.

Gomphosus varius, Green Bird Wrasse, transforming juvenile.

aggressive toward newly added labrids. I have seen them chase *Halichoeres* spp. and banana wrasses (*Thalassoma* spp.). Adults will not hesitate to capture smaller fishes (gobies, wormfishes, or dartfishes). If you want to attempt to keep smaller fishes with a *Gomphosus*, add them to the tank before the bird wrasse. Feed *Gomphosus* two to three times a day, unless natural fare (e.g., worms and crustaceans) are available in the tank. Because of their high metabolism, they tend to lose weight fairly quickly if given insufficient food. *Gomphosus varius* does not bury under the sand, so it does fine in a bare-bottom tank. This species is a very proficient jumper and will leap from an open tank.

Aquarium Size: 75 gallons. **Temperature:** 23° to 28°C (74° to 82°F).

Aquarium Suitability Index: 5.

Remarks: The large males have a dark head and a lime-green patch in the pectoral fin region. The females have black-edged scales on the anterior portion of the body, while the rear portion and tail are black.

The Slingjaw Wrasse (*Epibulus insidiator*): The Fastest Jaw in the West (Pacific)

Epibulus insidiator, Slingjaw Wrasse, male: cooperatively hunting with a Yellowsaddle Goatfish, *Parupeneus cyclostomus*.

The genus *Epibulus* currently contains two polychromatic species. The best-known species is the **Slingjaw Wrasse**, *Epibulus insidiator* (Pallas, 1770). It has been reported from New Britain and Palau and, as the vernacular label implies, attains a greater size than its relative; it is said to reach a size of around 25 cm (10 in.). *Epibulus insidiator* ranges from the Red Sea to the northwest Hawaiian and Tuamotu islands, north to southern Japan, and south to New Caledonia. It is usually found on reef faces and fore-reef slopes and around lagoon fringing and patch reefs. It is most often found in areas with rich stony coral growth. It occurs at depths ranging from 1 to 42 m (3 to 137 ft.) and attains a maximum length of 35 cm (14 in.).

The Slingjaw Wrasse displays striking sexual dichromatism. Sub-adults and some females are brown, while other females are bright yellow. Males are dark brown, with green edges on the scales, a yellow bar on the side, and a gray head with a black streak behind the eye. Brown individuals are the most commonly encountered form, followed by the terminal phase males. The yellow females are least common. *Epibulus insidiator* is a protogynous hermaphrodite (i.e., it changes from female to male), and transforming individuals displaying a combination of female and male characteristics are occasionally encountered. Terminal phase males are not only different in color from initial phase individuals, they are also considerably larger.

Juvenile *E. insidiator* are very similar in appearance, and behavior, to the possum wrasses (*Wetmorella* spp.). They are greenish brown with white lines on the head and body and a black spot on both the dorsal and anal fins. They are also very secretive, spending most of their time

Continued on following page

Epibulus insidiator, Slingjaw Wrasse, juvenile.

Epibulus insidiator, Slingjaw Wrasse, transforming female.

Epibulus insidiator, Slingjaw Wrasse, large male.

Epibulus insidiator, Slingjaw Wrasse, variant male.

among coral branches or in crevices. Brown subadult and small adult Slingjaw Wrasses (between 5 and 10 cm [2 to 4 in.]) have been observed to disperse from one reef to another using a very unusual behavior that has been dubbed "drift emigration." When the tide begins to go out, the Slingjaws swim to the surface, either singly or in groups of up to four individuals, and join floating plant debris. The plant material can include tree leaves, ferns, and seagrass. The Slingjaw Wrasse curls its tail toward its body, folds its fins up, and begins to float with the debris. Slingjaw Wrasses have even been observed to adopt the coloration of the plant material. For example, if the leaves are yellow, the fish will change to a yellowish hue overall. It has been suggested that this behavior may not only help these fish safely move from one area to another, but may also enable them to prey on small, elusive fishes that often associate with floating debris.

The second member of the genus is the **Dwarf Slingjaw Wrasse (*Epibulus brevis*) Carlson, Randall & Dawson 2008**, which is commonly known as the Dwarf Slingjaw Wrasse. This species is only slightly smaller than *E. insidiator*, reaches a total length of around 24 cm (9.4 in.) and has been reported from Palau, the Philippines, Papua New Guinea, Solomon Islands, Sulawesi, Bali, Lombok, and Flores in Indonesia. I recently observed the species in West Papua as well. It differs from *E. insidiator* in color. The males of this species are all brown with yellow on the throat area, on the caudal fin and a yellow marking at the opercular flap. Females vary in color from dark to light brown to yellow or almost white. The pectoral fins of the female almost always have black on the pectoral fins. The Dwarf Slingjaw also has longer pectoral fins than *E. insidiator*.

Carlson et al. (2008) examined the stomach contents of both Sling-

Epibulus insidiator, Slingjaw Wrasse: beautiful yellow female morph: extremely protrusible jaws allow them to snatch prey from tight hiding places.

jaw species. They examined the stomach contents of 20 *E. brevis* and found that crustaceans (crabs and shrimps) were dominant in the fishes' diet, with only one larger individual (17.2 cm [6.8 in.]) containing both fishes and crabs. They also examined the "gut" contents of 31 *E. insidiator* and observed that the stomachs yielded more fish than *E. brevis*, but also crabs, shrimps, and polychaete worms. The authors suggest that the larger size of the *E. insidiator* may explain its proclivity to ingest more fish (likewise, smaller *E. insidiator* tended to contain more crustaceans than larger conspecifics). In both species, prey was highly masticated as a result of the actions of the pharyngeal teeth.

Interesting Behavior

The Slingjaw Wrasse gets its name from its highly protrusible jaws, which can extend out to over half the fish's total body length. Unlike that of most other bony fishes, the lower jaw is not firmly attached to the skull. As a result, the Slingjaw Wrasse can project the upper and lower jaws simultaneously. This anatomical anomaly is employed to snatch their quarry out of narrow crevices and from between coral branches. In Fiji I followed a male that was searching for prey on a bottom composed of coral rubble and large slabs of coral rock. The Slingjaw would swim up to a coral slab and turn on its side to look underneath it. When it saw a prey item it shot its jaws into the narrow space. Then it swam up into the water column and spit out the inedible items, like sand and small pieces of rubble. The fish chewed its prey with its pharyngeal teeth, descended to the bottom, and resumed the hunt. I suspect that it rose well above the substrate to sort what it ingested so that if it accidentally spat out a prey item it would

Continued on following page

Epibulus brevis, Dwarf Slingjaw Wrasse, adult female, Sulawesi, Indonesia: a newly described species with females that exhibit black pectoral fins.

have a chance to recapture it before it could return to the bottom and hide. This particular individual was followed by an adolescent Lyretail Grouper (*Variola louti*). The grouper was taking advantage of potential feeding opportunities that might arise as a result of the Slingjaw's hunting. For example, if prey organisms were flushed from under the coral rocks by the slingjaw's projecting jaws, the grouper would pounce on it. It is not uncommon to see a Slingjaw slowly extend its jaws in an exaggerated yawn. I have seen them partially extend their jaws at a conspecific, causing the approaching fish to give the other a wide berth.

The Slingjaw Wrasse will also associate with other fishes in order to gain access to hidden or elusive prey. For example, in the Red Sea this wrasse will swim within schools of feeding Purple Tangs (*Zebrasoma xanthurum*). When the tangs descend to feed, the Slingjaw is in attendance to snap up any small fishes or crustaceans that are disturbed by the feeding herbivores. Occasionally it may even "take out" territory-holding damselfishes that rush out to confront the approaching school.

The form and coloration of the brown color phase of *E. insidiator* are similar to that of the herbivorous Dusky Surgeonfish (*Acanthurus nigricans*), while the yellow form resembles the zooplankton-feeding Golden Damsel (*Amblyglyphidodon aureus*). Their resemblance to these non-predatory fish may enable them to approach closer to their prey in areas where they co-occur with these species. Slingjaw Wrasses will also engage in cooperative, or joint, hunting. For example, I watched a Slingjaw and a Yellow Trumpetfish (*Aulostomus chinensis*) hunting together in the Maldives. The trumpetfish swam over the wrasse until they reached a large table coral; then the Slingjaw turned on its side and began to investigate the area under the coral platform, while the trumpetfish assumed a vertical orientation above the table coral and appeared to be waiting for flushed prey items. After about 20 seconds, the Slingjaw came out from under the coral, the trumpetfish assumed its position along the Slingjaw's back, and they moved on to the next coral colony. Another favorite Slingjaw hunting partner is the Yellowsaddle Goatfish

Epibulus brevis, Dwarf Slingjaw Wrasse, juvenile, Sulawesi, Indonesia.

Epibulus brevis, Dwarf Slingjaw Wrasse, male, West Papua.

(*Parupeneus cyclostomus*). These two fishes are often seen swimming above the reef together, with the goatfish swimming beneath the wrasse, searching for prey in a cooperative fashion.

Male *E. insidiator* will patrol high in the water column. When patrolling, the dorsal and anal fins are contracted, while the caudal fin is spread open. Terminal males sometimes swim over the reef with the anal fin extended like a rudder. Most of male Slingjaw activity occurs over prominent reef features such as coral promontories and large boulders, which apparently serve as sites where the fish rendezvous with potential mates. Females hover or swim slowly about these sites and occasionally bob up and down as they move near a male. According to Colin and Bell (in Carlson et al. 2008), *E. brevis* spawns at sunset. Males do swim around a territory and occasionally rise into the water column, but they engage in less flagrant displays than *E. insidiator* and usually remain nearer the seafloor. When attempting to entice a female to spawn, a male *E. brevis* will swim around his potential mate with all his fins collapsed. The median fins are spread as the pair rise into the water column to spawn (the spawning ascent may take a arch-like trajectory or a relatively short, casual rise over the substrate).

Keeping a Slingjaw

Epibulus insidiator makes a very interesting aquarium resident. It is an efficient predator that will snap up glass shrimp and feeder fish with incredible speed. One potential problem with keeping these fish with other species is that they are so quick that they may prevent more sluggish predators from getting enough to eat. Although they can be switched to frozen preparations or fresh or frozen seafood, including fresh or frozen table shrimp and strips of squid or clam, they prefer live food — live

fish, shrimps, and even live insects (e.g., feeder crickets) that are floating on the water's surface, as well as black worms and earthworms. Of course, feeder goldfish should not be a staple of the diet of this fish or any marine species. If you feed ghost shrimp, you should "gut-load" them with a nutritious frozen or flake food.

The adult Slingjaw Wrasse needs a large aquarium (135 gallons or larger) and should be provided with plenty of large refuge sites to hide in if threatened. In nature it this a shy species that is typically difficult to approach. They are also reclusive and nervous when first introduced to the aquarium, although this will change once they learn to recognize the aquarist as a provider rather than a potential threat. When this occurs the fish will not only rise to the surface of the tank when its keeper approaches, it will also take food from the aquarist's fingers. Juveniles will acclimate quickly to captive life if they are kept in a tank that does not contain aggressive fishes and has plenty of hiding places. They will spend most of their time slinking from crevice to crevice, but they will also swim in open areas if the tank is in a low-traffic area. Smaller individuals do well in reef aquariums, but as they mature, they are a threat to shrimps and smaller fishes. Be aware that these fish are capable of jumping out of open aquariums. This is most likely to occur if they are harassed by tankmates.

Epibulus insidiator is a solitary species and only one individual should be kept per aquarium. Although these individuals are not usually aggressive toward other fish species in the aquarium, I have seen them chase heterospecifics in the wild. For example, I observed an adult male *E. insidiator* persistently chase a snapper that was hanging in the water. Unfortunately, bright yellow females often turn brown in aquarium confines; this may be due to a lack of social interaction with conspecifics.

The genus *Halichoeres* is the largest in the family Labridae. There are approximately 70 species in the genus, with the vast majority (around 60) occurring in the Indo-Pacific. These wrasses are often encountered by divers and stalked by underwater photographers because of their brilliant colors—a feature that also makes them attractive to aquarists. Many of these fishes are not only beautiful, they can also help eliminate pestilent invertebrates from the reef aquarium. But there are many *Halichoeres* spp. that have a proclivity to dine on more desirable invertebrates as well.

Biology

The *Halichoeres* spp. are most common over sand or mixed sand and rubble substrates. They are frequently encountered near patch reefs or coral heads in lagoons, or over sand patches on the reef face or fore-reef slope. The majority of genus members are residents of shallow, inshore waters, although they can range to moderate depths. The *Halichoeres* spp. encountered in the aquarium trade that tend to inhabit deeper fore-reef walls include the Blackear Wrasse (*Halichoeres melasmapomus*), the Pale Wrasse (*H. pallidus*), and the White Wrasse (*H. trispilus*).

The *Halichoeres* spp. have well-developed pharyngeal teeth and jaws that they employ to masticate their prey. Most feed on a wide range of animals, including small crustaceans, polychaete worms, snails, small bivalves, and serpent stars. However, the makeup of the diet is somewhat dependent on the species and size of the wrasse. For example, one study demonstrated that certain *Halichoeres* spp. have larger jaw muscles, and thus greater crushing strength, than others. These wrasses are better able to crush more heavily armored prey items than their weaker jawed relatives. Smaller individuals have a small pharyngeal jaw gape and the jaws have less crushing strength; therefore, their diet consists primarily of polychaetes and small crustaceans. In many species the diet changes as the fish grows larger. The jaws become stronger and their pharyngeal gape increases, thus hard-bodied prey items, like larger crabs, bivalves, and snails, become more important in the diet. When they reach adulthood, many of the stronger-jawed wrasse species feed almost entirely on hard-bodied prey items, a niche utilized by relatively few coral reef fishes. Filamentous algae is not uncommon in the diets of some species, but in most cases it is probably taken incidentally as these fish pick at small crustaceans refuging in the algal mat.

Some *Halichoeres* spp. feed on zooplankton. These species often form shoals and move into the water column when feeding.

They also prefer current-prone habitats. A few species in the genus engage in cleaning behavior. Most are facultative cleaners, although one species (*Halichoeres cyanocephalus*) may be an obligate cleaner as a juvenile. Some of the other species known to clean include the Clown Wrasse (*H. maculipinna*), the Spinster Wrasse (*H. nicholsi*), the Atlantic Blackear Wrasse (*H. poeyi*), and the Rock Wrasse (*H. semicinctus*).

Most of the members of the genus *Halichoeres* use a special

other types of prey. For example, in the aquarium a larger specimen may grab a feeder fish in its mouth and break it into smaller pieces by smashing or rubbing it vigorously against hard substrate. The aquarist should be aware that even though a tankmate, whether a small fish or a crustacean, may appear too large for one these wrasses to ingest whole, it is still susceptible to being eaten.

These wrasses often associate with fishes that disturb the substrate as they feed, in order to exploit a resource that would normally be unavailable to them. This increases their predatory efficiency in this habitat. For example, a study conducted on the relationship between the Yellowhead Wrasse (*Halichoeres garnoti*) and the Spotted Goatfish (*Pseudupeneus maculatus*) and the Yellow Goatfish (*Mulloidichthys martinicus*) demonstrated that this wrasse makes more strikes when foraging in association with the goatfish.

The juvenile of at least one species of grouper (the Whitelined Grouper, *Anyperodon leucogrammicus*) is known to be an aggressive mimic of the initial phase of several *Halichoeres* spp. This enables the grouper to sneak up on prey items that are not threatened by the more common labrids.

The *Halichoeres* spp. are diandric protogynous hermaphrodites, with individuals displaying either the initial phase or terminal phase color pattern. At sexual maturity all of the *Halichoeres* spp. are initial phase individuals and can be either male or female. All terminal phase individuals are males resulting from female sex change. Terminal phase males are more spectacularly colored than initial phase specimens and are typically the individuals most sought after by hobbyists. They also tend to be the dominant individuals and usually have the greatest mating success.

Males of some species form permanent territories, others form small temporary territories during the spawning period, and still others live in large, overlapping home ranges and are not territorial. Initial phase specimens of several species form loose aggregations.

handling technique when feeding on prey items that are too large to fit into their pharyngeal jaws. If feeding on a large crab, for example, the wrasse will grasp one of the crustacean's legs or claws in its mouth, lift the crab off the bottom, and bash it against a rock until the appendage is separated from the body. After the wrasse removes all the appendages in this manner it will bite through the underside of the crab's carapace and ingest the internal organs. Wrasses use a similar technique to break up

Halichoeres garnoti, Yellowhead Wrasse, terminal male in courting or nuptial colors: striking colors of this genus attract divers and aquarium keepers alike.

These wrasses tend to have an internal clock that is triggered by ambient light levels. At night (or when threatened), they bury in the substrate. They do so by shoving their snouts in the sand or mud and rapidly undulating their bodies from side to side until they are covered with substrate. Then they emerge from their nocturnal shelter as the sun rises. When those species from the Indo-Pacific are transported and placed in a tank in the U.S., they often suffer from jet lag. That is, their biological clocks have to be "reset" to the day-night cycle in their new environment. This is why newly acquired *Halichoeres* spp. often bury in the sand when initially placed in the tank and reemerge later in the day or even in the middle of the night. It can take them a week or more to readjust their circadian rhythms to their new environment. To speed their adjustment to a new day-night cycle, keep them in a quarantine tank without sand.

Captive Care

The members of the genus *Halichoeres* are relatively hardy aquarium fishes once they make it through the shipping process. But many of these wrasses, especially large specimens, have difficulty recovering from the shock associated with shipping. When your dealer receives a *Halichoeres* spp., it is best to let it remain in the store's tank for at least a couple of days, or until it is swimming around the tank normally and is feeding. Check newly acquired specimens carefully for damage to the skin around the jaws, which is sometimes abraded when the wrasse frantically rubs its mouth against the bag while in transit. One way shippers can help alleviate this problem is to place a layer of fine substrate in the bottom of the bag, so the wrasse can bury under it during its long trip to the retailer.

Because the *Halichoeres* wrasses bury in the substrate at night

Halichoeres melanurus, Tailspot Wrasse, initial phase.

Halichoeres rubricephalus, Redhead Wrasse, initial phase.

Halichoeres cosmetus, Adorned Wrasse, initial phase.

Anyperodon leucogrammicus, Slender Grouper: mimics initial phase wrasses.

or when threatened, an aquarium that contains one of these wrasses must have a minimum of 5 cm (2 in.) of fine coral sand on the bottom. If you use a larger grade of crushed coral or dolomite the wrasse's jaws, fins, and scales may be damaged, which may lead to viral (e.g., *Lymphocystis*) or bacterial infections. To replicate the habitat occupied by the wrasses of this genus (i.e., lagoons near coral heads, at the edge of the fore-reef, or near sand patches on the reef slope), you should devote a significant amount of the aquarium's surface area to an open sand bottom.

The size of the tank that houses your *Halichoeres* spp. will depend on the species you intend to keep. Some species only reach 15 cm (5.9 in.) in length and can be housed in a standard 55-gallon tank. Others attain moderate lengths: For example, a terminal phase Pudding Wife Wrasse (*Halichoeres radiatus*) commonly attains a maximum length of 30 cm (12 in.) and needs

plenty of swimming room. A large *Halichoeres* spp. like this one should be kept in nothing smaller than a 100-gallon tank. Whether you are purchasing one of these wrasses for an existing tank or selecting a tank specifically for one of the *Halichoeres* spp., keep in mind that many of these fish are very active and larger specimens forage over an extensive home range. In the wild, a terminal phase Yellowhead Wrasse (*Halichoeres garnoti*) will move over a home range measuring from 2,500 to 5,000 m² (26,900 to 53,800 ft.²), which is at least as large as a football field. Another thing to consider is that these wrasses are more likely to misbehave (e.g., pick on more peaceful fishes) if crammed into an undersized tank.

The members of this genus vary considerably in their compatibility with other species. For example, some of the smaller species (e.g., the Golden Wrasse, *Halichoeres chrysus*) are very so-

Halichoeres melanurus, Tailspot Wrasse, terminal phase male displaying to members of his harem, with erect fins and intensified colors.

ciable and are rarely belligerent toward their tankmates, while the larger species (e.g., the Pudding Wife Wrasse) prey on smaller fish and may display aggression toward related species or other fish introduced after they have become well established in the aquarium. That said, even the less aggressive members of the genus can become bullies in certain situations. Some general trends that usually hold true for all members of the genus: they are more likely to behave aggressively toward newly introduced tankmates, they are more often aggressive toward closely related and similar-looking fishes, and terminal phase males tend to be more aggressive than initial phase individuals. If you are keeping more than one member of the genus in the same tank, it is best to add them at the same time.

While some of these wrasses will behave belligerently toward newcomers or smaller, more peaceful tankmates, they will have a difficult time acclimating to their new surroundings if they are being picked on by long-term aquarium residents. Fishes that are prone to picking on the smaller *Halichoeres* spp. include some dottybacks, pygmy angelfishes (e.g., the Cherubfish, *Centropyge argi*), the Eightline Wrasse (*Pseudocheilinus octotaenia*), Maori wrasses (*Cheilinus* and *Oxycheilinus* spp.), banana wrasses (*Thalassoma* spp.), larger damselfishes, hawkfishes, and sandperches. These wrasses are also potential prey for many morays, frogfishes, groupers, and triggerfishes.

Some of the smaller members of the genus can be kept in reef aquariums, although even they are a potential threat to fan worms, small snails, and ornamental shrimp. Not only do larger individuals have a greater dietary breadth, making them potentially dangerous to a wide range of motile invertebrates, but they will also flip over loose pieces of live rock and coral by grasping

Halichoeres argus, Peacock Wrasse, terminal phase.

Halichoeres biocellatus, Twospotted Wrasse, juvenile coloration.

Halichoeres biocellatus, Twospotted Wrasse, initial phase specimen.

Halichoeres biocellatus, Twospotted Wrasse, terminal phase.

them in their mouths when hunting hidden prey. One benefit of keeping these wrasses in a reef aquarium is that most species will feed on fire worms, pyramidellid snails, which are parasites of Tridacnid clams, and in some cases, flatworms.

Halichoeres Wrasse Species

Halichoeres argus (Bloch & Schneider, 1801)
Common Names: Peacock Wrasse, Argus Wrasse.
Maximum Length: 11 cm (4.3 in.).
Distribution: Sri Lanka to Fiji, north to Taiwan, and south to northern Australia.
Biology: The Peacock Wrasse is a resident of lagoons, rocky reef flats, and protected fringing reefs. It is often found in seagrass beds and over rocky areas with lush macroalgae growth. It is re-

ported at depths of 1 to 15 m (3.3 to 50 ft.). It is a microcarnivore, feeding on small motile invertebrates.
Captive Care: This is a hardy aquarium fish that is sold in the aquarium trade as an "assorted wrasse." For more husbandry information see the Captive Care section for the genus.
Aquarium Size: 55 gal. **Temperature:** 23° to 28°C (74° to 82°F).
Aquarium Suitability Index: 4.

Halichoeres biocellatus Schultz, 1960
Common Name: Twospotted Wrasse.
Maximum Length: 12 cm (4.7 in.).
Distribution: Philippines to Fiji, north to southern Japan, and south to the Great Barrier Reef.
Biology: The Twospotted Wrasse is found on coastal reefs, at the base of lagoon pinnacles, and on reef flats, crests, and reef faces

Halichoeres bivittatus, Slippery Dick, terminal phase male.

Halichoeres chloropterus, Green Wrasse, juvenile transforming to adult.

at depths of 7 to 35 m (23 to 116 ft.). It is often found over areas of mixed coral and reef rubble with the occasional sand patch. Its diet is probably similar to that of *H. melanurus.*

Captive Care: The Twospotted Wrasse is a durable species. For more information, see the Captive Care section for the genus.

Aquarium Size: 55 gal. **Temperature:** 23° to 28°C (74° to 82°F).

Aquarium Suitability Index: 4.

Remarks: *Halichoeres biocellatus* adults lack eyespots on the fins and have dusky bars on the posterior half of the body.

Halichoeres bivittatus (Bloch, 1791)

Common Name: Slippery Dick.

Maximum Length: 20 cm (7.9 in.).

Distribution: North Carolina and Bermuda to Brazil.

Biology: The Slippery Dick most commonly occurs over sand or mud substrates, with scattered coral heads and patch reefs, at a depth range of 1 to 15 m (3 to 50 ft.). It is a voracious predator that feeds on a wide variety of animal prey. It is very fond of crabs, urchins, polychaete worms, and snails (it tends to feed most on more brightly colored species of gastropods), but will also eat serpent stars, small bivalves, shrimp, chitons, mantis shrimp, hermit crabs, and fishes. One specimen was reported with a pipefish projecting from its mouth. Initial and terminal phase individuals roam over very large home ranges. During the breeding period, terminal phase males set up temporary territories at the edge of the reef, which contain two or three spawning sites. Groups of females aggregate in these areas, while terminal males rush from one site to the other, engaging in "looping" (rapid and continuous up-and-down movements above the substrate) and "quivering" (rapid lateral movements of the body). The Slippery Dick will engage in pair and group spawning, and

initial phase males may interfere with spawning attempts or join ("streak") with a spawning pair. The height of the spawning rush varies from 0.5 to 3 m (1.7 to 10 ft.) above the substrate. Spawning has been reported in the Slippery Dick from midday to the late afternoon. The eggs are 0.6 mm in diameter and hatch about 22 to 23 hours after they are fertilized at a temperature of 24.5°C (76°F). Newly hatched larvae measure 1.6 mm.

Captive Care: The Slippery Dick does best in a moderate-sized tank (75 gallons) with fish of similar size. Tankmates should be selected carefully, as this species will subdue smaller fishes, and even if they cannot be swallowed whole, *H. bivattatus* will grasp them in its mouth and attempt to beat them against aquarium decor to break them up into small pieces. Initial phase specimens can be kept together, or if you have a larger tank, a single initial phase specimen, or a small group of them, can be kept with a single terminal phase individual. Although this species will bury, it seems to do so less than many of its congeners. Because of this wrasse's polyphagous feeding habits, it is best not to house it with invertebrates, with the exception of large stinging anemones (e.g., *Condylactis* spp., *Stichodactyla* spp.).

Aquarium Size: 75 gal. **Temperature:** 23° to 28°C (74° to 82°F).

Aquarium Suitability Index: 4.

Halichoeres chloropterus (Bloch, 1791)

Common Names: Green Wrasse, Pastel Green Wrasse, Green "Coris."

Maximum Length: 19 cm (7.4 in.).

Distribution: Sumatra to the Solomon Islands, north to the Philippines, and south to the Great Barrier Reef.

Biology: *Halichoeres chloropterus* resides on protected coastal reefs and around lagoon patch reefs at depths from 0.5 to 10 m (1.7

Halichoeres chloropterus, Green Wrasse, initial phase specimen with shoal of Banggai Cardinalfish, *Pterapogon kauderni*.

Halichoeres chloropterus, Green Wrasse, terminal phase variant.

Halichoeres chloropterus, Green Wrasse, terminal phase male.

Halichoeres chlorocephalus, Greenhead Wrasse, terminal phase: rare fish.

Halichoeres chrysus, Golden Wrasse, terminal phase: hardy species.

to 33 ft.). It is found over mixed sand, rubble, live hard corals, and macroalgae. The Green Wrasse eats mollusks, crustaceans, and sea urchins.

Captive Care: The Green Wrasse is commonly encountered in the aquarium trade, where it is most often referred to as the Green Coris. Vivid green initial phase specimens are especially eye-catching and unusual. Although smaller *H. chloropterus* usually cause little trouble in the community tank, large individuals have been known to pick on small, more passive wrasses, like flasher wrasses and some of the more diminutive fairy wrasses. They are also likely to harass congeners introduced after them.

Aquarium Size: 75 gal. **Temperature:** 23° to 28°C (74° to 82°F).
Aquarium Suitability Index: 5.

Remarks: Terminal phase *H. chloropterus* has lavender markings on the head, while initial phase fish are green overall, often with small black spots. Juveniles have black lines along the body.

Halichoeres chlorocephalus Kuiter & Randall, 1995
Common Names: Greenhead Wrasse, Green "Coris."
Maximum Length: 12 cm (4.7 in.).
Distribution: Southeastern Papua New Guinea.
Biology: This beautiful wrasse is found near or on patch reefs in harbors, protected bays, and deep lagoons. It often occurs in silty habitats. The Greenhead Wrasse is reported to occur in micro-habitats with sponges and fine-branching stony corals.
Captive Care: For more husbandry information, see the Captive Care section for the genus. This species is very rare in the aquarium trade.
Aquarium Size: 55 gal. **Temperature:** 23 to 28°C (74 to 82°F).
Aquarium Suitability Index: 4.

Halichoeres chrysus Randall, 1981
Common Names: Golden Wrasse, Canary Wrasse, Yellow "Coris."
Maximum Length: 12 cm (4.7 in.).
Distribution: Christmas Islands to the Marshall Islands, north to southern Japan, and south to southeast Australia.
Biology: The Golden Wrasse is found near patch reefs and isolated coral heads, or in sand patches on coastal reef faces and slopes and in lagoons. It is usually found over sand or mixed sand and rubble. It has been reported at depths ranging from 2 to 60 m (7 to 198 ft.), but is most common in water deeper than 20 m (66 ft.). Small aggregations of female *H. chrysus* often forage together and sometimes follow feeding goatfishes.
Captive Care: *Halichoeres chrysus* is a great aquarium species, a not-too-large, nonaggressive species that can be housed with docile fish species like leopard wrasses, flasher wrasses, firefishes, and razor gobies. An aggregation of four or five specimens makes an especially attractive addition to a larger reef tank. The Golden Wrasse is quite resistant to *Cryptocaryon* and is not ill-affected by normal treatment levels of copper. I have seen *H. chrysus* clean other fish in captivity. One individual, for example, would pick at the body surfaces of several butterflyfishes. May be kept in groups of three or more inital fish and a single terminal male.
Aquarium Size: 55 gal. **Temperature:** 23° to 28°C (74° to 82°F).
Aquarium Suitability Index: 4.
Remarks: The initial phase has one or two eyespots on the dorsal fin and a black dot on the caudal peduncle.

Halichoeres cosmetus Randall & Smith, 1982
Common Name: Adorned Wrasse.
Maximum Length: 13 cm (5.1 in.).

Halichoeres cosmetus, Adorned Wrasse, terminal phase: sociable species.

Halichoeres cyanocephalus, Lightning Wrasse, initial phase.

Distribution: East Africa to the Chagos Archipelago and the Maldives, south to Mauritius and South Africa.

Biology: The Adorned Wrasse occurs at depths from 2 to 31 m (7 to 102 ft.) on fore-reef slopes and lagoon patch reefs. It is found over rubble, sand, and live hard coral substrates. The diet of this species is probably similar to that of *H. melanurus*.

Captive Care: This species is a hardy, sociable aquarium fish. One male and several females can be kept in a large aquarium. For more general husbandry information, see the Captive Care section for the genus.

Aquarium Size: 55 gal. **Temperature:** 23° to 28°C (74° to 82°F).

Aquarium Suitability Index: 4.

Remarks: Initial phase *H. cosmetus* have two ocelli on the dorsal fin.

Halichoeres cyanocephalus (Bloch, 1791)

Common Names: Lightning Wrasse, Yellowcheek Wrasse.

Maximum Length: 30 cm (11.8 in.).

Distribution: Florida and Antilles to Brazil; however, this fish is common only in the Florida Keys.

Biology: The Lightning Wrasse is a resident of deep coral and rocky reefs, occurring at depths from 27 to 91 m (89 to 300 ft.). It sometimes associates with tubular sponges and has been observed on shipwrecks. Young *H. cyanocephalus* (smaller than 8 cm [3.1 in.]) are obligatory cleaners that set up cleaning stations around isolated rocks on sand or gravel slopes or at the edges of patch reefs. To attract cleaning clients it will swim in a peculiar up and down ("seesaw") swimming motion. The stations are visited by a variety of reef fishes, including grunts, angelfishes, goatfishes, damselfishes, wrasses, parrotfishes, and surgeonfishes.

Halichoeres cyanocephalus, Lightning Wrasse, juvenile: deep-water species.

This wrasse tends to concentrate its cleaning on the fins and flanks of its clients and pick off crustacean parasites like gnathiid isopods. The Lightning Wrasse will feed on zooplankton as well as benthic invertebrates.

Captive Care: Once the Lightning Wrasse recovers from shipping it tends to do well in captivity. Thresher (1980) reports that this species is the most sensitive of the Atlantic *Halichoeres* spp. He states that it can be difficult to feed, and its large size makes it a threat to a wide variety of invertebrate tankmates. For more husbandry information, see the Captive Care section for the genus.

Aquarium Size: 100 gal. **Temperature:** 23° to 28°C (74° to 82°F).

Aquarium Suitability Index: 3–4.

Remarks: Initial phase *H. cyanocephalus* are bright blue with a yellow dorsum, while terminal phase specimens have a yellowish green back with a blue lateral band and a white belly.

Halichoeres garnoti, Yellowhead Wrasse, juvenile.

Halichoeres garnoti, Yellowhead Wrasse, initial phase.

Halichoeres garnoti, Yellowhead Wrasse: terminal male, courting colors.

Halichoeres garnoti (Valenciennes, 1839)

Common Name: Yellowhead Wrasse.

Maximum Length: 18 cm (7.1 in.).

Distribution: South Florida, Bermuda, northern Gulf of Mexico to southeast Brazil.

Biology: The Yellowhead Wrasse is most prevalent on patch reefs in lagoons and on fore-reef slopes, often in areas of rich hard and soft coral growth. It can be found at depths from 2 to 80 m (7 to 264 ft.). The major prey of *H. garnoti* include crabs, serpent stars, and snails, but it also consumes bivalves, polychaete worms, shrimp, hermit crabs, fish, urchins, chitons, and peanut worms. When feeding, this species inspects crevices, flips stones or rubble, and follows fish that disturb the substrate. These wrasses occasionally ingest planktonic organisms. An adult will sometimes use a rock as an anvil against which it bashes hard-shelled invertebrates into bite-sized pieces. One large male *H. garnoti* was seen to use a rock to break apart a scallop that was much too large to ingest. In this incident, initial phase individuals remained nearby and fed on smaller bits that were broken off the bivalve. The initial and terminal phase individuals usually occur singly. They live in a home range that covers an area of 1,500 to 2,000 m² (16,140 to 21,520 ft.²). Terminal phase individuals move over immense, overlapping home ranges measuring from 2,500 to 5,000 m² (26,900 to 53,800 ft.²). A size-based dominance hierarchy exists among terminal phase *H. garnoti* in an area. Initial phase individuals defer to terminal phase individuals in feeding situations. When exploiting a common food source, only the most dominant individual will retain its bright colors. Subordinate males will adopt a more subdued color pattern or wait until the dominant fish moves off. Intra- and interspecific aggression are rare in this species. Thresher (1979) reports that spawning occurs throughout the year from late morning to early afternoon. In his study, spawning was limited to calm days during slack tide. Males engage in "looping displays." A receptive female will move higher in the water column and hover as she waits for a male suitor. The two swim side by side and move upwards approximately 1 m (3.3 ft.) in the water column before releasing their gametes.

Captive Care: This is a durable aquarium species, but it tends to lose some of its brilliance in captivity. Large males tend to adopt the colors of the subordinate or even the initial phase when housed without conspecifics. If your tank is large enough (180 gallons or larger) you may be able to house a terminal phase individual with one or more initial phase fish. For more husbandry information, see the Captive Care section for the genus.

Aquarium Size: 75 gal. **Temperature:** 23° to 28°C (74° to 82°F).

Aquarium Suitability Index: 4.

H. hartzfeldii, Hartzfeld's Wrasse, initial phase specimen sheltering near sea anemone: wrasses do not "bathe" in the stinging tentacles as anemonefishes do.

Halichoeres hartzfeldii (Bleeker, 1852)

Common Names: Hartzfeld's Wrasse, Goldstripe Wrasse.

Maximum Length: 18.0 cm (7.1 in.).

Distribution: Indonesia to Micronesia, north to southern Japan, and south to the Great Barrier Reef.

Biology: The Hartzfeld's Wrasse is found on outer reef faces and slopes at depths of 10 to 70 m (33 to 231 ft.). It is usually found in areas of sand or mixed sand and rubble. Like many of this genus, the juveniles and females occur in loose groups, with an attendant male patrolling over large areas. Males are apparently territorial.

Captive Care: This is an attractive wrasse that occasionally is offered under the title of "assorted wrasse." The colors of terminal males usually fade in captivity, but it is a hardy aquarium resident. Large individuals will pick on smaller conspecifics and possible congeners. For more husbandry information, see the Captive

Halichoeres hartzfeldii, Hartzfeld's Wrasse, initial phase.

Halichoeres hartzfeldii, Hartzfeld's Wrasse, terminal phase male.

Halichoeres hortulanus, Checkerboard Wrasse, young initial phase fish.

Halichoeres hortulanus, Checkerboard Wrasse, terminal phase.

Halichoeres hortulanus, Checkerboard Wrasse, small juvenile.

Care section for the genus.
Aquarium Size: 75 gal. **Temperature:** 23° to 28°C (74° to 82°F).
Aquarium Suitability Index: 4.
Remarks: This wrasse is very similar to *Halichoeres zeylonicus*, which replaces it in the western Indian Ocean. Male *H. hartzfeldii* have a black spot below the median body stripe, while male *H. zeylonicus* have a spot above this stripe.

Halichoeres hortulanus (Lacepède, 1801)
Common Name: Checkerboard Wrasse.
Maximum Length: 27 cm (10.6 in.).
Distribution: Red Sea to the Marquesas and Tuamotus, north to southern Japan, and south to the Great Barrier Reef.
Biology: The Checkerboard Wrasse is a solitary species that is common in lagoons, often near the coral-rich back barrier reef and on fore-reef slopes, at depths from 1 to 30 m (3 to 98 ft.). It is a very opportunistic predator that frequently associates with fish that disturb the substrate when they feed, like goatfishes and stingrays. Its main food source is small, sand-dwelling snails, which it crushes with its well-developed pharyngeal teeth. It also feeds on hermit crabs, polychaete worms, small infaunal clams, crustaceans, and even bony fishes on rare occasion. Adult *H. hortulanus* are active fish that typically out-swim predators rather than burying in the substrate. They do bury in the sand at night, however.
Captive Care: This is a large, active species that will require a moderate-sized aquarium (e.g., 70 gallons). It is rarely aggressive toward other fish housed with it, but larger specimens may eat fish that are small enough to subdue. It can be kept with other wrasses, although conspecifics may fight unless they are kept in large tanks and introduced to the tank simultaneously. Although juvenile *H. hortulanus* do minimal damage in a reef aquariums,

Halichoeres hortulanus, Checkerboard Wrasse, terminal phase male.

Halichoeres iridis, Orangehead Wrasse, terminal phase.

adults will feed on many of the motile, desirable invertebrates that we house in our reef tanks, including algae-eating snails and ornamental shrimp. They will also flip pieces of coral over when searching for prey items.

Aquarium Size: 100 gal. **Temperature:** 23° to 28°C (74° to 82°F).

Aquarium Suitability Index: 4.

Remarks: The Indian Ocean form of this fish, which ranges from the Red Sea to Bali and was formerly known as *H. centriquadrus*, may be a distinct species. Indian Ocean adults lack the second yellow spot under the middle of the dorsal fin, which is present in the Pacific form.

Halichoeres iridis Randall & Smith, 1982

Common Names: Orangehead Wrasse, Iridis Wrasse, Radiant Wrasse.

Maximum Length: 11.5 cm (4.5 in.).

Distribution: Southern Red Sea, East Africa to the Seychelles, Chagos, Mauritius, and the Maldive Islands, south to southern Africa.

Biology: The Orangehead Wrasse is a resident of steep reef slopes at depths from 6 to 43 m (20 to 142 ft.), but is most common below 20 m (66 ft.). This wrasse is most abundant over sand or rubble substrates. Its diet is probably similar to that of *H. melanurus*.

Captive Care: This species can be kept in a tank as small as 20 gallons. It is a sociable species that does well in a peaceful community tank. An occasional *H. iridis* will ship poorly or die for no apparent reason after being kept in the home aquarium, however. This species has recently become more common in the aquarium trade.

Aquarium Size: 55 gal. **Temperature:** 23° to 28°C (74° to 82°F).

Aquarium Suitability Index: 4.

Remarks: Initial phase *H. iridis* have eyespots at the base of the dorsal fin, which are lacking in terminal phase specimens. Terminal phase individuals also have green and yellow markings on their faces.

Halichoeres leucoxanthus Randall & Smith, 1982

Common Names: Lemon Meringue Wrasse, Indian Ocean Yellow "Coris."

Maximum Length: 11 cm (4.3 in.).

Distribution: Maldives to western Indonesia.

Biology: The Lemon Meringue Wrasse occurs on fore-reef slopes, over rubble and sand bottoms, at depths between 10 and 60 m (33 and 198 ft.). Like its relative the Golden Wrasse (*H. chrysus*), this species often forages in small groups. I have even seen it feeding in heterospecific groups, along with the Vermiculate Leopard Wrasse (*Macropharyngodon bipartitus*).

Captive Care: This desirable smaller species is similar in its husbandry requirements and disposition to the Golden Wrasse. It is nonaggressive and initial phase individuals can be kept in small groups. However, you should only place one terminal phase specimen per aquarium. (If you purchase a group of younger *Halichoeres* wrasses, one dominant terminal phase male should emerge as they mature.)

Aquarium Size: 55 gal. **Temperature:** 23° to 28°C (74° to 82°F).

Aquarium Suitability Index: 4.

Remarks: The terminal phase individuals have yellow and green bands on the head and lack the three spots on the dorsal fin that are present in initial phase specimens. Females have solid yellow dorsal fins. If buying a group, choose one male and two or more females.

Halichoeres leucoxanthus, Lemon Meringue Wrasse, initial phase: this Indian Ocean, group-forming species is distinguished from *H. chrysus* by a white ventrum.

Halichoeres leucurus (Walbaum, 1792)

Common Names: Greyhead Wrasse, Silty Wrasse.

Maximum Length: 15 cm (5.9 in.).

Distribution: Java east to New Guinea, north to the Yaeyama Islands, and south to Flores, Indonesia; Palau in Micronesia.

Biology: The Greyhead Wrasse is found in lagoons, protected coastal reef slopes, and reef channels. It typically occurs in coral-rich habitats or microhabitats with macroalgae and is more often found on silty, turbid habitats than some of its close relatives (e.g., *H. richmondi*). It occurs at depths of 2 to 15 m (7 to 50 ft.). It is a microcarnivore that feeds on a variety of benthic invertebrates.

Captive Care: *Halichoeres leucurus*, like many in the genus, do well in the aquarium if they bounce back from the initial shipping stress. This species will eat fire worms, but may also take out ornamental shrimp and crabs. Specimens have been known to jump out of open aquariums. Keep a cover in place.

Aquarium Size: 55 gal. **Temperature:** 23° to 28°C (74° to 82°F).

Aquarium Suitability Index: 4.

Remarks: The Greyhead Wrasse is very similar to Richmond's Wrasse (*Halichoeres richmondi*). This species is synonymous with *Halichoeres purpurescens* (Linnaeus, 1758).

Halichoeres maculipinna (Müller & Troschel, 1848)

Common Name: Clown Wrasse.

Maximum Length: 18 cm (7.1 in.)

Distribution: North Carolina and Bermuda to Brazil.

Biology: The Clown Wrasse is a resident of reef flats and shallow rocky areas, at depths from 2 to 24 m (7 to 79 ft.). This species hunts primarily over soft substrates where it looks for prey in loose sediment. It feeds heavily on polychaete worms, but will also eat copepods, small pistol shrimp, other small crustaceans, snails, octopuses, crabs, small bivalves, chitons, and peanut worms. Copepods are a preferred food of smaller clown wrasses. Initial phase individuals are often seen in loose, feeding aggregations that can number from several to as many as 40 individuals. These groups of *H. maculipinna* are joined by young *H. garnoti*, small *H. bivittatus*, Bluehead Wrasse (*Thalassoma bifasciatum*), juvenile surgeonfish, and small parrotfish. Such shoals of initial phase individuals remain in a home range of from 70 to 150 m² (753 to 1,614 ft.²). Individuals within these groups form a size-related linear dominance hierarchy. Thresher (1979) reports that terminal phase individuals are either subordinate or dominant. Dominant individuals spend more of their time in the water column (from 0.75 to 1.25 m [30 to 49 in.] above the bottom) and less of their time feeding. They move around large, overlapping territories (500 to 1,100 m³ [5,380 to 11,836 ft.³] in area) that include the home ranges of three to six initial phase herds. The territory of the dominant terminal phase individual also contains one to three subordinate terminal phase specimens. These individuals move about the territory and attempt to avoid the dominant territory holder (which often engages in chasing the subordinates). The subordinates stay close to the substrate, rarely display the bright color phase, and never court or spawn. A dominance hierarchy also exists among subordinate terminal phase males that utilize the same territory. Subordinate males participate in territory defense and will help repel intrusion by neighboring terminal phase males. Occasionally, dominant males mix with initial phase herds, chasing subordinates and courting with females. When dominant males meet near territory boundaries, they engage in a number of motor patterns. These include "head-stand" (territory defender adopts a head-down position and swims back and forth at the territory boundary), "parallel swimming" (two fish rapidly swim side by side along their mutual boundary), and "gaping" (two fish orient head-to-head with their mouths agape). These bouts of displaying rarely, if ever, result in physical combat. The Clown Wrasse almost never engages in interspecific aggression.

Thresher (1979) reports that spawning in this species occurs throughout the year from late morning to early afternoon. In his study, spawning was limited to calm days during slack tide. During courtship, dominant males actively court females, chasing subordinates and actively patrolling territory boundaries. Males engage in "looping displays." When a female is ready to spawn,

Halichoeres leucurus, Greyhead Wrasse: beautiful terminal phase male exceeds its bland-sounding common name.

Halichoeres maculipinna, Clown Wrasse, initial phase: this species is common in many parts of the Caribbean. Terminal phase fish on next page.

it rises slightly off the substrate while being chased by a dominant male. The pair then swim side by side, dash about 1 m (3.3 ft.) into the water column, release gametes, and dart back to the seafloor. As the pair rises off the seafloor, they are joined by one to five initial phase individuals. These could be "streakers"—initial phase males that dart in to release their gametes simultaneously with the dominant male.

Captive Care: *Halichoeres maculipinna* is a hardy, inexpensive

Halichoeres maculipinna, Clown Wrasse, terminal phase.

Halichoeres maculipinna, Clown Wrasse, TP male in spawning colors.

Halichoeres margaritaceus, Weedy Surge Wrasse, initial phase.

Halichoeres margaritaceus, Weedy Surge Wrasse, terminal phase.

aquarium species. Initial phase specimens can be kept in small groups, but only one terminal phase specimen should be kept per aquarium. Unfortunately, larger terminal phase specimens, which are typically more colorful, sometimes have more difficulty acclimating to aquarium confines.

Aquarium Size: 75 gal. **Temperature:** 23° to 28°C (74° to 82°F).
Aquarium Suitability Index: 4.
Remarks: The initial phase *H. maculipinna* has a dark lateral band with a yellow band above it. It is white below and has short red bands on the top of the head. Terminal phase individuals are green overall with pink markings on the head and pink stripes on the body. They also develop a large black spot on the side and smaller black spots on the dorsal fin.

Halichoeres margaritaceus (Valenciennes, 1839)
Common Name: Weedy Surge Wrasse.
Maximum Length: 15 cm (5.9 in.).
Distribution: Cocos Island in the eastern Indian Ocean to the Line and Tuamotu islands, north to southern Japan, south to New South Wales and Lord Howe Island, southern Japan and Taiwan.
Biology: This is a shallow-water species, having been reported at depths of less than 1 to 5 m (3.3 to 17 ft.). It is found on fringing coral reefs, reef flats, reef margins, and along rocky shorelines, often in areas with rich macroalgae growth. These wrasses are often found in surgy microhabitats. The diet of the Weedy Surge Wrasse includes benthic crustaceans, mollusks, polychaetes, forams, fishes, and fish eggs.
Captive Care: This species is regularly sold in the aquarium trade as an "assorted wrasse." For more husbandry information, see the Captive Care section for the genus.

Halichoeres marginatus, Dusky Wrasse, juvenile: known as the "Black Coris."

Halichoeres marginatus, Dusky Wrasse, terminal phase male.

Aquarium Size: 55 gal. **Temperature:** 23° to 28°C (74° to 82°F).
Aquarium Suitability Index: 4.
Remarks: It is replaced by *Halichoeres nebulosus* in the western Indian Ocean (the two species occur together in parts of the western Pacific).

Halichoeres marginatus Rüppell, 1835
Common Names: Dusky Wrasse, Black "Coris" (initial phase individuals).
Maximum Length: 17 cm (6.7 in.).
Distribution: Red Sea to the Line and Tuamotu islands, north to southern Japan, and south to the southern Great Barrier Reef and the Austral Islands.
Biology: The Dusky Wrasse lives in lagoons, near patch reefs and the back of the barrier reef, and on fore-reef slopes. It occurs at depths from less than 1 to 30 m (3 to 99 ft.) and is usually found in areas with healthy hard coral growth. This species feeds primarily on small crustaceans (e.g., isopods and copepods), chitons, and polychaetes (including terebellid worms), and to a lesser degree on small snails, shelled protozoa known as foraminiferans, sea cucumbers, peanut worms, fish and invertebrate eggs, barnacles, and algae filaments. Plant material is probably ingested incidentally as this fish feeds on small animals living in the algal mat. I have seen specimens pull tufts of algae off hard substrate, spit it out, inspect it, and then shake it from side to side. Although they don't eat the algae, they may use this feeding technique to try and flush small prey items out of the algae. During the morning and early afternoon, solitary adult male and female individuals feed on hard substrates. This species often visits Bluestreak Cleaner Wrasse (*Labroides dimidiatus*) cleaning stations. In southern Japan, the spawning season for this species is between early May and early November. Larger terminal phase males set up mating territories in late afternoon (between 3:00 and 6:30 P.M.) near prominent coral heads on the fore-reef slopes. At approximately 4:00 P.M., females begin migrating to the breeding territories. Smaller females will often follow larger consexuals as they make this migration to the spawning area (groups of as many as nine females may move together to the spawning area). However, smaller females tend to move to closer areas to spawn rather than to areas farther from their home ranges. One study demonstrated that females are more likely to select a particular spawning site, rather than a specific male (males do not occupy the same site night after night). Larger females tend to prefer to spawn at down-current sites, which would increase the likelihood that their newly fertilized gametes would survive in offshore habitats (there are more small mouths that would feed on the gametes near the reef). At between 5:00 and 6:00 P.M. males and females pair and begin to court. Those terminal phase males that have not set up mating territories, as well as initial phase males, will try to "sneak" spawnings or join spawning groups. Females spawn once per night, while males spawn with multiple females. Large females have been observed to change sex within 3 to 4 weeks of spawning as females.
Captive Care: This species will readily bury when threatened and at night. This wrasse rarely bothers its tankmates and can be kept with less aggressive species like flasher wrasses, fairy wrasses, and firefishes. I had a juvenile specimen that would pick at the side of a posing Bluespotted Angelfish (*Chaetodontoplus caeruleopunctatus*). This species can be kept in reef aquariums, although large adults may nip at algae-eating snails. I observed a terminal phase specimen picking the viscera out of a snail shell, for example, although I cannot be sure it was responsible for the demise of the

Halichoeres melanochir, Orangefin Wrasse: terminal phase male.

Halichoeres melanochir, Orangefin Wrasse: initial phase.

gastropod and its soft parts. It will pick at live rock, sending clouds of sediment into the water that can be removed by external filters. It will eat pyramidellid snails and the prolific commensal flatworms that can infest hard corals, soft corals, and mushroom anemones.

Aquarium Size: 55 gal. **Temperature:** 23° to 28°C (74° to 82°F).
Aquarium Suitability Index: 3.

Remarks: Terminal phase individuals vary somewhat in their coloration from one location to the next. For example, in many parts of the Pacific there is a yellow bar present on the pectoral fin in terminal phase individuals. In Palau, specimens lack this yellow bar; instead, they have a white spot with dark edges on the tip of the pectoral fin. In some areas the terminal phase Dusky Wrasse may have a red blotch behind the pectoral fin (Lieske & Myers, 1994). Initial phase specimens are dark brown with faint stripes along each scale row and a whitish caudal fin. Juveniles have alternating dark brown and pale yellow stripes. Kuiter (2001) suggests that *H. marginatus* should apply to the population of *H. marginatus* in the Red Sea, while populations in the Indian Ocean and Pacific should be referred to as *Halichoeres lamarii* (Valenciennes, 1839).

Halichoeres melanochir Fowler & Bean, 1928

Common Names: Orangefin Wrasse, Black Wrasse.
Maximum Length: 10 cm (3.9 in.).
Distribution: Philippines to Taiwan, north to southern Japan, and south to northwestern Australia.
Biology: *Halichoeres melanochir* is most common on sand patches on the fore-reef slope. It occurs at depths ranging from 5 to at least 25 m (17 to 83 ft.). This species feeds most heavily on snails,

chitons, crabs, amphipods, and errant polychaetes, but will also eat foraminiferans, bivalves, planktonic fish eggs, copepods, serpent stars, shrimp, sponges, fish larvae, peanut worms, barnacles, and algae filaments. It prefers mollusks. It typically occurs singly.
Captive Care: This is one of the smaller members of the genus. It is therefore less of a threat to certain invertebrate tankmates. That said, based on the dietary habits of *H. melanochir* listed above, you can see it is still likely to damage a number of invertebrates. I have seen this fish behave aggressively toward inoffensive wrasse species, like leopard wrasses (*Macropharyngodon* spp.). For more on its general husbandry, see the Captive Care section for the genus.
Aquarium Size: 55 gal. **Temperature:** 23° to 28°C (74° to 82°F).
Aquarium Suitability Index: 4.
Remarks: *Halichoeres melanochir* has orange pelvic fins. This species also has a black spot at the pectoral fin axil. The juveniles have dark stripes along the body and white blotches, with ocelli on the dorsal fin.

Halichoeres melanurus (Bleeker, 1851)

Common Names: Tailspot Wrasse, Hoeven's Wrasse.
Maximum Length: 10.5 cm (4 in.).
Distribution: Indonesia to Samoa, north to the Ryukus, and south to the southern Great Barrier Reef.
Biology: The Tailspot Wrasse is most common in protected lagoons, usually near the base of patch reefs or on fringing reef slopes, over sand or rubble. It occurs at depths from 2 to 15 m (7 to 50 ft.). This species feeds most heavily on amphipods, snails, algae filaments, copepods, snails, crabs, errant polychaete worms, and crabs, but it will also eat chitons, barnacles, foraminiferans,

bivalves, fish eggs, fan worms, terebellid worms, peanut worms, sponges, sea cucumbers, and, on rare occasions, small anemones. Males of this species are solitary, but females will sometimes forage in small, loose groups.

Captive Care: *Halichoeres melanurus* is a smaller member of the genus that is ideally suited for home aquariums of various sizes. It can be housed with a wide range of fish species and rarely bothers its tankmates. Initial phase individuals can be kept in small groups in the aquarium and will not bother other wrasses, including closely related species. Terminal phase specimens, on the other hand, should not be housed together, and if you want to keep them with females, introduce them all together or place the initial phase specimens in the tank first. Terminal phase individuals are very fond of small bristleworms and will even tear up

larger specimens. I have found damaged fireworms in the pre-filter and sump of my aquarium, the results of a large Tailspot Wrasse attack. This species will also feed on pyramidellid snails and commensal flatworms. The downside of the Tailspot Wrasse's dietary proclivities is that it will nip at feather dusters and may harass small algae-eating snails and ornamental crustaceans. I have also seen them tear *Caulerpa* blades off the rhizome, not to feed on the plant, but possibly in search of small crustaceans.

Aquarium Size: 55 gal. **Temperature:** 23° to 28°C (74° to 82°F).

Aquarium Suitability Index: 4.

Remarks: The initial phase Tailspot Wrasse is orange-yellow overall with fine blue pinstripes and a blue-trimmed black spot at the end of the caudal fin. Older literature may refer to this species as *Halichoeres hoevenii*, a name originally applied to initial phase

Halichoeres melanurus, Tailspot Wrasse, terminal phase male: ideal aquarium community tank member that will eat a variety of nuisance invertebrates.

Halichoeres melanurus, Tailspot Wrasse, initial phase transforming.

Halichoeres timorensis, Timor Wrasse, terminal phase.

Halichoeres binotopsis, Saowisata Wrasse, initial phase.

Halichoeres binotopsis, Saowisata Wrasse, terminal phase male.

Halichoeres vrolikii, Vrolik's Wrasse, terminal phase.

individuals. This species is a member of a complex that includes a number of very similar wrasse species, in which the female color forms are nearly identical. **Vrolik's Wrasse** (*Halichoeres vrolikii*) (**Bleeker, 1855**) is a very similar species that is known from the Maldives to Java. It is found in lagoons and on protected coastal reefs. The males of this species differ from *H. melanurus* in having green spots on the caudal fin. It reaches 12 cm (4.7 in.) in length. The females of *H. kallochroma, H. chlorocephalus, H. leucurus, H. richmondi,* and *H. rubricephalus* are very similar to *H. melanurus.* The **Saowisata Wrasse** (*Halichoeres binotopsis*) (**Bleeker, 1849**) is also similar, although the female color pattern is more distinct. It has been reported from coastal reef flats, where females form loose groups and males patrol their territories. It gets 12 cm (4.7 in.) long. The **Timor Wrasse** (*Halichoeres timorensis*) (**Bleeker, 1852**) is most similar to *H. binotopsis.* This species is found from Sri Lanka to the Andaman Sea. It is a resident of coastal coral or rocky reefs. It reaches 12 cm (4.7 in.) in length. Females have broken orange stripes on the body.

Halichoeres melasmapomus Randall, 1981

Common Names: Blackear Wrasse, Earmuff Wrasse.
Maximum Length: 24.0 cm (9.4 in.).
Distribution: Cocos (Keeling) Islands and Rowley Shoals in the eastern Indian Ocean to the Marquesas and Pitcairn Islands, north to the Philippines.
Biology: This wrasse is found in relatively deep water. It is reported at depths of 10 to 55 m (33 to 182 ft.), but most occur at depths in excess of 33 m (109 ft.). Although it has been reported from coastal bays, it is most common on outer reef dropoffs. It is usually found around caves that support rich sessile invertebrate growth or on patches of rubble on steep slopes. Adults of this species are usually found in small groups.
Captive Care: Because of its propensity for deep water, *H. melasmapomus* is not commonly observed in the aquarium trade. It tends to be a durable aquarium species that will require a sand bed in which to bury. Although this species is often found in groups in nature, individuals are likely to fight in the aquarium (especially males). For more on general husbandry, se the Captive Care section for the genus.
Aquarium Size: 100 gal. **Temperature:** 23° to 28°C (74° to 82°F).
Aquarium Suitability Index: 3.
Remarks: *Halichoeres melasmapomus* is different from many in the genus in that the females and males are quite similar in color (males are slightly more colorful than females). The juveniles differ in having three ocelli on the dorsal fin. Those individuals that are found in habitats near shore are reported to be more reddish overall, while those from offshore areas are pink. Kuiter (2001) refers to this species as *Halichoeres xanti* (Karoli, 1882).

Halichoeres nebulosus (Valenciennes, 1839)

Common Names: Nebulous Wrasse, Cloudy Wrasse.
Maximum Length: 12 cm (4.7 in.).
Distribution: Red Sea to Papua New Guinea, north to southern Japan, and south to the Great Barrier Reef.
Biology: The Nebulous Wrasse is a resident of reef flats, fore-reef slopes, and rocky shorelines. It is often in seagrass meadows or areas exposed to surge. Although it is most abundant in shallow water, it has been taken as deep as 40 m (132 ft.). The Nebulous Wrasse feeds most on chitons, snails, crabs, small clams, amphipods, sponges, and errant polychaetes. Dietary items of lesser importance include mantis shrimp, peanut worms, planktonic fish eggs, sea spiders, and filamentous algae.

Halichoeres malasmapomus, Blackear Wrasse, TP: deep-water species.

Halichoeres nebulosus, Nebulous Wrasse, TP: distinctive head markings.

Captive Care: This is another species that is sold in the aquarium trade as an "assorted wrasse." It can be kept in a community tank with small, docile fish species. It rarely behaves belligerently toward its tankmates, with the possible exception of smaller fish introduced into the aquarium after it. It can be kept in a reef aquariums; however, as it grows it may begin to prey on snails and ornamental crustaceans.
Aquarium Size: 55 gal. **Temperature:** 23° to 28°C (74° to 82°F).
Aquarium Suitability Index: 4.
Remarks: The Nebulous Wrasse has a boomerang-shaped pink mark on the cheek below the eye, which distinguishes it from *H. margaritaceus*. Males of this species are similar to the **Circle Cheek Wrasse (*Halichoeres miniatus*) (Valenciennes, 1839)**. This species ranges from Japan to northeastern Australia, where it is found on algae-covered rocky reefs. The males of this species

Halichoeres ornatissimus, Ornate or Christmas Wrasse, juvenile: young have distinct eyespots on the dorsal fin to deflect piscivores from attacking the head.

have pink bands on the lower cheek that form a ring (in some individuals it is not a complete ring).

Halichoeres ornatissimus (Günther, 1864)

Common Names: Ornate Wrasse, Christmas Wrasse.
Maximum Length: 17 cm (6.7 in.).
Distribution: Ryukus, southern Japan, Marianas, Marquesas, Society, Tuamotu, and Hawaiian Islands.
Biology: The Ornate Wrasse is a resident of lagoon patch reefs and outer reef slopes, where there is rich coral growth and occasional sand patches. It occurs at depths of 1.5 to 22 (5 to 73 ft.). This species feeds mainly on small benthic crustaceans and mollusks.

Captive Care: Although *H. ornatissimus* occasionally ships poorly, especially larger specimens, once it has shaken off the rigors of spending hours in a small shipping bag it does quite well in the home aquarium. It should not be placed in an aquarium with aggressive tankmates and should be left alone while it acclimates. The Ornate Wrasse rarely displays aggression toward its tankmates. However, terminal males should not be housed together and may chase and nip closely related species introduced after them, especially if kept in a small tank.

Aquarium Size: 55 gal. **Temperature:** 23° to 28°C (74° to 82°F).

Aquarium Suitability Index: 4.

Remarks: Juvenile Ornate Wrasses have more green on the body than the adults and a dark black spot on the middle of the dorsal fin. Individuals from the Hawaiian Islands tend to display a darker green and a more brilliant red than their western Pacific counterparts. This species is not sexually dichromatic. The **Oriental Wrasse** (*Halichoeres orientalis*, **Randall, 1999**) is a similar species from southern Japan and Taiwan. It reaches 15 cm (5.9 in.) in length and is found at a depth range of 2 to 30 m (7 to 99 ft.).

Halichoeres pallidus Kuiter & Randall, 1995

Common Names: Pale Wrasse, Babi Wrasse.

Maximum Length: 10 cm (3.9 in.).

Distribution: Eastern Indonesia east to Palau and the Line Islands.

Biology: The Pale Wrasse is found at depths of 37 to 74 m (122 to 244 ft.) on steep outer reef slopes. It often occurs in or near invertebrate-encrusted caves. This species occurs in small groups consisting of mainly females with one dominant male.

Captive Care: This species is rare in the trade because of its proclivity to deep water. It would be best to keep *H. pallidus* in a deepwater reef aquarium. Keep only one male per tank. In many respects, the care of this species is similar to the captive care of other *Halichoeres* spp.

Aquarium Size: 55 gal. **Temperature:** 23° to 28°C (74° to 82°F).

Aquarium Suitability Index: 4.

Remarks: Juveniles and females have three ocelli on the dorsal fin. The **White Wrasse** (*Halichoeres trispilus*) **Randall & Smith, 1982** is a similar species that have been reported from Sodwana Bay, South Africa, the Maldives, and Mauritius, east to south Java. It is also a deep-water species, having been reported from depths of 25 to 56 m (83 to 185 ft.). It typically associates with invertebrate-encrusted caves. Females form small groups, while males patrol a territory, occasionally visiting females.

Halichoeres pictus (Poey, 1860)

Common Names: Painted Wrasse, Rainbow Wrasse.

Maximum Length: 13.0 cm (5.1 in.).

Distribution: Southern Florida and Bahamas, to northern South America.

Biology: *Halichoeres pictus* is found on reef faces and slopes at depths of 5 to 25 m (17 to 83 ft.). It is often found among gorgonians or on patch reefs. It is different from many in the genus in that it is often found in loose aggregations up in the water column where it feeds on zooplankton. Juveniles live near deep walls, often associating with the Masked Goby (*Coryphopterus personatus*). Adults occur in loose groups that often consist of 20

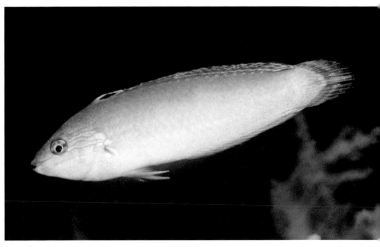

Halichoeres pallidus, Pale Wrasse, TP: deep-water species.

Halichoeres pictus, Painted Wrasse, initial phase: common Caribbean fish.

to 40 individuals. The males "flash" brighter colors when they display toward females, with the black spot on the caudal peduncle becoming very prominent. Groups of *H. pictus* often mix with the Bluehead Wrasse (*Thalassoma bifasciatum*) and small Clown Wrasses (*Halichoeres maculipinna*).

Captive Care: The Painted Wrasse is not regularly collected for the home aquarium, even though terminal individuals are quite colorful. It is a durable aquarium species that can be kept in groups in larger tanks. Only keep one male per tank, unless the tank is 180 gallons or larger. Also, make sure you feed this species at least once a day, as it feeds mainly on zooplankton. This species will readily jump out of open aquariums.

Aquarium Size: 75 gal. **Temperature:** 23° to 28°C (74° to 82°F).

Aquarium Suitability Index: 4.

Halichoeres pictus, Painted Wrasse, terminal phase: zooplankton picker.

Halichoeres pictus, Painted Wrasse, terminal phase variant.

Halichoeres podostigma, Whitetail Wrasse, IP: nice aquarium species.

Halichoeres poeyi, Atlantic Blackear Wrasse, terminal phase: rarely collected.

Halichoeres podostigma (Bleeker, 1854)

Common Names: Whitetail Wrasse, Axilspot Wrasse.
Maximum Length: 18.5 cm (7.3 in.).
Distribution: Philippines and Indonesia.
Biology: The Whitetail Wrasse is found on outer reef flats, reef faces, and slopes at depths of 2 to 25 m (7 to 83 ft.). It often occurs in areas of rich coral and hydrozoa growth. *Halichoeres podostigma* is a solitary species.
Captive Care: This is a nice aquarium wrasse. It is best kept in a fish-only aquarium or in a reef aquarium that lacks ornamental crustaceans and worms. Its husbandry is similar to that of other members of the genus (see the Captive Care section for the genus).
Aquarium Size: 75 gal. **Temperature:** 23° to 28°C (74° to 82°F).
Aquarium Suitability Index: 4.
Remarks: The juvenile coloration differs greatly from that of the adults. It is tan overall with five to nine white stripes on the anterior half of the body and green toward the tail.

Halichoeres poeyi (Steindachner, 1867).

Common Name: Atlantic Blackear Wrasse.
Maximum Length: 20 cm (7.8 in.).
Distribution: Southern Florida and Bahamas, Caribbean and tropical western Atlantic to Rio de Janeiro, Brazil.
Biology: The Atlantic Blackear Wrasse is found at depths of less than 1 to 15 m (3 to 50 ft.). It is occasionally found on coral reefs but is most common in seagrass beds. *Halichoeres poeyi* feeds mainly on crabs and snails but also eats serpent stars, urchins, peanut worms, hermit crabs, fish, chitons, bivalves, polychaete worms, sea cucumbers, isopods, and mantis shrimp. It is a shy

Halichoeres prosopeion, Twotone Wrasse, juvenile. Often ships poorly.

Halichoeres prosopeion, Twotone Wrasse, transforming juvenile.

species that will flee or bury in the sand at the first signs of danger. This species is a facultative cleaner.

Captive Care: *Halichoeres poeyi* is not common in the aquarium trade. It is similar in its husbandry requirements to others in the genus (see the Captive Care section for the genus).

Aquarium Size: 75 gal. **Temperature:** 23° to 28°C (74° to 82°F).

Aquarium Suitability Index: 4.

Halichoeres prosopeion (Bleeker, 1853)

Common Name: Twotone Wrasse.

Maximum Length: 13 cm (5.1 in.).

Distribution: Indonesia to Samoa, north to the Ryukus, and south to the Great Barrier Reef.

Biology: The Twotone Wrasse is found at depths ranging from 2 to 40 m (7 to 132 ft.) on lagoon reefs, back barrier reefs, in reef channels, and on fore-reef slopes. It is a solitary species that is usually most prolific in areas with rich hard and/or soft coral growth. I have seen adults of this species chasing congeners in the wild.

Captive Care: *Halichoeres prosopeion* often ships poorly, but once it adjusts after this traumatic process it will usually do quite well in captivity. Large specimens may behave aggressively toward smaller fishes, especially those introduced into a tank after it. It is most likely to display aggression toward closely related species. Although it can be kept in reef aquariums, it is a threat to small snails, ornamental crustaceans such as shrimps and small crabs, and tube worms.

Aquarium Size: 55 gal. **Temperature:** 23° to 28°C (74° to 82°F).

Aquarium Suitability Index: 4.

Remarks: Juvenile *Halichoeres prosopeion* have four black longitu-

Halichoeres prosopeion, Twotone Wrasse, terminal phase male.

dinal stripes, which graudally disappear as they age; the sexes are similar in coloration.

Halichoeres radiatus (Linnaeus, 1758)

Common Name: Pudding Wife Wrasse.

Maximum Length: 51 cm (20 in.).

Distribution: North Carolina and Bermuda, the northeast Gulf of Mexico and to Brazil, and east to St. Paul Rocks.

Biology: The Pudding Wife Wrasse is most prevalent on reef flats and lagoon patch reefs but is also reported from the edge of the fore-reef. It occurs at depths ranging from 2 to 55 m (7 to 182 ft.) over sand and rubble substrate. It is reported to be most common at depths of less than 12 m (40 ft.). This opportunistic carnivore feeds mainly on bivalves, snails, urchins, and crabs, but

Halichoeres radiatus, Pudding Wife Wrasse, juvenile: Caribbean species is very hardy but grows too large and rowdy for most community aquariums.

Halichoeres radiatus, Pudding Wife Wrasse, initial phase, Bonaire.

it also eats serpent stars, hermit crabs, polychaete worms, mantis shrimp, and chitons. *Halichoeres radiatus* is often followed by the Bar Jack (*Caranx ruber*). The jack will swim above and to the side of the wrasse as they move over the seafloor. The jack's rate of food intake apparently increases when it is following this wrasse. The wrasse's feeding activity exposes hidden invertebrates that both fish feed upon. However, the jacks rarely pilfer food from their wrasse associates. Jacks will behave aggressively toward conspecifics that approach their *H. radiatus* feeding partners. Studies have also shown that wrasse feeding rates increase when a jack is present, indicating that this relationship has benefits for both partners. In fact, *H. radiatus* will sometimes initiate contact with these jacks and are never aggressive toward them. It has yet to be explained why their food intake increases when a jack is present. The Pudding Wife Wrasse moves over a large home range.

Captive Care: This is a durable but very large wrasse that will need

Halichoeres radiatus, Pudding Wife Wrasse, initial phase, Cozumel.

Halichoeres richmondi, RIchmond's Wrasse, initial phase fish.

a moderately deep sand bed and plenty of swimming room to thrive. Many people are attracted to the colorful juveniles but are unaware of how large this fish gets. *Halichoeres radiatus* can be somewhat aggressive toward conspecifics and congeners. It will also eat small fishes and a wide range of invertebrate tankmates. It is not suitable for the reef aquarium. What it does not eat, it will flip or knock over when looking for food.
Aquarium Size: 135 gal. **Temperature:** 23° to 28°C (74° to 82°F).
Aquarium Suitability Index: 4.

Halichoeres richmondi Fowler & Bean, 1928
Common Names: Richmond's Wrasse, Chainlined Wrasse.
Maximum Length: 19 cm (7.4 in.).
Distribution: Java and the Philippines, south to the Marshall Islands, and north to the Ryukus.
Biology: Richmond's Wrasse occurs on coastal reefs, in lagoons, and in reef channels, at depths from 2 to at least 12 m (3.3 to 40 ft.). It often is found in habitats with rich stony and/or soft coral growth. While males occur singly, females are sometimes seen in loose groups.
Captive Care: Richmond's Wrasse does not fare well during the shipping process, but if you can acquire a specimen that has been in a dealer's tank for a week or more and it is eating, then your chances of successfully keeping this species long-term is very good. It is an active fish that should be provided with plenty of swimming space.
Aquarium Size: 75 gal. **Temperature:** 23° to 28°C (74° to 82°F).
Aquarium Suitability Index: 4.
Remarks: Richmond's Wrasse is similar to *H. leucurus*. The initial phase color pattern of the two species are difficult to tell apart. In Sumatra and the Andaman Sea, both *H. richmondi* and *H. leucu-*

Halichoeres richmondi, RIchmond's Wrasse, terminal phase male.

rus are replaced by the **Pinksnout Wrasse** (*Halichoeres kallochroma*) (Bleeker, 1853). In the latter species, the male has a pink snout as well as other subtle color differences.

Halichoeres rubricephalus Kuiter & Randall, 1995
Common Name: Redhead Wrasse.
Maximum Length: 10 cm (3.9 in.).
Distribution: Irian Jaya east to Flores and Banggai Islands, Indonesia.
Biology: Where it occurs, the Redhead Wrasse has been found in very specific microhabitats. It occurs on protected inner reefs in areas with rich growths of finely branched corals. It is known from a depth range of 10 to 35 m (33 to 116 ft.).
Captive Care: This beautiful species has started showing up in the aquarium trade, although relatively few are collected. Reports

Halichoeres rubricephalus, Redhead Wrasse, terminal phase male.

Halichoeres scapularis, Zigzag Wrasse, initial phase.

Halichoeres scapularis, Zigzag Wrasse, terminal phase: a fish with personality.

Halichoeres schwartzii, Schwartz's Wrasse, TP: displaying to female.

from aquarists who have kept them suggest that they are similar to most other *Halichoeres* spp. in their husbandry requirements (see the Captive Care section for the genus).

Aquarium Size: 55 gal. **Temperature:** 23° to 28°C (74° to 82°F).

Aquarium Suitability Index: 4.

Remarks: The male *H. rubricephalus* is unmistakable—it is one of the most spectacular wrasses in this genus. The females are somewhat similar to *H. melanurus* and its close relatives.

Halichoeres scapularis (Bennett, 1832)

Common Name: Zigzag Wrasse.

Maximum Length: 20 cm (7.9 in.).

Distribution: Red Sea to Vanuatu, north to southern Japan, and south to the Great Barrier Reef.

Biology: This opportunistic wrasse is found on the edges of coastal reefs, in lagoon seagrass beds and sandy areas, and on reef flats at depths of 1 to 25 m (3.3 to 83 ft.), but is usually found at depths of less than 5 m (17 ft.). This species regularly follows goatfishes and other fishes that disturb the sand bed, pouncing on invertebrates that are flushed from hiding. Although food habitat data is lacking, it probably feeds on a large variety of invertebrates and small fishes.

Captive Care: *Halichoeres scapularis* is an interesting aquarium inhabitant. It has lots of "personality," quickly learning to recognize its keeper as a source of food. It will flip benthic debris and follow tankmates that stir the substrate. This species will eat fireworms, but may also take out ornamental shrimp and crabs. Larger *H. scapularis* are also a potential threat to smaller fish.

Aquarium Size: 75 gal. **Temperature:** 23 to 28°C (74 to 82°F).

Aquarium Suitability Index: 4.

Halichoeres schwartzii (Bleeker, 1849)

Common Name: Schwartz's Wrasse.

Maximum Length: 10 cm (3.9 in.).

Distribution: Flores, Banda Sea, and Bali, Indonesia.

Biology: Schwartz's Wrasse is a resident of shallow water habitats. It is found at depths of 2 to 10 m (7 to 33 ft.) in bays and lagoons and on reef flats. It is found in seagrass beds and over sand and rubble. It typically occurs singly. Males will behave aggressively toward one another. It feeds on small crustaceans by picking them off the sandy bottom.

Captive Care: This is often available as an "assorted" wrasse. It is a durable species whose husbandry requirements are similar to those of congeners. As noted above, males will fight and may pick on females. This species will eat fire worms, but may also take out ornamental shrimp and crabs.

Aquarium Size: 55 gal. **Temperature:** 23 to 28°C (74 to 82°F).

Aquarium Suitability Index: 4.

Remarks: Dussumier's Wrasse (*Halichoeres dussumieri*) (Valenciennes, 1839) is a similar species that occurs throughout the Indian Ocean east to Bali. The **Hong Kong Wrasse** (*Halichoeres exornatus*) (Richardson, 1846) is found around Hong Kong, east to the Philippines, and west to Borneo. Like *H. schwartzii*, it is a resident of shallow, protected habitats. Both of these fishes get larger than *H. schwartzii*, attaining a maximum length of 16 cm (6.3 in.). Due to their size this species needs to be kept in a larger tank. It will be a threat to a larger number of invertebrates.

Halichoeres solorensis (Bleeker, 1853)

Common Name: Solor Wrasse.

Maximum Length: 18 cm (7.1 in.).

Distribution: Flores to West Papua, Indonesia.

Biology: The Solor Wrasse is found at depths of 10 to 15 m (33 to 50 ft.). It occurs around *Acropora* thickets and over sand and rubble bottoms on coastal reefs and in lagoons. Juveniles and females form small, loose groups; adult males occur singly, occasionally visiting female social units and chasing off intruding males.

Captive Care: The male *H. solorensis* is a striking aquarium fish. Its general husbandry requirements are similar to others in the genus. While juveniles and females can be kept together, males will fight. If you want to keep more than one *H. solorensis* in a tank, it should hold 100 gallons or more.

Aquarium Size: 75 gal. **Temperature:** 23° to 28°C (74° to 82°F).

Aquarium Suitability Index: 4.

Halichoeres trimaculatus (Quoy & Gaimard, 1834)

Common Name: Threespot Wrasse.

Maximum Length: 27 cm (10.6 in.).

Halichoeres solorensis, Solor Wrasse, juvenile: note ocelli or eyespots.

Halichoeres solorensis, Solor Wrasse, terminal phase: can become a strikingly beautiful aquarium species. Color-enhancing rations benefit all wrasses.

Distribution: Christmas Island to the Line and Ducie Islands, north to southern Japan, and south to Lord Howe Island.

Biology: The Threespot Wrasse is found over sand, or mixed sand and mud, on reef flats, in lagoons, and on protected coastal reefs at depths from less than 1 to 18 m (3 to 59 ft.). The preferred prey of this species are snails, crabs (including hermit crabs, swimming crabs, galatheid crabs, and xanthid crabs), and amphipods. However, it is also known to feed on chitons, bivalves, fish larvae, invertebrate eggs, polychaete worms, urchins, isopods, shrimp, and algae fronds and filaments. In one study a single specimen also contained hard coral fragments. This species is frequently seen following foraging goatfishes.

Captive Care: This is a large, active species that needs plenty of

Halichoeres trimaculatus, Threespot Wrasse, terminal phase: very active; not reef-safe.

Halichoeres zeylonicus (Bennett, 1833)
Common Names: Goldstripe Wrasse, Sri Lanka Wrasse.
Maximum Length: 15 cm (5.9 in.).
Distribution: Red Sea to northern Bali, north to the Arabian Gulf.
Biology: The Goldstripe Wrasse is found on open sand and rubble areas of outer slopes or flats. It occurs at depths of 11 to over 34 m (36 to 112 ft.). The females occur in small groups, while males are solitary and move about over large territories. Initial phase individuals are often found living amid and making contact with the tentacles of *Macrodactyla doreensis*.
Captive Care: This is a medium-sized member of the genus that will do well in an aquarium with a sand bottom. For more general husbandry information, see the Captive Care section for the genus.
Aquarium Size: 75 gal. **Temperature:** 23° to 28°C (74° to 82°F).
Aquarium Suitability Index: 4.
Remarks: Juvenile specimens sport a yellow longitudinal stripe. It is very similar to Hartzfeld's Wrasse (*H. hartzfeldii*). The colors of the two species differ. **Pelicier's Wrasse (*Halichoeres pelicieri*) Randall & Smith, 1982** is a deep-water species that has been reported only from Mauritius. It has been reported from depths of 20 to 85 m (66 to 281 ft.). This species differs from *H. zeylonicus* in that the males have black on the dorsal fin.

swimming room. Adult specimens should be housed in aquariums of 100 gallons or larger, with ample open space, relatively little aquarium decor and one inch or more of fine sand substrate on the aquarium bottom. Because of its large size and catholic diet, it should not be housed in a reef aquarium.
Aquarium Size: 100 gal. **Temperature:** 23° to 28°C (74° to 82°F).
Aquarium Suitability Index: 4.

Halichoeres trimaculatus, Threespot Wrasse, initial phase, with goatfish.

Halichoeres zeylonicus, Goldstripe Wrasse, terminal phase male.

Hemigymnus fasciatus, Barred Thicklip Wrasse: although attractive and fascinating to watch, these wrasses are not ideal aquarium subjects.

GENUS *HEMIGYMNUS* (THICKLIP WRASSES)

This genus of handsome wrasses is best observed in the wild, rather than in the home aquarium. While they may be housed in an extra-large vessel, they present husbandry challenges that many are not able or willing to take on. That said, the unusual feeding behavior and attractive colors do make it a tempting aquarium inhabitant or underwater photographic subject.

Biology

All three species of this small genus of labrids have large, rubbery lips. The lips are not that pronounced in juveniles, but grow larger as these fishes mature. The thicklip wrasses also have a pair of protruding canine teeth, nodular teeth in the upper jaw, and large pharyngeal teeth. Their specialized dentition, along with their fleshy lips, are important in their acquisition of nutrients. The adults use their lips to literally "scrub" the seafloor. They ingest large quantities of sediment along with various inverte-

brate prey items, then rise up into the water column and then sort the edible from the inedible. As they filter the substrate, a cloud of debris streams from their gill openings—or they spit out the inedible bits and pieces. They do this high in the water column so that they can re-ingest any edible food items they accidentally spit out. Adults ingest a wide range of benthic invertebrates, including lots of hard-shelled invertebrates, using their strong dentition to masticate these armored animals. The juveniles feed most heavily on planktonic crustaceans, which they individually target.

The genus is represented throughout the Indo-Pacific. The adults are active, moving around large sections of reef and fringing rubble flats and slopes. Small juveniles sometimes associate with longspine sea urchins (genus *Diadema*). The young fish often resemble pieces of floating algae as they swim in a twisting motion with their heads down and tails curled. The *Hemigymnus* spp. wrasses are often attacked by a variety of different parasites. A study conducted on *Hemigymnus melapterus* on the Great Barrier Reef showed that this species was a host for 26 parasite species, 6 of which were abundant (a gnathiid isopod, a copepod, a

Hemigymnus fasciatus, Barred Thicklip Wrasse, large male: an active fish that forages over a wide territory to hunt benthic invertebrates.

digenean, and 3 tetraphyllidean cestode larvae). Larger individuals had a higher richness, abundance, and biovolume of parasites, although the density of parasites was higher on smaller wrasses. The ectoparasite load on Blackedge Thicklip Wrasses increases significantly when they sleep in reef crevices at night. Grutter and Hendrikz (1999) reported that the number of gnathiid isopods increased by 50% overnight. The nocturnal burying behavior of some labrids may be an adaptation to reduce parasite infestation, and not only a tactic to hide from predators while they slumber. In one study, wild *H. melapterus* had an average of 13 to 21 isopods per adult fish. Gnathiid larvae feed on blood and can become engorged in as little as 30 minutes after attaching to a host. Studies have shown that an excessive load of isopods can significantly reduce the blood volume in *Hemigymnus melapterus*. These parasites are highly mobile and often drop off the host to refuge and molt soon after they are satiated with the host's blood. Because the *Hemigymnus* is so often targeted by external parasites, it is a favorite client of cleaner wrasses (*Labroides* spp.).

These wrasses are protogynous hermaphrodites. They have been reported to migrate to specific spawning sites and reproduce in groups.

Captive Care

The genus *Hemigymnus* is one of those groups of reef fishes that has a questionable aquarium reputation. If you look at some of the books written on marine fishes over the last several decades, you will see these wrasses variously described as "easy to keep," "more difficult to maintain," "difficult to feed," a fish that "often wastes away," and "excellent aquarium fish when young." It seems that all these descriptions can be correct, depending on the age of the specimen in question and the husbandry practices of the aquarist.

The young *Hemigymnus* spp. will usually take a variety of aquarium foods, such as live brine shrimp, mysid shrimp, chopped seafood, and frozen preparations. The key to success with these fishes is to feed them often. In fact, most of them perish because of a lack of food. They need to be fed small portions, as often as four or five times a day—even more often, if possible.

If they are kept in a tank with a productive inline refugium, you will not have to add food as often. But make sure you keep a close eye on the fishes' girths. If they begin to look thin, feed them more. You cannot count on live substrate to keep juvenile *Hemigymnus* well fed, as they will quickly demolish microinvertebrate populations. However, the small animals associated with live substrate can be a helpful nutrient source, at least initially. Adding an adult thicklip wrasse to your aquarium is a more challenging proposition. The larger *Hemigymnus* are less likely to take aquarium foods, and live food will often be needed to initiate feeding in adults.

Another thing to consider before acquiring a thicklip wrasse is aquarium size. The *Hemigymnus* spp. get large (45 cm [18 in.] or longer) and are active, so they will outgrow most home aquariums. An aquarium of 240 gallons or larger is required to house a full-grown adult. In some cases, tanks as small as 180 gallons may suffice if the fish grows up in captivity. The tank should also have plenty of swimming room—don't pack it with life rock. The thicklip wrasse does not bury in the substrate, so a sand bed is not necessary.

As mentioned above, these fishes often suffer from infestations of ectoparasites, including gnathiid isopods and flukes (e.g., *Benedenia* sp.). It is a good idea to give a newly acquired *Hemigymnus* a formalin bath or freshwater dip to help rid it of these noxious hitchhikers. A Bluestreak Cleaner Wrasse (e.g., *Labroides dimidiatus*) or cleaner shrimps (e.g., *Periclimenes*) can also be used to help control or get rid of isopod larvae and flukes. Grutter et al. (2002) demonstrated that small *H. melapterus* (under 11.5 cm [4.5 in.] in length) had 100 times more of the monogenetic trematodes, *Benedenia lolo*, when held in captivity than individuals just taken from the wild had. Larger captive individuals had about 15 times more monogeans than similarly sized, freshly caught individuals. The researchers concluded that small fish have a lower resistance to these parasites and thus are more susceptible to infection by the motile, infectious stage.

How about compatibility? When it comes to fish tankmates, the *Hemigymnus* are not usually aggressive toward nonrelated heterospecifics. However, they will quarrel with one another and with congeners; therefore, only one *Hemigymnus* should be kept in a tank. On rare occasions, a resident thicklip wrasse may chase a newly added fish (e.g., another wrasse), but this is the exception, not the rule.

These wrasses can cause big problems for invertebrates. As you will see from the list of food items they consume in the species accounts below, the *Hemigymnus* spp. will eat a variety of motile invertebrates. In the reef tank, they can perform some useful functions. When they feed on sand-dwelling prey, they will take

Hemigymnus fasciatus, Barred Thicklip Wrasse, juvenile.

Hemigymnus fasciatus, Barred Thicklip Wrasse, initial phase.

mouthfuls of substrate and during the sorting process produce large clouds of sediment. In the aquarium, this will help keep the substrate free of detritus, putting sediment into suspension, where it can be removed by external filters and may help to feed certain soft corals. But the fish's sand-sifting activities may cover corals with sediment, which can be difficult for some species to shed.

Thicklip Wrasse Species

Hemigymnus fasciatus (Bloch, 1792)
Common Name: Barred Thicklip Wrasse.
Maximum Length: 80 cm (31.5 in).
Distribution: Red Sea and East Africa east to Line and Ducie Is-

Hemigymnus melapterus, Blackeye Thicklip Wrasse, juvenile.

Hemigymnus melapterus, Blackeye Thicklip Wrasse, adult male.

seen in areas of mixed rubble, sand, and small coral colonies. Juveniles feed most on demersal, planktonic crustaceans, while adults prey on crustaceans, polychaete worms, brittle stars, sea urchins, mollusks, and forams. Adults are regularly seen hunting over mixed sand-rubble substrate. *Hemigymnus fasciatus* usually occurs singly, but occasionally forms loose assemblages. During courtship and spawning, the colors of the male intensify.

Captive Care: Although the adult *H. fasciatus* is spectacular, it is not a great aquarium fish. First, it is not a good shipper. Your chances of success will increase if you acquire a juvenile and keep it in a tank with a productive refugium. Tiny juveniles may have a more difficult time adjusting than young fish over 3 cm (1.5 in.) in length, since they may be more difficult to feed. These fish need to eat five or more times a day. The juvenile Barred Thicklip will accept a variety of meaty foods, but adults are likely to ignore all but live foods. This fish will fight with conspecifics and congeners. It usually ignores other fish tankmates.

Aquarium Size: 240 gal. **Temperature:** 23° to 28°C (74° to 82°F).
Aquarium Suitability Index: 2–3.
Remarks: The **Red Sea Thicklip Wrasse** (*Hemigymnus sexfasciatus*) (**Rüppell, 1835**) is endemic to the Red Sea. It reaches a length of 45 cm (17.7 in.) and is a resident of reef faces and slopes, usually over rubble bottoms. Juveniles are black with white bars on the body, while adults have more white on the head and the bars are wider.

Hemigymnus melapterus (Bloch, 1791)
Common Names: Blackeye Thicklip Wrasse, Half-and-Half Wrasse.
Maximum Length: 90 cm (35 in).
Distribution: Red Sea east to the Society Islands, north to they Ryukus, and south to southeastern Australia and Lord Howe Island.
Biology: This wrasse is found in a variety of different reef habitats, from fringing reefs and lagoon patch reefs to fore-reef faces and slopes. It has been reported at depths of 1 to at least 30 m (3.3 to 98 ft.). Juvenile *H. melapterus* are most often found in shallow water habitats (often among branching stony corals), while adults are more often found in deep water over mixed sand and rubble with scattered coral colonies. This fish is also found in lagoon or reef flat seagrass meadows. The young *H. melapterus* feeds mainly on planktonic crustaceans that live near the seafloor. They feed more on amphipods, copepods, small crabs, tanaids, mantis shrimps, forams, cumaceans, polychaetes, invertebrate eggs, algae (which is probably ingested incidentally), mysids, sponges, and sand. As they grow larger, they ingest more snails, which they crush with their large pharyngeal teeth, as well as larger crabs,

lands, north to southern Japan, and south to southeastern Australia, Lord Howe Island, and Rapa Island.
Biology: The Barred Thicklip Wrasse is found on coastal fringing reefs, reef flats, outer reef faces, and reef slopes at depths of 1 to 40 m (3.3 to 132 ft.). Juveniles are more reclusive than adults and often take shelter in ramose stony corals. Adults are more often

Hemigymnus melapterus, Blackeye Thicklip Wrasse, displaying male: this species feeds on a wide assortment of motile invertebrates and gets very large.

decapod shrimps, and mantis shrimps. The adults also eat chitons, hermit crabs, serpent stars, sea urchins, and fish. This is a solitary species. It is reported to form spawning aggregations.

Captive Care: *Hemigymnus melapterus* is a very large, active fish that will need a huge aquarium to live out its life span—that is, if you are able to keep it until it reaches adulthood. Most juveniles die in a relatively short time after being placed in the aquarium. Even though this species feeds on a wide range of prey items, it is often difficult for aquarists to meet its dietary needs. This may have more to do with quantity than with quality. In the wild, these fish continually "browse" on the many invertebrates that make up its diet. In the aquarium, they are lucky to have access to a limited food supply two or three times a day. *Hemigymnus melapterus* will do better in a tank with live rock, although it will not take them long to decimate natural prey stocks in a small tank. Few aquarists would want to throw this wrasse in a reef aquarium because of its catholic diet, which includes most varieties of motile invertebrates. It is best to keep one per tank. This wrasse is rarely aggressive toward nonrelated tankmates. This species also hosts numerous ectoparasites (see biology in general genus account).

Aquarium Size: 240 gal. **Temperature:** 23° to 28°C (74° to 82°F).

Aquarium Suitability Index: 2–3.

Remarks: The juvenile/adolescent and adult color patterns of *H. melapterus* are very different. The young fish are bicolored: dark posteriorly, white anteriorly. Individuals less than 8 cm (3.1 in.) in size have a yellow tail. Adults have a color pattern on the head consisting of blue and pink markings.

Hologymnosus doliatus, Candycane Wrasse, terminal phase: the business end of a voracious predator that hunts crustaceans and small fishes.

GENUS *HOLOGYMNOSUS* (RING WRASSES)

The genus *Hologymnosus* contains just four described species, all residents of the Indo-Pacific. Two species are not uncommon in the marine aquarium trade, and the Candycane Wrasse or Pastel Ring Wrasse (*Hologymnosus doliatus*) can often be found in aquarium stores. Altough very interesting to watch, these wrasses are not suitable for every aquarium venue. They are large and active and require a fairly strict bill of fare.

The *Hologymnosus* spp. are torpedo-shaped, with long snouts and relatively large jaws. Unlike some of their cousins, these wrasses have poorly developed pharyngeal teeth and typically feed on prey items they can swallow whole. However, that does not stop them from feeding on a wide array of invertebrates and fishes. The various species have been reported to prey on polychaete worms, snails, crustaceans (including shrimp, crabs, and mantis shrimp), brittle stars, and small fishes. They are highly opportunistic. I have seen them following large Day Octopuses (*Octopus cyaneus*) as these cephalopods hunted among rocks or coral heads. When prey items were flushed and missed by a hunting octopus, the Ring Wrasse (*Hologymnosus annulatus*) would pounce on them. For the same reason, they will also follow divers as they move over the substrate.

These wrasses are diandric, protogynous hermaphrodites. Juveniles of some species will form small groups and usually do not venture far from the substrate. Initial phase fishes form loose aggregations, while terminal phase individuals are solitary and territorial. The *Hologymnosus* spp. bury in the substrate at night or when threatened. The ring wrasses are so named because the two common species have ringlike stripes on the body in the initial and terminal color phases.

Captive Care

These large predatory wrasses will readily acclimate to an extra-large aquarium. Juveniles typically ship better and make the transition to captivity more readily than adults. It is not uncommon for these fishes to damage the end of their snouts and lower jaws by rubbing against the shipping bag and they sometimes perish in transit. One common problem with these wrasses is that they will launch themselves out of an open tank if harassed or startled.

When initially introduced to the aquarium, ring wrasses may hide (buried in the substrate) for several days before coming out to search for food. They will eat any fish tankmates that can be swallowed whole. They will also make short work of ornamental shrimps and small crabs, which they render into bite-sized morsels by bashing them against rocks or coral. Snails are not immune to *Hologymnosus* attacks, either. I have seen ring wrasses knock these invertebrates off the glass and wrest the foot and organs from their shells. They will also flip pieces of rubble over with their mouths when searching for prey. They may disturb smaller pieces of live coral when hunting in this manner.

Ring Wrasse Species

Hologymnosus annulatus (Lacepède, 1801)
Common Name: Ring Wrasse.
Maximum Length: 40 cm (15.7 in.).
Distribution: Red Sea and East Africa east to Pitcairn Island and French Polynesia, north to southern Japan, and south to southeast Australia.
Biology: The Ring Wrasse is a resident of coastal reefs and outer reef slopes at depths of 8 to 40 m (26 to 132 ft.). Juveniles form small groups, while adults are usually solitary. This species feeds principally on small fishes, but occasionally eats shrimps and small crabs. It has been suggested that the juvenile *H. annulatus* may mimic the Striped Blanquillo (*Malacanthus latovittatus*). The latter species may resemble the Bluestreak Cleaner Wrasse (*Labroides dimidiatus*) to reduce the likelihood it will be eaten by piscivores. It may be that young *H. annulatus* benefit in the same way. Small specimens bury under the sand.
Captive Care: See the notes for Captive Care above.
Aquarium Size: 180 gal. **Temperature:** 23° to 28°C (74° to 82°F).
Aquarium Suitability Index: 4.
Remarks: Juveniles are black or dark brown with yellow stripes on the back, while initial phase individuals, which can be either male or female, are brown with dark brown body bars and white caudal fin margins. Terminal phase individuals, which are always male, are green to blue-green, with purplish red body bars.

Hologymnosus doliatus (Lacepède, 1801)
Common Names: Candycane Wrasse, Pastel Ring Wrasse, Longface Wrasse.
Maximum Length: 38 cm (15 in.).

Hologymnosus annulatus, Ring Wrasse, juvenile: resembles cleaner wrasse.

Hologymnosus annulatus, Ring Wrasse, adult: needs a large aquarium.

Distribution: East Africa to Samoa, east to the Line Islands, north to southern Japan, and south to southeast Australia.
Biology: This wrasse is found on fringing reefs, in lagoons, on rubble reef flats, and on fore-reef slopes, over sand, rubble, and coral. It occurs in the shallow waters of the surge zone to depths of at least 30 m (98 ft.). The Candycane Wrasse feeds on small fishes and crustaceans, including shrimp, crabs, and mantis shrimp. They also eat brittle stars and polychaete worms, but these are not an important part of their diet. Juveniles are often seen in small groups and usually do not venture far from the substrate. Initial phase individuals will form loose aggregations, sometimes associating with foraging goatfish or other members of the genus. Terminal males are usually solitary and territorial. They swim high into the water column and sometimes associate with hunting octopuses or grubbing goatfishes.

Hologymnosus doliatus, Candycane Wrasse, juvenile specimen.

Hologymnosus doliatus, Candycane Wrasse, adolescent coloration.

Hologymnosus doliatus, Candycane Wrasse, initial phase.

Hologymnosus doliatus, Candycane Wrasse, terminal phase male.

Captive Care: Juvenile Candycane Wrasses are regularly seen in the aquarium trade. They are durable, attractively marked, and interesting to watch. They can be kept in small groups (three to five individuals) in tanks that are 135 gallons or larger, but they will eventually outgrow a tank of this size. All specimens should be introduced simultaneously. *Hologymnosus doliatus* will eat snails and any fish or ornamental shrimps small enough to fit into its mouth. They bury at night; therefore, a fine coral sand or live sand should be used as substrate.

Aquarium Size: 180 gal. **Temperature:** 23° to 28°C (74° to 82°F).

Aquarium Suitability Index: 4.

Remarks: Juvenile *H. doliatus* are white with three red stripes. Those between 7.5 and 10 cm (2.9 and 3.9 in.) in length change into the initial phase, which is pale green, blue, or pink overall with 20 to 23 orange-brown or yellowish brown bars. Terminal phase males are usually larger than 22 cm (8.7 in.). The initial phase of the **Redback Ring Wrasse (*Hologymnosus rhodonotus*) Randall & Yamakawa, 1988** has three or four red stripes along the body. It ranges from the Timor Sea, Indonesia, to the Philippines and southwestern Japan. This fish commonly occurs over macroalgae beds at depths of 15 to 40 m (50 to 132 ft.). It is a fascinating aquarium resident that will turn rubble with its snout when searching for food.

Hologymnosus rhodonotus, Redback Ring Wrasse: makes a personable pet.

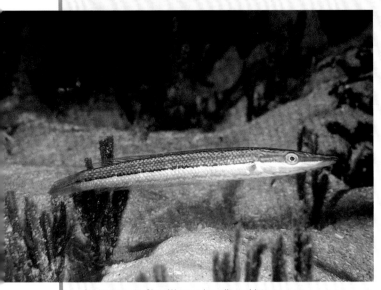

Cheilio inermis, Cigar Wrasse, juvenile amidst seagrass.

Cheilio inermis, Cigar Wrasse, adult, yellow phase specimen.

Genus *Cheilio*
(The Cigar Wrasses)

Cheilio inermis (Forsskål, 1775)

Common Name: Cigar Wrasse.

Maximum Length: 50 cm (19.7 in.).

Distribution: Red Sea to the Hawaiian Islands and Easter Island.

Biology: The Cigar Wrasse is most common in seagrass and macroalgae beds but also occurs over reef pavement or sand substrates. It occurs in lagoons, reef flats, and on outer reef faces and slopes at depths of less than 1 to 30 m (3.3. to 98 ft.). I have observed this species hunting by riding and following fishes that disturb the substrate. For example, I observed an adult *C. inermis* following a foraging Snowflake Moray (*Echidna nebulosa*). It will also engage in "hunting by riding" on the reef flat, where it positions itself alongside or just above the Sohal Surgeonfish (*Acanthurus sohal*), which it uses as a moving blind to get close to prey. Other predators (e.g., Yellowsaddle Goatfish, *Parupeneus cyclostomus*) will also shadow this labrid as it hunts.

Captive Care: *Cheilio inermis* is a durable aquarium fish. The juveniles are especially malleable, readily acclimating to the captive environment. They are not overly shy and will spend a considerable amount of time swimming about in the open. If harassed by aggressive tankmates, however, they will hide all the time. At night, and when threatened, they bury under the substrate. The Cigar Wrasse will happily eat chopped seafood, mysid shrimp, and frozen preparations (krill, reef plankton, carnivore rations). While the yellow color form is the most highly sought after, it is not always easy to find, and is also likely to lose its brilliance after it has been in the aquarium for a while. This fish is prone to jumping from an open aquarium.

Aquarium Size: 200 gal. **Temperature:** 23° to 28°C (74° to 82°F).

Aquarium Suitability Index: 4.

Remarks: This wrasse could easily be mistaken for one of its elongate cousins in the genus *Hologymnosus*. The initial phase individuals are green with a dark stripe down the middle of the flank. The juvenile and initial phase fish is lime green or brown above the stripe, and silvery gray below it. It is capable of instantaneous color change, which occurs when its mood changes (e.g., it is startled), at night, or when it moves from one microhabitat to another. The terminal phase is darker overall, lacking the mid-lateral stripe, with pink, orange, yellow, black, or white blotches behind the pectoral fin. There is also a xanthic (gold) color phase. It is a large labrid reaching a length of 50 cm [19.7 in.].

TRIBE LABRICHTHYINI (CLEANER WRASSES)

Left: A pair of Bluestriped Cleaner Wrasses, *Labroides dimidiatus*, busily grooming a Longfin or Tiera Batfish, *Platax tiera*.
Above: *Balistoides viridescens*, Titan Triggerfish, having its gill preened by obligate cleaner wrasse, *Labroides dimidiatus*, while a juvenile *Bodianus bimaculatus* acts as a facultative cleaner on its flanks.

Not only do the labrids exhibit considerable variation in size, shape, and coloration, they also employ a number of different feeding strategies. For example, some are microcarnivores that feed on shelled protozoa, while others prey on large invertebrate prey like sea stars and sea urchins. Some of the most specialized of the microcarnivores feed on ectoparasites that live on their piscine neighbors. Wrasses, and other fish species that engage in this behavior, are known as "cleaners." The most specialized of the ectoparasite feeding wrasses belong to the tribe Labrichthyini and the genus *Labroides* (the Cleaner Wrasses). These wrasses feed almost exclusively on crustacean parasites, as well as slime and scales removed from their clients. There are other members of the tribe that clean extensively only when young or that are part-time cleaners as either juveniles or adults.

Unfortunately, most cleaner wrasses seldom find enough to eat in an aquarium setting and typically waste away over a period of weeks or months. For this reason alone, most conscientious aquarium keepers resist the temptation to buy these fishes when they are available.

Additionally, these wrasses perform an important service in

Diproctacanthus xanthurus, Wandering Cleaner Wrasse: unlike many cleaners, this species does not set up a "cleaning station," but goes in search of clients.

the reef communities where they are found, and collecting them can impact the healthy balance of a local area that loses its parasite-picking species. Informed, ethical collectors are increasingly leaving the cleaner wrasses on the reef and discouraging their capure and sale. Additionally, some species described in this section are cleaners as juveniles but mature to prey primarily on live coral polyps, making less than desirable for the reef aquarium.

GENUS DIPROCTACANTHUS (WANDERING CLEANER WRASSE)

The Cleaner Wrasses vary somewhat in their feeding strategies. Some of the best known of this group set up defined cleaning stations that are visited by their parasitized clients. There are others that "clean on the go." Such is the case with the only species

in the genus *Diproctacanthus*, the **Wandering Cleaner Wrasse** (***D. xanthurus***) (**Bleeker, 1856**). As the common name implies, this species does not set up permanent cleaning stations, but moves about its home range, cleaning fishes that it encounters. Preliminary evidence suggests it may clean more territorial species, like damselfishes, that do not leave their defended areas to visit stationary cleaners. As *D. xanthurus* gets larger, it feeds more on stony coral polyps and their mucus.

The young *D. xanthurus* is black with white stripes along the sides, a color pattern seen in some of the other cleaner species, like certain *Labropsis* spp. and the Oneline Wrasse (*Labrichthys unilineatus*). This color pattern may signal to potential predators that it is a cleaner. It is not totally immune to becoming a hungry piscivore's meal. For example, I once observed a Graceful Lizardfish (*Saurida gracilis*) capture and ingest an adult individual. It resides on coastal fringing reefs, in shallow lagoons, and on protected outer reef faces at depths of 3 to 25 m (7 to 83 ft.). As a result of its scleractinian diet, it is typically found in areas with rich stony coral growth. It ranges from Java and the Philippines east to Vanuatu and south to the Great Barrier Reef. This wrasse attains a length of 8 cm (3.1 in.).

Captive Care

The Wandering Cleaner Wrasse, like most in this tribe, is not well suited to captivity. An occasional individual may take normal aquarium foods, but most starve to death unless natural foods (e.g., live stony corals) are provided. If they are in a large enough tank, with a substantial fish population, they may acquire enough food by "grazing" on the slime of their piscine tankmates. They will pick at small-polyped stony corals and may nip at clam mantles (this is not uncommon in the related *Labroides* spp.).

If you are inclined to attempt to keep this fish, only one should be kept per tank, as they will fight. They may also quarrel with other "cleaner" wrasses. As mentioned above, they do occasionally fall prey to piscivores, especially in the aquarium.

Therefore, it is best not to house them with morays, lizardfishes, frogfishes, and groupers. They are sometimes the target of territorial species like dottybacks, large damsels, and triggerfishes as well. If you want to keep *D. xanthurus* with predators, add it to the tank first.

GENUS *LABRICHTHYS* (TUBELIP WRASSE)

While many species have been placed in this genera in the past, currently it is considered to be monotypic. The single species, the **Tubelip** or **Oneline Wrasse** (*Labrichthys unilineatus*) (Guichenot, 1847), is a wide-ranging fish that is found from the east African coast east to Samoa, north to southern Japan, and south to tropical Australia. The juvenile phase of this species is dark brown to black with a white median stripe from the tail to the head. The

Proof that cleaner wrasses are not immune to predation: *Diproctacanthus xanthurus*, Wandering Cleaner Wrasse, being swallowed by a lizardfish.

Labrichthys unilineatus, Tubelip or Oneline Wrasse: juveniles may clean.

Labrichthys unilineatus, Tubelip or Oneline Wrasse, adult male.

This species is found on coastal fringing reefs, in lagoons, and on semiprotected outer reefs. It is typically associated with rich, branching stony coral growth. Both juveniles and adults feed almost exclusively on small-polyped stony corals and their mucus, in particular members of the genus *Acropora*. They incidentally ingest foraminiferans, invertebrate eggs, and tiny gastropods. Juveniles have been reported to clean other fishes but do so less frequently than others in the tribe.

McIlwain and Jones (1997) studied the predator/prey relationship between this labrid and scleractinian corals. They found that juveniles, and to a lesser degree female *Labrichthys unilineatus*, were usually found around patches of *Acropora nobilis* and *A. elseyi*. The males are more wide-ranging, with their territories being dominated by *Montipora* spp. and *Acropora hyacinthus*. The juveniles are more particular about the corals they feed on, usually choosing corals that are found at lower densities. Adult males are less selective, feeding on the most readily available *Acropora* spp. in their territories. McIlwain and Jones also found that damaged coral tissue was an important component of the adult *L. unilineatus* diet. When a coral colony was disturbed, the feeding rate of male *L. unilineatus* increased by 50%. They concluded that "the reason for selection of damaged corals is unknown but a loss of nematocysts or release of mucous or chemical attractants may be involved."

This species is a protogynous hermaphrodite. It is a pelagic spawner, with the larval phase lasting from 17 to 24 days.

Captive Care

This species is not common in aquarium stores. Juveniles are sometimes sold as "assorted wrasses." Like the others in the tribe that feed on corals as adults, they will be unwanted residents in the stony coral tank. While juveniles may behave themselves with scleractinians, adults will feed on both small-polyped and large-polyped corals. They are also not likely to do well in captivity if these foods are not present.

If you are willing to provide an adult Tubelip Wrasse with a proper diet, you can keep one, but you should be aware that both juveniles and adults will fight with each other. You can keep a juvenile with an adult, but fighting may break out as the younger fish matures. Another possibility is that the juvenile will mature into a female, while the dominant adult will develop male sexual organs. In this case, the two fish should get along if they have plenty of space.

stripe disappears when the juveniles reach an approximate length of 6.5 cm (2.6 in.). Initial and terminal phase individuals are very similar in color, but the former has yellow lips and the latter has a yellow patch behind the pectoral fin. Both are dark green to brown with blue lines and reticulations on the head and body. It is a fairly large species, attaining a maximum length of 17.5 cm (6.9 in.).

GENUS *LABROIDES* (CLEANER WRASSES)

The first record of a wrasse in the genus *Labroides* cleaning another fish appeared in the literature rather belatedly, in 1940. In this reference, the author, L. F. de Beaufort, stated, "In the aquarium of Amsterdam I observed that *Labroides dimidiatus* cleans the surrounding of the mouth and the gill openings of large fishes...." It was nine years later when the famous ichthyologist J. L. B. Smith said of the Bluestreak Cleaner Wrasse (*L. dimidiatus*), "Feeds on minute organisms on rocks and has been observed to nibble over the mouth parts and gill cover of large rock-cods [groupers]." It was not until 1955 that a more detailed description of *Labroides* cleaning behavior appeared in a paper written by Dr. John Randall, who did a taxonomic revision of the genus

in 1958. Since those original descriptions of the symbiosis that occurs between cleaner wrasses and other fish clients, scores of papers have been written about this amazing relationship. In this section, I have tried to synthesize all that is currently known about the biology and behavior of these unusual fishes. If you are looking for more detailed information regarding their biology, check out the exhaustive list of reference material provided at the end of the book.

Cleaning Behavior

The cleaner wrasse genus *Labroides* comprises five very distinguishable species. Unlike their relatives in the tribe Labrichthyini, the members of this genus rely almost entirely on cleaning to obtain nutrients as both juveniles and adults. Cleaning behavior is defined as a mutualistic relationship that exists between certain parasite-picking fishes and their piscine neighbors (the

Juvenile Bluestriped Cleaner Wrasse, *Labroides dimidiatus*, picks at a Kikado Moray Eel, *Gymnothorax kikado*: morays are heavily coated in slime and cleaners will feed on this nutrient-rich mucus, sometimes in preference to parasites. They also pick at the edges of wounds.

client or host species). So what are the benefits to the cleaner and the client?

The most important prey of the *Labroides* spp. are crustacean ectoparasites that attach to the fish and feed on their body fluids and tissue—namely, gnathiid isopod larvae and calagoid, lernaeid, and lichomolgid copepods. The importance of each of these two groups varies from one location to the other. In locations where isopods are the most common parasite on reef fishes, adult *Labroides* selectively feed on larger gnathiids. Of secondary importance in the cleaner wrasse's diet are parasitic flatworms (e.g., *Benedenia* spp.). I should point out that flatworms may be more important in cleaner diets than they are currently thought

Labroides bicolor, Bicolor Cleaner Wrasse (juvenile), grooming a Regal Angelfish, *Pygoplites diacanthus*, this is a mobile cleaner that often services fishes that hide in caves and under overhangs, like this angel species.

to be. Because they are soft-bodied and hence digested more rapidly than hard-bodied crustaceans, they would be more difficult to find in cleaner guts. All of these ectoparasites can certainly have an impact on the fitness of their host. Therefore, having them removed by a cleaner would have definite benefits.

Cleaner wrasses will also feed on the infected and dead tissue of an injured client. A study on Caribbean cleaner gobies (genus *Gobiosoma*) indicates that injured fishes may seek out cleaners to aid in wound healing. In this study, it was shown that wounded fishes, namely the Blue Tang (*Acanthurus coeruleus*), spent more time seeking out cleaner services than healthy conspecifics did. These injuries were reported to heal quickly because the gobies kept the wounds free of infected tissue. Although this same quantitative data does not exist for *Labroides*-client interactions, there is no doubt the cleaning services of the *Labroides* might fulfill a similar function.

What is the benefit to the cleaner wrasses? There are hundreds of small fishes, like the *Labroides*, that feed on small crustacean prey, but because these wrasses are able to utilize this highly specialized food resource, there is less competition with their neighbors.

Mucophagy

This is where a confounding element enters this otherwise nice, simple story. Not only do the *Labroides* prey on ectoparasites, they also feed heavily on the scales and mucus of their clients. Consider the Hawaiian Cleaner Wrasse (*Labroides phithirophagus*). This species can ingest up to 2 ml (.07 oz.) of host mucus during an hour of cleaning. That is a lot of slime for such a small fish!

Food preference studies have indicated that cleaners prefer slime over ectoparasites. In one such study, captive *L. dimidiatus* were trained to take mashed prawns and fish flakes from Plexiglass plates. They were then offered a choice of parrotfish mucus, monogenean flatworms, parasitic gnathiid isopod larvae, and flour glue (the control) on the plates, in equal amounts. The wrasses fed most heavily on mucus and monogeneans, while gnathiids were eaten only slightly more than the control. These findings are very interesting when you consider that gnathiid isopods are reported to be the most important component in the diet of this population of Bluestreak Cleaner Wrasse. (They make up 85% of the diet of adult *L. dimidiatus* from Lizard Island.)

The amount of mucus consumed varies between the *Labroides* spp. and from one geographical area to the next. In part, mucus ingestion is a function of parasite abundance. In locations where crustacean ectoparasites are not as common, clients spend less time posing, and cleaners do more inspecting and take more bites and "swipes" at their clients. "Swiping" is when the *Labroi-*

Defying the usual rules predator and prey, cleaner wrasses routinely groom around and even within the mouths of piscine neighbors, even large piscivores that normally eat other fish.

des swims against the side of the client with its jaws open, a behavior thought to be associated with mucus ingestion.

Cleaner wrasses tend to ingest more mucus from fish that produce it in copious amounts. For example, at Heron Island, Great Barrier Reef, 7 of the 10 species most often subjected to swiping behavior were wrasses and parrotfishes—species known to produce heavy mucus coatings. There are also interspecific differences in the quality (e.g., caloric value) of client mucus. For example, parrotfish mucus is thought to be more nutrient-rich than surgeonfish mucus. These factors apparently have some role in determining which fish a cleaner wrasse selects to clean (e.g., parrotfishes over surgeonfishes) or whether the cleaner invests its time and energy ingesting mucus or searching for parasites on a particular client.

The act of feeding on another fish's slime is known as "mucophagy," and is considered to be a form of parasitism. Fish mucus is rich in nutrients, like nitrogen and carbon. It is a valuable food resource, to be sure. But by removing this protective mucus,

the cleaner wrasses may render their clients more susceptible to bacterial or protozoan infections. Mucus also facilitates swimming by reducing drag as the fish moves through the water; removing it may increase the fish's energy expenditure. It would seem that if a cleaner engaged in too much mucus feeding and harmed its clients, there would be selective pressure against frequenting cleaning stations, or at least against visiting those cleaners that included more mucus than parasites in their diets.

Cleaning Strategies

The foraging strategies of cleaner wrasses vary somewhat. Species like the Bluestreak Cleaner Wrasse maintain a specific site, which clients visit when in need of cleaning. Their cleaning stations are often on or near a conspicuous coral head or reef promontory that can be easily located by clients. In contrast to *L. dimidiatus*, the adult Bicolor Cleaner Wrasse (*Labroides bicolor*) moves over a large home range searching out potential hosts. Studies conducted in French Polynesia demonstrated that while there is some overlap in the types of clients these two species service, their most important clients differ significantly. The three most frequently cleaned clients of *L. bicolor* were Hardwick's Wrasse (*Thalassoma hardwicke*), the Yellow Longnose Butterflyfish (*Forcipiger flavissimus*), and the Floral Maori Wrasse (*Cheilinus trilobatus*), while the three most popular piscine clients of *L. dimidiatus* were the Pinktailed Triggerfish (*Melichthys vidua*), the Green Bird Wrasse (*Gomphosus varius*), and the Vagabond Butterflyfish (*Chaetodon vagabundus*). Juveniles of both species maintain relatively small territories that are often formed under ledges or in caves.

TABLE 1.	
Bluestreak Cleaner Wrasse (*Labroides dimidiatus*) Stats from Great Barrier Reef	
The *Labroides* spp. spend a large portion of the daylight hours inspecting and ingesting parasites, as you can see from the table below (adapted from Grutter, 1996).	
Amount of time active each day	12.65 hours
Mean duration of host inspection per day	256 minutes
Estimated number of fish inspected per day	2297 fish
Diet	99.7% gnathiid isopods
Number of parasites eaten per minute	4.8 parasites
Number of parasites eaten per day	1,218 parasites
Number of parasites removed per inspection	0.5 parasites
Number of bites taken for every parasite eaten	6 bites
Time required for food to pass through the gut	3.7 hours
Percent of total body weight consumed per day	7%

Soliciting by Cleaner and Host

Cleaner wrasses actively solicit business by exhibiting conspicuous swimming displays. These displays differ somewhat between the various species. The Bluestreak Cleaner Wrasse will swim in a circle with the tail flared and lifted slightly. This is known as the "undulating dance display." It has been reported that the intensity of this display is greater when the cleaner is attempting to attract a more desirable client.

When a fish desires the attention of a cleaner wrasse, it may adopt a specific pose. For example, some parrotfishes hang motionless in the water column and adopt a heads-up posture. Other piscine clients may perform a headstand as they are inspected by a cleaner. Most species will raise their fins, but some also open their mouths or flare their gill covers in order to give the cleaner access to these chambers. Clients, even piscivorous species, will allow the cleaner to enter their gill cavities and mouths to rid them of irritating hitchhikers. Studies have shown that client species that engage in posing are more likely to be cleaned and will be inspected for longer than those species that do not. When a host fish wants to terminate the cleaning behavior it will perform specific body, fin, or mouth movements, just swim away, or chase the cleaner. Chasing often occurs after the client "jolts" (a negative response thought to be associated with the cleaner picking mucus or scales from the client).

Some host species will also facilitate cleaning by changing color. For example, when being inspected by a cleaner wrasse, the Sleek Unicornfish (*Naso hexacanthus*) changes from a dark brown to light blue. Color changes may serve to advertise that the client wants to be serviced, and also may make the ectoparasites more conspicuous to the cleaner.

Tactile Stimulation, Cleaner Manipulation, and Annoying Irritation

One proximate cause for fishes to seek out cleaners is the tactile stimulation the wrasses provide; you might say it's analogous to a back rub or foot massage. The cleaner wrasse gently drags its

This goatfish has adopted a dark red coloration while being cleaned, possibly to make any ecotoparasites more visible to the wrasse.

pelvic fins over the client's body, especially the dorsal surface, or gently rubs against the client's belly with its dorsal fin. This behavior, sometimes referred to as "stabilizing the host," may serve several different functions. Bshary and Würth (2003) state that this behavior is important for social manipulation, preconflict management, and reconciliation. Let's look at each of these in detail.

• **Social manipulation.** *Labroides* use tactile stimulation, along with swimming displays, to entice clients into being cleaned, especially when attempting to lure a fish that is moving past a cleaning station. It is not uncommon for a cleaner to intercept passing fish and get them to stop for inspection by stabilizing them with pelvic fin contact, giving the wrasse a feeding opportunity. The cleaner also uses this positive reinforcement to influence how long the client remains at the cleaning station.

• **Preconflict management.** Studies indicate that *L. dimidiatus* engages in more tactile stimulation when inspecting piscivores than when inspecting fishes that are not potential predators. This positive reinforcement may help discourage predatory fishes from eating the cleaners.

• **Reconciliation.** After a cleaner wrasse engages in a behavior that causes a client to jolt, such as "cheating" behavior (feeding on mucus or tissue, which not only has no benefit to the host but may even cause harm), the *Labroides* usually engages in more tactile stimulation to reestablish a positive relationship between itself and the client. This is more common when the client is larger and a nonresident (see the side bar on "The Nuances of the Cleaner-Client Relationship" on page 235 for more on the difference between choosy and resident clients). Research has shown that larger clients are provide more nutrients than smaller fishes (for more information on cleaner preferences see page 229). It has also been reported that tactile stimulation is more effective at stopping a client from behaving aggressively toward a cleaner after a jolt than simply swimming rapidly away.

While tactile stimulation may be one reason that clients visit *Labroides*, irritation caused by external parasites has also been

Klein's Butterflyfish, *Chaetodon kleinii*, leans to the side to attract two Bluestreak Cleaner Wrasses, *Labroides dimidiatus*. Communication between client and cleaners is very complex.

Floral Maori Wrasse, *Cheilinus chlorourus*, flares its gill covers, an invitation for this Bluestreak Cleaner Wrasse to inspect and remove parasites that may be irritating its gill filaments (red).

shown to motivate a fish to seek out these services. Although fishes that are totally free of ectoparasites will invite cleaning, those infested with parasites are more likely to visit cleaners. Aquarists should not assume that a fish is parasite-infested just because it poses for a cleaner. However, captive fishes will often

Piscivorous (fish-eating) clients do not always play by the rules: young Volitans Lionfish, *Pterois volitans*, swallowing an unfortunate *Labroides* cleaner wrasse.

Labroides spp. wrasses are lifelong cleaners. Here a juvenile attempts to groom a Redcheek Anthias.

in 60 different genera), certain clients are preferred over others. In fact, sometimes a cleaner will break off a cleaning bout with one species to attend to a preferred client. These preferences may be related to the probability that the host will be infected with parasites, the host's willingness to be cleaned, or possibly the nutrient value of the host's body mucus. Recent studies indicate that clients with access to more than one cleaning station are more attractive to a cleaner wrasse than those that do not have a choice and cannot switch from one cleaner to another (see sidebar on page 235).

The Bluestreak Cleaner Wrasse prefers large clients. A study done with two butterflyfish models that were similar in every way except for size demonstrated that *L. dimidiatus* inspected and picked food from every large model presented, but did the same to only 27% of the smaller models introduced. Larger fish may be more attractive to cleaners because the surface area of the host is directly proportional to the size of the parasite population and mucus availability.

A cleaner's success in finding and feeding on parasites is also host specific; the morphology and behavior of the host influences the predatory success of the cleaner. On the Great Barrier Reef, *L. dimidiatus* prefers to clean the Blackedge Thicklip Wrasse (*Hemigymnus melapterus*), while on reefs off the island of New Caledonia its preferred clients were *H. melapterus* and the Twolined Spinecheek (*Scolopsis bilineatus*). The adults of these two species (especially *H. melapterus*) are often infested by gnathiid isopods—a favorite food of these cleaners. One study suggested that the Hawaiian Cleaner Wrasse prefers hosts that have more nutrient-rich mucus. Its "favorite" client was the Saddleback Wrasse (*Thalassoma duperrey*), which produces larger quantities of high-calorie mucus.

Cleaners often prefer to inspect and pick at certain areas of the body, and this varies from one host to another. When the Bluestreak Cleaner Wrasse inspects snappers, it cleans the tail first and moves up the body until it reaches the anterior portion of the first dorsal fin. When cleaning goatfishes, this wrasse usu-

increase their rate of posing and visiting cleaner species when they have ectoparasites.

Client Types and Preferences

While cleaner wrasses will service a wide variety fish species from sharks and Manta Rays to porcupinefishes (at one site on the Great Barrier Reef *L. dimidiatus* was found to clean 132 species ally starts with the gill area and then cleans the mouth. This preference may reflect differences in the distribution of nutrients (parasites, scales, and slime) on the host.

Immunity from Predation

Cleaner wrasses and other parasite-pickers enjoy almost total immunity from predation. However, piscivores, like lizardfishes and the Stocky Hawkfish (*Cirrhitus pinnulatus*), will occasionally eat *Labroides*. A study carried out on another grouper of cleaners (cleaner gobies, genus *Elactinus*) demonstrated that they are more likely to be eaten by juvenile predators than by adults, possibly because the predators have not yet learned to associate the cleaners with the service they provide. The *Labroides*' color pattern, and possibly their swimming behavior, may signal that they are cleaners, and this may make them less desirable piscivore targets.

Impact of Cleaning

There has been some debate concerning the impact cleaner fishes have on the reef community. Depopulation studies, which remove cleaner fish from a reef, have given conflicting results. The first study of this type demonstrated that the number of potential hosts on a depopulated reef decreased substantially. It was suggested that the hosts left the location and moved to areas where cleaners were still present. In contrast, a second study carried out on the Hawaiian Cleaner Wrasse reported that the absence of these fish on patch reefs had little impact on the reef's fish community. Another study on the Bluestreak Cleaner Wrasse that confined its observations to one host, the Princess Damselfish (*Pomacentrus vaiuli*), it was demonstrated that cleaning behavior reduced the weight of parasites on a host fish, but removing the cleaners did not affect host fish numbers. A more recent study showed that the Bluestreak Cleaner Wrasse did reduce gnathiid isopod loads on one particular species of host (the Thicklipped Wrasse, *Hemigymnus melapterus*), but the hosts were reinfested during the night while they were torpid.

Labroides cleaning stations are well known to be centers of fish activity, where great diversity and concentration of fishes occur. Off Ras Mohammed, Egypt, studies were conducted on how cleaner wrasses impacted fish diversity. In this study, when Bluestreak Cleaner Wrasses were removed or disappeared from a cleaning station, there was no major immediate impact on fish abundance. But after 4 to 20 months, there was a significant decline in piscine diversity. If a cleaner wrasse moved back into the neighborhood, the diversity in that area increased within the first few weeks. The impact was especially pronounced for more free-ranging species that utilized multiple patch reefs in a large home range.

An adult Bluestreak Cleaner Wrasse calms a potential damsel host by grazing its pelvic fins over the client's body, a tactic used to stabilize and reassure.

Cleaner Parasites

Cleaner wrasses are occasionally parasitized by protozoa (e.g., *Cryptocaryon irritans*) and at least two species of bucephalid flatworms (i.e., *Rhipidocotyle labroidei*, *Rhipidocotyle* sp.). These flatworms are transmitted in a very unique way: the wrasses pick the flatworms off clients and are thus parasitized by them. Infection rates are high, with from 51% to 67% of all *L. dimidiatus* examined (from various locations) and 100% of *L. bicolor* from French Polynesia being infected by bucephalid digeneans.

Sexuality and Social Behavior

The cleaner wrasses are protogynous hermaphrodites with a sex ratio biased toward females. All but one member of the genus (*L.*

Indian Longnose Parrotfish solicits cleaning by a pair of *Labroides dimidiatus* by adopting a tail-down position. It will hang in this pose until a cleaner "cheats" and nips the client or the wrasses swim off.

Barrier Reef, as it has been well studied and is thought to be similar to that exhibited by some of the other *Labroides*. (For more specifics, see the individual species accounts.)

Labroides dimidiatus vigorously defends a permanent territory from neighboring males. Males have been observed to defend the same site for over two years. The typical *L. dimidiatus* social unit in this region consists of a single male, with three to six mature females and several juveniles living within the male's larger territory. The male is larger than the females and his dominance apparently suppresses sex change in the most dominant (usually the largest) female. The male actively patrols his territory, visiting females and scouting the borders of his "turf." When the male *L. dimidiatus* encounters a female (especially more dominant females), he often performs a unique aggressive display. If he encounters a member of his harem at the border of or outside of his territory, he will vigorously drive her back in.

There is size-related, linear dominance hierarchy among female *L. dimidiatus*. If there are two similarly sized females, they may be co-dominant and each may defend an area within the male's larger territory. The dominant female usually resides in the center of the male's territory and more often interacts with the male. Smaller adult females and juveniles are less site-attached, moving about within the larger male's territory. If a high-ranking female should die, the next highest ranking consexual takes her place in the pecking order. Female Bluestreak Cleaner Wrasses within a territory will exclude larger females that attempt to join their harem.

When the male *L. dimidiatus* dies, the most dominant female will begin to change sex and attempt to take over his territory—that is, if she can deflect similar attempts by neighboring males. In some cases, the male neighbors will succeed in commandeering the newly available territory. Adjacent males are more likely to take over a territory if they are considerably larger than the dominant male in that harem.

Female behavior begins to resembles that of a male within hours after his disappearance. Within 1.5 to 2 hours after he has gone, the female will begin to exhibit the specific male-to-female aggressive display toward consexuals in the harem. The sex-changing female is able to spawn as a male within 2 to 4 days. If

bicolor) are sexually monochromatic. Two species in the genus *Labroides* (*L. bicolor* and *L. dimidiatus*) are known to be territorial and haremic. That said, the social structure of some species may vary from one population to the next. We will examine the social system of the Bluestreak Cleaner Wrasse from the Great

Nuances of the Cleaner-Client Relationship

The relationship that exists between cleaner and client is not as straightforward as it might appear. Instead, a variety of selective pressures are at work on both participants as their interactions play out. Recent studies by Bshary and Grutter (2002), Bshary and Noe (2003), and Bshary and Würth (2003) have resulted in some interesting hypotheses about this relationship.

The Players

Before we go further, we need to define some of the "players" in the "cleaning game." First of all, there are the cleaners—the wrasses of the genus *Labroides*. Then there are three groups of potential clients. There are the **piscivorous clients** and **nonpiscivorous clients**. The latter can be broken down into **resident clients** and **choosy clients**. Resident clients occupy a small territory or home range that typically includes only one cleaning station, while the choosy clients live in a larger home range that includes multiple cleaning stations. Another important fact is that the *Labroides* can recognize repeat clients, and clients remember experiences with individual cleaners.

The Cleaner's Choice

These wrasses eat parasites and/or remove mucus, tissue, and scales from their clients. Feeding on a client's mucus and tissue is referred to as "cheating," because rather than providing a benefit to the client, it may cause the client harm. It has been demonstrated that when a cleaner cheats, clients often engage in "jolting"—darting forward or violently twitching. When inspecting a client, the cleaner has a choice: either search for and remove parasites or nip off mouthfuls of the client's slime and/or scales. The latter takes less energy than searching for parasites, but it may cost the cleaner repeat clients.

The Client's Choice

Likewise, potential clients that can choose between more than one cleaning station (choosy clients), are likely to avoid cleaners that have cheated them in the past. Also, when waiting to be cleaned, the choosy client is less likely to utilize a cleaner's services if it sees the cleaner cheat another fish. So there are two factors that work to keep cleaner wrasses honest—cheating may impact not only whether a choosy client returns but also whether a waiting client hangs around to be cleaned. In short, choosy fish are more likely to return to a cleaner that gives them good services than to one prone to cheating.

Things are very different for clients who do not have the option to visit other cleaning stations (the resident clients). When it comes to grooming, the resident fishes take what they can get. Of course, if cleaners were always cheating residents, you would predict that these clients would stop visiting their local cleaners. One way residents reduce the likelihood of cheating is to punish cleaners by behaving aggressively toward them if they cheat. When a cleaner causes a resident fish to jolt, the resident fish will often turn on and chase the cleaner. This negative reinforcement apparently helps reduce the amount of cleaner cheating that goes on against residents. The clients that have a choice are more attractive to cleaners than resident fishes. When a choosy client swims up to a cleaner that is servicing a resident client, the *Labroides* will usually switch from the resident to the choosy client. If resident and choosy

Cleaning involves a complex set of learned behaviors for client and cleaner.

clients simultaneously pose for cleaning, the labrid will almost always opt to clean the choosy individual. There may be several reasons for this. The choosy client may be preferred because it hosts a larger parasitic load than the resident fish, but laboratory experiments do not bear this out. Data suggests that if a choosy client is ignored in favor of another fish, it is less likely to return to the same cleaning station. It makes sense that the *Labroides* should attempt to appease the choosy client before the resident; the cleaner may not get another crack at a choosy client that is ignored, but the resident has no option but to return to the same cleaner.

Cleaner wrasses rarely, if ever, cheat on piscivorous clients. Researchers have also noted that one rarely sees a piscivorous fish engage in jolting behavior when being cleaned. Cleaner wrasses are probably careful not to elicit a negative reaction in the predatory species, as the consequences could be severe—they could be eaten. Piscivores refrain from the short-term advantage of eating the cleaner wrasse because of the long-term benefit of repeated parasite removal.

Dr. Alexandra Grutter, the leading researcher on *Labroides* behavior, states that cleaning behavior "involves some of the most complex and highly developed interspecific communication signals known."

Labroides bicolor, Bicolor Cleaner Wrasse (juvenile), busily inspects the gill filaments of a patient soldierfish, removing parasitic isopods and trematodes.

the male "next door" should succeed in taking over the territory after a female has begun the process of sex change, she can revert back to being a functional female. If there are co-dominant females, they may both change sex simultaneously and split the vacating male's territory and harem.

Large female *L. dimidiatus* within a harem may also change sex if they live at the periphery of a male's territory. These females are not as frequently visited by the male, so the sexual suppression that comes with male aggressive interactions is not as effective. Among the females in a social unit, more dominant females suppress sex change in those females lower down on the social ladder. (See the species account for *L. dimidiatus* for more information on its social structure and behavior in other locations.)

Captive Care

Although the *Labroides* vary somewhat in their aquarium suitability, most members of this genus are considered difficult to maintain long-term in the home aquarium. There may be one exception to this: the Bluestreak Cleaner Wrasse. Although we have long considered it difficult to keep this species in North America, unless it was held with numerous fishes on which to "graze," the Europeans consider it a good beginner's fish. It is so popular there that in 2002 it was one of the top ten species exported to the European Union. The Europeans report some encouraging longevity records. For example, the Nancy Aquarium, France, has kept *L. dimidiatus* for more than 11 years, while a lifespan of more than 6 six years has been reported to me by several European reef-keepers.

The biggest problem with the *Labroides* involves feeding. With the possible exception of *L. dimidiatus*, most species reject captive fare. As a result, they rely totally on the ectoparasites and slime present on their fish tankmates to meet their nutritional needs. If you have a large tank that has lots of potential clients, the cleaner wrasse may be able to acquire enough nutrients by grazing slime and the occasional parasite. But if there is relatively little grazing surface (i.e., fish bodies), then the cleaner will not get enough food to stay alive. Also, some hosts do not produce as much slime as others and are not as valuable as food sources as others, so the types of fishes you keep with the cleaner may have an impact on its chances of survival as well. Those species of cleaner wrasses (e.g., *L. phithirophagus*) that rely heavily on fish slime as a nutrient source will usually perish in short order in most home aquariums. The occasional cleaner wrasse (usually individual *L. dimidiatus*) will accept foods like finely chopped shrimp, mysid shrimp, frozen brine, freeze-dried tubifex worms, black worms, or even frozen prepared foods and flake foods. One way to induce a finicky cleaner to feed is to present it with a live or fresh mussel that has had the valves forced open so that they can pick at the "meat" within.

Cleaner Wrasse Pros and Cons

Unfortunately for the aquarist, cleaner wrasses do not consume the most problematic aquarium parasites—the protozoa and dinoflagellates. Therefore, cleaners are not recommended as a means of biological control of ich (*Cryptocaryon irritans*) or Velvet (*Amyloodinium ocellatum*) outbreaks. But cleaner wrasses *will* control another group of parasites that frequently infect our fishes. It has been shown that the cleaning behavior of the Bluestreak Cleaner Wrasse can reduce the number of the monogenetic flatworms (*Benedenia lolo*) in aquarium-held fishes. (Food choice studies have shown that when given a choice of four different foods—mucus, parasitic monogenean flatworms, gnathiid isopods, and a control—the Bluestreak Cleaner Wrasse fed more on mucus and monogeneans.) In one study the *L. dimidiatus* did not eliminate all of the flatworms, but they did

help keep their numbers in check. There is also evidence that indicates these wrasses will pick off the cyst phase of the flatworm (*Paravortex* sp.), which is commonly referred to as Black Ich (a.k.a. Yellow Tang disease). As a result, the *Labroides* spp. may also aid in controlling outbreaks of this ectoparasite in a closed system. Finally, Bluestreak Cleaner Wrasses will remove the cauliflower-like growths associated with the viral infection *Lymphocystis*.

But adding a cleaner wrasse to a tank of fishes also has a downside. As we discussed previously, there are some "costs" associated with visiting a cleaner wrasse. The *Labroides* feed on host mucus, scales, and skin, especially when ectoparasites are in short supply. Because most of the parasites on the cleaner's bill of fare are in short supply in the home aquarium, the captive *Labroides* will ingest larger quantities of fish slime and scales in order to survive. When it loses its external protection, a "captive client" is likely to be more susceptible to bacterial infections and infections by protozoa and dinoflagellate parasites. It is only logical that a cleaner is going to be more of a menace than a benefit in a small tank that contains fewer potential clients to feed from. Therefore, if you are going to keep a *Labroides*, it would be wise to house it

Industriously picking under the gill cover of a Yellowback Fusilier, *Caesia teres*, a pair of Bluestreak Cleaner Wrasses, *Labroides dimidiatus*, provide a unique parasite removal service.

Labroides bicolor, Bicolor Cleaner Wrasse, adult: sexes are the same color, but males grow larger. Two juveniles placed in an aquarium will become a pair.

Labroides dimidiatus, Bluestreak Cleaner Wrasse, variant in Papua New Guinea displaying yellow or gold highlights along its streak.

in a large tank with a relatively large fish community. A large tank will also make it easier for potential clients to avoid the attentions of a cheating cleaner wrasse.

As mentioned above, a client fish that gets nipped by a cheating *Labroides* may retaliate by chasing it off. This behavior is commonly seen in the aquarium and can be problematic for the cleaner, as certain tankmates may persistently attack it any time it comes near. On rare occasions, an exasperated fish will turn on the cleaner and kill it. For example, triggerfishes have been known to dispatch an annoying cleaner wrasse. On the other hand, *Labroides* will sometimes hound less maneuverable species, like puffers, trunkfishes, and porcupinefishes, causing them great duress. This pestering may even make an *Ostracion* trunkfish

emit its deadly toxins and wipe out a whole captive community. A confused cleaner might also persistently attempt to nip at and chase fishes with small spots. In some cases, it appears that the cleaner is attempting to feed on the "parasite-like" markings.

Compatibility

Adult cleaner wrasses of the same species will often fight in aquarium confines. This is especially true when space is limited. The key to keeping more than one per tank is to acquire a heterosexual pair. Unfortunately, most *Labroides* do not exhibit sexual chromatism. If you want to keep more than one in the same tank, purchase two juveniles or subadults and add them to the tank simultaneously. If you do this, the dominant fish should transform into a male and the subordinate will mature and remain female. However, even juveniles will fight if crowded, so make sure you have a tank of at least 100 gallons. It is possible to add a smaller cleaner into a tank that contains a larger individual, or vice versa, but if the tank is not large enough (135 gallons or more), the large individual may harass the smaller fish to death. It is safer to add two juvenile fish (3 to 5 cm [1.2 to 2.0 in.] in length) and let them mature into male and female. If you add a trio of cleaners to a tank, it is not uncommon for one fish to grow rapidly (the male) followed closely by another individual (the female). The third individual often grows very little. Remember, the more cleaners you have in a tank, the more stress they may cause to their piscine tankmates.

Cleaner wrasses of different species are likely to fight in small tanks. *Labroides* may also quarrel with closely related species, especially those that sport similar colors (e.g., *Larabicus quadrilineatus*, juvenile *Pseudodax moluccensis*). They have also been known to behave aggressively toward other labrids that have a longitudinal stripe (e.g., young *Thalassoma amblycephalum*).

While the *Labroides* enjoy some degree of immunity from predation in the wild, this same courtesy is not necessarily given them in captivity. Wobbegongs, trumpetfishes, frogfishes, scorpionfishes (including lionfishes), and groupers have all been known to eat cleaner fishes in the aquarium. (As mentioned above, lizardfishes and hawkfishes have been observed eating them in the wild.) To reduce the changes of predation, the *Labroides* should be added to the tank before the piscivore. They are normally eaten when added to a tank that already contains one of the predators listed above. Of this group of predators, the frogfishes are more likely than any of the others to eat cleaners, no matter when they are introduced to the tank. Pugnacious tankmates, like dottybacks, larger damsels, and triggerfishes, may aggressively attack and damage a cleaner.

These wrasses do not bury in the sand but hide in reef crevices at night. They often "slumber" in the confines of a mucus cocoon, which may help prevent them from being detected by nocturnal predators. The Bluestreak Cleaner Wrasse has spawned in the aquarium, although to the best of my knowledge the larvae have never been raised in captivity.

Cleaner Wrasse Species

Labroides bicolor Fowler & Bean, 1928
Common Name: Bicolor Cleaner Wrasse.
Maximum Length: 14 cm (4.7 in.).
Distribution: East Africa to the Line, Marquesan and Society Islands, north to southern Japan, and south to Lord Howe Island.
Biology: *Labroides bicolor* is found near lagoon patch reefs, on reef flats, outer

Labroides dimidiatus, Bluestreak Cleaner Wrasse, Fiji variant, attempts to clean a *Cirrhilabrus rubrimarginatus*. The Fiji form of this species has a yellow patch on the caudal peduncle.

reef faces, and slopes at depths of 2 to 40 m (7 to 132 ft.). Unlike *L. dimidiatus*, adult Bicolor Cleaner Wrasses wander over a large area looking for clients and will swim well off the bottom to clean schooling fish. I have observed large adults cleaning members of schools of Oriental Sweetlips (*Plectorhinchus orientalis*) that were milling in water up to 2 m (7 ft.) deep over the reef. In French Polynesia, *Labroides bicolor* is sometimes found near *L. dimidiatus* cleaning stations. In fact, adults of the two species have been observed simultaneously cleaning the same large client. Adults are usually observed in male-female pairs. Juveniles are more site-specific, occupying a similar habitat to that of the young *L. dimidiatus* (i.e., caves or crevices). The juveniles are reported to clean less frequently than adults and some of the other young *Labroides*. As a result, young *L. bicolor* may feed more heavily on nonparasitic copepods than adults (food habit data does not exist to back this hypothesis up). Adults feed on caligid copepods, gnathiid isopod larvae, and fish scales and mucus. The juvenile fish engages in a solicitation dance or display to attract clients, but adults do not. Adults seek out clients in their large home range.
Captive Care: This is the largest cleaner wrasse and, like many in the genus, it has a dubious husbandry record. Some individuals may accept regular aquarium foods, but most individuals require a large population of fish tankmates to feed from if they are to survive. It is an "aggressive" cleaner that is likely to bother fish tankmates, especially those that are not as fleet-of-fin (e.g., boxfishes, puffers). To reduce tankmate harassment, you should keep

it in a large tank (300 gallons or more). See the Captive Care section for the genus for more general information on the husbandry of *Labroides*.
Aquarium Size: 75 gal. **Temperature:** 23° to 28°C (74° to 82°F).
Aquarium Suitability Index: 2.
Remarks: Juvenile *L. bicolor* are a different color than the adults. This fish is also sexually dichromatic. Females are gray anteriorly, with a black stripe on the side and yellowish white toward the tail area. Males have a royal blue head; they are black toward the middle of the body and yellow or yellowish cream posteriorly.

Labroides dimidiatus (Valenciennes, 1839)
Common Name: Bluestreak Cleaner Wrasse.
Maximum Length: 11.5 cm (4.5 in).
Distribution: Indo-Pacific, except Hawaiian Islands.
Biology: The Bluestreak Cleaner Wrasse is found on rocky and coral reefs. On coral reef habitats it occurs on coastal fringing reefs, in lagoons, reef flats, outer reef faces, and fore-reef slopes at depths of less than 1 to 40 m (3.3 to 132 ft.). The social structure of the Bluestreak Cleaner Wrasse varies from one location to the next (possibly a function of population density). The following social behavior has been reported in Aldabra, Indian Ocean, by Potts (1973): The newly settled *L. dimidiatus* (which are less than 1 cm [0.4 in.] in length and are sometimes called wrigglers) live in protected microhabitats—in crevices or between rocks and boulders. Wrigglers engage in intense bouts of territorial aggres-

Labroides dimidiatus, Bluestreak Cleaner Wrasse: variant from Fiji with yellow coloration.

which is a promontory or some conspicuous feature. This is the main cleaning station and is where the adult *L. dimidiatus* spend most of their time. Adult pairs defend their territory from subadults and neighboring adults. The territory covers an average area of around 36 m² (387 ft.²) and tends to be in more exposed conditions than that of any other size class. When currents are the strongest, adults remain in more sheltered portions of their territory. *Labroides dimidiatus* populations on the Great Barrier Reef may exhibit a unique social structure, as described in the section on Sexuality and Social Behavior (page 233). When an intruder enters an adult pair's territory they will chase, charge, and ram or bite it. The intruding individual often retreats, or may engage in submissive behavior (raising its head to expose its belly) before aggression escalates to physical contact. Along territory boundaries, individuals more often display toward one another.

Gnathiid isopod larvae (usually ranging in length from 0.3 to 2.7 mm [0.01 to 0.12 in.) and client mucus are the most important components of this species' diet. They also eat parasitic copepods, parasitic flatworms, and nonparasitic copepods. Grutter (2000) reported ontogenetic changes in the feeding behavior of *L. dimidiatus*. While adults and juveniles both feed most heavily on isopods, adults feed more on scales, while juveniles eat more nonparasitic copepods. Adults consume up to seven times more isopods and four times more scales than small juveniles. Client slime is regularly ingested during cleaning bouts, but *L. dimidiatus* will also engage in more overt forms of mucophagy. Adults have been observed to dash into groups of parrotfish, taking swipes (a behavior associated with mucophagy) at the scarids as they passed.

Cleaning begins in *L. dimidiatus* soon after they settle from the plankton (at a size of about 1 cm [0.4 in.] in length). Wrigglers often clean less mobile species, like *Cirripectes* blennies. Juveniles (between 2 and 3 cm [0.8 and 1.2 in.] in length) clean diurnal fishes as well as nocturnal species that share the crevices where they often live. The Bluestreak Cleaner Wrasse may share its territory with other cleaner fishes. For example, I once saw a Sleek Unicornfish (*Naso hexanchus*) being cleaned by a pair of *L. dimidiatus* and 10 juvenile Diana's Hogfish (*Bodianus diana*) at a cleaning station in the Maldives. The Bluestreak Cleaner would usually spend most of its time inspecting the gills and pectoral fin regions, while most of the hogfish picked at the surgeonfish's tail.

sion. These conflicts often consist of parallel swimming, lateral displays, tail flips, and frontal displays (where individuals face off and open their mouths). If aggression escalates, the wrigglers will come to blows, charging and thrusting their jaws at one another. This behavior acts to disperse the young fish within suitable habitats.

Juveniles (between 2 and 3 cm [0.8 and 1.2 in.] in length) co-occur with wrigglers, but can also be found in more exposed habitats. Individuals in this size class exhibit site attachment, defending a specific area for days or even weeks, but they also regularly move to different sites. Juvenile territory size can range from 4.3 to 9.0 m² (46 to 97 ft.²). While they will exclude each other from this territory, they usually ignore wrigglers. Subadults, between 4 and 7 cm (1.6 to 2.8 in.) in length, differ in color from the adults. They occur singly and are territorial. They are found in some of the same habitats as the juveniles (i.e., more sheltered areas), but will range farther out into more current-prone, exposed habitats. Territorial adults exclude subadults from the most preferred habitats. Subadults are more site-attached than wrigglers or juveniles and occupy a territory smaller than that of an adult (typically about 23 m² [247 ft.²]). The subadult territory contains a central focal point where the fish spends the majority of its time. This is where most of the cleaning behavior occurs, and it is defended aggressively against juveniles and other subadults.

A pair of adults will occupy a territory, the focal point of

Pair of *Labroides dimidiatus*, Bluestreak Cleaner Wrasses, the large male above, calm and groom a temporarily hovering parrotfish that appears mesmerized.

Labroides dimidiatus has also been observed cleaning clients along with *L. bicolor* and the Redlipped Cleaner Wrasse (*L. rubrolabiatus*). In New Caledonia this species has been reported to inspect and clean an average of around 60 individual clients per 15 minutes of observation and spends about 26% of the day engaged in this activity. Off Aldabra Atoll, this species prefers to clean goatfishes and parrotfishes.

Labroides dimidiatus exhibits little interspecific aggression. In the Indian Ocean, it will behave aggressively toward the Ocellated Toby (*Canthigaster solandri*), apparently because this puffer will hang around cleaning stations and nip the cleaner's clients as they wait to be serviced. Because this behavior "hurts business," the cleaners will display toward and vigorously ram these puffers with their mouths open until the offenders leave the cleaning station. The Bluestreak Cleaner Wrasse will also display at and possibly attack those fishes that mimic it (e.g., False Cleaner Blenny [*Aspidontus taeniatus*], Bluestriped Fang Blenny [*Plagiotremus rhinorhynchus*]).

This fish, like others in the genus, is a protogynous hermaphrodite. Sex change is controlled by social factors (the presence of a dominant male or female) and may also be a function of age. Kuwamura (1981, 1984) found that females typically change to

Breastspot Cleaner Wrasse seduces and stabilizes a damselfish client into a relaxed state as it searches for items or mucus to pick at.

males before they reach three years of age, but can occur in individuals as young as one year in the right social context (for instance, when dominant males or females are lacking in the social unit). Females can reach sexual maturity at an age of one year. In some regions, *L. dimidiatus* will spawn throughout the year on every day throughout the lunar cycle. They may spawn at any time during the day, but prefer to release gametes on an outgoing tide or in an area where there is a strong current. At the more northern limits of their range, they have distinct spawning seasons. For example, in Japan, spawning occurs in the warmer months of May to early September. Cleaner wrasses spawn within their territories. In *L. dimidiatus*, the female initiates spawning. She will arch her body into an S-shape (sigmoid posturing), exhibiting her belly, which is distended with hydrated ova. She will also change her color, fading from black to brown on the anterior portion of the body. In turn, the male engages in "flutter-swimming." He approaches the female and curls his body in front of her while expanding and fluttering his caudal fin. On the Great Barrier Reef, females spawn exclusively with the male that monopolizes their harem, while 2% to 3% of male spawning events involve females outside of the haremic group.

Captive Care: This is the most common and durable cleaner wrasse. It often does best when kept with a large community of fish from which to browse mucus and parasites. One reason this species may do slightly better than its congeners is that it is more likely to ingest other foods, although it rarely does so with gusto. They are usually not aggressive toward other fish species, unless

they are similar in shape and color. For example, they may chase smaller wrasses that have a broad lateral stripe similar to theirs. Occasionally you will see this species nipping at the substrate on the reef. Not only will these wrasses nip slime from fish, in captivity they will also pick at tridacnid clam mantles and may cause their demise. This species has been observed spawning in captivity. Before spawning, the genital opening was noticeably expanded. For 20 minutes, the male and female swam together and the female cleaned her partner. A second female in the tank with the spawning pair was driven off by the courting female when she approached the male. The pair swam around together, moving in and out of the decor, for over and hour; then the male began tightly circling the female and cleaning her. After more courtship, the male and female finally dashed toward the aquarium surface, dispersing their gametes at the top of the ascent. See the Captive Care section for the genus for more information on the general husbandry of the *Labroides*.

Aquarium Size: 55 gal. **Temperature:** 23° to 28°C (74° to 82°F).
Aquarium Suitability Index: 2–3.

Remarks: There are no chromatic differences between the sexes, but juvenile color differs from that of the adults. This chromatic disparity prevents larger individuals from attacking the youngsters. If larger juveniles (over 3 cm [1.2 in.] in length) are isolated from adults, they will usually take on the adult color pattern in about 3 days' time. If they are then exposed to adults again, and subsequently attacked by them, most will revert back to the juvenile coloration in as little as 5 minutes. There is an advantage to exhibiting the adult color pattern: The dark lateral stripe of the adult has been shown to be the color pattern most attractive to

Labroides pectoralis, Breastspot Cleaner Wrasse, adult.

Hawaiian Cleaner Wrasse, *Labroides phthirophagus*: a beauty, but notoriously hard to keep well nourished and in long-term good health in an aquarium.

potential clients. There are several different color variants of *L. dimidiatus*. One of these, known as the Fiji form, has a broad yellowish orange section on the posterior part of the body.

Labroides pectoralis Randall & Springer, 1975

Common Name: Breastspot Cleaner Wrasse.

Maximum Length: 8 cm (3.1 in).

Distribution: Christmas Keeling Islands and Rowley Shoals east to Micronesia, north to the Ogasawara Islands, and south to the Great Barrier Reef and New Caledonia.

Biology: This attractive species is found on fringing reefs, lagoons, outer reef faces, and outer slopes at depths of 2 to 28 m (7 to 92 ft.). It occurs singly or in pairs. In most respects, its behavior is similar to that of *L. dimidiatus*.

Captive Care: In the aquarium it is difficult to provide this wrasse with enough host fish (whose mucus it eats) to prevent starvation, although some individuals will accept alternative foods, like mysid shrimps, finely chopped shrimp, and even flake foods. See the Captive Care section for the genus for more information on the husbandry of *Labroides*.

Aquarium Size: 30 gal. **Temperature:** 23° to 27°C (74° to 80°F).

Aquarium Suitability Index: 2.

Remarks: The Breastspot Cleaner Wrasse gets its name from the black spot at the base of the pectoral fin. This species has been known to hybridize with the Bicolor Cleaner Wrasse (*L. bicolor*).

Labroides phthirophagus Randall, 1958

Common Name: Hawaiian Cleaner Wrasse.

Maximum Length: 10 cm (3.9 in).

Distribution: Hawaiian Islands.

Biology: The Hawaiian Cleaner Wrasse is found on rocky and coral reef faces and slopes at depths of less than 1 to 90 m (3.3 to 297 ft.). It is rarely found in the turbulent surge zone. This species is territorial and haremic. Juveniles are often solitary, while adults occur singly or in pairs. They have also been seen in groups of up to five individuals (these groups apparently consist of one male

Labroides rubrolabiatus, Redlip Cleaner Wrasse, adult.

ium. Youngbluth (1968) starved several individuals for 4 days and then attempted to feed them planktonic copepods and several other types of zooplanktors. The fish were sacrificed and the stomachs of all individuals were found to be empty. This same author does report keeping a juvenile for 2 months on a diet of frozen brine shrimp and zooplankton. But this species usually does not do well in the home aquarium and is best left in the wild. See the Captive Care section for the genus for more general *Labroides* husbandry information.

Aquarium Size: 40 gal. **Temperature:** 23° to 27°C (74° to 80°F).

Aquarium Suitability Index: 1.

Remarks: Males and females are identical in color; juveniles are all black with a purple stripe on the back. Youngsters adopt the adult color when about 4 cm (1.5 in.) in length. Females may reproduce when they are around 4.5 cm (1.8 in.) in length.

and several females and/or juveniles). Adults occupy stable cleaning stations, but individuals may move from one station to another. It feeds primarily on parasitic copepods and gnathiid isopod larvae, and may rely on host mucus more than any other cleaner wrasse. It has been suggested that these wrasses feed more on slime because ectoparasites are less common on Hawaiian fishes. It also eats nonparasitic cyclopoid copepods and fish eggs. This species engages in an undulating dance display when attempting to attract clients, but does so less often than *L. dimidiatus*. It cleans a wide range of hosts, from trumpetfishes to porcupinefishes.

The Hawaiian Cleaner Wrasse reproduces throughout the year, with peaks in spawning in January and February and in late September. While solitary adults occupy a cleaning territory during much of the year, pairs are often seen during the reproductive season. They spawn throughout the day, with courtship lasting for days or even weeks before reproduction occurs. During pair formation the male passes in front of the female and quivers, while she engages in a sigmoid posturing (arching the body into an S-shape). Just before spawning, the female's abdomen swells, all cleaning ceases, and courtship intensifies. The male circles the female and engages in more passing and quivering, while the female performs more sigmoid postures. The pair rushes into the water column 30 to 60 cm (12 to 24 in.) over the substrate to release their gametes. A pair may spawn more than once a day.

Captive Care: In the aquarium it is difficult to provide this fish with enough host fish (and therefore, mucus) to prevent starvation. While these fishes sometimes eat nonparasitic copepods in the wild, they tend not to accept these types of food in the aquar-

Labroides rubrolabiatus Randall, 1958

Common Name: Redlip Cleaner Wrasse.
Maximum Length: 9 cm (3.5 in).
Distribution: Samoa to the Line and Society Islands, French Polynesia and the Pitcairn Group.
Biology: *Labroides rubrolabiatus* is known from outer reef crests, faces, and slopes at depths of 1 to 32 m (3.3 to 106 ft.). It is often observed in pairs and sometimes found near *L. dimidiatus* cleaning stations. In fact, it has been observed cleaning larger clients along with the Bluestreak Cleaner Wrasse. The Redlip Cleaner Wrasse cleans a variety of fishes, from small herbivores to large carnivores like the Napoleon Wrasse (*Cheilinus undulatus*). Limited stomach content data has revealed that the Redlip feeds heavily on gnathiid isopods and fish mucus and scales. This species performs a less exaggerated version of the undulating dance display employed by *L. dimidiatus*.
Captive Care: The Redlip Cleaner Wrasse, like others in the genus, presents feeding problems in captivity. A large population of fish kept in the same tank may help meet this species' nutritional needs, since it "grazes" on the mucus and scales of its tankmates. Tankmates that produce a lot of slime (like other wrasses and parrotfishes) provide more grazing surface area. See the Captive Care section for more general information on *Labroides* husbandry.
Aquarium Size: 30 gal. **Temperature:** 23° to 27°C (74° to 80°F).
Aquarium Suitability Index: 2.
Remarks: No color differences exist between the sexes, but juveniles are bright blue with a black band in the middle of the body.

MODEL: *Larabicus quadrilineatus*, Fourline Wrasse.

MIMIC: *Pseudochromis springeri*, Springer's Dottyback.

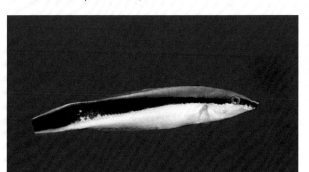

MODEL: *Labroides dimidiatus*, Bluestreak Cleaner Wrasse.

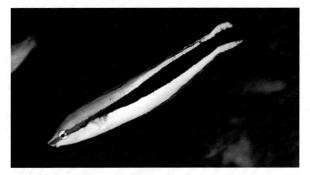

MIMIC: *Aspidontus taeniatus*, Sabertoothed Cleaner Mimic Blenny.

Cleaner Look-Alikes

A number of noncleaner species have evolved color patterns that are similar to those of cleaner fishes, apparently to benefit from the cleaners' alliance with most predators. For example, Springer's Dotty-back (*Pseudochromis springeri*) has a color pattern similar to that of the sympatric Fourline Wrasse (*Larabicus quadrilineatus*), and the juvenile Striped Blanquillo (*Malacanthus latovittatus*) looks like the Bluestreak Cleaner Wrasse (*L. dimidiatus*). This color mimicry may help to protect the mimics from some predators.

But some cleaner look-alikes may not only benefit from the protection afforded by this resemblance, but also attract potential hosts close enough so they can bite off a mouthful of scales. Such is the case with the Sabertoothed Cleaner Mimic (*Aspidontus taeniatus*). This crafty little blenny not only looks like a Bluestreak Cleaner Wrasse—it acts like one, performing the undulating dance display. When a fish approaches to be cleaned, the blenny darts forward and bites it, taking a mouthful of scales, fin, or mucus. Most of this blenny's victims are younger fish. After

being duped by this impostor on a number of occasions, experienced fish learn to distinguish it from the true Bluestreak Cleaner Wrasse and are less likely to fall victim to its savage attacks. The aquarist can tell the difference by looking at the position of the mouth: in the cleaner mimic the mouth is under the snout (subterminal), and in the cleaner wrasse it is at the end of the head (terminal). It should be pointed out that the cleaner mimic only nips at other fish to supplement its diet. Its main foods are tubeworms and fish eggs.

At least one study has shown that the presence of a cleaner mimic that fed on the mucus and tissue of the cleaner's potential clients (*Plagiotremus rhinorhynchus*) reduced the number of fishes visiting the cleaning stations of juvenile *L. dimidiatus*, which engaged in less cleaning as a result. The *P. rhinorhynchus* also increased its number of strikes on victims when close to a cleaning station. In short, having this nipping neighbor is detrimental to the Bluestreak Cleaner Wrasse, significantly impacting the adults' food source.

GENUS *LABROPSIS* (TUBELIP WRASSES)

These unusual wrasses get their name from their tubelike mouths and pleated lips. Their pharyngeal teeth are also unique in that they are smaller than those of other labrids and are conical in shape rather than molarlike. These adaptations are associated with their diet, which consists of coral polyps and their mucus. They do not need the larger, more robust pharyngeal dentition of their kin to handle these soft-bodied prey items.

These fishes are also parasite-pickers/mucus feeders. They (as well as the *Diproctacanthus* and *Labrichthys*) have raptorial teeth that they may use to damage coral polyps in order to induce

Labropsis manabei, Northern Tubelip Wrasse, juvenile: juveniles may clean.

Labropsis alleni, Allen's Tubelip Wrasse, adult: adults feed on coral polyps.

more mucus production. These wrasses then slurp up the mucus in their tubelike mouths. Like others in this tribe, the juveniles clean, while the adults typically do not. However, some *Labropsis* spp. are also facultative cleaners as adults. Unlike the *Labroides* spp., the Tubelip Wrasses do not set up permanent cleaning stations. The bold stripes are a characteristic they share with many cleaners. It may be a general signal to other fishes of their parasite-picking services. These fishes do not bury, but hide in reef crevices at night.

All these fishes are protogynous hermaphrodites—all males result from female sex change. Two species (*Labropsis polynesica* and *L. micronesica*) exhibit marked sexual dichromatism. The males of these two species also develop emarginate caudal fins (it is rounded in juveniles and females). In three species (*Labropsis australis*, *L. manabei*, and *L. micronesica*) there are no color differences between the sexes, but the males have very elongated pelvic fins. The sixth species exhibits very little dichromatism and no difference in finnage between the sexes.

Captive Care

Although not common, some of the six species in this genus occasionally make their way into the aquarium hobby. These fishes tend to do poorly in the reef tank because of their specialized diets. Many members in this genus feed exclusively on the polyps of small-polyped stony corals when they reach adulthood. As is the case with a number of obligatory corallivores, switching them to an artificial diet is difficult. Of course, if you keep the corals they normally eat (e.g., *Acropora* spp.), you will probably want to avoid adding them to the same aquarium. The more advanced aquarist who wants to attempt keeping one of these fishes in a reef tank should keep in mind that members of the same species are likely to fight, and congeners might also quarrel. Sand depth or grain size is not an issue with these wrasses, as they "sleep" in reef interstices.

Tubelip Wrasse Species

Labropsis alleni Randall, 1981
Common Name: Allen's Tubelip Wrasse.
Maximum Length: 10 cm (3.9 in.).
Distribution: Indonesia, Philippines, New Guinea, Solomon Islands, and Micronesia.
Biology: Allen's Tubelip Wrasse is found in lagoons and on outer reef faces and slopes at depths of 4 to 52 m (13 to 172 ft.). Juveniles are parasite-pickers, having been observed to pick clean Chromis Damsels. Adults are not known to be cleaners, but feed mostly on stony coral polyps.

Labropsis australis, Southern Tubelip Wrasse, juvenile transforming.

Labropsis australis, Southern Tubelip Wrasse, small adult.

Captive Care: This is the most common member of the genus in the aquarium trade. Husbandry success has been mixed. Some individuals (younger fish) sometimes accept aquarium fare, and as long as it is varied, they have been known to survive in captivity for some time. However, there are also those individuals that never eat or feed and still fade away. Keep one per tank.
Aquarium Size: 30 gal. **Temperature:** 23° to 27°C (74° to 80°F).
Aquarium Suitability Index: 2.
Remarks: There are slight color differences between larger males and females. The juveniles exhibit two yellow stripes from head to the tail.

Labropsis micronesica Randall, 1981
Common Name: Micronesian Tubelip Wrasse.
Maximum Length: 12 cm (4.7 in.).
Distribution: Micronesia, including Palau, Caroline, Mariana, and Marshall Islands.
Biology: This wrasse is found in clear lagoons and on outer reef faces and slopes at depths of 7 to 33 m (23 to 109 ft.). It occasionally is seen over sand and rubble areas near the reef. Young fish live among branching corals and seek shelter within them if threatened. Adults stray into the water column, up to a couple of meters (feet) above the coral cover. Juveniles and, to a lesser degree, adults are cleaners.
Captive Care: While these fish can be successfully kept in the home aquarium, they often present potential feeding problems because of the specialized diet of the adults.
Aquarium Size: 55 gal. **Temperature:** 23° to 27°C (74° to 80°F).
Aquarium Suitability Index: 2.
Remarks: At less than 40 mm (1.6 in.), this species is black with two white stripes. The initial phase individuals have juvenile

Labropsis micronesica, MIcronesian Tubelipe Wrasse, male.

stripes but the body changes to brownish or gray. This species is very similar to the **Southern Tubelip** (*Labropsis australis*) **Randall, 1981** and the **Northern Tubelip** (*L. manabei*) **Schmidt, 1931**. The juveniles of the three species are difficult to distinguish from each other. The terminal phase of both *L. australis* and *L. manabei* have a black spot at the pectoral base. The Northern Tubelip also has a large yellow area on the caudal peduncle that is lacking in the other two species. The Southern Tubelip ranges from the Great Barrier Reef and Lord Howe Island to New Caledonia, Fiji, and Samoa. The Northern Tubelip is found in eastern Indonesia and Papua New Guinea, and north to southern Japan. *Labropsis australis* reaches a maximum length of 11 cm (4.3 in.), with females ranging in size from 4.2 to 6.5 cm (1.7 to 2.6 in.), while males are between 7.4 and 11 cm (2.9 to 4.3 in.). *Labropsis manabei* attains a length of 13 cm (5.1 in.). The ecol-

Labropsis manabei, Northern Tubelip Wrasse, male.

Labropsis xanthonota, Yellowback Tubelip Wrasse, juvenile.

Labropsis xanthonota, Yellowback Tubelip Wrasse, male.

ogy of these two species is similar to that of *L. micronesica*. The Southern Tubelip is found in lagoons and on outer reef faces and slopes at depths of 2 to 55 m (7 to 182 ft.), where it occurs singly or in pairs. The Northern Tubelip is found on reef faces and slopes at depths of 15 to 38 m (50 to 125 ft.). Both species prefer habitats with rich stony coral cover—the main food for adults.

Labropsis xanthonota Randall, 1981

Common Names: Yellowback Tubelip Wrasse, Wedge-tailed Wrasse, Comet Wrasse.
Maximum Length: 14 cm (5.5 in.).
Distribution: East Africa to the Mariana, Marshall, and Samoa Islands, north to southern Japan, and south to the Great Barrier Reef and New Caledonia.
Biology: This is typically a solitary fish. This species usually re-

sides in clear, coral-rich habitats. It has been found in lagoons and outer reef faces and slopes at depths of 4 to 55 m (13 to 182 ft.) in areas with rich stony coral growth. As with others in the genus, the juveniles are cleaners, picking at the bodies and fins of damsels, anemonefishes, other wrasses (including *Labroides*), parrotfishes, and surgeonfishes. Subadults and adults are stony coral feeders.
Captive Care: This species is occasionally available in the aquarium trade. The juveniles tend to do better than the coral-feeding adults. In some cases, the adults will accept other foods, like mysid shrimps and shaved seafood. It is risky to place them in a reef tank with stony corals, but they can be housed with most soft corals. The tank should be covered, as males are accomplished leapers. Keep one per tank. If your aquarium is large enough (180 gallons or larger) you may keep a male in the same tank with a female or juvenile.
Aquarium Size: 55 gal. **Temperature:** 23° to 27°C (74° to 80°F).
Aquarium Suitability Index: 2.
Remarks: Females are typically under 7.2 cm (2.8 in.) SL, while males measure from 6.8 to 10 cm (2.7 to 3.9 in.) SL. Females have a rounded caudal fin, while this fin is emarginate in males. The similar **Polynesian Tubelip Wrasse (*Labropsis polynesica*) Randall, 1981** is known from the Polynesian Islands, where it is reported from depths of 15 to 38 m (50 to 125 ft.). Adolescents and adults feed on stony coral polyps. Juveniles clean other fishes. The male color phase differs from *L. xanthonota* in having a larger yellow patch on the opercular area and no white wedge on the caudal fin. The female phase has three white lines down the body and yellow spots on the scales. The female *L. xanthonota* has more blue stripes down the sides and back (approximately six) and a distinct black spot on the anterior dorsal fin.

The **Red Sea Cleaner Wrasse** or **Fourline Wrasse** (*Larabicus quadrilineatus*) (Rüppell, 1835) is the single member of the genus. Juveniles and females are black overall with two blue stripes running from the head to the tail. Males of this species are dark blue or black overall, with blue on the median fins, and a bright blue line under the eye. This species is a protogynous hermaphrodite. The Red Sea Cleaner Wrasse is known from the Red Sea and the Gulf of Aden and attains a maximum length of 11.5 cm (4.5 in.). *Larabicus quadrilineatus* occurs on fringing reefs, around scattered patch reefs, or on coral-rich reef walls. Adults are always associated with stony corals, their primary source of food. As a juvenile it is a cleaner; at least, it engages in this activity on a part-time basis. It also eats tiny crustaceans and may pick at corals. As an adult, it feeds more extensively on stony corals, especially small-polyped species. It is typically a solitary species.

Captive Care

The Red Sea Cleaner Wrasse is more likely to acclimate to aquarium life than many of the other cleaners, but it is by no means easy to keep. Juveniles are occasionally seen in the aquarium trade and most individuals will adapt to aquarium care and fare. But because of its diet, an adult is an unwelcome addition to the stony coral aquarium. Not only will it feed on small-polyped species like *Acropora* and *Pocillopora*, it has also been known to feed on large-polyped stony corals. This includes members of the genus *Euphyllia*. (It has been known to decimate whole heads of *E. parancora* in a relatively short period of time.) It has also been known to nip at the pigment spots on clam mantles, causing them to close. The Red Sea Cleaner Wrasse has also been reported to feed on *Aiptasia* anemones. In most cases it will behave itself in a soft coral aquarium, but keep a close eye on it in case it exhibits a dietary shift. It is more likely to pick at xeniids and clavulariids than the "tree-like" soft corals. It has also been known to pick at feather dusters. It is not a threat to ornamental crustaceans, snails, or sea stars.

You should attempt to feed this fish mysid shrimps, live brine shrimp, and frozen *Cyclops*. Some individuals will eat these foods and do well in the aquarium. Others—especially adult specimens—will reject them and waste away. Keep only one *L. quadrilineatus* per tank unless the aquarium is large, as they tend to fight. It is possible to keep them in pairs, but males are not common in the aquarium trade. If you place two younger specimens in a large tank, one is likely to change into a male; the other should remain as a female.

Larabicus quadrilineatus, Red Sea Cleaner Wrasse, juvenile: may take aquarium foods.

Labrichthys unilineatus, Tubelip or Oneline Wrasse, adult: will eat coral polyps.

There are 10 species in the genus *Macropharyngodon*, all of which are not only ideally suited to the reef aquarium, but require this type of aquarium venue to survive. While beautiful and relatively dainty, the leopard wrasses are not for everyone. They are more temperamental than many labrids and will do best in captivity if kept in a tank where natural fodder is regularly available.

They have special requirements that must be met if you are going to have success keeping them. They are active grazers of small crustaceans, worms, and other substrate-dwelling invertebrates, and an established aquarium with healthy live rock and a productive bed of live sand is essential. Without natural hunting opportunities, supported with the feeding of appropriate live and frozen meaty foods, *Macropharyngodon* spp. wrasses are almost certainly destined to starve in the aquarium.

Biology

Members of the genus *Macropharyngodon* are characterized by deep, laterally compressed bodies, exceptionally large pharyngeal teeth (hence the genus name), two pairs of large canines toward the front of the jaws, smaller conical teeth on the sides of the jaws, and canines that point forward at the back of the upper jaw. Their chromatic attire varies greatly from one species to the next, but all of them display spots or blotches of one form or another. For this reason I have chosen to use the name leopard wrasse to refer to all members of the genus. Some species are sexually dimorphic—and all species are sexually dichromatic.

The leopard wrasses are distributed from Hawaii to the east coast of Africa, with several species having very restricted ranges. All of these fish are reef dwellers, and because of their small size and lack of anatomical defenses they spend most of their days moving among the branches of hard corals or near coral rubble. They refuge under the sand at night or when they are threatened. Juveniles often drift over the seafloor like floating debris, possibly to avoid the attention of predators. The leopard wrasse's diet is composed almost entirely of shelled protozoa (i.e., foraminiferans) and small snails, which they pick off hard reef substrates with their canines and grind up with their large pharyngeal teeth. Copepods and amphipods make up minor components of the diet.

The leopard wrasses are hermaphrodites, with at least some of the males in a population resulting from female sex change. At least some species also display a haremic social system. In these species the territory of a male usually contains several females. If the male in one of these groups dies or is displaced, the most dominant female changes sex and fills his position in the pecking order. Several species in this genus are also commonly observed in pairs, but whether or not they form long-term pair bonds has yet to be demonstrated.

Captive Care

Leopard wrasses often suffer greatly from poor collection and handling practices, as well as the subsequent shipping stress. They will do much better if shipped in a bag that has a thin layer of fine sand on the bottom. This enables them to bury and feel more secure, and may alleviate the mouth damage that can result from the wrasse rubbing its jaws against the sides of the bag as it attempts to escape. Marine fish wholesalers and retailers should keep a layer of sand in the tank where they hold these fishes to help reduce stress. Retailers should also avoid placing them in a tank with aggressive fishes that will pick on them and hinder the acclimation process. The potential leopard wrasse buyer should make sure the flesh around the jaws is not abraded and that the fish has been in the store a few days. Some aquarists argue that because the *Macropharyngodon* spp. are slow to take introduced food, it is best to purchase the fish immediately and get it into a tank with live substrates.

Once you get your leopard wrasse, the next challenge is to ensure it gets enough to eat. It will usually take a while before a leopard wrasse begins eating normal aquarium fish fare, but they will typically start pecking at the substrate soon after they pop out of the sand for their first look around. A leopard wrasse that has been eating and seems acclimated to aquarium life may slowly lose weight and subsequently perish. One theory is that they harbor intestinal parasites that compete with them for the limited amount of nutrients they can find in the aquarium. Although this may be true, to the best of my knowledge no one has conclusively demonstrated this to be the case. Many marine fishes are parasitized by these worms, but in natural situations they infrequently succumb and die.

If you are worried that your wrasse has intestinal parasites, you may want to give it a dewormer. The best of these are fenbendazole, a drug you will have to get from your veterinarian, and piperazine (e.g., Pipzine by Aquatronics). In the case of the leopard wrasses, the best way to administer it is to add it to their food.

Most individuals who have successfully kept these wrasses have done so by housing them in a tank with healthy live rock and live sand. In fact, I would suggest that keeping leopard wrasses in a tank that contains these two types of substrate is mandatory due to their specialized diets. Although leopard

Macropharyngodon ornatus, Ornate Leopard Wrasse, female: a very appealing reef fish, but it needs advanced husbandry and ideal conditions and feeding.

wrasses will eat and should be fed a variety of prepared and live foods, the live rock and live sand will enable them to continually forage on the associated micro-invertebrate fauna like foraminiferans (shelled protozoa), small snails, and minute crustaceans. In this respect they are similar to the mandarin fish, *Synchiropus* spp. In fact, it is probably not a good idea to house the two food competitors in the same tank, unless you are sure there is enough food to go around. Your leopard wrasse should have supplemental food at least twice a day (and preferably more often). Good foods include mysid shrimp, live black worms, and finely chopped seafood. It is also a good practice to occasionally replace some of your live rock and/or live sand with a new batch to replenish natural stocks of leopard wrasse food.

Another way to ensure your leopard wrasse gets enough to eat is to use a refugium. This can consist of a small tank placed below or alongside the aquarium or a specially designed unit that hangs inside the tank. In the former type the water and associated planktors are typically pumped into the main aquarium. In an internal refugium, water is slowly pumped (e.g., 10 to 15 gallons per hour) from the display tank into the refugium. Water, along with some of the small animals that it contains, pours directly into the tank over an overflow. This prevents the zooplanktors from being disabled or destroyed by the pump's impeller (although this may not really be a concern). Zooplankton culture, like mysid shrimp, copepods, and amphipods, may be added to the refugium. These small crustaceans can be fed aquarium flake food and plant material and are typically very prolific. They provide a natural, constant, and nutritious food source for any wrasse housed in an aquarium with them. Another advantage to having a well-stocked refugium is that you will not have to introduce food so frequently to assure your leopard wrasse gets enough to eat. I know individuals that have productive refugia containing fat and happy leopard wrasses.

If you have a tank filled with live rock, live sand, and a refugium, the next step is to successfully acclimate your wrasse. To ensure success with this process it is important to purchase a healthy specimen. A fit leopard wrasse will be swimming around the dealer's tank scanning the substrate for food. The dorsal musculature should not be atrophied (i.e., the back should not look concave when the fish is viewed from the front and the head should not appear enlarged) and the stomach should not be pinched in. As is also the case with mandarin fish, an emaciated specimen will handicap the aquarist's attempts at husbandry from the outset. I have had more success acclimating large juveniles or subadult specimens than larger individuals or tiny juveniles.

To avoid acclimation difficulties, a leopard wrasse should not be introduced into a tank that contains aggressive fish. For example, dottybacks, wrasses of the genus *Pseudocheilinus*, *Halichoeres*, and *Thalassoma*, pygmy angels, and hawkfishes may harass a newly introduced leopard wrasse and reduce its chances of sur-

vival. It should be noted that some fish appear to avoid those leopard wrasse species that possess eyespots (such as juvenile *Macropharyngodon meleagris* and *M. ornatus*). The potential aggressor may mistake the lateral view of the wrasse for the front of a predatory fish. It has been documented that the eyespots of many potential prey species serve to deceive would-be predators in this way. Smaller leopard wrasses may fall prey to adult boxer shrimps (*Stenopus* spp.), large hermit crabs, arrow crabs, and cancrid crabs.

A sand substrate will increase your chances of success with a leopard wrasse—or any other species of wrasse that buries. When wrasses attempt to bury in large, sharp, calcareous substrates they often damage the areas around the mouths and fins, resulting in redness or receding skin. These injuries can result in viral infections and the cessation of feeding. Although sand will make leopard wrasse care easier, it is possible to keep them in tanks without sand. In this situation, a leopard wrasse will hide between the rocks at night. Another potential hazard is the overflow of the wet-dry prefilter; leopard wrasses have been known to swim between the teeth of an overflow box or get sucked through them.

When introduced into the aquarium, a leopard wrasse may spend a day or two hiding under the sand. During this critical

Trio of *Macropharyngodon bipartitus*, Vermiculate Leopard Wrasses, graze for small invertebrate prey in the company of a shoal of *Halichoeres* wrasses.

acclimation period you should not dig the wrasse up to show your friends or to check on its condition. Eventually it will emerge from the substrate and begin to forage. It is not uncommon for a leopard wrasse to appear at a specific time each day—initially, this may be late in the day, long after the aquarium lights first come on. This is apparently caused by a sort of "piscine jet lag." Since the wrasse is still on Indo-Pacific time, it comes out of hiding when it would be early morning in the area where it was collected. With time these wrasses usually adjust their internal clocks to the day-night cycle in your aquarium. One way to get your leopard wrasse on local time is to keep it in a quarantine tank for a week that contains no substrate. In this way, it will be forced to comply with its new day-night cycle. The downside of this practice is it is likely to cause the fish more stress during acclimation.

Leopard wrasses are peaceful community fish. They are cordial toward other fish species and juveniles and initial phase fish rarely pester their own kind. On several occasions I have introduced more than one initial phase specimen into the same tank simultaneously and observed little overt aggression between them. However, terminal phase fish can be quite cantankerous and may even kill other males or, on rare occasions, females. If you want to keep more than one individual in your tank, it is still advisable to add them all at the same time and keep only one male per tank. A leopard wrasse should be one of the first fish introduced after the tank has cycled, because it is such a passive fish. Another positive attribute of this genus is that they rarely succumb to protozoan and dinoflagellate infections.

Leopard Wrasse Species

Macropharyngodon bipartitus Smith, 1957
Common Names: Vermiculate Leopard Wrasse, Splendid Leopard Wrasse, Divided Wrasse.
Maximum Length: 12 cm (4.7 in.).
Distribution: Red Sea south to Natal, east to the Maldives and Mauritius.
Biology: This wrasse is found in lagoons and on reef faces and slopes at depths of 3 to 30 m (10 to 98 ft.), usually over rubble or sand. Adult males occur singly; females and initial phase fish often forage in small groups. I have observed up to five juveniles foraging together along with several Lemon Meringue Wrasses (*Halichoeres leucoxanthus*)—see photo on opposite page.
Captive Care: See the Captive Care section in the genus account above for husbandry tips. Although a group of these wrasses would make an interesting display in a large aquarium, it may be difficult to provide them with enough to eat.
Aquarium Size: 55 gal. **Temperature:** 23° to 28°C (74° to 82°F).

Macropharyngodon bipartitus, Vermiculate Leopard Wrasse, female: younger fish may be introduced to the aquarium in groups. Adult males will fight.

Macropharyngodon bipartitus, Vermiculate Leopard Wrasse, female.

Macropharyngodon bipartitus, Vermiculate Leopard Wrasse, male.

Macropharyngodon choati, Choat's Leopard Wrasse, female.

Macropharyngodon choati, Choat's Leopard Wrasse, male.

Aquarium Suitability Index: 2.
Remarks: Male *M. bipartitus* are very different from the females. They are dark brown to dull orange-red in overall color, with green bands on the head, body, and fins. The juveniles and females are orangish brown over much of the body, with white spots. The head is yellowish white with black spots, and there is an area of black on the abdomen. The **Bluespotted Leopard Wrasse** (*Macropharyngodon cyanoguttatus*) **Randall, 1978** is a similar species that occurs from South Africa to Réunion and Mauritius. The females of this species are brown with blue spots on each scale, and have a yellow head with blue bands. The males are brownish yellow with blue spots and a pale orangish yellow head with blue bands. It is reported from rubble areas at

depths of 15 to 50 m (50 to 165 ft.). It reaches 12 cm (4.7 in.) in length.

Macropharyngodon choati Randall, 1978
Common Names: Choat's Leopard Wrasse, Choat's Wrasse.
Maximum Length: 11 cm (4.3 in.)
Distribution: Great Barrier Reef and New South Wales.
Biology: Choat's Leopard Wrasse is found at depths of 1 to 28 m (3.3 to 91 ft.) on the reef flat and over coral rubble at the base of reef dropoffs. It is also common in areas with good macroalgae growth and in seagrass habitats. Adult *M. choati* occur singly and in pairs, while juveniles may form groups.
Captive Care: See the Captive Care section in the genus account above.
Aquarium Size: 75 gal. **Temperature:** 22° to 27°C (72° to 80°F).
Aquarium Suitability Index: 2.
Remarks: *Macropharyngodon choati* is white overall with orange to red bands and blotches with a dark opercular patch trimmed with yellow. The males have bluish cheeks. **Vivien's** or the **Madagascar Leopard Wrasse** (*Macropharyngodon vivienae*) **Randall, 1978** is yellowish orange with a large black spot over the pectoral base. It is only known from Madagascar and the east coast of Africa, where it occurs at depths down to 40 m (132 ft.).

Macropharyngodon geoffroyi (Quoy & Gaimard, 1824)
Common Names: Potter's Leopard Wrasse, Shortnose Leopard Wrasse, Geoffroy's Wrasse.
Maximum Length: 16 cm (6.3 in.)
Distribution: Hawaiian Islands.
Biology: Potter's Leopard Wrasse is found on boulder and coral reefs, on the reef face and fore-reef slopes at a depth range of 6 to 32 m (20 to 104 ft.). It occurs singly or in pairs, and moves close to the substrate picking at benthic invertebrates. Like other *Macropharyngodon* spp., it feeds mainly on prosobranch gastropods and foraminiferans, but will also consume copepods and amphipods.
Captive Care: Because this species is collected and shipped from Hawaii, *M. geoffroyi* usually suffers less from collecting and handling than other leopard wrasses collected further afield. However, it still might succumb to shipping-related stress. See the Captive Care section in the genus account above for more husbandry tips.
Aquarium Size: 75 gal. **Temperature:** 23° to 28°C (74° to 82°F).
Aquarium Suitability Index: 2–3.
Remarks: *Macropharyngodon geoffroyi* exhibits color differences between the sexes. The females are yellowish orange overall with dark-edged blue spots and a dark spot at the front of the dorsal

Macropharyngodon geoffroyi, Potter's Leopard Wrasse, terminal phase male, full courting coloration. Compare to adult male, below.

Macropharyngodon geoffroyi, Potter's Leopard Wrasse, female.

Macropharyngodon geoffroyi, Potter's Leopard Wrasse, adult male.

Macropharyngodon geoffroyi, Potter's Leopard Wrasse, juvenile.

M. kuiteri, Kuiter's Leopard Wrasse, female, New South Wales, Australia.

Macropharyngodon kuiteri, Kuiter's Leopard Wrasse, female, Vanuatu.

Macropharyngodon kuiteri, Kuiter's Leopard Wrasse, male, Vanuatu.

fin. Males have reddish orange median fins and blue lines (as opposed to the spots characteristic of the female) on the face.

Macropharyngodon kuiteri Randall, 1978

Common Name: Kuiter's Leopard Wrasse.
Maximum Length: 10 cm (3.9 in.)
Distribution: Southern Queensland, New South Wales, Australia, New Caledonia, Vanuatu.
Biology: Kuiter's Leopard Wrasse is found at depths of 10 to 30 m (33 to 99 ft.), but is most common at depths in excess of 20 m (66 ft.). It is found on rocky and algal reefs, most often over sand and rubble substrate or among macroalgae.
Captive Care: See the Captive Care section in the genus account for husbandry information.
Aquarium Size: 75 gal. **Temperature:** 22° to 27°C (72° to 80°F).

Aquarium Suitability Index: 2–3.
Remarks: There are minor differences in the colors of the male and female *M. kuiteri*. The male has pink bands on the cheek. Juveniles have ocelli on the dorsal and anal fins. This species is similar to **Moyer's Leopard Wrasse (*Macropharyngodon moyeri*) Shepard & Meyer, 1978**, which is limited in distribution to the Izu Islands south to the northern Ryukus. It has been reported at depths of 5 to 20 m (17 to 66 ft.) over sand and rubble substrates.

Macropharyngodon meleagris (Valenciennes, 1839)

Common Name: Leopard Wrasse.
Maximum Length: 15 cm (5.9 in.)
Distribution: Cocos-Keeling Island in the Indian Ocean east to the Marquesas and Pitcairn Islands, north to southern Japan, and south to southeastern Australia.

Macropharyngodon meleagris, Leopard Wrasse, juvenile.

Macropharyngodon meleagris, Leopard Wrasse, male.

Biology: The Leopard Wrasse occurs at depths of less than 1 to 28 m (3 to 91 ft.) and inhabits lagoons, reef flats, faces, and slopes. It is also found in the turbulent areas of the reef crest. This fish feeds mainly on foraminiferans and gastropods. It also eats copepods and invertebrate eggs. Filamentous algae, detritus, and sand are ingested incidentally. *Macropharyngodon meleagris* usually occurs singly but is also found in pairs and groups.

Captive Care: See the Captive Care section in the genus account for husbandry information.

Aquarium Size: 100 gal. **Temperature:** 23° to 28°C (74° to 82°F).

Aquarium Suitability Index: 2–3.

Remarks: Female *M. meleagris* have dark brown spots on a pale green body, while the males are orangish red overall with black-edged green spots on the body, green bands on the head, and a black shoulder patch that contains several small yellow spots. The females were once thought to be a different species and were referred to as *Macropharyngodon pardalis*.

Macropharyngodon ornatus Randall, 1978

Common Name: Ornate Leopard Wrasse.

Maximum Length: 12 cm (4.7 in.).

Distribution: Sri Lanka to Papua New Guinea, south to northwestern Australia, and north to the Andaman Sea.

Biology: The Ornate Leopard Wrasse occurs at depths of 3 to 20 m (10 to 65 ft.) on the reef crest, reef face, and reef slope. It is often found over rubble or mixed rubble and sand. Male *M. ornatus* typically occur singly, while females and juveniles will form small groups.

Captive Care: See the Captive Care section in the genus account for husbandry information.

Aquarium Size: 75 gal. **Temperature:** 23° to 28°C (74° to 82°F).

Macropharyngodon ornatus, Ornate Leopard Wrasse, male.

Aquarium Suitability Index: 2–3.

Remarks: Males have green bands and spots on the face, body, and fins, and lack the black spot on the shoulder that is present in *M. meleagris*. Females have similar markings, but they are lighter in color.

Macropharyngodon negrosensis Herre, 1932

Common Name: Black Leopard Wrasse.

Maximum Length: 12 cm (4.7 in.).

Distribution: Andaman Sea to Samoa, north to Japan, and south to the Great Barrier Reef.

Biology: The Black Leopard Wrasse occurs at depths from 8 to 32 m (26 to 104 ft.), with most being reported from 15 m (49 ft.) or deeper. It is found in lagoons and on reef faces and slopes. Adults are found singly or in pairs. Juvenile *M. negrosensis* form

Macropharyngodon negrosensis, Black Leopard Wrasse, female.

Macropharyngodon negrosensis, Black Leopard Wrasse, male.

loose groups that are sometimes joined by other small wrasses.
Captive Care: See the Captive Care section in the genus account for husbandry information.
Aquarium Size: 75 gal. **Temperature:** 23 to 28 ºC (74 to 82 ºF).
Aquarium Suitability Index: 2.

Remarks: The females of *M. negrosensis* have many pale spots on a black background. The males are black overall with a dark purple thorax, broad lines on the face (rather than spots), and scales edged with light green. The light tail will turn black during courtship.

TRIBE NOVACULINI (RAZORFISHES)

THE SAND FLATS AND SLOPES ADJACENT TO CORAL REEFS ARE home to a very interesting fish community. The piscine residents of this habitat exhibit unusual adaptations for living in this structurally impoverished environment. Many of the fishes from the sand slope community bury in the sediment when they are threatened. The masters of this predator avoidance tactic are the razorfishes. When in danger, they dive head first into the sand. While many members of the razorfish tribe are not the most chromatically blessed of the reef's ichthyfauna, their behaviors make them worthy residents of the extra-large sand/reef interface-biotope tank.

Biology

The razorfish tribe is represented in rocky and coral reef habitats around the world. Some species are wide ranging (e.g., *Iniistius pavo*), while others have a very limited distribution. Several species that fall into this latter group have been described in recent years. For example, *Xyrichtys koteamea* is a species that is only known from Easter Island and was described in 2004. It is one of

the most colorful members of the tribe, sporting a bright red coloration. Another attractive, newly described species is Halstead's Razorfish (*Xyrichtys halsteadi*). This fish is a resident of Papua New Guinea, the Mariana Islands, Wake Island, and the Society Islands, and is known from water depths of 21 to 49 m (69 to 162 ft.). The genus *Xyrichtys* is well represented in the Eastern Pacific. There are six species found in this area and five of them are endemic to the region: the Mundiceps Razorfish (*Xyrichtys mundiceps*), which is found in Baja California and in Panama, the Blackspot Razorfish (*X. victori*), which is only known from the Galapagos and Cocos Islands, and Wellington's Razorfish (*Xyrichtys wellingtoni*), which is endemic to Clipperton Atoll. There is also an undescribed species that occurs around the Galapagos Islands and one that has been observed around Revillagigedo Islands.

The razorfishes are residents of sand flats, sand slopes, and

Cymolutes torquatus, Finescale Razorfish, male, emerging from sand, where it dives head first whenever threatened.

Iniistius pavo, Blue or Pavo's Razorfish, color variant: a fish noted for its ability to "swim" buried in soft sand, sometimes diving in and traveling a meter (3.3 ft.) or more to escape a threat. Note pair of eyespots (ocelli) on dorsal fin that may confuse predators and deflect attacks.

seagrass beds. They share these habitats with garden eels, sand divers, and flatfishes. Razorfishes are well known from their sand-diving and "sand-swimming" behavior. When they are threatened by predators and at night, when they are most vulnerable, they dive head first into the sand. They can also "swim" under soft sand; many divers have watched a razorfish disappear into the sand, then reemerge one meter (3.3 ft.) or more away from the entry point. The razorfishes seem to prefer to initiate their dives at a certain spot (referred to by one author as their "dive sites") and will typically hover above this site before plunging into the sand. At least some razorfishes (and other burying labrids) prepare the sand at this location so that they can dive into it more rapidly. For example, the Finescale Razorfish (*Cymolutes torquatus*) will move rubble, bits of seagrass, and twigs from a location in its territory where it typically dives when threatened. The Green Razorfish (*Xyrichtys splendens*) will soften up the substrate in areas with coarse sand and rubble by repeatedly diving into the sand in a specific location (these are known as "maintenance dives"). This makes it easier for the fish to penetrate when danger threatens. It has been suggested that the mucus that the fish exudes also softens the sand.

The Rockmover Wrasse (*Novaculichthys taeniourus*) has been observed to use a different strategy when preparing nocturnal resting sites. This wrasse will use its mouth to move coral rubble and form a mound comprising 4 to 71 bits of debris. As the sun sets, the wrasse buries in the sand under these mounds. The purpose of this behavior may be to make it more difficult for nocturnal predators to locate and extract the wrasse from the sand, or to dissuade other burying wrasses from using that particular spot on the seafloor.

To avoid predators, razorfishes do not always dive into the sand. Studies have shown that most species of razorfish are reluctant to sand-dive in response to predators and usually only do this as a last resort, when the predator comes too near. When a razorfish buries itself, it can no longer keep track of the predator's activities. It may find itself in a more precarious situation when it reemerges from the sand than it was in when it dove in. Indeed, some predators will remain in the area and wait out burying prey species like razorfishes. The length of time that a razorfish remains buried after diving to escape a predator may be anywhere from less than a minute to over an hour (this varies between individuals and species). Some species are more nervous and engage in sand-diving more readily than others. Some razorfishes, rather than sand-diving, hide in the seagrass or rapidly swim away from a threat. The juveniles of some species mimic benthic debris. The juvenile Rockmover Wrasse (*Novaculichthys taeniourus*) and the young Blue or Pavo's Razorfish (*Iniistius pavo*) will sway back and forth and drift just over the seafloor in an apparent attempt to resemble free-floating plant material.

The razorfishes feed on benthic invertebrates and zooplankton. The substrate-bound invertebrates they feed on tend to be small relative to the razorfish's body size. An ontogenetic change in diet has been demonstrated in at least one species (the Pearly Razorfish, *Xyrichtys novacula*), and probably occurs in all razorfishes. In this species, juveniles eat more smaller, soft-bodied prey items (e.g., amphipods and copepods), while adults consume more hard-shelled invertebrates (e.g., bivalves, crustaceans, and sea urchins). Those species that feed heavily on zooplankton rise into the water column to search for food and often form loose feeding groups. But most razorfishes stay within 1.5 m (5 ft.) of the bottom.

At least some razorfishes live in groups or colonies because of the threat that exists on open sand bottoms. By living in groups, they increase their chances of detecting predators. When one razorfish detects an approaching predator, it signals others in the colony with its behavioral response. For example, when Rosy Razorfish (*Xyrichtys martinicensis*) at the edge of a colony detect a jack, they rapidly move to the substrate. This response instantaneously moves through the colony until all members of the group have adopted their predator-avoidance response.

The razorfishes are monandric, protogynous hermaphrodites (the only males are secondary males that result from female sex change). They are also sexually dimorphic (the male is larger than the female) and sexually dichromatic. They are also haremic, and the territory of the male includes the territories or home ranges of one or more females. The males vigorously defend their territory boundaries and their females from consexuals and regularly visit the members of their harem. The razorfish are all broadcast (pelagic) spawners. They are also pair spawners. The male initiates courtship, which usually involves some form of S-curve posturing (the fish holds its body in an S-shape) and a slow spawning ascent into the water column. At the top of the ascent, the fish "snap," at which time they release their gametes, then dash back to the seafloor.

An interesting phenomenon has been observed in spawning razorfishes of the genus *Xyrichtys*. In the Caribbean, the males of two species of zooplankton-feeding razorfishes (*X. martinicensis* and *X. splendens*) have been observed to eat their mates' eggs. After the male and female release their gametes at the apex of the

Xyrichtys victori, Galapagos Razorfish, adult male: haremic species.

spawning ascent, the male will turn and feed on ova before the gamete cloud dissipates. This is known as filial cannibalism. Nemtzov and Clark (1994) report that in 40% of the spawning bouts observed in these two species, the males ate some of the ova emitted by their partners. The males of the sympatric Pearly Razorfish (*X. novacula*), which normally feeds on benthic invertebrates, did not engage in this feeding behavior.

Captive Care

While a number of the razorfishes are attractive and many are very interesting to watch, most home aquarists are not familiar with members of this group. The species that are most often seen and sought are the members of the genus *Novaculichthys*. The other razorfishes are sporadically available. These fascinating fishes often prove to be nervous aquarium inhabitants (especially the *Iniistius* and *Xyrichtys*), at least until they fully acclimate to aquarium living. For this reason, they are best housed in tanks in low-traffic areas. For example, they are probably not the best fish for the display aquarium in a doctor's office. In this venue, they may spend most or all of their time hiding under the substrate. It is important to cover the top of the aquarium, as razorfish are likely to leap out of an open tank. This is especially true the first night or two after being added to a tank and/or when the lights are turned off for the night.

Another requirement for most of the razorfishes is a tank with lots of open sand substrate. The sand should have a fine grain size. While you can mix some rubble and shells with the sand, it is best to keep these larger chunks to a minimum, as they can impede sand-diving. These fishes may injure themselves on larger, coarser pieces of debris. Those species that generally spend their lives in seagrass will appreciate either live

Iniistius aneitensis, Yellowblotch Razorfish, adult male: creatures of sand flats and reef slopes, all the razorfishes need a spacious expanse of deep sand.

seagrass or stands of macroalgae (e.g., *Caulerpa prolifera*) in the tank. The latter is easy to grow in the home aquarium. Because these fishes spend most of their lives near the seafloor, a tank with more surface area is also better than a very high aquarium. That said, they do rise up in the water column to feed, so a tank with some height is good.

The razorfishes need to be fed several times a day to ensure their good health, unless they are kept in an aquarium that has good micro-invertebrate fauna (which they will most likely quickly deplete) or a productive refugium. Feed them a meaty food, such as mysid shrimps, table shrimp shavings, frozen preparation for carnivores, and live black worms. The juveniles of some species may have difficulty competing for food.

As far as disposition is concerned, many in the tribe tend to be rather aggressive. For this reason, it is often best to house them on their own (e.g., a male with one or more females) or with other aggressive wrasses. Of course, the larger the tank, the less

problem you will have with aggression. Juveniles are more tolerant of tankmates, but as they grow so too does their attitude. For example, the juvenile Rockmover or Dragon Wrasse (*Novaculichthys taeniourus*) is a relatively placid fish, but the adults are hellions. Adults of the larger species may not only bully their neighbors, they will also feed on them. For example, *Iniistius pavo* and *Xyrichtys novacula* will prey on small fishes. The more diminutive Green Razorfish (*Xyrichtys splendens*) can be housed with other fishes, although it, too, may pick on smaller species added to a tank where they are already residents.

There are two ways to acquire a male and female razorfish. You can find and purchase a specimen of each sex or you can purchase two females or two juveniles and the larger, more dominant fish is likely to change sex to a male. It is also possible to keep small groups of these fishes in large tanks (at least a 180-gallon tank for the smaller species and preferably more for larger razorfishes). Refer to the species accounts below; some species are

Cymolutes praetextatus, Knife Razorfish.

Cymolutes torquatus, Finescale Razorfish, juvenile.

Cymolutes torquatus, Finescale Razorfish, adult female.

less tolerant of conspecifics than others.

If you are willing to devote a substantial portion of an extra-large reef tank's bottom to open sand, you can successfully keep these fishes. They will need a fine sand substrate at least 8 cm (3 in.) in depth. Their sub-sand activities will help aerate and turn the sand bed. One problem with razorfish, especially adults, is that they will eat ornamental crustaceans, some beneficial worms, snails, and serpent stars.

Genus *Cymolutes*

Cymolutes praetextatus (Quoy & Gaimard, 1834)
Common Name: Knife Razorfish.
Maximum Length: 20 cm (7.9 in).
Distribution: East Africa to the Society Islands, south to Rowley Shoals.
Biology: This razorfish is found in shallow lagoons and on reef flats at depths of 2 to 10 m (7 to 33 ft.), over sand, rubble, macroalgae, and seagrass, often in current-prone areas.
Captive Care: This active razorfish should be housed in a tank with a relatively deep sand bed (8 cm [3.1 in.]). A good crop of *Caulerpa* will also help it feel at home in captivity. Keep only one male per tank. Adding more than one female to a tank will result in the larger fish transforming to a male. It may fight with other razorfishes and smaller wrasses. It needs a tank devoid of reef structure and will eat a number of different motile invertebrates. It is similar in husbandry requirements to the Finescale Razorfish (*C. torquatus*).
Aquarium Size: 135 gal. **Temperature:** 23° to 28°C (74° to 82°F).
Aquarium Suitability Index: 3.
Remarks: This machete-shaped wrasse is yellowish green with a

white line along the dorsal fin base. There are three species in the genus. The third species in the genus is the **Hawaiian Knifefish** (*Cymolutes lecluse*) (**Quoy & Gaimard, 1824**), which is endemic to the Hawaiian Islands.

Cymolutes torquatus (Valenciennes, 1840)
Common Names: Finescale Razorfish, Collared Knifefish.
Maximum Length: 20 cm (7.9 in).
Distribution: East Africa and the Marquesas, north to southern Japan, and south to Lord Howe Island.
Biology: This species is found on sand flats or slopes adjacent to coastal reefs, in lagoons, or on reef flats at depths of 2 to 15 m (7 to 50 ft.) in seagrass beds. They are often found over sand, seagrass, and rubble. This wrasse commonly clears pieces of debris

Cymolutes torquatus, Finescale Razorfish, male.

Novaculichthys macrolepidotus, Seagrass Razorfish, adult: hardy in captivity.

from a specific site on the bottom, apparently to prepare a spot where it can dive head first into the sand at night or when threatened. The Finescale Razorfish has been observed being cleaned by the Goldstripe Wrasse (*Halichoeres zeylonicus*). The male *C. torquatus* is haremic, defending a territory that is about 10 to 14 m² (108 to 151 ft.²), which is subdivided into smaller territories occupied by the females. A male's harem usually consists of four or five females. Males patrol their territories and visit the females that live within their borders. To test a female's receptivity, the male will engage in looping, where it swims in a loop up to 30 cm (12 in.) into the water column and quivers. If the female is receptive to the male's advances, she will curve her body toward the male and change colors. A sexually receptive female develops a lavender-pink swelling on the abdomen and when approached by the male, her yellow body markings turn black. The pair as-

cends into the water column, side by side, and release their gametes at the top of the spawning ascent (about 1 m [3.3 ft.] above the substrate). Just prior to the spawning ascent, the area around the anus turns yellow. Spawning in this species occurs midmorning (between 9:38 and 10:50 A.M.).

Captive Care: The Finescale Razorfish is an attractive member of the tribe that is not common in the aquarium trade. Like others in the group, this wrasse requires a sand bed of at least 5 to 8 cm (2 to 3 in.) to burrow in. It will do best in a tank with lots of uncluttered, open sand bottom. Juveniles can be kept with a variety of tankmates, but adults can have a rather belligerent disposition. For this reason, it is best to keep it with larger tankmates or moderately aggressive fishes. For example, adults can be kept with larger members of these groups: gobies (e.g., *Valenciennea* spp.), sea bream, sand perches, flatfishes, and cowfishes (these fishes co-occur with it on open sand slopes as well). It is best to add these fish before the *C. torquatus*. It is likely to quarrel with other razorfishes.

Aquarium Size: 135 gal. **Temperature:** 23° to 28°C (74° to 82°F).
Aquarium Suitability Index: 3.

Remarks: Female Finescale Razorfish are pale overall with dark bands and a reddish dorsal fin. The males are bright green with red dorsal and caudal fin margins. The male also has a conspicuous dark bar behind the gill cover (hence the alternate common name).

Genus *Novaculichthys*

Novaculichthys macrolepidotus (Bloch, 1791)
Common Name: Seagrass Razorfish.
Maximum Length: 15 cm (5.9 in.).
Distribution: Red Sea to Papua New Guinea, north to the Ryukyus, and south to Lord Howe Island.
Biology: This is a shallow-water wrasse that is typically associated with seagrass and macroalgae. It is found in mangrove habitats, lagoons, and channels at depths of less than 1 to at least 4 m (3.3 to 13 ft.). It lurks among underwater vegetation and is easily overlooked. Adult *N. macrolepidotus* often occur in groups, which probably consist of a single male and a harem of females.
Captive Care: The Seagrass Razorfish is a fairly durable aquarium species. An ideal habitat tank for this species would contain dense stands of long-bladed *Caulerpa* spp. The wrasse can slink about the macroalgae as it does in seagrass beds in the wild. It can be pugnacious in a small aquarium and toward smaller, more docile fishes. It is best to house it with moderately aggressive tankmates. Like most reef fishes, if added to a tank of bullies, the Seagrass Razorfish may have a difficult time adapting. Keep one per tank.

Novaculichthys macrolepidotus, Seagrass Razorfish, large adult: an accurate biotope for these fish would include stands of long-bladed green *Caulerpa* macroalgae.

You may be able to keep a heterosexual pair or a group of females in a very large aquarium (180 gallons or larger) with lots of seagrass or *Caulerpa*. This fish has been known to jump out of an open aquarium.

Aquarium Size: 75 gal. **Temperature:** 23° to 28°C (74° to 82°F).
Aquarium Suitability Index: 4.
Remarks: Juvenile *N. macrolepidotus* vary from brown to green, usually with darker blotches. The female is bright green with a dark stripe along the side of the body. The male is green with dark lines radiating from the eyes and several spots at the base of the tail.

Novaculichthys taeniourus (Lacepède, 1801)
Common Names: Rockmover Wrasse, Dragon Wrasse, Reindeer Wrasse.
Maximum Length: 27 cm (10.6 in).
Distribution: Red Sea to Panama, north to the Ryukyu and Hawaiian Islands, south to Lord Howe and Tuamotu Islands.

N. taeniourus, Rockmover Wrasse, juvenile: cute, but it becomes destructive.

Novaculichthys taeniourus, Rockmover Wrasse, subadult: a fascinating species for a large aquarium where it is free to rearrange rock and rubble.

Biology: The Rockmover Wrasse is found in lagoons, reef flats, channels, reef faces, and reef slopes at depths of 1 to 20 m (3.3 to 66 ft.). It is most often found over mixed sand-rubble bottoms. The young *N. taeniourus* occur singly and sometimes mimic a piece of floating debris. They move in a sinusoidal fashion, with the head down, just over the seafloor. Adults most often occur singly. This fish gets is common name from its habit of grasping rubble with its jaws and lifting and moving the debris or flipping it over in an attempt to find concealed prey items.

They can move relatively large pieces of rubble or rock—in some cases, these bits of debris often outweigh the fish. After moving a piece of rubble, these fish will visually examine the exposed substrate and may shovel further in the sediment by taking mouthfuls of sand and throwing it to one side. The Rockmover Wrasse feeds on bivalves, snails, sea urchins, brittle stars, polychaete worms, and crabs. Because of its habit of disturbing the substrate, this wrasse is regularly followed by opportunists. For example, jacks will often follow *N. taeniourus* as it flips over coral rubble or rocks. The jacks remain just behind and above the wrasse's gill openings. From this position, they dart forward to grab prey flushed by the wrasse's feeding activities. Although up to four Bluefin Jacks (*Caranx melampygus*) may follow a single *N. taeniourus*, some individuals guard the Rockmover Wrasse that they are following. The labrid-associating jacks will change to a darker color, possibly to warn conspecifics that they will attack if the heterospecific pair is approached too closely. Other wrasses and goatfishes are also drawn to the Rockmover Wrasse's feeding activities. This labrid pair spawns.

Captive Care: Although ornate, interesting, and relatively well be-haved as a juvenile, the young *N. taeniourus* can become destruc-tive and undesirable aquarium inhabitants as they mature. They can be very aggressive toward fish tankmates and should be kept in a fish-only tank with aggressive tankmates. Juveniles are not aggressive and some aquarists have even housed more than one in the same tank. Keep subadult and adult *N. taeniourus* singly, as they will fight. The Rockmover Wrasse is not suitable for the reef aquarium because of its habit of flipping rubble and corals and its proclivity to eat all kinds of motile invertebrates. If you have a medium-sized tank (e.g., 75 gallons) you can keep an adult *N. taeniourus* on its own. It is a very interesting fish to watch—just place patches of rubble on the bottom and watch the wrasse redecorate the aquarium. Placing live ghost shrimp in a tank with a rubble bottom can encourage more rubble flipping. This species buries and will require a fine sand bed (5 to 10 cm [2 to 4 in.] deep) in which to hide. If adults bury near rockwork, they may topple reef structure. They have been known to jump from uncovered aquariums. They will eat almost any meaty food offered, and grow fast if well fed.

Aquarium Size: 135 gal. **Temperature:** 23° to 28°C (74° to 82°F).
Aquarium Suitability Index: 4.
Remarks: Juvenile *N. taeniourus* can be brown or green with white blotches. Adults are dark brown with a white line on each scale. This species was formerly placed in the genus *Hemipteronotus*.

Genus *Iniistius*

Iniistius aneitensis (Günther, 1862)
Common Names: Yellowblotch Razorfish, Whiteblotch Razorfish.
Maximum Length: 24 cm (9.4 in.).
Distribution: Zanzibar, Maldives and Chagos Archipelago east to Hawaiian Islands, north to the Ryukyus.
Biology: This razorfish is found on sand flats and slopes adjacent to fringing reefs, in lagoons and outer reef slopes at depths of 6 to 92 m (20 to 304 ft.). In the Hawaiian Islands, it is most com-mon on sand flats and slopes at depths of around 15 m (50 ft.).

Novaculichthys taeniourus, Rockmover Wrasse, large juvenile green morph.

Novaculichthys taeniourus, Rockmover Wrasse, adult: becomes aggressive.

Iniistius aneitensis, Yellowblotch Razorfish, small juvenile.

Iniistius aneitensis, Yellowblotch Razorfish, large juvenile: seldom collected.

Iniistius aneitensis, Yellowblotch Razorfish, adult male.

Iniistius celebicus, Celebes Razorfish, juvenile.

Iniistius celebicus, Celebes Razorfish, female: need a deep sand bed.

This species is haremic, with the territory of a male containing 2 to 10 females.

Captive Care: The Yellowblotch Razorfish occasionally makes it into the ornamental fish trade and can be successfully kept in the home aquarium. Feed this and other razorfishes several times a day or more. For more on keeping this and other razorfishes, see the Captive Care section for the tribe.

Aquarium Size: 135 gal. **Temperature:** 23° to 28°C (74° to 82°F).

Aquarium Suitability Index: 3.

Remarks: The young *I. aneitensis* can be uniform green, dark brown, or black, but more often is light with dark bars. Adults have a white blotch on the abdomen. Most members of the genus *Iniistius* were placed in the genus *Xyrichtys* in the past. Now it is thought that the genus *Xyrichtys* is limited to the Eastern Pacific and Atlantic Oceans (with the exception of *Iniistius pavo*, which ranges to Panama, and *Xyrichtys halsteadi*, which is found in the Western Pacific). (See terminal phase male, page 262.)

Iniistius celebicus (Bleeker, 1856)

Common Names: Celebes Razorfish, Bronzespot Razorfish.

Maximum Length: 19 cm (7.5 in).

Distribution: Indonesia to the Hawaiian Islands, north to the Philippines, and south to Middleton Reef in the Coral Sea.

Biology: The Celebes Razorfish is found in clear lagoons and on outer reef slopes at depths of 8 to 20 m (26 to 66 ft.). In the Hawaiian Islands, this species inhabits current-prone sand slopes. It is a shy species that dives under the sand at the slightest disturbance. The females move about in loose groups. Males will join these females as they forage and dash around among them. When the male engages in this behavior it also exhibits a distinct color

Iniistius celebicus, Celebes Razorfish, male: smaller member of its genus.

Iniistius pavo, Blue Razorfish, black juvenile.

phase, which is bluish with two broad, light stripes. When the pair rises into the water column to spawn, the male rolls around the female at the apex of the ascent.

Captive Care: *Iniistius celebicus* is one of the smaller members of the genus and thus is better suited to the home aquarium than many of its relatives. As for others in the genus, a tank with little or no reef structure and a medium to deep sand bed is essential to successful husbandry of this species. See the general recommendations in the Captive Care section for the tribe for more information.

Aquarium Size: 135 gal. **Temperature:** 23° to 28°C (74° to 82°F).
Aquarium Suitability Index: 3.

Remarks: The male of *I. celebicus* is pale overall, with a black patch behind the pectoral fin.

Iniistius pavo (Valenciennes, 1840)

Common Names: Blue Razorfish, Pavo's Razorfish, Indianfish.
Maximum Length: 41 cm (16.1 in).
Distribution: Red Sea to Mexico, north to southern Japan and the Hawaiian Islands, and south to Lord Howe Island and the Society Islands. In the Eastern Pacific, it ranges from the Gulf of California to Panama and the Galapagos Islands.
Biology: The Blue Razorfish is found in clear lagoons and outer reef sand slopes. It is most common in areas with large sand expanses adjacent to coral reefs. These razorfish tend to prefer a coarse sand substrate. In the Indo-West Pacific, juveniles are found as shallow as 2 m (7 ft.), while the adults are not common at depths of less than 30 m (98 ft.). In the Galapagos Islands, they are more common at shallow depths, between 5 and 12 m (17 to 40 ft.). Juveniles swim in a head-down, sinusoidal fashion and apparently attempt to mimic benthic plant debris. They often

Iniistius pavo, Blue Razorfish, brown juvenile.

Iniistius pavo, Blue Razorfish, white juvenile.

Iniistius pavo, Blue Razorfish, striped subadult: best in a species tank.

Iniistius pavo, Blue Razorfish, striped subadult: needs deep sandy bottom.

Iniistius pavo, Blue Razorfish, adult: aggressive toward most tankmates.

hover near bits of coral rubble or benthic debris. This species will forage over the sand and on hard reef substrate. The adult male *I. pavo* defends a large territory that contains a harem of three to five females. The territory of the male can cover an area of 25 to 50 m² (269 to 538 ft.²). In areas where this species is less abundant, adults range over large home ranges. The Blue Razorfish spawns about 4 hours before dusk. In the Red Sea, the black color phase of this fish has been reported to occur singly most of the time, occasionally pairing at dusk. The males of this species sometimes squabble with male sand divers (*Trichonotus* sp.).

Captive Care: If provided with the appropriate aquarium venue, *I. pavo* can be a fairly hardy aquarium resident. One problem with this fish is that it can be quite aggressive toward fish tankmates, especially related species and fishes added to a tank where it already resides. It will attack garden eels and sand divers. For this reason, it is best to devote a tank to a male and one or more females of this species. The tank should have a sand bed at least 8 cm (3 in.) deep to facilitate sand-diving. The Blue Razorfish is a threat to a wide variety of motile invertebrates and will do better in a tank devoid of live rock or other structure. For more on keeping this and other razorfishes, see the Captive Care section for the tribe.

Aquarium Size: 240 gal. **Temperature:** 23° to 28°C (74° to 82°F).

Aquarium Suitability Index: 3.

Remarks: Juveniles under 6 cm (2.4 in.) are a solid color (greenish brown, tan brown, dark brown, or black). As they get larger they take on a banded color pattern. There is an ocellus on the dorsal fin. Adults over about 14 cm (5.5 in.) are light gray to brownish gray overall with three obscure body bars and a bar across the caudal fin. There are one or two small, dark spots below the anterior portion of the dorsal fin. Males have a blue marking on each scale on the lower half of the body. The scientific name *Xyrichtys niger* has been used for the black or melanistic juvenile phase of this species (an occasional adult may be all black as well). *Iniistius tetrazona* is also a synonym of this species. There are 16 scientific names used for this species.

Iniistius pentadactylus (Linnaeus, 1758)

Common Name: Fivefinger Razorfish.

Maximum Length: 25 cm (9.8 in).

Distribution: Red Sea to Papua New Guinea, north to the Ogasawara Islands, and south to Natal.

Biology: This species is found in open sand stretches, often near coastal reefs, at depths of 2 to 18 m (7 to 59 ft.). The male territory, which can cover an area of 8 to 30 m² (86 to 323 ft.²), includes the smaller territories of one to six females. Larger females are dominant over smaller consexuals. Nemtzov (1985) demonstrated that all males in a Red Sea population studies were derived from female sex change. If a male is removed from a population, the largest female in the area will change sex. The second largest female may also begin to change sex, but the change is suppressed by the larger, more dominant female. This species pair spawns, with courtship beginning about 15 minutes after sunset and continuing until it gets dark. Males will mate once or up to eight times during an evening. Males approach females, who respond by swimming off (if unreceptive) or performing an S-curve with her body. The male circles around the S-curving female for about 2 minutes. The pair then adopts a parallel orientation and engages in the spawning ascent. At about 2 m (6.6 ft.) from the substrate, the pair "snaps" (releases their gametes) and dashes back to the seafloor. The males of this species sometimes fight with male sand divers (*Trichonotus* sp.).

Captive Care: If a female is placed in an aquarium without a male, it will change sex. For more on keeping this and other razorfishes, see the Captive Care section for the tribe.

Aquarium Size: 135 gal. **Temperature:** 23° to 28°C (74° to 82°F).

Aquarium Suitability Index: 3.

Remarks: The female *I. pentadactylus* has a patch of white scales with red edges on the abdomen. The males are greenish gray overall with four or five spots behind the eye.

Iniistius umbrilatus (Jenkins, 1901)

Common Name: Hawaiian Razorfish.

Maximum Length: 19 cm (7.5 in.).

Distribution: Hawaiian Islands.

Biology: The Hawaiian Razorfish occurs on sand flats and slopes at depths of 6 to 40 m (20 to 132 ft.). Randall (2002) provides details regarding its biology. He reports that it is one of the most abundant species in the Hawaiian Islands. It settles out of the plankton at a size of about 12 mm (0.5 in.), with peak numbers occurring in March and April (although new recruits are reported from all months of the year). The young fish form loose groups. They are preyed upon by lizardfishes (mostly *Tachinocephalus myops*). Adult males are territorial. The females defend an area within the male's larger territory. The male moves about his turf, occasionally visiting his harem members, and displays at territory boundaries. Spawning occurs in the late afternoon, when a male begins to approach females from behind. Unreceptive females will swim away; a female that is ready to spawn slowly rises into the water column, side by side with the male, and the pair releases its gametes. The pair then abruptly wiggles and returns to the seafloor. The height of spawning ascent is 0.5 to 1 m (20 to 39 in.).

Captive Care: This is medium-sized razorfish that is similar in behavior and husbandry requirements to others in the genus. For more on keeping this and other razorfishes, see the Captive Care section for the tribe.

Aquarium Size: 100 gal. **Temperature:** 23° to 28°C (74° to 82°F).

Aquarium Suitability Index: 3.

Remarks: The small juveniles of this species are pale with patches of various shades of brown or green. As they grow, the patches become bars on the body. There are also two ocelli on the dorsal fin. Adults males are gray with white-edged scales, and have a black patch on the mid-back.

Iniistius pentadactylus, Fivefinger Razorfish, adult male: females are larger.

Iniistius umbrilatus, Hawaiian Razorfish, juvenile.

Xyrichtys martinicensis, Rosy Razorfish, female: needs space and deep sand.

Xyrichtys martinicensis, Rosy Razorfish, female: Caribbean native.

Genus *Xyrichtys*

Xyrichtys martinicensis Valenciennes, 1840

Common Name: Rosy Razorfish.

Maximum Length: 5.9 in. (15 cm).

Distribution: Southern Florida and Bahamas, west to the Yucatan and south to Venezuela.

Biology: The Rosy Razorfish is found on sand flats and slopes, over wide sand expanses, in lagoons, and adjacent to outer reefs. It has been reported from depths of 5 to 15 m (17 to 45 ft.). It prefers fine, nonsilty sand to areas of mixed sand and rubble. This preference is, no doubt, due to its sand-diving behavior. Victor (1987) did an extensive study on the behavioral ecology of this species. He found that it lives in colonies of 5 to 100 or more individuals, mainly females. The males in each colony defends a particular area that contains a group (harem) of females. Harem size may range from 3 to 35 females. Male *X. martinicensis* patrol the boundaries of their territories and engage in lateral displays with consexuals along their territory borders. Males will also regularly attack trophic competitors, like small flounders, Mojarras, and goatfishes. Females occupy a small, defined home range (maybe 2 m [7 ft.] in diameter), which includes a preferred dive site. While they do not defend their entire home range from neighboring females, they will vigorously defend a portion of it from consexuals. Larger females usually initiate aggression toward smaller ones. Before overt aggression occurs, females of similar size engage in ritual display—they line up side by side and curve their bodies into an exaggerated S-posture. The female *X. martinicensis* spend most of their time either foraging on zooplankton in the water column or searching for small benthic in-vertebrates. When feeding on plankton, they hold their position in the water column about 1 m (3.3 ft.) over the bottom. Females also perform maintenance dives at their preferred dive sites and remove bits of debris (e.g., coral rubble) from the area. Male Rosy Razorfish have also been observed to chase and steal food from females in their harem. While individuals maintain their position in the colony relative to their neighbors, the whole colony will occasionally move up or down the slope. Occasionally, colonies may merge with neighboring groups.

This species pair-spawns. Spawning occurs in late afternoon (between 2:30 and 4:00 P.M.). A male courts females by engaging in a headstand, erecting all his fins, and intensifying in color. He then quivers and dashes around the female with his head up. If receptive, she will slowly rise into the water column and the male will position himself alongside her. At a height of about 1 m (3.3 ft.) over the seafloor, the pair releases its gametes and dashes back to the bottom. If female is not receptive, the male moves on to another member of his harem. Larger females may change sex; this transformation takes about 2 weeks. Sex change has been reported in females of 7 cm (2.8 in.) SL. The sex-changing female will attempt to secure a portion of the harem it was a formerly a member of. When fast-moving predators come into the area, all members of the colony initiate a fright response: they immediately move to the bottom, lie on their sides, and adopt a mottled color pattern. They will dive into the sand if the predator should close to within 1 m (3.3 ft.). Once the predator passes, things quickly return to normal in the razorfish colony. In the late afternoon (5:30 P.M.), these wrasses take shelter in the sediment.

Captive Care: Keep one Rosy Razorfish male per tank. If the reef tank is large enough (180 gallons or more), a male and one or

Xyrichtys novacula, Pearly Razorfish, adult female: will get quite large.

Xyrichtys novacula, Pearly Razorfish, adult male.

more females may be included. As for others in this group, provide a deep, open sand bed in which it can bury. This species is sexually dichromatic. It feeds on small benthic invertebrates and is likely to feed on worms, small snails, ornamental shrimps, and juvenile serpent stars. Feed meaty foods, including shredded frozen seafood, mysid shrimp, frozen preparations, and pigment-enriched flake food, at least once a day—unless you have a healthy stock of crustaceans and worms for them to feed on, in which case you can feed every other day.

Aquarium Size: 100 gal. **Temperature:** 23° to 28°C (74° to 82°F).
Aquarium Suitability Index: 3.
Remarks: The juveniles and females have an orange stripe along the side. This fish has a dark patch at the base of the pectoral fin.

Xyrichtys novacula (Linnaeus, 1758)

Common Name: Pearly Razorfish.
Maximum Length: 38 cm (15 in).
Distribution: North Carolina and northern Gulf of Mexico, south to Brazil, and east to West Africa and the Mediterranean.
Biology: This fish is found on sand flats and slopes at depths of 2 to 80 m (7 to 264 ft.) and is most common on deep sand slopes. Off North Carolina, it occurs on offshore scallop beds. It lives over and in several different types of sediment. In the eastern Mediterranean, the highest densities of *X. novacula* occur over substrate with moderately to well-sorted coarse or very coarse sand grains. In the Tyrrhenian Sea, it prefers fine, well-sorted sand. This species feeds on benthic invertebrates that frequent the sand bottoms it lives over and in. In the Caribbean, this species feeds most heavily on small gastropods (including *Batillaria* sp., *Caecum* sp., *Drillia* sp., and juvenile *Natica* sp.) and bivalves (*Er-vila nitens*, *Pitar* sp.), with polychaetes, shrimps, amphipods, isopods, scaphopods, serpent stars, sea urchins, and small fishes being of secondary importance. Pearly Razorfishes regularly ingest sand when feeding. In the Mediterranean, studies have shown that there is a trophic shift as this species grows larger. Young fish feed more on small prey items, like copepods and amphipods, while adults feed more on bivalves (e.g., *Acanthocardia tubercolata*), decapods, and sea urchins. Pearly Razorfish between 12 and 14 cm (4.7 to 5.5 cm) are reported to feed on the greatest diversity of prey items. This species is haremic, with the male territory including the home ranges of four to six females. There is evidence to suggest that they exhibit different color patterns at different sizes. This enables the male to determine the female's age and size, and whether or not she is sexually mature, by her chromatic attire. (Age and size will determine how many eggs she can produce.) Spawning occurs seasonally: in the southern Mediterranean the species spawns from late May until late September. Males and females spawn numerous times during the spawning period. It has been suggested that during the cooler months of the year this species spends most of its time hidden under the sand, but recent studies indicate that this is not the case.

Captive Care: *Xyrichtys novacula* is a large razorfish that will require a very spacious tank devoid of much reef structure, with a deep substrate bed (at least 13 cm [5 in.] in depth for adults) of fine-grained sand. It will do best in a low-traffic area. The juveniles may be kept with other fish species, but adults can be quite aggressive and will even eat small fishes. The general husbandry requirements are similar to others in the tribe. See the Captive Care section for more information.

Aquarium Size: 240 gal. **Temperature:** 23° to 28°C (74° to 82°F).

Xyrichtys splendens, Green Razorfish, adult male: good aquarium choice.

Aquarium Suitability Index: 3.
Remarks: *Xyrichtys novacula* adopts a barred pattern when drifting over the seafloor. Females reach sexual maturity at a length of around 10 to 12 cm (4 to 4.7 in.).

Xyrichtys splendens Castelnau, 1855
Common Name: Green Razorfish.
Maximum Length: 5.9 in. (15 cm).
Distribution: Southern Florida and Bermuda, south to the Yucatan and Brazil.
Biology: The Green Razorfish is found in shallow water, usually on sand flats in seagrass meadows. It also occurs in areas with soft sand or in microhabitats with mixed sand and coral rubble. This species, even large adults, feeds mainly on planktonic copepods. It will feed on some benthic prey (especially those individuals that reside in seagrass meadows), including amphipods, crustaceans, tiny snails, and minute clams. Females rise in the water column to forage and when a potential threat approaches, return to the seafloor. When approached by a predator, fish of both sexes will hover near a rock or piece of rubble with the body curved (the best posture to be in to instigate a fast dash into the sand) and their lateral bars darkened. If they are attacked, they will dive into a depression next to the rock or rubble. The fish prepare these depressions by repeatedly diving in and out of the sand (Nemtzov [1994] refers to them as "dive sites"). In other habitats, the zooplankton-feeding individuals may shelter among the branches of gorgonians (e.g., *Muricea muricata*, *Plexaura homomalla*, and *Eunicea* spp.) or staghorn coral when threatened. In seagrass beds, the Green Razorfish will hide among the grass blades when threatened, diving into the sand if the threat persists. Nemtzov (1994) found that this species usually stayed under the sand for just over 4 minutes when attacked by a predator. Male *X. splendens* are territorial, excluding consexuals from their turf. They ignore most heterospecifics, attack some, and steer clear of a few. The species that are regularly attacked include snake eels, lizardfishes, the Peacock Flounder (*Bothus lunatus*), the Slippery Dick (*Halichoeres bivittatus*), and the Rosy Razorfish (*X. martinicensis*). These are trophic competitors or predators of *X. splendens*. Females rarely attack intruders. The fishes that the Green Razorfish avoids are all piscivores and include Tarpons, jacks, tunas, snappers, groupers, and barracudas. Females live within the territories of the males and occasionally squabble. In some cases, a male may break up female fights. The Green Razorfish is a haremic species that spawns late in the afternoon. During courtship, the male swims rapidly past a female and flips

onto his side (this behavior is known as "flipping"), and swims 1 to 2 m (3.3 to 7 ft.) off the bottom and vibrates the rear portion of his body ("rising"). When predators are in the area, males engage in fewer courtship displays and the height of the spawning ascent is lower.
Captive Care: This attractive razorfish is one of the best for the reef tank, as it does not attain a large size and readily adapts to

captive life. It also feeds on smaller prey than razorfishes of similar size. It is primarily a zooplanktivore (e.g., copepods). That said, larger individuals may eat newly introduced ornamental shrimps, and this species can be aggressive toward other labrids and may pick on more docile species in a smaller tank. As for others in this group, provide a deep, open sand bed in which they can bury. Feed it meaty foods, including finely shredded frozen seafood, mysid shrimp, frozen preparations, and pigment-enriched flake food. Feed it two to three times a day.

Aquarium Size: 75 gal. **Temperature:** 23° to 28°C (74° to 82°F).

Aquarium Suitability Index: 4.

Remarks: When the Green Razorfish drifts in the water column, it often takes on a barred pattern. This species was formerly placed in the genus *Hemipteronotus*.

Paracheilinus flavianalis, Yellowfin Flasher Wrasse: male displaying flashing behavior: among the ideal fishes for the reef aquarium, beautiful and well behaved.

FLASHER WRASSES (GENUS *PARACHEILINUS*)

Many wrasses are extremely colorful, sporting resplendent hues and ornate patterns. Some of the most chromatically dramatic species, however, belong to the genus *Paracheilinus*—the flasher wrasses. Unfortunately, few divers actually take note of these beauties. They often occur at moderate depths, which means their brilliant colors are usually less conspicuous, and they are smaller in size than other wrasses. Flasher wrasses are most abundant in areas less frequented by the average diver, like rubble slopes or over beds of macroalgae. Aquarists, too, have a tendency to overlook these stunning fishes because they are often displayed improperly in aquarium stores. However, once you see a male flasher wrasse display, or "flash," you will never overlook this group again.

The genus *Paracheilinus* contains 16 described species. Due to individual and geographical variation, as well as the possibility that some forms may hybridize, the exact number of flasher wrasses is still under debate among aquarists. As a result of their small size and predilection for deep water, the majority of flasher wrasses were only recently discovered. The first species, the Eightlined Flasher Wrasse (*Paracheilinus octotaenia*), was described in 1955, while the second species, the Filamented Flasher (*P. filamentosus*), was not named until 1974. Seven of the known species have been named since 1999 (with at least one awaiting formal description).

All of the flasher wrasses are sexually dimorphic and dichromatic, with the males displaying more vibrant colors, attaining greater size, and, in most species, having more elongate dorsal fin filaments. In some flasher wrasses the color of the juveniles varies from that of the adults. All the flasher wrasses are protogynous hermaphrodites and haremic. Flasher wrasses often occur in mixed groups. In the Philippines, I have seen up to three species of *Paracheilinus*, as well as several *Cirrhilabrus* spp., in the same mixed aggregation. A number of flasher wrasse species hybridize. I observed congeners of mixed groups in the Philippines chasing one another and males courting with heterospecifics. I also observed several male hybrids. This can make identifying some individuals quite difficult. Kuiter and Allen (1999) suggested that males of certain species may exhibit intensified nuptial colors and more fin filaments in areas where they occur with congeners. In this way, they may be better able to attract conspecific females, as these features make the males more visible to females.

Flasher wrasses occur in aggregations, in which females greatly outnumber males. These groups usually occur over coral rubble bottoms, often in association with macroalgae and soft corals. They hang in the water column and feed on zooplankton carried by the current. Flasher wrasses are sometimes found in association with their relatives, the fairy wrasses. Like the fairy wrasses, they form a mucous cocoon that envelops their bodies while they sleep.

Captive Care

These wrasses adapt readily to captivity, especially if housed with other peaceful fishes. They can be kept in groups and, in fact, in some cases they do best if a male and one or more females are kept together. One of the most rewarding things about keeping flasher wrasses in groups is that the males will display more. These colorful displays are important in courtship and defending females from neighboring rivals. Solitary males will occasionally "flash" at their reflections in the aquarium glass. If you decide to keep more than one flasher wrasse in the same aquarium, it is important to introduce all individuals to the tank at the same time, or introduce the less aggressive females before the male(s). I have successfully kept more than one male in the same aquarium, but they must be introduced simultaneously, whether the males are of the same or different species. Your chances of successfully keeping two males together are greatly increased if the tank is of larger dimensions. I would not recommend keeping two males of the same species in a tank smaller than the standard 135 gallons, and in some cases a tank with this surface area may be too small.

Except for the Eightlined Flasher Wrasse (*Paracheilinus octo-*

Paracheilinus filamentosus, Filamented Flasher Wrasse: a shoal of females sheltering among soft corals.

Paracheilinus cyaneus, Blue Flasher Wrasse, Derawan, male at center, erects fins among a group of conspecifics and fairy wrasses.

taenia—see species account), there do not appear to be any significant differences in aggressiveness between species. In most cases the largest or first male in the aquarium will be the dominant individual. For example, I had a lovely group of flasher wrasses that were all introduced to a 100-gallon aquarium at the same time. The group consisted of three different species. All was

Paracheilinus lineopunctatus, Dot-and-Dash Flasher Wrasse, male flashing: flasher wrasses are generally peaceful except with perceived *Paracheilinus* rivals.

copacetic for the first couple of weeks, except for occasional short chases. Then the problems began. The largest of the group (a Carpenter's Flasher Wrasse, *Paracheilinus carpenteri*) began chasing smaller males (a conspecific male as well as males of other species) all the time, until a couple of its consexual rivals jumped out of the tank into the overflow chamber and another male began to hide incessantly.

With the possible exception of their close relatives (e.g., fairy wrasses) or other small planktivores (e.g., fire gobies), flasher wrasses are rarely aggressive toward other fishes. These infrequent bouts of aggression usually consist of displaying or, on rare occasions, chasing a newly introduced fish. These wrasses are not a threat to invertebrates, with the possible exception of small anemone shrimp (*Periclimenes* spp.), and for this reason they are welcome introductions to the invertebrate tank. They are also great for reef tanks because they spend most of their time in the water column and serve as "dither" fish, encouraging other small, shy fish to spend more time in the open.

Although your chances of success are reduced, I have seen flasher wrasses in reef tanks with larger or more aggressive fishes. For example, a friend of mine has several flasher wrasses in a large tank (180 gallons) with eight species of surgeonfish, a Flameback Angelfish, smaller dottybacks, basslets, and other wrasses. But their enemies do include aggressive pygmy angelfishes, aggressive anthias (e.g., *Pseudanthias squamipinnis* and *P. rubrizonatus*), dottybacks, damselfishes, hawkfishes, large fairy wrasses (especially if these wrasses are introduced before them), wrasses in the genus *Pseudocheilinus*, *Thalassoma*, and larger *Halichoeres* spp., tangs, pufferfishes, and, of course, any fish that can swallow them (e.g., frogfishes, scorpionfishes, groupers). Flasher wrasses are particularly vulnerable to combative species in smaller aquariums. If they are persistently harassed when introduced to a tank, they will hide and never come out to feed. Therefore, if you are going to keep flasher wrasses with potentially quarrelsome fish, they should be the first fish added to the tank after it has cycled.

Ideal flasher wrasse tankmates include Lori's Anthias (*Pseudanthias lori*), Dispar Anthias (*P. dispar*), assessors (*Assessor* spp.), juvenile sand tilefishes (*Hoplolatilus* spp.), gobies, dartfishes, blennies (sometimes *Ecsenius midas*, the Midas Blenny, will harass them), small fairy wrasses, leopard wrasses (*Macropharyngodon* spp.), and pencil wrasses (*Pseudojuloides* spp.). Flasher wrasses also have invertebrate foes; they have been known to fall victim to predatory crustaceans (e.g., large hermit crabs, cancrid crabs), elephant ear polyps (*Amplexidiscus fenestrafer*), and carpet anemones (*Stichodactyla* spp.).

A content flasher wrasse should be out and feeding within 48 hours of being introduced to its new home. If individuals hide for longer than three days, chances are they will never acclimate. Flasher wrasses are not picky feeders and should be given a varied diet to ensure the maintenance of good health and vibrant coloration. Finely chopped seafoods and frozen preparations with added amino acids and pigments are great staple foods for your wrasses. Avoid feeding them only brine shrimp or flake foods. Flasher wrasses should be fed at least once a day in order to maintain their body weight. Since they feed on zooplankton and rarely pick at organisms on live rock, they will not thrive in the reef tank if they are fed infrequently. A good protein skimmer and live sand will help decrease the buildup of dissolved organics that may result from this more regular feeding regime. Avoid purchasing specimens that show signs of emaciation, like a pinched-in stomach or atrophied dorsal musculature. Although they can contract ich, they are not especially susceptible to this infection. Like all your newly acquired specimens, flasher wrasses should be quarantined before they are added to the display tank.

Flasher Wrasse Species

Paracheilinus angulatus Randall & Lubbock, 1981
Common Names: Sharpfinned Flasher Wrasse, Angular Flasher Wrasse, Lyretail Flasher Wrasse, Royal Flasher Wrasse.
Maximum Length: 8 cm (3.1 in.).
Distribution: Northern Indonesia and the Philippines.
Biology: The Sharpfinned Flasher Wrasse is found at depths of 5 to at least 20 m (17 to 66 ft.). It is reported from coastal reefs with extensive coral and macroalgae growth. At Batangas, in the Philippines, it is typically found on coastal sand slopes. This species aggregate in channels that are filled with rocks, macroalgae, debris, and *Diadema* sea urchins, sharing this habitat with several fairy (*Cirrhilabrus lyukyuensis, C. rubripinnis*) and flasher wrasses (*Paracheilinus carpenteri, P. lineopunctatus*). The males engage in displays where their color intensifies and they dash through the water column and rapidly circle heterosexuals. This fish will hybridize with the Carpenter's Flasher Wrasse (*Paracheilinus carpenteri*), Blue Flasher Wrasse (*P. cyaneus*), Filamented Flasher Wrasse (*P. filamentosus*), and Dot-and-Dash Flasher

Paracheilinus angulatus, Sharpfinned Flasher Wrasse, large male, Philippines.

Paracheilinus angulatus, Sharpfinned Flasher Wrasse, young male, Philippines.

Wrasse (*C. lineopunctatus*).
Captive Care: This is a durable aquarium wrasse. Males will behave aggressively toward consexuals, and larger individuals will chase congeners that are smaller or introduced after they have become established. See the Captive Care section for the genus for more general husbandry information.
Aquarium Size: 30 gal. **Temperature:** 23° to 28°C (74° to 82°F).
Aquarium Suitability Index: 4.
Remarks: The Sharpfinned Flasher is readily available in the U.S. aquarium trade. This species has a lunate tail like *P. filamentosus* but lacks filaments on the dorsal fin. Adult males sport a rainbow

Paracheilinus togeanensis, Togean Flasher Wrasse, male displaying, Sulawesi.

Paracheilinus attenuatus, Attenuate Flasher Wrasse, male.

Togean Islands, Indonesia. This species has a lunate tail and lacks filaments on the dorsal fin.

Paracheilinus attenuatus Randall, 1999

Common Name: Attenuate Flasher Wrasse.
Maximum Length: 7 cm (2.8 in.).
Distribution: Amirante Islands in the Seychelles and Kenya.
Biology: The Attenuate Flasher has been taken at depths of 21 to about 50 m (68 to 163 ft.), on rubble or hard bottoms. Like the other members of the genus, *P. attenuatus* is usually found in small groups, which comprise primarily females. The females stay near the bottom, while males may move higher into the water column to display at each other and to potential mates.
Captive Care: See the Captive Care section for the genus for more general husbandry information.
Aquarium Size: 20 gal. **Temperature:** 22° to 27°C (72° to 80°F).
Aquarium Suitability Index: 4.
Remarks: This recently described wrasse is very distinct from others in the genus in that the adult males have a lanceolate (pointed) caudal fin. (In young specimens and females the tail is rounded.) In this species the first soft ray of the dorsal fin extends into a filament and the color consists of four longitudinal lavender bands on an orange body. The **Fairy Flasher Wrasse** (*Paracheilinus piscilineatus*) (**Cornic, 1987**) is known only from Mauritius. It is very similar in appearance to a fairy wrasse, hence the common name. It lacks filaments on the dorsal fin and has a truncate caudal fin. The Fairy Flasher Wrasse usually occurs at depths in excess of 35 m (116 ft.).

Paracheilinus bellae Randall, 1988

Common Name: Bell's Flasher Wrasse.
Maximum Length: 8 cm (3.1 in.).
Distribution: Kwajalein Atoll, Marshall Islands.
Biology: Bell's Flasher lives among beds of macroalgae (e.g., *Halimeda*, *Padina*, *Caulerpa*, and *Dictyota*) in Kwajalein Atoll lagoon. It occurs at depths of 18 to 31 m (59 to 101 ft.), but is most common in the deeper portion of this range. It feeds on zooplankton. The fish swims just above the bottom when feeding or interacting with conspecifics, retreating into the dense algae when threatened. It shares this habitat with Johnson's Fairy Wrasse (*Cirrhilabrus johnsoni*).
Captive Care: *Paracheilinus bellae* is rare in the aquarium trade. When available, it commands a high price. The one individual I kept was similar in its requirements and behavior to *P. filamentosus*. See the Captive Care section for the genus for more general husbandry information.
Aquarium Size: 20 gal. **Temperature:** 23° to 28°C (74° to 82°F).

of colors; they have an orange body with seven violet stripes and red, yellow, and green highlights on the fins. The color of the females is more subdued. This fish is closely related to the **Comoro Flasher Wrasse** (*Paracheilinus hemitaeniatus*) **Randall & Harmelin-Vivien, 1977**, which is known only from Madagascar and KwaZulu, South Africa. The Comoro Flasher Wrasse has a slightly emarginate caudal fin as a juvenile, but in adult males the fin is very lunate with filaments on the edge of each lobe. It also has six longitudinal purple lines on the body. *Paracheilinus hemitaeniatus* is found on outer reef slopes at depths of 25 to 50 m (83 to 165 ft.). The very rare **Togean Flasher Wrasse** (*Paracheilinus togeanensis*) **Kuiter & Allen, 1999** is known only from the

Paracheilinus bellae, Bell's Flasher Wrasse, male.

Paracheilinus bellae, Bell's Flasher Wrasse, male, displaying.

Aquarium Suitability Index: 4.

Remarks: This is an exquisite fish. The body color is a mix of red, orange-yellow, and dull blue violet. There are blue markings on the orange-yellow dorsal fin, and the caudal fin is red with a yellow crescent in the center. It is most similar to the Filamented Flasher Wrasse (*Paracheilinus filamentosus*).

Paracheilinus carpenteri Randall & Harmelin-Vivien, 1977

Common Names: Carpenter's Flasher Wrasse, Redfin Flasher Wrasse.

Maximum Length: 8 cm (3.1 in.).

Distribution: Philippines to southern Japan and Palau.

Biology: The Carpenter's Flasher Wrasse occurs at a depth range of 7 to 40 m (23 to 130 ft.). In the original description of this species, it was reported to be found on coral rubble slopes, among soft corals and mushroom corals (*Fungia* spp.). Off the coast of Batangas, Philippines, it is observed in rocky channels or gutters, often swimming or hiding among macroalgae, debris, and *Diadema* sea urchins. It shares this habitat with other flasher and fairy wrasses (see *Paracheilinus angulatus*, above). I observed males of this species chasing conspecifics as well as congeners. The male *P. carpenteri* will dash up and down in the water column when displaying. I also observed them spawning at midday. The spawning ascent took the pair less than 40 cm (16 in.) above the bottom. This species will hybridize with the Sharpfinned Flasher (*P. angulatus*). I observed one such male hybrid spawning with a female *P. carpenteri* and chasing males of the two parent species.

Captive Care: *Paracheilinus carpenteri* is a durable aquarium fish if provided with a quiet aquarium in which to acclimate. (Using a quarantine tank to get new arrivals well fed and accustomed to

Paracheilinus carpenteri, Carpenter's Flasher Wrasse, male, Philippines.

P. carpenteri, Carpenter's Flasher Wrasse, male, Philippines.

Paracheilinus carpenteri, Carpenter's Flasher Wrasse: an unusual color variant. Paracheilinus, often poorly displayed in shops, can be overlooked by aquarists.

Paracheilinus carpenteri, Carpenter's Flasher Wrasse, male, Philippines.

your water is a good practice.) Once settled, adult males may behave aggressively toward conspecifics and male congeners. It may be slightly more aggressive than many *Paracheilinus* spp.

Aquarium Size: 20 gal. **Temperature:** 23° to 28°C (74° to 82°F).

Aquarium Suitability Index: 4.

Remarks: This species is most similar to McCosker's Flasher Wrasse and is one of the most common flasher wrasses in U.S. aquarium stores. (To repeat: these fish may not look their best in a crowded retail display tank, where their potential coloration and spectacular finnage may not be apparent to the casual passerby.) Carpenter's Flasher has two to four prolonged dorsal rays, a slightly rounded caudal fin, two stripes running from the eye to the posterior part of the body, and two short stripes starting under the pectoral fins. It has a yellow-orange or red-orange body with blue stripes and a red anal fin that often has blue spots.

Paracheilinus cyaneus, Blue Flasher Wrasse, West Papua: when flashing, the back turns blue and the dorsal fins turn white and yellow.

Paracheilinus cyaneus Kuiter & Allen, 1999

Common Name: Blue Flasher Wrasse.

Maximum Length: 8 cm (3.1 in.).

Distribution: Derawan Island, Tomini Bay (Togean Islands), Lembeh Strait (Sulawesi), and Banggai Island (Sulawesi).

Biology: In Lembeh Strait, Sulawesi, *P. cyanea* is found in current-prone habitats. It occurs over rubble, sponge, and macroalgae beds at depths of 20 to 26 m (65 to 85 ft.). In Lembeh, it often mixes with Filamented Flasher Wrasses (*P. filamentosus*) and Tono's Fairy Wrasses (*Cirrhilabrus tonozukai*). In other regions, it has been reported from shallow reef crests and on sheltered reefs at depths of 6 to 35 m (20 to 114 ft.). It will hybridize with *P. filamentosus*.

Captive Care: This fish is similar to *P. filamentosus* in its husbandry requirements. See the Captive Care section for the genus for

Paracheilinus cyaneus, Blue Flasher Wrasse, male: note lyretail.

Paracheilinus nursalim, West Papua: identified by black patches on dorsum and caudal peduncle.

more general husbandry information.
Aquarium Size: 20 gal. **Temperature:** 23° to 28°C (74° to 82°F).
Aquarium Suitability Index: 4.
Remarks: *Paracheilinus cyaneus* is unique in have eight or nine filaments on the dorsal fin (some populations of Indonesian *P. filamentosus* have up to nine, but most have six or fewer), and fine lines or rows of spots between the larger violet lines on the body. Flashing males are bright iridescent blue to white over most of head onto the dorsal fin, although the dorsal filaments are red. *Paracheilinus nursalim* **Allen and Erdmann, 2008** is known from the Bird's Head Peninsula, Western, New Guinea. It is similar to *P. cyaneus* and *P. filamentosus*, but has black patches under the dorsal fin and caudal peduncle. It resides on rubble slopes at depth of 5 to at least 50 m (16 to 163 ft.) (most common between 20 and 35 m [65 to 114 ft.]).

Paracheilinus filamentosus Allen, 1974
Common Name: Filamented Flasher Wrasse.
Maximum Length: 10 cm (3.9 in.).
Distribution: Indonesia, New Guinea, the Solomon Islands, the Philippines, and Belau.
Biology: The Filamented Flasher Wrasse is found on coastal reefs at a depth range of 3 to 35 m (10 to 114 ft.). It usually occurs at depths in excess of 20 m (65 ft.). It occurs in aggregations numbering from a few individuals to more than 30. These groups usually consist mainly of females with fewer males. However, on

several occasions I have seen large groups of adult males moving over rubble slopes. Off Flores, Indonesia, this species mixes with Lubbock's Fairy Wrasse (*Cirrhilabrus lubbocki*), while in Lembeh Strait, this species will aggregate with large groups of Bluehead Fairy Wrasse (*Cirrhilabrus solorensis*). In this same region, it is also found over macroalgae beds, where it will mix with the Blue Flasher Wrasse (*P. cyaneus*) and Tono's Fairy Wrasse (*Cirrhilabrus tonozukai*). (This population of *P. filamentosus*-type wrasses may represent a different, undescribed species). In Milne Bay, Papua New Guinea, this species will form mixed aggregations with juvenile Finespotted Fairy Wrasses (*Cirrhilabrus punctatus*) and the Yellowstripe Anthias (*Pseudanthias tuka*). Small juveniles that have only recently settled out of the plankton are sometimes found among rubble around the bases of large carpet anemones. This species will hybridize with the Sharpfinned (*P. angulatus*) and the Yellowfin Flasher Wrasse (*P. flavianalis*). It might also hybridize with *C. carpenteri*. In areas where it co-occurs with other flasher wrasses, male *P. filamentosus* exhibit more spectacular, intense colors when they display. This phenomenon may occur so that females are better able to recognize consexual males in order to prevent excessive hybridization.

Captive Care: This species is occasionally seen in the aquarium trade. It is not aggressive toward nonrelated species, but males will fight and it may quarrel with congeners. Female *P. filamentosus* are more difficult to come by in aquarium stores than the more attractive males. See the Captive Care section for the genus for more general husbandry information.
Aquarium Size: 30 gal. **Temperature:** 23° to 28°C (74° to 82°F).
Aquarium Suitability Index: 4.
Remarks: Adult *P. filamentosus* are readily identified by their elongate dorsal fin filaments (numbering from two to nine, but usually fewer than six) and their lunate (half-moon-shaped) tail. Males are usually orange overall, with purple lines radiating from the eyes, fuchsia stripes on the sides and back, a pink abdomen, and red caudal and anal fins. A flashing male may display all these colors, plus blue and yellow. There is some evidence that suggests there may be more than one species that has been classified as *P. filamentosus*. For example, the population of flashers from Sulawesi referred to as *P. filamentosus* are different in coloration and may represent a distinct species.

Paracheilinus filamentosus, Filamented Flasher Wrasse, female, Sulawesi.

Paracheilinus filamentosus, transforming female, Sulawesi.

Paracheilinus filamentosus, male at cleaning station, Sulawesi.

Paracheilinus filamentosus, male: "full flash" displaying mode.

Paracheilinus filamentosus, male, Papua New Guinea.

Paracheilinus sp., Sulawesi: possible new species. Note larger median fins.

Paracheilinus cyaneus x *P. filamentosus*, Hybrid Flasher Wrasse, Derawan.

Paracheilinus flavianalis, Yellowfin Flasher Wrasse, male.

Paracheilinus flavianalis, Yellowfin Flasher Wrasse, male.

Paracheilinus flavianalis, Yellowfin Flasher Wrasse, male.

Paracheilinus flavianalis, Yellowfin Flasher Wrasse, male.

Paracheilinus rubricaudalis, Redtail Flasher Wrasse, male.

Paracheilinus flavianalis Kuiter & Allen, 1999
Common Name: Yellowfin Flasher Wrasse.
Maximum Length: 8 cm (3.1 in.).
Distribution: Isolated reefs off the coast of northwestern Australia, east to Bali, and north to Sulawesi, Indonesia.
Biology: The Yellowfin Flasher is found at water depths of 6 to 35 m (20 to 114 ft.), where it occurs on current-prone rubble slopes and flats. In some cases it associates with macroalgae (e.g., *Halimeda*). This flasher wrasse has also been taken from estuaries and shallow lagoons. It typically occurs in small groups and often mixes with groups of Filamented Flashers (*P. filamentosus*) and fairy wrasses (*Cirrhilabrus* spp.). It will hybridize with *P. filamentosus*.
Captive Care: This fish is similar to *P. mccoskeri* in its husbandry requirements. See the Captive Care section for the genus for more general husbandry information.
Aquarium Size: 20 gal. **Temperature:** 23° to 28°C (74° to 82°F).

Aquarium Suitability Index: 4.
Remarks: Male *P. flavianalis* have one to three long, red dorsal fin filaments, and a yellow anal fin that is plain or bisected by metallic blue spots. It has been misidentified as a variant of *P. mccoskeri* or *P. carpenteri*, but is now considered a valid species. The **Redtailed Flasher Wrasse (*Paracheilinus rubricaudalis*) Randall & Allen, 2003** has long been confused with this species. The Redtailed Flasher is only known from Vanuatu and the Fiji Islands. It is very similar to *P. flavianalis* but differs in having a red caudal fin.

Paracheilinus lineopunctatus Randall & Lubbock, 1981
Common Names: Dot-and-Dash Flasher Wrasse, Spotlined Flasher Wrasse.
Maximum Length: 6.5 cm (2.6 in.).
Distribution: Okinawa and the Philippines.
Biology: *Paracheilinus lineopunctatus* occurs at the bases of steep

Paracheilinus rubricaudalis, Redtailed Flasher Wrasse, male: a species very similar to the Yellowfin Flasher Wrasse, but with a distinct red caudal fin.

Paracheilinus lineopunctatus, Dot-and-Dash Flasher Wrasse, male displaying.

Paracheilinus lineopunctatus, Dot-and-Dash Flasher Wrasse, male, Philippines.

Paracheilinus mccoskeri, McCosker's Flasher Wrasse, young male.

Paracheilinus mccoskeri, McCosker's Flasher Wrasse, male flashing.

outer reef slopes and on coastal sand slopes at depths of 12 to 40 m (39 to 130 ft.). It is often found in small aggregations over rubble bottoms but is also seen with other flasher and fairy wrasses in areas with a mixture of rocks and macroalgae. In Batangas, Philippines, it is one of the least common members of the genus in mixed *Paracheilinus/Cirrhilabrus* groups. Solitary males or small groups of females have been observed in rocky channels or rocky, low-profile spurs. Males will dash around these groups displaying toward females and congeners. When flashing, the body takes on a more violet hue, a blue patch on the dorsal fin intensifies, and a metallic blue line appears at the base of the dorsal fin.

Captive Care: The Dot-and-Dash Flasher seems to be the most peaceful member of the genus. I have had adult males that were dominated by males of other flasher wrasse species. Like others in the genus, if it is harassed it will often jump out of the tank or into overflow boxes. See the Captive Care section for the genus for more general husbandry information.

Aquarium Size: 20 gal. **Temperature:** 23° to 28°C (74° to 82°F). **Aquarium Suitability Index:** 4.

Paracheilinus mccoskeri, McCosker's Flasher Wrasse, flashing male: an Indian Ocean species recognized by its red anal fin and single dorsal fin filament.

Remarks: Male *P. lineopunctatus* have four to six elongate soft dorsal rays and longitudinal rows of dots and short dashes on the body. The body is orange-red with dark brown lines, while the dorsal fin has purplish rays and orange-red and blue mottling.

Paracheilinus mccoskeri Randall & Harmelin-Vivien, 1977

Common Name: McCosker's Flasher Wrasse.
Maximum Length: 7 cm (2.8 in.).
Distribution: Gulf of Oman, Comores, Maldives, Similan Islands, Sumatra.
Biology: McCosker's Flasher is found on sloping coral rubble bottoms at depths of 20 to 50 m (66 to 163 ft.). This fish occurs in aggregations, with males maintaining harems of up to 10 females. In Indonesia, where it is infrequently seen, it is usually observed shoaling with the Filamented Flasher.
Captive Care: This is an amazing aquarium fish if kept in a relatively peaceful aquarium. It is not commonly seen in North American fish stores. See the Captive Care section for the genus for more general husbandry information.

Aquarium Size: 20 gal. **Temperature:** 23° to 28°C (74° to 82°F).
Aquarium Suitability Index: 4.
Remarks: Male *P. mccoskeri* are usually easy to distinguish from the closely related *P. carpenteri* by the presence of only one elongated dorsal filament. Males are orange on the back and sides and yellow on the ventrum, with interrupted bright blue lines on the body and along the base of the dorsal fin. Most of the anal fin and the posterior part of the dorsal base are bright red.

Paracheilinus octotaenia Fourmanoir, 1955

Common Names: Eightlined Flasher Wrasse, Red Sea Flasher Wrasse.
Maximum Length: 9 cm (3.5 in.).
Distribution: Northern Red Sea.
Biology: The Eightlined Flasher Wrasse is found on rubble slopes on back barrier reefs or reef face margins. It is found at depths of 8 to 25 m (26 to 81 ft.). *Paracheilinus octotaenia* occurs in loose aggregations in which males maintain harems of 4 to 12 females. Juveniles often refuge among soft corals. Adults will rise

Paracheilinus octotaenia, Eightlined Flasher Wrasse, male: one of the more pugnacious of the flasher wrasses when housed with other *Paracheilinus* species.

up to 3 m (10 ft.) off the bottom to feed and may join schools of Lyretail Anthias (*Pseudanthias squamipinnis*). During aggressive displays and courtship the male's pink fins turn bright red and the blue lines become more intense. Persistent males have been observed to court females for as long as 20 minutes in an attempt to get them to spawn. At night the aggregations disperse

Paracheilinus octotaenia, Eightlined Flasher Wrasse, female, Red Sea.

and individuals hide in the reef.

Captive Care: The Eightlined Flasher Wrasse is a welcome addition to the reef aquarium or peaceful fish tank. However, I have found this to be one of the most aggressive members of the genus, and males usually dominate other flasher wrasses if they are kept in mixed aggregations. This species has also been known to behave aggressively toward smaller *Cirrhilabrus* spp. If you are interested in keeping more than one *P. octotaenia* in the same aquarium, it is best to keep only one male unless the tank is very large (200 gallons or larger). They can be kept in pairs, but I recommend housing one male with several females so that the male's aggression is dispersed among several individuals. See the Captive Care section for the genus for more general husbandry information.

Aquarium Size: 30 gal. **Temperature:** 23° to 27°C (74° to 80°F).

Aquarium Suitability Index: 4.

Remarks: The head of *P. octotaenia* has a deeper profile than that of other flasher wrasses and males have a slight hump on the forehead. The body is orange-red with blue stripes and the caudal fin is rounded. Males have eight pronounced stripes on the side of the body, while females have four or five. Males may also have dark lines near the soft portions of the dorsal and anal fins and the posterior of the caudal fin. A similar, deep-bodied species has been discovered off Komodo Island by Dr. Gerald Allen.

HYBRID: *Paracheilinus carpenteri* X *Paracheilinus angulatus*

HYBRID: *Paracheilinus angulatus* X *Paracheilinus lineopunctatus*

HYBRID: *Paracheilinus flavianalis* X *Paracheilinus filamentosus*

HYBRID: *Paracheilinus angulatus* X *Paracheilinus cyaneus*

Paracheilinus Hybrids

There are a number of flasher wrasse species that can be found living together in mixed groups. These may include two or more *Paracheilinus* spp. as well as fairy wrasses (*Cirrhilabrus* spp.) and/or other zooplanktivores. All the flasher wrasses studied to date spawn in the late afternoon/early evening. Most spawn daily. It therefore, should not be surprising, that in mixed *Paracheilinus* groups, cross-spawning sometimes occurs. At least some of the resulting hybrids have been observed spawning with parent species; however, at this time it has not been determined if these flasher "mutts" are fertile or not.

It has been suggested that where flasher species co-occur, they exhibit even more spectacular flashing displays and that those species that possess long dorsal fin filaments may have more than they do in areas where they do not mix with congeners. Both of these characteristics may enable conspecific females to recognize members of their own kind rather than "waste" their gametes spawning with congeners.

While they are not common in the aquarium trade, these hybrids do show up from time to time. Identifying a hybrid can be a challenge. They will share characteristics of both parents, usually looking more like one parent than the other. If you look closely at the accompanying hybrid photos, you will clearly see characteristics of both parents.

Pseudocheilinus ocellatus, Whitebarred Wrasse, Marshall Islands.

GENUS PSEUDOCHEILINUS (LINED WRASSES)

The genus *Pseudocheilinus* comprises seven small, colorful species. Like other family members, these wrasses are diurnal. All of these diminutive fishes are relatively secretive, remaining under ledges, in large crevices, among rubble, or amid the branches of stony corals. Because of their small size, they are very wary. Even still, they fall prey to morays, groupers, goatfishes, and other piscivores. Their inherently cautious demeanor makes them very tricky to photograph underwater (this especially true for the smaller species). Patience is required to add shots of the lined wrasses to your fish photo portfolio. In an attempt to get a good shot, I have waited as long as 20 minutes for a Sixline Wrasse (*Pseudocheilinus hexataenia*) to emerge from a stony coral colony, only to give up in the end!

Some members of this genus display distinct habitat separation where they occur sympatrically. For example, on massive coral pinnacles off the Island of Beqa, Fiji, the tops of the coral heads, which start at a depth of about 6 m (19 ft.), are covered with fire coral, hard corals (like *Acropora* spp.), some soft corals (leather corals and *Dendronephthya* spp.), and anemones. This is the habitat where one finds groups of Sixline Wrasses (*Pseudocheilinus hexataenia*). Along the steep coral head walls, where gorgonians, *Dendronephthya* spp., and cup corals predominate, one finds the Eightline Wrasse (*Pseudocheilinus octotaenia*), while near the base of the coral heads, at a depth of about 18 m (60 ft.), solitary Striated Wrasses (*Pseudocheilinus evanidus*) are more common on rubble slopes adjacent to these coral pinnacles.

Unlike some of the other labrids, the *Pseudocheilinus* spp. do not usually bury at night or when danger threatens—instead, they hide in reef interstices. A few reputable aquarists have told me that their *Pseudocheilinus* spp. bury in fine sand at night. However, I have never seen this. These wrasses will often form a mucous cocoon when they slumber. They are protogynous hermaphrodites. There is little information on their mating systems or reproductive behavior, although at least some species appear to be haremic. I have seen male Striated Wrasse (*Pseudocheilinus evanidus*) visiting females late in the afternoon. The male would display for one of its potential mates before moving on to the next. The male was larger than the females it visited.

Food habit data show that these fishes feed primarily on crustaceans, mollusks, tiny sea urchins, serpent stars, and fish eggs. At least one species (i.e., *P. hexataenia*) serves as a facultative cleaner, nipping parasitic isopods and copepods off the fins and bodies of other fishes. The eyes of the *Pseudocheilinus* (and some of their kin) may facilitate capturing small prey items. They have a specialized optic system, consisting of a "double pupil" (i.e., an "oblique division of the sclera cornea into two near-equal parts" [Springer and Randall, 1974]) that may enable them to better locate small prey (it has been suggested that that one portion of the lens may serve to magnify potential prey as they feed near the substrate).

Captive Care

If you get a healthy individual to begin with, the *Pseudocheilinus* spp. tend to be very durable little fishes. When feeding, provide *Pseudocheilinus* spp. with a varied diet that includes finely chopped seafoods, frozen mysid shrimp, frozen preparations for carnivores, and a color-enhancing flake food. In a reef aquarium, they will only need to be fed once every other day, as they will forage on micro-invertebrates on the live rock. In a fish-only tank that lacks live substrate, feed them at least once a day. Once a lined wrasse acclimates to the aquarium, it is an aggressive

Pseudocheilinus octotaenia, Eightline Wrasse: an unusual color form and an aggressive pose.

Pseudocheilinus ocellatus, Whitebarred or Tailspot Wrasse: member of a genus of interesting reef-safe fishes that hunt incessantly for small invertebrates.

feeder that can compete with most fish tankmates. However, make sure newly acquired individuals get enough to eat if housed with boisterous fishes. If picked on, they will skulk around among the aquarium decor and may not get enough to eat (this is especially true in a tank that lacks live rock).

Pseudocheilinus wrasses can also be aggressive toward closely related or similarly shaped species. One they have been in a aquarium for a while, especially if the tank is smaller, they may chastise an new piscine addition to their "territory." I have even seen the diminutive Sixline Wrasse (*Pseudocheilinus hexataenia*) become the bane of many a reef aquarist that placed it in a small to medium-sized community tank (under 75 gallons). Therefore, if your aquarium is of modest size, it is best if your lined wrasse is

the last fish introduced. There tends to be a correlation between aggressiveness and size (this may also be related to sex as larger individuals are most likely males)—larger individuals tend to be more prone to bouts of thuggery. It is also a bad idea to keep more than one species of *Pseudocheilinus* in the same aquarium. (While it has been done in very large reef tanks, it is a risky proposition.) It is possible to keep conspecifics together, but the tank must be very spacious, with loads of hiding places and the individual wrasses must be of the opposite sex. To increase the odds of acquiring a male-female pair, buy individuals that vary greatly in length to ensure you have a female (or possibly a juvenile which will develop into a female if a male is present) and a male—the latter are likely to be highly combative if kept together. Adults of the larger lined wrasse species (e.g., *Pseudocheilinus octotaenia*) will prey on small fishes, like "nanogobies" (*Eviota*, *Trimma*, *Trimmatom*) and wormfish (*Gunnelichthys* spp.).

Another *Pseudocheilinus* downside is that larger specimens may thin out your shrimp and crab stocks. I have had them eat a variety of shrimp species (even larger *Stenopus* spp., which are most vulnerable to labrid attacks when they are molting), anemone crabs, and small hermit crabs. They will occasionally leap out of an open aquarium when the lights are extinguished or when they are harassed by other fishes. When selecting a specimen, avoid those that are producing excessive amounts of slime and that have cloudy eyes—this usually indicates a parasitic skin infection.

The members of the genus *Pseudocheilinus* are well known for their habit of feeding on pyramidellid snails (small gastropods that are parasites of *Tridacna* clams). The parasitic snails are nocturnal, spending the day near the base of the clam or between the scutes of certain species of clams (Delbeek and Sprung, 1994). As a result, these wrasses are not likely to encounter the snails and have the opportunity to prey upon them very often. Delbeek and Sprung (1994) suggest manual removal is still the most effective way to rid clams of these parasites. The *Pseudocheilinus* spp. will also feed on Acoel flatworms. That said, do not expect them to eradicate these pests if your tank is already infested with them.

Lined Wrasse Species

Pseudocheilinus evanidus Jordan & Evermann, 1903
Common Names: Striated Wrasse, Secretive Wrasse.
Maximum Length: 9 cm (3.5 in.).
Distribution: Red Sea to the Hawaiian Islands and Tuamotus, north to the Izu Island.
Biology: The Striated Wrasse is known at depths of 6 to 61 m (20 to 201 ft.) on the reef face, reef slope, and occasionally in lagoons. In some parts of its range, it is most common at depths in excess of 20 m (65 ft.). It is usually observed over coral rubble bottoms near the reef face or large coral heads, although it is occasionally observed swimming amid live hard corals. This species is secretive, but it is occasionally seen swimming just over the bottom as it moves from one crevice to another. It has been reported from the stomach of the Manybar Goatfish (*Parupeneus multifasciatus*), which uses its barbels to drive small fish from rubble interstices. The Striated Wrasse is known to feed on small benthic crustaceans, worms, serpent stars (it may bite off the appendages of larger brittle stars), and small fishes.
Captive Care: Like others in the genus, this species often becomes very stressed during shipping and may have trouble acclimating to its aquarium home. If it is kept in relatively peaceful confines

Pseudocheilinus evanidus, Striated Wrasse: male, front, initiates courtship.

Pseudocheilinus evanidus, Striated Wrasse: secretive, bottom-hugging fish.

Pseudocheilinus evanidus, Striated Wrasse: individual exhibits banded phase.

Pseudocheilinus hexataenia, Sixline Wrasse: males will do battle, and it will often bully more peaceful wrasses and mild-mannered gobies and blennies.

initially, *P. evanidus* settles in and begins showing itself on occasion. The Striated Wrasse will battle fiercely with its own kind, as well as other *Pseudocheilinus* wrasses, and should be kept with larger, more aggressive fishes. Like all the members of this genus, it will eat a wide range of foods in captivity. Adult *P. evanidus* are also known predators of small gobies. It will leap from open aquariums.

Aquarium Size: 20 gal. **Temperature:** 22° to 27°C (72° to 80°F).
Aquarium Suitability Index: 4.
Remarks: Randall (1999), individuals 7.2 to 7.4 cm (2.8 to 2.9 in.) were males, while individuals 5.6 to 6.1 cm (2.2 to 2.4 in.) were females. Adults have long filaments on the first two spines of the anal fin.

Pseudocheilinus hexataenia (Bleeker, 1857)

Common Name: Sixline Wrasse.
Maximum Length: 7.5 cm (2.9 in.).
Distribution: Red Sea and East Africa to the Tuamotus and Johnston Island, north to the Ryukyu Islands, and south to Lord Howe Island and Austral Island.
Biology: *Pseudocheilinus hexataenia* occurs in lagoons but is most common on fore-reef slopes in water as shallow as 1 m up to at least 35 m (3.3 to 114 ft.). It is most common at depths of less than 20 m (66 ft.). Sixline Wrasses usually swim within the calcareous "forest" of branching corals, and they also refuge near the bases of large sea anemones. I have seen them associating most frequently with the Magnificent Sea Anemone (*Heteractis mag-*

nifica). This fish is haremic, with one male defending a small group of females. I have seen loose aggregations of as many as four Sixline Wrasses in an area of 142 cm² (22 ft.²) on the reef. Its natural bill of fare consists mainly of crustaceans (shrimps, mysids, isopods, amphipods, copepods, crab megalops), foraminiferans (minute, shelled protozoa), polychaete worms, and small gastropods. (It feeds on the substrate as well as on demersal plankton.) *Pseudocheilinus hexataenia* will also pick crustacean parasites off the fins and bodies of other fishes. I have seen this wrasse clean a Giant Moray Eel (*Gymnothorax javanicus*), a butterflyfish, and a *Stegastes* damselfish in the wild.

Captive Care: This species is better suited to the community tank than either *P. octotaenia* or *P. evanidus*. However, it will often behave aggressively toward more docile wrasses (e.g. flasher, fairy, and leopard wrasses), and toward shy, inoffensive species (e.g., small gobies, dart gobies), especially if these fishes are introduced after *P. hexataenia*. Several individuals can be housed in the same aquarium, but fighting may occur if population densities are too high (i.e., the aquarium is too small) and if more than one male is present in the tank. If you are placing more than one Sixline Wrasse into your tank, it is important to introduce them simultaneously and that there are size differences between individuals (add one larger individual and one or two smaller specimens). In cases where squabbles do occur, the conflicting individuals are probably males. Because this is a secretive species, it should be provided with numerous hiding places. Once established it will thrive if fed a varied diet. The Sixline Wrasse is a good candidate for the reef aquarium, but large specimens may consume ornamental shrimps.

Aquarium Size: 20 gal. **Temperature:** 22° to 28°C (72° to 82°F).
Aquarium Suitability Index: 4.

Remarks: Randall (1999) found that in a sample of 27 specimens from Fiji, individuals 2.5 to 3.0 cm SL (that is from the tip of the nose to the beginning of the tail) were females, while all fish he examined over 3.5 cm SL were male. Individuals between 2.1 and 2.7 cm SL were juveniles. (Be aware, that while this may be the case for the Fijian population of *P. hexataenia*, the size range as related to gender may vary somewhat between localities—that said, males from any population are going to be larger than females.)

Pseudocheilinus hexataenia, Sixline Wrasse: cleaning a Giant Moray Eel, *Gymnothorax javanicus*, in the Red Sea. This species is a facultative cleaner.

Pseudocheilinus ocellatus, Whitebarred Wrasse: from deeper waters.

Pseudocheilinus ocellatus, Whitebarred Wrasse: note color variation.

P. ocellatus, Whitebarred Wrasse: larger specimens may have white bars.

Pseudocheilinus ocellatus Randall, 1999

Common Names: Whitebarred Wrasse, Tailspot Wrasse, Mystery Wrasse.

Maximum Length: 12 cm (4.7 in.).

Distribution: Cocos Keeling Islands, the Great Barrier Reef, Fiji Islands, Japan, Marshall Islands, Cook Islands, Pitcairn Island, and Johnston Atoll.

Biology: The Whitebarred Wrasse tends to be more common in oceanic environments, usually on clear coastal reefs or outer reef slopes. It is a resident of deep reef walls and slopes and has been reported at depths of 20 to 58 m (65 to 189 ft.). It most often occurs at depths in excess of 30 m (98 ft.). *Pseudocheilinus ocellatus* lives on rubble slopes, at the bases of dropoffs, and often in caves, crevices, or among hard corals. It is a secretive species that is probably most similar to the Eightline Wrasse (*P. octotaenia*) in its habits.

Captive Care: The Whitebarred Wrasse is not only magnificent in appearance, it is also a hardy addition to the fish-only or reef aquarium. Like any member of the genus *Pseudocheilinus*, it should be provided with plenty of caves and overhangs to hide in. When first introduced it will spend most of its time lurking among the aquarium decor. But once it acclimates to its new home (which usually occurs relatively quickly if there are no larger, more aggressive fishes in the aquarium), it will make frequent forays into the open. I have had *P. ocellatus* leap out of an open aquarium when harassed by other fish. This species may also jump out of the aquarium when the lights are turned off. The Whitebarred Wrasse does not appear to be as aggressive as some of its relatives (e.g., *P. octotaenia*). I have kept it with a range of fish species without incident, but have noticed (and been told) that individuals get more aggressive as they get larger—I observed one individual catch and eat a small goby. *Pseudocheilinus ocellatus* is likely to behave aggressively toward more docile species introduced after it has become well established in its aquarium home. This wrasse may be harassed by other fishes; I have seen other wrasses chase it incessantly. I had a Pacific Redstriped Hogfish (*Bodianus* sp.) that attacked a *P. ocellatus* every time they met. The hogfish did not bother any of the other fishes in the tank, including fairy wrasses and a small Pinkstreaked Wrasse (*Pseudocheilinops ataenia*), but for some reason, the hogfish targeted the *P. ocellatus*. The Whitebarred Wrasse will scan live rock, searching for small prey items. (Its diet, described above, is probably similar to that of *P. octotaenia*.) It is a minimal threat to ornamental invertebrates, including crustaceans. I have kept it with several different species of cleaner shrimps without incident. That said, I should point out that large *P. ocellatus* might eat ornamental shrimps and crabs.

Pseudocheilinus octotaenia, Eightline Wrasse, juvenile.

Pseudocheilinus octotaenia, Eightline Wrasse: pink color form.

Aquarium Size: 30 gal. **Temperature:** 23° to 28°C (74° to 82°F).
Aquarium Suitability Index: 4.
Remarks: The chromatic attire changes somewhat as the fish matures. Young fish sport conspicuous white lines along the flanks. These gradually become thinner and may even disappear in adults. At all sizes, *P. ocellatus* has a distinct ocellus on each side of the caudal peduncle. This may serve to deflect the attack of a piscivore from the vulnerable head region to the tail. (Predators usually are more successful at catching their prey if they attack the head.) The head of *P. ocellatus* is a fluorescent yellow with pink tattoos. The overall color can be magenta to reddish. Randall (1999) reports possible sexual dichromatism—in at least some males the fin spines and fin rays are purple.

Pseudocheilinus octotaenia Jenkins, 1901
Common Name: Eightline Wrasse.
Maximum Length: 13.5 cm (5.3 in.).
Distribution: East Africa to Hawaiian and Pitcairn Islands, north to Ryuku Islands, and south to the Great Barrier Reef.
Biology: *Pseudocheilinus octotaenia* is found on rocky and coral reefs at depths of 4 to 60 m (13 to 198 ft.). It occurs on reef faces, fore-reef slopes, and steep dropoffs. It is a common fish over much of its geographical range, but because of its reclusive lifestyle it is infrequently encountered. It is typically a solitary fish that is seen moving about under ledges or in crevices. It feeds primarily on small brachyuran crabs, copepods, shrimps, mollusks (including small snails), sea urchins, fish eggs, and small fishes. A 7-cm (2.8-in.) individual examined by Randall (1999) had intact and crushed snails in its stomach, including an intact snail that was 5 mm (0.2 in.) in length.
Captive Care: The Eightline Wrasse is one of the most common members of the genus in the aquarium trade. It is an attractive species that is aggressively inclined; it frequently assaults tank-

Pseudocheilinus octotaenia, Eightline Wrasse: orange color form.

Pseudocheilinus octotaenia, Eightline Wrasse: blotchy color form.

Pseudocheilinops ataenia, Pinkstreaked Wrasse: a likeable small wrasse that makes a commendable reef or nano-reef addition.

Pseudocheilinops ataenia, Schultz, 1960
(Pinkstreaked Wrasse)

I have always had a soft spot for wrasses, especially the smaller species that make interesting additions to reef tanks. My friend and colleague, Dennis Reynolds (owner of Aquamarines, a fish wholesaler), is always sending me amazing wrasses. One of these, which I had seen in the wild and always hoped to keep in my aquarium, is the Pinkstreaked Wrasse (*Pseudocheilinops ataenia*). This lovely little fish only gets 6.5 cm (2.6 in.) long (and is usually is smaller than this). It is sexually dichromatic, with the males sporting more pronounced yellow lines down the body and bluish-gray markings on the gill cover.

This wrasse is known from the Southern Philippines, Indonesia and Palau. It is usually found on sheltered fringing reefs, in areas with rich growths of delicate, branching stony corals and plate-like coralline algae. I have seen it in large beds of staghorn coral rubble, living alongside groups of Green Mandarinfish (*Synchiropus splendidus*). I have also seen loose groups living within mixed "gardens" of *Anacropora* stony coral and *Halimeda* algae. This wrasse eats amphipods and other micro-inverte-brates. It is a very secretive species that typically occurs in small groups. It has been reported from depths of 5 to 30 m (17 to 99 ft.).

The Pinkstreaked Wrasse is a small, colorful fish that is a welcome addition to any reef aquarium (even the nano-reef). While it is very shy initially, it gradually becomes quite bold and spends a considerable amount of time in the open. It is a good feeder, taking frozen foods and flake foods. It is ignored by most of its tankmates, although I have seen the related *Pseudocheilinus* wrasses chase it. If the tank is large enough and there are plenty of hiding places, the *P. ataenia* will simply dive between the branches of soft or hard corals. I have never seen it behave aggressively toward any other fishes, including two smaller possum wrasses (*Wetmorella* spp.) I introduced to a tank where the *P. ataenia* was well established. The possum wrasses are very similar in shape to the Pinkstreaked, and one would think they would elicit aggression. On a couple of occasions, one Pinkstreaked Wrasse I kept inspected a larger fairy wrasse as if it was going to clean it. However, I have yet to see actual cleaning.

Pseudocheilinus dispilus, Spotcheek Wrasse: Mauritian rarity.

Pseudocheilinus tetrataenia, Fourline Wrasse: small but feisty.

mates like firefishes, dart gobies, other wrasses, basslets (especially the similarly shaped *Liopropoma* spp.), and tobies, shredding fins and removing scales quite effectively with its large canine teeth. It is best to keep the Eightline Wrasse with larger or more belligerent fishes like butterflyfishes, angelfishes, larger dottybacks, damselfishes, and tangs; however, when kept with aggressive tankmates it should be the first fish introduced. I would not recommend placing more than one specimen in your home aquarium, and it should not be kept with any of its close relatives. Usually Eightline Wrasses are initially shy and hide most of the time, but after acclimating they become quite bold. They will eat flake food, baby guppies, brine shrimp, and frozen preparations. Although larger *P. octotaenia* will eat ornamental shrimp, they also prey on bristleworms, capturing and consuming polychaetes up to 8 cm (3 in.) in length, and urchins that have tests about the size of a marble.

Aquarium Size: 30 gal. **Temperature:** 22° to 28°C (72° to 82°F).
Aquarium Suitability Index: 4.
Remarks: The color of this species is variable (see accompanying photos). The base color can be orange, pink, lavender, or gray. The **Spotcheek Wrasse** (*Pseudocheilinus dispilus*) **Randall, 1999** is only known from Mauritius and Réunion Island. It is very similar to *P. octotaenia*. This species is yellow with eight pink stripes down the body and two purple spots on the operculum. It is found at depths of 15 to 37 m (50 to 122 ft.) and reaches 8 cm (3.1 in.) in length. The **Citron Wrasse** (*Pseudocheilinus citrinus*) **Randall, 1999** is another similar species. This fish is orange overall with a pink stripe on the cheek. It is found off the Pitcairn Islands, an atoll in the southern Tuamotus, Rapa, and the Austral Islands, on rocky and coral reefs at depths of 23 to 48 m (79 to 158 ft.). It attains a length of at least 6.6 cm (2.6 in.) and differs from all species except *P. tetrataenia* in having prolonged filaments on the first two dorsal spines. Both of these species are rare in the aquarium trade.

Pseudocheilinus tetrataenia, Fourline Wrasse, adult, displaying.

Pseudocheilinus tetrataenia Schultz, 1960

Common Name: Fourline Wrasse.
Maximum Length: 7.3 cm (2.9 in.).
Distribution: Palau to the Hawaiian Islands and Tuamotus, south to the Austral Islands.
Biology: This little wrasse is most common on exposed outer reef faces and slopes. It spends its time moving about and hiding near the base of stony coral colonies (e.g., *Pocillopora* spp.). In Hawaii, *P. tetrataenia* is collected at depths of 6 to 45 m (20 to 146 ft.), but it tends to be more common in the shallow parts of this range (less than 12 m [39 ft.]). Off the Pitcairn Islands, the Fourline Wrasse tends to occur at greater depths, having been reported at depths of 30 m (98 ft.) or more. This species feeds on demersal plankton (including eggs, larval shrimps and crabs, copepods, and larval gastropods) and benthic crustaceans (snapping shrimp [*Alpheus* sp.] and amphipods).

Pseudocoris heteroptera, Torpedo False Coris Wrasse, terminal male: built for speed, to capture zooplankton in midwater.

The Plankton Pickers
Genus *Pseudocoris* (False Coris Wrasses)

There are a number of wrasse groups that specialize in feeding on zooplankton. These include two genera coveted by aquarists, the fairy wrasses (*Cirrhilabrus*) and the flasher wrasses (*Paracheilinus*).

Another group of plankton pickers that fills this trophic niche is the genus *Pseudocoris*. These fishes spend much of their time swimming in the water column (in some cases up to 10 m [33 ft.] over the seafloor), where they pick off passing planktors. They also tend to occur in small- to medium-sized shoals and often form mixed groups with other zooplankton-feeding fishes.

One clue to their open water life style is their lunate caudal fin. A tail like this is indicative of speed and is a characteristic shared by many small, open water feeders. They are torpedo-shaped—another physical clue that they are speedsters. Their shoaling behavior is also an adaptation to being more vulnerable high above the reef. At least some species are known to refuge under the sand at night.

While these wrasses are not commonly encountered in the aquarium store, the five species in the genus make interesting introductions to the moderate- to large-sized home aquarium. Not only are they active fishes

Pseudocoris yamashiroi, Redspot False Coris Wrasse, initial phase: classic zooplankton feeder and a great reef aquarium species.

Pseudocoris yamashiroi, Redspot False Coris Wrasse, terminal phase male: unusual variant from the Maldives, Indian Ocean.

that will need plenty of swimming space, but some are also very colorful and will spend most of their time in full view, dashing about in the water column. A tank of at least 135 gallons is a minimum requirement for a small group.

When first acquired, the false corises may spend much of their time buried in the substrate. It is important to get their biological clock reset to the new light-dark regime in your aquarium. I have had individuals that continually come out at night and stay hidden during the daylight hours. In time, they usually will recover from their "jet lag." If you find your *Pseudocoris* does not start to adjust after a week, you may want to try and encourage them to come out of the sand by gently probing the sand with your finger or rigid airline tubing. (Make sure you do this gently, as you don't want to injure your labrid charge.) Some aquarists place newly acquired wrasse species that bury in the sand at night in a quarantine tank that lacks a sand bed. In this way, the fish are forced to adapt to a new light-dark cycle before being placed in a tank with sand to bury in.

The *Pseudocoris* tend not to be overly aggressive, although males may pester other zooplankton-feeding labrids. Keep only one male per tank. Juveniles and females can be housed in small groups and may do best if kept in shoals or with other zooplankton-feeding wrasses (e.g., *Paracheilinus*). That said, I have had females that were picked on by larger fairy wrasses (*Cirrhilabrus* spp.). These wrasses (especially males or females that are being harassed by more bellicose neighbors) will jump out of open aquariums. If harassed by tankmates they typically

hide incessantly and will not survive. Feed them frequently, at least three times a day. They greedy accept frozen mysid shrimp, finely minced table shrimp, and smaller individuals will snap up frozen *Cyclops*.

The most common in aquarium stores is the **Redspot False Coris** (*Pseudocoris yamashiroi*) (**Schmidt, 1931**). The male of this species has a white ventrum and is gray, green, and yellow on the upper third of the body with scattered dark spots. Females are pink to gray overall with silver or blue lines on the head that can extend onto the body, especially in smaller individuals. It reaches a length of just over 15 cm (5.9 in.).

Pseudocoris yamashiroi ranges from East Africa to Samoa, south to the Kermadec Islands and north to the Philippines. It is found over lagoon patch reefs, in reef channels, on fore faces and slopes at depths of 2 to at least 25 m (7 to 83 ft.). This species forms aggregations as juveniles and adults. Groups of the latter are composed mainly of females with the occasional male. It is a zooplankton feeder that ingests copepods and mysid shrimps. The Redspot False Coris is a wonderful addition to the reef tank. Only one male should be housed per tank and a male is best introduced with or after a group of females. This species will leap from an open aquarium. Feed a meaty food (e.g., chopped seafood, mysid shrimp) three or more times a day.

Bleeker's False Coris (*Pseudocoris bleekeri*) (**Hubrecht, 1876**) is a lovely fish that is known from Indonesia north to the Ryuku Islands.

Continued on following page

Pseudocoris yamashiroi, Redspot False Coris Wrasse: group of initial phase fish showing the tendency of this genus to gather in clusters offering some safety in numbers as they feed away from cover. There is typically one terminal phase male riding herd over a number of initial phase fish.

Female *P. bleekeri* are green, while the male has a distinct bright yellow band on the side (this is more conspicuous when these fishes feed over the substrate). It reaches a length of 15.0 cm (5.9 in.). This false coris is found over coastal sand and rubble reefs and over coral pinnacles, usually in current-prone areas. It feeds on zooplankton and often forms mixed assemblages with other zooplanktivores. When the male rises into the water column to feed, the yellow blotch appears on the side. Its husbandry requirements are similar to *P. yamashiroi*.

The **Torpedo False Coris** or **Torpedo Wrasse** (*Pseudocoris heteroptera*) (**Bleeker, 1857**) is distributed from the Seychelles to the Society Islands, north to south Japan. It reaches a length of 16 cm (6.3 in.). The males exhibit an attractive color pattern consisting of a bluish gray head and anterior body. The posterior section of body is green with dark bars. Females are white to tan with a dark brown stripe along the back and a thicker stripe running down the center of the body. The anal fin is often orange. The Torpedo False Coris is a resident of outer reef crests and reef faces where it occurs at depths of 2 to 54 m (7 to 178 ft.). It is often found over open bottoms composed of a mixture of sand and rubble, with scattered coral heads. *Pseudocoris heteroptera* resides in small groups, which are comprised of many initial phase fish and a single terminal phase male. When initial phase fish move up in the water column to feed, they will often lose their stripes and become a monochromatic gray, which will make them less conspicuous to roving piscivores. Males exhibit rapid color change when interacting with rivals or potential mates. Its husbandry is similar to others in the genus.

Pseudocoris bleekeri, Bleeker's False Coris Wrasse, terminal phase male, Cebu.

Captive Care: This wrasse's behavioral and husbandry characteristics are similar to those of the Sixline Wrasse (*P. hexataenia*). It is a smaller species than *P. hexataenia*, but it is equally aggressive. I have seen it harass gobies, assessors, and other wrasses in small reef aquaria.

Aquarium Size: 20 gal. **Temperature:** 22 to 27 ºC (72 to 80 ºF).

Aquarium Suitability Index: 4.

Remarks: Adult *P. tetrataenia* have prolonged filaments on the first two dorsal spines. This characteristic is not related to sex but to size (larger females and males exhibit these filaments). That said, if a fish lacks this filaments it is probably a juvenile or a female.

GENUS *PSEUDODAX* (CHISELTOOTH WRASSE)

This genus has a single species that sometimes shows up in aquarium stores. This fish, the **Chiseltooth Wrasse** (*Pseudodax moluccanus*) (**Valenciennes, 1840**), is usually sold as an "assorted wrasse." It reaches a length of 25 cm (9.8 in.). It ranges from the Red Sea and South Africa east to the Society, Marquesas, and Tuamotu Islands, north to southern Japan, and south to the Great Barrier Reef.

The Chiseltooth Wrasse is found near lagoon patch reefs, in reef channels, and on reef faces and reef slopes at depths of 3 to 40 m (9 to 132 ft.). Juveniles typically occur at depths greater than 18 m (59 ft.). Adults are often found near cave entrances or on dropoffs and are solitary fish. Juveniles also occur singly and are faculative cleaners that will engage in this activity in captivity (they will also take introduced foods). Dietary studies do not exist for this species, but they probably feed on small, motile invertebrates, which they pluck from the substrate with their protruding teeth.

Captive Care

The Chiseltooth Wrasse tends to ship poorly, but once acclimated, it usually does quite well. Juveniles recover much more readily from shipping than adults. They need a sand bed at least 5 cm (2 in.) in depth in which to bury. Feed this fish meaty foods, including frozen preparations, mysid shrimps, and finely chopped/shaved seafood (e.g., shrimp). Feed at least twice a day in a reef tank (more often in a tank without live substrate). It will probably not harm sessile invertebrates, but adults may eat ornamental shrimps, a variety of worms, small clams, and tiny snails. As mentioned above, the food habits of this species have not been studied, so keep an eye on it if you add it to a stony coral tank.

Pseudodax moluccanus, Chiseltooth Wrasse, juvenile: part-time cleaner.

Pseudodax moluccanus, Chiseltooth Wrasse, transforming juvenile.

Pseudodax moluccanus, Chiseltooth Wrasse, adult: invert predator.

It may jump from an open tank if startled.

Unless you have a large aquarium, keep one per tank. Juveniles will squabble with each other, as will adult males. If you have a large aquarium (180 gallons or larger), it is possible to keep two females (one will probably eventually change sex) or a male and a female in the same tank. Juveniles are likely to quarrel with other cleaner wrasses, especially those that are similar in color (e.g., *Labroides* spp. and *Labropsis* spp.). This wrasse more readily acclimates to captive life than the full-time cleaners. **Aquarium Size:** 100 gal. **Temperature:** 23° to 28°C (74° to 82°F). **Aquarium Suitability Index:** 3.

GENUS *PSEUDOJULOIDES* (PENCIL WRASSES)

The genus *Pseudojuloides* comprises gorgeous labrids that pose special husbandry problems for aquarists. Like the genera *Anampses* and *Stethojulis*, the members of this genus often pine away in captivity. While dietary studies do not indicate specialized feeding habits, they regularly appear to starve in the home aquarium. We will discuss this problem and some possible solutions in the Captive Care section that follows.

Biology

There are 10 described species in this genus and several that are awaiting formal description (only a couple of species regularly show up in the aquarium trade). All members of the genus are residents of the Indo-Pacific. While some species are more wide-ranging, more than half of the *Pseudojuloides* have relatively limited distributions. For example, *P. argyreogaster* is an all-green species that is only known from Tanzania and the Seychelles, while the Golden Pencil Wrasse (*P. xanthomos*) is only known from a single specimen collected off the island of Mauritius. Most are residents of the tropical coral reef ecosystem, but there are a handful of species found on subtropical, rocky reefs. The Elongate Pencil Wrasse (*P. elongatus*), for instance, is known from eastern and western Australia, Lord Howe Island, Norfolk Island, and New Zealand.

The pencil wrasses are most often found over mixed sand-rubble-algae habitats adjacent to coral reefs, often on moderate to deep rubble slopes. The spectacular Flaming Pencil Wrasse (*P. pyrius*) is found at depths of 14 to 41 m (46 to 135 ft.), while the Sidespot Pencil Wrasse (*P. mesostigma*) occurs at depths greater than 30 m (98 ft.). They often share this habitat with fungid corals, perchlets (*Plectranthias* spp.), fairy wrasses (*Cirrhilabrus* spp.), and flasher wrasses (*Paracheilinus* spp.). Those

Pseudojuloides cerasina, Smalltail Pencil Wrasse, terminal phase: a gloriously pigmented species that, sadly, has a history of failing to thrive in the aquarium.

species from subtropical seas live among the macroalgae that characterize these rocky reefs. When threatened, the fishes will hide among the rubble, bury in the sand, or try to out-swim their adversaries.

These wrasses feed on small, benthic invertebrates (including fan worms, small crustaceans) that they pluck from the substrate without disrupting it. They are apparently diandric, protogynous hermaphrodites. Although there are no specific studies on the social and mating behaviors of this fish, they regularly occur in small groups of initial phase individuals. The terminal phase males usually occur singly and are typically quite gaudy in their coloration.

Captive Care
Although they would seem to be ideally suited for the reef aquarium, the *Pseudojuloides* spp. are difficult to keep. Food habit studies do not indicate that they have a specialized diet, but even so, they tend to become emaciated and perish in the aquarium. Like other wrasses that present feeding challenges (e.g., Tamarin wrasses, leopard wrasses, and ribbon wrasses), they usually do

Pseudojuloides mesostigma, Sidespot Pencil Wrasse, pair, male foreground.

Pseudojuloides atavai, Polynesian Pencil Wrasse, IP: Society Islands.

better in a reef tank, where they will find some natural fodder, than in a more sterile aquarium that lacks "live" substrate.

One key to keeping them alive is to provide them with a varied diet and feed them frequently. They will eat *Cyclops* (especially small individuals), mysid shrimp, and vitamin-enriched brine shrimp (alive or frozen). Add them to a large, established tank with live substrate. A productive refugium will increase your chances of success. Although its use is not encouraged by most reef keepers, a mat of filamentous algae often encourages the growth of the amphipods that these fishes feed on.

Pseudojuloides are proficient jumpers that will leap from open tanks. It is important to provide them with a layer of fine sand, at least 5 cm (2 in.) deep, to bury under. I would keep them in a larger reef tank (or at least an aquarium with lots of live rock) to ensure there are enough micro-invertebrates for them to feed on. They will compete with other fishes in this trophic group, including mandarin dragonets (*Synchiropus picturatus* and *S. splendidus*).

You can keep an initial phase individual and a terminal phase individual in the same tank, or more than one initial phase fish. In the latter case, one of the IP individuals is likely to change to the terminal phase. This can occur in as short a time as 2 weeks. It is best not to house these wrasses with more aggressive fish tankmates. Avoid housing them with larger dottybacks, *Paracirrhites* hawkfishes, pugnacious damsels, banana wrasses (genus *Thalassoma*), larger sand perches, and triggerfishes. Of course, in a larger tank, you may be able to get away with keeping the *Pseudojuloides* with potential bullies, but make sure the pencil wrasses are in the tank first. Their elongate form makes them easy prey for a wide range of piscivores, including frogfishes, scorpionfishes, and groupers.

Pencil Wrasse Species

Pseudojuloides atavai Randall & Randall, 1981
Common Name: Polynesian Pencil Wrasse.
Maximum Length: 13 cm (5.1 in.).
Distribution: Guam to the Society, Tuamotu, and Austral Islands and Ducie Island.
Biology: *Pseudojuloides atavai* is found on reef faces and slopes at depths of 12 to at least 31 m (40 to 102 ft.). It is found over rubble bottoms.
Captive Care: This species is rarely seen in the North American aquarium trade. Most that are collected end up in Japan. For husbandry, see the Captive Care section for the genus.
Aquarium Size: 75 gal. **Temperature:** 23° to 28°C (74° to 82°F).
Aquarium Suitability Index: 2.
Remarks: Initial phase fish are white with a copper-colored dorsum, while terminal phase males are spectacular, with a network of pink lines on the head and pink spots on the orange body.

Pseudojuloides cerasinus (Snyder, 1904)
Common Name: Smalltail Pencil Wrasse.
Maximum Length: 12.3 cm (4.8 in.).
Distribution: East Africa to the Hawaiian, Society, and Austral Islands, north to the Izu Islands, and south to Lord Howe Island.
Biology: This is the most common member of the genus. It is found in clear lagoons and on outer reef faces and slopes at depths of 2 to 61 m (7 to 201 ft.). It is not common at depths of less than 20 m (66 ft.). The Smalltail Pencil Wrasse is usually found over coral rubble with patches of macroalgae. It is also found in areas of rich stony coral growth.
Captive Care: See the Captive Care section for the genus.

Pseudojuloides cerasinus, Smalltail Pencil Wrasse, initial phase.

Pseudojuloides cerasinus, Smalltail Pencil Wrasse, transforming to TP.

Aquarium Size: 75 gal. **Temperature:** 23° to 28°C (74° to 82°F).
Aquarium Suitability Index: 2.
Remarks: Females are all orange with a white spot on the nose. This initial phase coloration is common among all the *Pseudo-juloides* spp., except *P. atavai*. The **Flaming Pencil Wrasse** (*Pseudojuloides pyrius*) **Randall & Randall, 1981** is a remarkable species that is only known from the Marquesas Islands. It is found at moderate depths, having been reported from 18 to 41 m (59 to 133 ft.) over rubble and sand. It is bright reddish or-ange overall.

Pseudojuloides kaleidos Kuiter & Randall, 1995
Common Name: Bluenose Pencil Wrasse.
Maximum Length: 10 cm (3.9 in.).
Distribution: Maldives and Indonesia.
Biology: The Bluenose Pencil Wrasse is found in reef channels and reef faces at depths to at least 25 m (83 ft.). It occurs over mixed rubble, algae, and invertebrate growth and is often found in current-prone habitats. The initial phase individuals often form small groups, while males are solitary.
Captive Care: This wrasse is not commonly encountered in the aquarium trade. See the Captive Care section for the genus.
Aquarium Size: 75 gal. **Temperature:** 23° to 28°C (74° to 82°F).
Aquarium Suitability Index: 2.

Pseudojuloides cerasinus, Smalltail Pencil Wrasse, male variant.

Pseudojuloides mesostigma Randall & Randall, 1981
Common Names: Sidespot Pencil Wrasse, Black Patch Wrasse.
Maximum Length: 8.5 cm (3.3 in.).
Distribution: Papua New Guinea north to southern Japan. Re-cently recorded from Tonga.
Biology: This pencil wrasse occurs at moderate depths, and has

Pseudojuloides kaleidos, Bluenose Pencil Wrasse, terminal phase male.

P. mesostigma, Sidespot Pencil Wrasse, TP male, Papua New Guinea.

Pseudojuloides severnsi, Severn's Pencil Wrasse, terminal phase male.

Pseudojuloides severnsi, Severn's Pencil Wrasse, TP male variant.

P. erythrops, Redeye Pencil Wrasse, TP male: rare deep-water fish.

been reported from 30 to 40 m (98 to 132 ft.). It is usually found on rubble slopes with scattered small coral colonies.

Captive Care: See the Captive Care for the genus.

Aquarium Size: 75 gal. **Temperature:** 23 to 28°C (74 to 82°F).

Aquarium Suitability Index: 2.

Remarks: The terminal phase of *Pseudojuloides mesostigma* is easily recognized by its midback black patch that extends onto the dorsal fin.

Pseudojuloides severnsi Bellwood & Randall, 2000

Common Name: Severn's Pencil Wrasse.

Maximum Length: 11 cm (4.3 in.).

Distribution: Sri Lanka, Ryukyu Islands, and Indonesia.

Biology: *Pseudojuloides severnsi* is found on rubble slopes, often adjacent to reef dropoffs, at depths of 12 to 50 m (39 to 165 ft.). It is more often found at the deeper end of this range. The initial phase fish are found in small groups, while terminal phase males often occur singly, occasionally visiting their harems of females.

Captive Care: This is one of the more common species in the aquarium trade. See the Captive Care section for the genus.

Aquarium Size: 75 gal. **Temperature:** 23° to 28°C (74° to 82°F).

Aquarium Suitability Index: 2.

Remarks: The Redeye Pencil Wrasse (*Pseudojuloides erythrops*) **Randall & Randall, 1981** is a species that has only been found around Mauritius. It is a deep-water species reported at depths of 50 to 60 m (165 to 198 ft.).

GENUS *PTERAGOGUS* (SECRETIVE OR SNEAKY WRASSES)

The taxonomy of this genus appears to be in a state of flux. Currently, there are seven described species. But in his treatise on various labrid genera, Rudie Kuiter (2002) lists 10 species in the genus *Pteragogus*, three of which are in need of formal description. Although Kuiter has long been known as a splitter in taxonomic circles, he is also a very perceptive fish expert. He suggests that all three of the new species have been mislabeled as *Pteragogus cryptus* in the past. (His claims are discussed in more detail in the *P. cryptus* species account.) I will leave this debate to those who have the time and inclination to count scales, fin spines, and rays, and research the historical documents that may have originally ascribed binomials to these labrids.

Biology

When it comes to their life history, there is no debate—relatively little is known about these stealthy reef dwellers. The genus is limited in distribution to the Indo-Pacific. These fishes are most common on shallow coastal reefs at shallow to moderate depths. They are quite cryptic, spending most of their time moving among algae, seagrass, or sessile invertebrates. They often live among rubble, in crevices, or among rich invertebrate growth on coastal reef walls. At least two species (*Pteragogus aurigarius* and *P. taeniops*) are more often found on rocky reefs in warm-temperate regions (southern Japan and South Africa, respectively). The Seagrass Secretive Wrasse (*Pteragogus pelycus*) and the Malachite Secretive Wrasse (*P. aurigarius*) are regularly encountered in seagrass meadows.

Food habit studies are unavailable for *Pteragogus*, but it is suspected that they prey upon crustaceans and small fishes. While most occur singly, at least one species (*P. pelycus*) is sometimes

Pteragogus aurigarius, Malachite Secretive Wrasse, male: while this gorgeous Japanese species is not often seen in the trade, others in the genus are.

Pteragogus cryptus, Cryptic Wrasse: an unusual aquarium species.

Pteragogus cf. cryptus, Cryptic Wrasse, Lembeh Strait, Sulawesi.

observed in aggregations. There is some information available on the reproductive behavior of genus members. The males of at least one species (*P. flagellifer*) are known to form temporary territories during the spawning period, especially when a population consists primarily of females. They pair spawn, engaging in courtship behaviors similar to those exhibited by other labrids. (See the species account of *P. cryptus* for more details). A number of species exhibit sexual dimorphism and/or dichromatism. For example, there are several species in which the males develop elongate filaments on the anterior-most dorsal spines. Male Cockerel Wrasses (*P. enneacanthus*) and Japanese Secretive Wrasses (*P. aurigarius*) are more colorful than the females.

Captive Care

These wrasses, none of which exceed 20 cm (7.9 in.) in length, are ideal for the medium to large home aquarium. One thing you should be aware of before purchasing a secretive wrasse is that, as the name implies, they are very shy when first added to the aquarium. However, if not harassed, they will become more brazen as they adjust to captive life.

Provide these fishes with as varied a diet as possible. It is possible that certain individuals will not eat or won't get enough to eat, especially if they are housed with overbearing tankmates like angelfishes or triggerfishes. Live food (ghost shrimps, live-bearing fishes) can be useful to initiate a feeding response in finicky individuals. Feed them at least once a day. Keep only one member of the genus per tank, as aggressive interactions are likely to occur. In the wild, they tend to be solitary.

It is possible to keep *Pterogogus* in a reef aquarium, but they will feed on some motile invertebrates, including ornamental crustaceans. They usually spend most of their time slinking around live rock and among corals (they will even rest among the polyps of soft corals). They are usually not a threat to fishes of equal or larger size, but they may feed on piscine tankmates that can be swallowed whole.

Secretive Wrasse Species

Pteragogus cryptus Randall, 1981
Common Name: Cryptic Wrasse.
Maximum Length: 9.5 cm (3.7 in.).
Distribution: Red Sea, Taiwan to the Great Barrier Reef and New Caledonia, east to the Samoa Islands and Micronesia. Randall (2005) reports that there are no Indian Ocean records for this species. See Remarks for more on the enigmatic distribution and taxonomy of this fish.
Biology: This species resides on coastal fringing reefs at depths of 4 to 67 m (13 to 221 ft.). It hides most of the time, occasionally coming out of cover to move from one hiding place to another. It often rests and swims among soft corals and macroalgae. Spawning has been observed. A male and female will rendezvous at a prominent landmark and begin hovering just above the site at about 3:30 P.M., the male maintaining a slightly higher position in the water column. The male swims back and forth above the female (this is known as "sway swimming"). When the female *P. cryptus* is ready to spawn, she will rise up and swim parallel to the male as he continues his zigzag trajectory. The pair then ascends sharply approximately 15 to 20 cm (5.9 to 7.9 in.), levels out, and swims parallel to each other for a short distance, then engages in a final spawning ascent of about 1 m (3.3

Pteragogus cryptus, Cryptic Wrasse, Philippines.

Pteragogus enneacanthus, Cockerel Wrasse, red variant.

ft.). They release their gametes at the point when they suddenly dash back down toward the reef. Males are mature at as small as 4.5 cm (1.8 in.), while females mature at a smaller size, about 3.6 cm (1.4 in.).

Captive Care: See the Captive Care section for the genus.

Aquarium Size: 30 gal. **Temperature:** 23° to 28°C (74° to 82°F).

Aquarium Suitability Index: 4.

Remarks: This species exhibits no sexual dichromatism. Kuiter (2002) suggests that there are three species that are currently mis-identified as this species. The Lembeh Sneaky Wrasse (*Pteragogus* sp.) is an undescribed species that differs in having 10 dorsal spines, but the males lack the elongated dorsal filaments on the spines found on the other *Pteragogus* with 10 spines. The Lem-beh has a red bar below the eye and an ocellus trimmed with yellow on the gill cover. This species is only known from Lembeh Strait, Sulawesi (its range is no doubt larger). Kuiter refers to the second species as the Pacific Sneaky Wrasse (*Pteragogus* cf. *cryptus* 1). He states this species is only known from the western Pacific. It has 10 dorsal spines but lacks the ocelli on the gill covers. The male has elongated fin filaments. It usually has a white line from the tip of the snout over the eye to the rear edge of the opercu-lum. The Indian Sneaky Wrasse (*Pteragogus* cf. *cryptus* 2), which is found throughout the Indian Ocean, from the east coast of Africa to Bali, is similar to the last species, but the white line runs past the gill cover along the side of most of the body, and the scales on the body are edged in white. Kuiter suggests that "real" *Pteragogus cryptus* may be limited in distribution to the Red Sea (where the holotype for the species was collected by Dr. John Randall).

Pteragogus enneacanthus, Cockerel Wrasse, brown variant.

Pteragogus enneacanthus (Bleeker, 1853)

Common Name: Cockerel Wrasse.

Maximum Length: 15 cm (5.9 in.).

Distribution: Taiwan to the Great Barrier Reef, New South Wales, east to Tonga.

Biology: This member of the genus is often found moving or resting among the large, stinging hydroids of the genus *Aglao-phenia*. It is sometimes also seen, like others in the genus, amid macroalgae and soft corals. The Cockerel Wrasse is a resident of fringing coastal reefs, where it occurs at depths of 3 to 25 m (10 to 83 ft.).

Pteragogus enneacanthus, Cockerel Wrasse, tan variant.

Pteragogus aurigarius, Malachite Secretive Wrasse: initial phase.

Pteragogus guttatus, Whitebarred Sneaky Wrasse, male.

Pteragogus aurigarius, Malachite Secretive Wrasse, male.

Captive Care: The larger size of this species means it is more likely to prey on a wider array of tankmates. Other than the size difference, its care requirements are similar to others in the genus. **Aquarium Size:** 75 gal. **Temperature:** 23° to 28°C (74° to 82°F). **Aquarium Suitability Index:** 4.

Remarks: The Cockerel Wrasse has nine dorsal spines. In males, the first two dorsal spines have filaments. This species differs from its kin in having white stripes running along the flanks. It is wide-ranging, occurring from east Africa to Papua New Guinea, north to southern Japan, and south to the Great Barrier Reef. Like *P. enneacanthus*, the adult males have very elongate filaments on the first two dorsal spines. It is most often found in shallow seagrass beds.

Pteragogus guttatus (Fowler & Bean, 1928)

Common Name: Whitebarred Sneaky Wrasse.
Maximum Length: 9.0 cm (3.5 in.).
Distribution: Malaysia to Micronesia, also Philippines and Indonesia.
Biology: Like others in the genus, this species is often found on coastal fringing reefs, slinking among soft corals, macroalgae beds, or the spines of long-spined urchins (*Diadema* spp.). It has been reported at depths of 4 to 67 m (13 to 220 ft.), but is most common at depths of less than 10 m (33 ft.). It is often found over rubble substrates.
Captive Care: See the Captive Care section for the genus.
Aquarium Size: 30 gal. **Temperature:** 23° to 28°C (74° to 82°F).
Aquarium Suitability Index: 4.
Remarks: This species has nine dorsal spines and thin white bars on the dorsal fin and dorsum under the fin. *Pteragogus guttatus* also has a row of dark spots running along the lateral line. The **Malachite Secretive Wrasse** (*Pteragogus aurigarius*) **Richardson, 1845** is a colorful species from subtropical Japan and China.

Stethojulis interrupta, Cut Ribbon Wrasse, terminal phase fish: members of this genus are prone to starve in the aquarium and need six or more feedings per day.

GENUS *STETHOJULIS* (RIBBON WRASSES)

Some wrasses present the aquarist with a husbandry enigma that is difficult to explain or solve. Such is the case with the *Stethojulis* spp. (commonly known as ribbon wrasses). Unlike many of the challenging fish species, the members of this genus do not have specialized diets; quite the contrary. These wrasses feed on a wide range of demersal and planktonic invertebrates. So what is it that makes these wrasses quite difficult to keep in the aquarium? We will investigate that quandary here.

Many divers overlook the ribbon wrasses, especially when they are sporting their initial phase livery. Not only are they not that colorful, they are very active and not very large. But while the initial phase fish may be easy to pass by, the color of the terminal phase males can be striking.

Biology

The members of the genus *Stethojulis* are all found in the tropical Indo-Pacific. Some, like the Redspot Ribbon Wrasse (*Stethojulis bandanensis*), are found over a wide geographical range, while others, like the Belted Ribbon Wrasse (*S. balteata*), are very limited in distribution (this species is only found on Hawaiian and Johnston Island reefs). The Spotted Ribbon Wrasse (*S. maculata*) is another species with limited range—only in southern Japan.

The members of this genus are typically found in shallow water, most often at depths of less than 10 m (33 ft.), near coastal fringing reefs, in lagoons, on reef flats, and on the reef face. They are very active and some frequent more turbulent habitats, such as the reef crest. The species studied thus far all have similar food habits and prefer tiny invertebrates that live on or near the seafloor, including minute crustaceans, worms, and tiny sea urchins. (See the species accounts for more specifics regarding diet.)

While few details on their social habits are available, most species occur in groups comprising mainly initial phase individuals. A single terminal phase male often escorts these groups as they move over what appear to be extensive home ranges. These fish are diandric protogynous hermaphrodites. That is, initial phase fish can be either female or male, while the terminal phases are males that result from female sex change or initial phase male transformation.

Stethojulis bandanensis, Redspot Ribbon Wrasse, initial phase.

Stethojulis bandanensis, Redspot Ribbon Wrasse: terminal phase male.

Stethojulis interrupta, Cut Ribbon Wrasse, initial phase.

Stethojulis interrupta, Cut Ribbon Wrasse, terminal phase.

Stethojoulis interrupta, Cut Ribbon Wrasse, transforming to terminal phase.

the eye and one that runs along the pectoral axil onto the caudal peduncle. The terminal phase of this species has blue to greenish lines radiating from the eye and a reddish orange patch above the pectoral fin. This fish is replaced by *Stethojulis balteata* in the Hawaiian Islands and by *S. albovittata* in the western Indian Ocean.

Stethojulis interrupta (Bleeker, 1851)

Common Name: Cut Ribbon Wrasse.

Maximum Length: 13 cm (5.1 in).

Distribution: Red Sea to the Solomon Islands, north to the Philippines, and south to southeastern Australia and Lord Howe Island.

Biology: This ribbon wrasse is found near coastal reefs in areas of mixed, rubble, sand, and rock coral. It occurs in small groups to about 20 m (66 ft.) depth. Feeding is done by sorting small animals from mouthfuls of sand and detritus.

Captive Care: See the Captive Care section for the genus.

Aquarium Size: 100 gal. **Temperature:** 23° to 28°C (74° to 82°F).

Aquarium Suitability Index: 2.

Remarks: Coloration of this species seems to be highly variable. There appear to be a number of different transitional color forms between the initial phase and terminal phase. Females are often orange above and pale below with a dark reticulated pattern. There is a yellow stripe from the tip of the snout to the base of the pectoral fin; in some cases, part of the yellow line may be blue. Terminal phase individuals have a blue line above and below the eye and a single blue line running along the dorsal base and the midflank.

Stethojulis notialis Randall, 2000

Common Name: South Pacific Ribbon Wrasse.

Maximum Length: 13 cm (5.1 in).

Distribution: New Caledonia, Norfolk Island, Fiji and Tonga.

Biology: This fish is found on reef flats and reef faces at depths down to 6 m (20 ft.). It is most often seen over mixed sand, rubble, and coral habitats. It is also seen among macroalgae. The diet is probably similar to that of other members of the genus.

Captive Care: This is not a common species in the trade, but may be occasionally exported from Fiji and Tonga. See the Captive Care section for the genus.

Aquarium Size: 100 gal. **Temperature:** 23° to 28°C (74° to 82°F).

Aquarium Suitability Index: 2.

Remarks: The dorsum of the initial phase fish is green, becoming pale down toward the stomach. There are fine reticulations on the ventrum. There is a yellow stripe on the top of the head that extends to the caudal peduncle. The terminal phase fish are similar but have four dark bars on the side.

Stethojulis strigiventer (Bennett, 1833)

Common Name: Three Ribbon Wrasse.

Maximum Length: 15 cm (5.9 in).

Distribution: South Africa east to the Tuamotu Islands, north to southern Japan, and south to New South Wales, Australia.

Biology: The Three Ribbon Wrasse inhabits seagrass beds and areas of mixed sand, rubble, and algae on inner reef flats and in shallow lagoons at depths of 2 to 15 m (7 to 50 ft.). The diet of *S. strigiventer* is predominantly made up of demersal and planktonic invertebrates, including harpacticoid copepods, gammaridean amphipods, tanaids, and forams. It also ingests (in order of importance): errant polychaetes, sea spiders, snails, cumaceans, cyclopoid copepods, invertebrate eggs, sedentary polychaetes, crab megalops, ostracods, isopods, sponges, acarids, fish eggs,

Stethojulis notialis, South Pacific Ribbon Wrasse, initial phase.

Stethojulis strigiventer, Three Ribbon Wrasse, terminal phase.

barnacle larvae, crabs, galatheid crabs, calanoid copepods, caprellid amphipods, bivalves, and shrimps. When feeding off the substrate, it incidentally ingests sand and algae.

Captive Care: See the Captive Care section for the genus.

Aquarium Size: 135 gal. **Temperature:** 23° to 28°C (74° to 82°F).

Aquarium Suitability Index: 2.

Remarks: The initial phase of *S. strigiventer* is pale blue to gray with white spots and lines above, broader white lines below, and a white line under the eye. The initial phase Three Ribbon Wrasse has an ocellus on the posterior part of the dorsal fin. The terminal phase is green above and white below. There is also a black spot on the upper operculum, a blue line along the dorsal base, a blue line that runs from in front of the eye onto the caudal fin, and a blue line that runs from the snout, under the eye, to just beyond the pectoral base.

Stethojulis trilineata, Threelined Ribbon Wrasse, terminal male.

Stethojulis trilineata (Bloch & Schneider, 1801)
Common Name: Threelined Ribbon Wrasse.
Maximum Length: 14 cm (5.5 in).
Distribution: Maldives east to Samoa, north to southern Japan, and south to the Great Barrier Reef.
Biology: *Stethojulis trilineata* is a shallow-water reef-dweller. It is found in lagoons and on reef flats and exposed reef faces at depths of less than 1 to 8 m (3.3 to 26 ft.). It is often seen on reef crests or above reef dropoffs. The main components of the Threelined Ribbon Wrasse's diet include harpacticoid copepods, gammaridean amphipods, and ids. It also eats the following (in order of importance): ostracods, errant polychaetes, cumaceans, fish eggs, snails, forams, crabs, stomatopods, peanut worms, invertebrate eggs, isopods, bivalves, caprellid amphipods, chitons, hydroids, sea spiders, and sedentary polychaetes.
Captive Care: See the Captive Care section for the genus.
Aquarium Size: 100 gal. **Temperature:** 23° to 28°C (74° to 82°F).
Aquarium Suitability Index: 2.
Remarks: The terminal phase is green overall with a red dorsal fin. There are four blue lines, of varying length, on the head and body and the area in front of the pectoral base is yellowish-orange (this extends onto the head).

GENUS *THALASSOMA* (BANANA WRASSES)

While all the wrasses are quite athletic, the members of the genus *Thalassoma* are hyperactive. In the wild they are often seen dashing over the turbulent reef flat, and in captivity they dash from one end of the tank to the other. Watching one of these fishes isn't usually a relaxing experience.

There are 27 species of banana-shaped wrasses in this genus,

which are represented worldwide. The majority of members are found in the Indo-Pacific. The anatomical features that characterize the *Thalassoma* include the presence of 26 lateral line scales, conical teeth (those in the front of the jaw project slightly from the mouth), the lack of canine teeth in the corners of the jaw, and an emarginate to lunate tail, which can be more truncate in young fish. While at first glance they may look very different, molecular studies suggest that the bird wrasses (genus *Gomphosus*) should be included in the genus *Thalassoma*. The former differs only in the elongate snout present in adults, and *G. varius* is known to hybridize with *Thalassoma* species. (This crossbreeding is often a good indicator of relatedness.) Nonetheless, I have followed most other authors in keeping the two genera separate. (For more on *Gomphosus* see page 172.)

Many of the banana wrasses fall into the category of "the bold and the beautiful," displaying attractive colors that can dazzle the most jaded aquarist. But they can also be very belligerent and predatory, making short work of an array of different invertebrates as well as small fish tankmates. However, they definitely have a place in an aquarium housing more aggressive fish, and some of the smaller species can also be trusted in the reef tank.

Biology
Several species in the genus are quite limited in their geographical ranges. For example, the St. Helena Wrasse (*Thalassoma sanctaehelenae*) is only found around the southeastern Atlantic island of St. Helena. Likewise, Heiser's Wrasse (*Thalassoma heiseri*) is only known from the Pitcairn Group and the Tuamotu Archipelago, and the Ascension Wrasse (*Thalassoma ascensionis*) is only known from Ascension Island and the St. Helena Islands. Newton's Wrasse (*Thalassoma newtoni*) is only found around the small island of São Tomé in the eastern Atlantic. As you might expect, because these species live in such remote locations, they rarely make it into the aquarium trade.

All of these species are diurnal carnivores. Food habit studies indicate ontogenetic changes in diet, especially those species that attain a larger size. The trend is that smaller individuals feed on smaller, soft-bodied invertebrates like amphipods, small crabs, shrimps, polychaete worms, and peanut worms. As they grow they are better able to handle small, hard-shelled species like chitons, small bivalves, and small urchins. Finally, large adults can manage more heavily armored prey and feed on gastropods, bivalves, and sea urchins of varying sizes. Most of the *Thalassoma* spp. have well-developed pharyngeal teeth, which enable them to grind up these armored prey items. But when prey are too large to swallow whole, these fishes may use hard substrate (rock or coral) as an anvil to beat them into smaller pieces. The fish grasps the prey toward the front of the jaws and throws its head from side to side as it bashes the prey against the substrate. Many of these wrasses will invade the nests of demersal spawners, such as damselfishes, to feed on their eggs. They often overcome the defending parent by attacking the nests in large groups. For this reason, these wrasses are often attacked with great vigor by damselfishes and other nesting species.

Some of the *Thalassoma* spp. are also facultative cleaners when young, while a few continue to clean, at least on occasion, into adulthood. Unlike some of the obligate cleaners, these wrasses regularly become the victims of predators. For example, the Noronha Wrasse (*Thalassoma noronhanum*) is preyed upon by the Coney (*Cephalopholis fulva*) when away from its cleaning station. Likewise, it has been suggested that Bluehead Wrasses (*T.*

bifasciatum) refrain from cleaning piscivores because they are regularly eaten by them, especially by younger predators that have yet to "learn the rules."

There are several *Thalassoma* spp. that regularly associate with sea anemones. Initial phase individuals of two of these, the Twotone Wrasse (*Thalassoma amblycephalum*) and the Bluehead Wrasse (*T. bifasciatum*), will carefully maneuver between the tentacles of sea anemones or lie on the nematocyst-free oral disc. Juvenile Moon Wrasses (*Thalassoma lunare*) will also hang around large sea anemones.

Social and Reproductive Behavior

The *Thalassoma* spp. are diandric protogynous hermaphrodites. There are two primary color forms: the initial phase and the ter-

Thalassoma rueppellii, Klunzinger's Wrasse, terminal phase male: the so-called "banana wrasses" include many active, colorful species that may turn thuggish.

Bluehead Wrasses, adult and juveniles, with *Condylactis* anemone.

Moon Wrasse, rear, follows a goatfish burrowing for food in the sand.

Moon Wrasse shadows a smaller goatfish on the prowl for prey items.

minal phase. (Some species also have a juvenile color phase.) Initial phase individuals are either females or males; those individuals that hatch and develop as males are referred to as primary males. The terminal phase fishes are males that result from female sex change (secondary males) or, more often, from the transformation of an initial phase male. In the Sea of Cortez, Rainbow Wrasse studies indicate that sex change is not common, with only about 30% of the terminal phase males being derived from females. In this shoaling species, the initial phase population exhibits an equal sex ratio (50% females: 50% primary males). The terminal phase individuals are larger than the initial phase fish and are sometimes referred to as "super males." Sex change is controlled by social status, age, and size. In many species, initial phase females change to terminal phase males when the number of the latter reaches some critical point. The presence of the terminal phase males suppresses sex change. An interesting study carried out by Schärer & Vizoso (2003) demonstrated that female Bluehead Wrasses (*T. bifasciatum*) whose ovaries are infected by the myxozoan *Kudoa ovivora* have lower reproductive success (the eggs are rendered infertile by the parasite) and change sex earlier and at a smaller size than females not infected by this parasite.

The *Thalassoma* spp. are promiscuous and nonharemic, and exhibit two different spawning strategies: they spawn in pairs or in groups. In pair spawning, a female usually seeks out and spawns with a terminal phase male. These males form temporary spawning territories that are very similar to the lek-like mating arenas exhibited by certain birds. While the female will spawn once per day, the male may spawn with numerous females. Territorial males engage in various displays to attract females to their territories and entice them to spawn. They engage in such behavior as "looping" (swimming in loops), which enables females to locate the male's territory from some distance; "quivering" (shuddering of the body); and "pectoral fluttering" (a male rapidly beats the pectoral fins to communicate to the female that he is ready to engage in the spawning ascent). Some terminal phase males also exhibit color changes, which help attract the attention of potential mates. While there is some data that indicates that females prefer larger males (with whom they enjoy the greatest reproductive success), other studies show that females select a mating site to spawn at rather than the male that occupies it. Larger males may successfully occupy the sites that are preferred by females. The accruing of mates by terminal phase individuals is also a function of population density. In larger populations, interference from initial phase males significantly reduces terminal phase male reproductive success. In fact, when population densities reach a certain level, terminal phase males of some species may abandon their territories and engage in group spawning with initial phase males.

In group spawning, females and initial phase males gather over a prominent reef feature, rise into the water column *en masse* and shed their gametes. Some initial phase males engage in an interesting strategy known as "streaking": they will quickly dash in and join a spawning pair (e.g., a terminal phase male and a female) near the top of the spawning ascent and shed their gametes. These shrewd initial phase males will hang around near the territories of terminal phase individuals in order to engage in streaking, and the terminal phase males often attempt to chase them off.

The rapid spawning ascent of the *Thalassoma* spp., and other small reef-dwelling species, provides some protection from marauding piscivores. A study conducted on the interaction of spawning Cupido Wrasses (*Thalassoma cupido*) and their predators demonstrated that only about 1.9% of piscivore attacks directed toward these spawning labrids were successful. (Seven species of fishes were observed attempting to eat these fish during spawning, including morays, lizardfishes, trumpetfishes, two types of scorpionfishes, groupers, and Cigar Wrasses [*Cheilio inermis*].) While adults might avoid predators, their gametes are eaten by a variety of zooplanktivores. The wrasses do little to

Thalassoma bifasciatum, Bluehead Wrasse, initial phase: the model.

Mycteroperca tigris, Tiger Grouper, juvenile: the mimic.

Aggressive Mimics of *Thalassoma* spp.

In the tropical Western Atlantic there is a cleaner mimic known as the Wrasse Blenny (*Hemiemblemaria simulus*). This clinid blenny (family Clinidae) looks like the initial phase of the Bluehead Wrasse (*Thalassoma bifasciatum*) and may gain some protection as a result. However, as mentioned in the text, these labrids are not immune to predation during the cleaning phase of their life cycle. The primary function of this mimetic relationship is to enable the Wrasse Blenny to sneak up on the newly settled wrasses, damselfishes, and dart gobies that are a major part of its diet. Because the initial phase Bluehead Wrasse does not feed on small fishes, it does not elicit an avoidance response. The Sabertooth Blenny (*Runula azalea*) makes its living by biting bits of skin and mucus off passing fishes. It usually launches its attacks while hovering amid groups of initial phase Rainbow Wrasses (*Thalassoma lucasanum*). It appears to be an aggressive mimic of this wrasse, as the two species are very similar in color and shape.

The other proposed aggressive mimic of a *Thalassoma* spp. is a member of the grouper family. The juvenile Tiger Grouper (*Mycteroperca tigris*) is also thought to mimic the initial phase Bluehead Wrasse to gain a tactical advantage over its prey. The grouper feeds on large prey items that do not take shelter when one of these benign labrids appears on the scene. Also, as you will see in the species account for *T. bifasciatum* (page 327), this wrasse is very abundant. As a result, those organisms that are not threatened by it are likely to become habituated to its presence. This gives the similar-looking *M. tigris* a real hunting advantage.

Hybridization happens: Apparent cross of *Thalassoma lutescens* and *Thalassoma duperrey*, the Sunset Wrasse and the Saddle Wrasse. Such hybrids may or may not be fertile.

prevent this and in some cases they will spawn right in the middle of groups of planktivorous (egg-eating) damsels. Important egg predators include anthias, pygmy angelfishes (e.g., *Centropyge interruptus* and *C. tibicen*), and a number of different damselfishes (e.g., *Amphiprion clarkii*, *Chromis* spp., *Dascyllus trimaculatus*, *Pomacentrus coelestis*, and *P. nagasakiensis*). The spawning cycle may be dependent on the tidal cycle or it may occur at a fixed time of day. In most cases, eggs are released when there is maximum water movement off the reef so that the eggs will be carried out into the open sea and away from the highest concentrations of egg-eating fishes and invertebrates.

Captive Care

The *Thalassoma* spp. are durable aquarium fishes that will readily adjust to captive life. While younger fishes will suffer less from shipping stress and acclimate to aquarium living more readily, most adults will also adjust if given places to hide and plenty of swimming room. These are very active fishes that will "pace" back and forth in the aquarium, so lots of swimming space is essential. Because they get quite large, a large aquarium is needed to keep them "happy." The larger species should be housed in tanks of over 100 gallons. There are a few Goliaths in the group that require tanks on the order of 180 gallons or larger. While these wrasses can deftly maneuver around aquarium decor, create open swimming space to facilitate their active lifestyle.

At night, most of the *Thalassoma* spp. will hide in reef crevices. However, there are some species (or individuals) that have been observed to bury under the sand. They are more likely to do this when greatly stressed. That said, a sand substrate is not required to keep these labrids healthy. These wrasses are also accomplished jumpers, so make sure the aquarium has some type of top.

The *Thalassoma* spp. are usually not too picky about the fare that they will accept in captivity. Chopped seafood (e.g., shrimp) that has been rinsed is a favorite, as well as frozen mysids and frozen preparations. Most can also be trained to take flake or freeze-dried foods. Because they are so active, it is a good idea to feed them three times daily.

Many aquarists prefer the color of the "super males." If you purchase an initial phase individual and keep it by itself, it may or may not change into a terminal phase fish. Some species (e.g., *T. duperrey*) require the presence of a smaller initial phase conspecific in order to induce sex change. Others (e.g., *T. lucasanum*) will change from initial phase to terminal phase if kept alone. If you keep a group of initial phase individuals, the largest fish in the group (whether female or male) will typically transform into a terminal phase male if there is not already a terminal phase male in the tank. In captivity, initial phase individuals often develop into terminal phase males at smaller sizes than they would in the wild. This transformation from initial phase to terminal phase can occur in fewer than 11 days or may take as long as 103 days. Keep only one terminal phase male in a tank.

These fishes do vary somewhat in their aggressiveness. Some of the larger species (e.g., *Thalassoma lutescens*, *T. purpureum*) can be pugnacious to their neighbors when they reach adulthood. Large males are most likely to behave antagonistically toward newly introduced fish tankmates and have been known to consume smaller fishes, especially more slender species (e.g., dartfishes). Adult males are best housed with larger or more aggressive fishes. However, if they are added to a tank that already contains bullies, they may have a hard time acclimating. For example, I added an adult Moon Wrasse (*Thalassoma lunare*) to a tank with a resident Arc-eyed Hawkfish (*Paracirrhites arcatus*) and the hawkfish prevented the labrid from acclimating (the wrasse had to be removed because the hawkfish kept beating on it). Male congeners (especially terminal phase individuals) are likely to clash unless the tank is very large.

While these fishes can be an interesting addition to the reef tank, larger species/individuals can cause problems with your motile invertebrate community. For example, they have been known to consume snails, small bivalves, worms (including fan worms), urchins, serpent stars, and sea stars. On the other hand, members of the genus *Thalassoma* may be useful in controlling certain coral parasites and predators. For example, the Saddle Wrasse (*Thalassoma duperrey*) preys on the *Porites*-eating nudi-

Thalassoma amblycephalum, Blunthead Wrasse, terminal phase male: durable species that does not require a large aquarium to flourish.

branch, *Phestilla sibogae*. This wrasse tends to prefer larger individuals (between 1.5 to 3.5 cm [0.6 to 1.4 in.] in length). It may feed on other slug predators and also on predatory/parasitic snails (e.g., pyramidellid snails). *Thalassoma* spp. will also eat both good and noxious polychaete worms, but rarely bother corals.

Banana Wrasse Species

Thalassoma amblycephalum (Bleeker, 1856)
Common Names: Blunthead Wrasse, Pacific Bluehead Wrasse.
Maximum Length: 14 cm (5.5 in).
Distribution: Somalia and South Africa east to the Marquesas Islands, north to southern Japan, and south to Rowley Shoals and northern New Zealand.
Biology: The Blunthead Wrasse is found on fringing reefs, lagoon patch reefs and pinnacles, and outer reef faces at depths of 1 to 15 m (3.3 to 50 ft.). Juveniles and initial phase individuals sometimes associate with sea anemones (e.g., *Heteractis magnifica*).

Thalassoma amblycephalum, Blunthead Wrasse, initial phase.

Thalassoma ballieui, Blacktail Wrasse, terminal phase: a large, subtly colored fish believed to be the oldest species in the genus, dating back 8 to 13 million years.

Thalassoma ballieui, Blacktail Wrasse, female: a clear threat to invertebrates.

Thalassoma ballieui, Blacktail Wrasse, juvenile: Hawaiian endemic species.

Thalassoma amblycephalum forms large feeding groups in current-prone areas. These fishes feed principally on planktonic crustaceans (the most important of these are cyclopoid copepods, shrimp and crab larvae, and mysids). This species most often group spawns. Groups of up to 40 initial phase fish will assemble 4 m (13 ft.) over the substrate. Individuals jockey for position in the group until a single individual begins to swim erratically and rises into the water column. Other fish will follow this individual until the whole group rapidly rises 1 to 2 m (3.3 to 7 ft.) higher into the water. Suddenly, the group will rapidly turn downward (this is when gametes are released) and race toward the seafloor. In some areas, spawning occurs near prominent landmarks. Spawning can occur in the late morning until the late afternoon and may be tidally influenced. This juveniles, and occasionally adults, will engage in cleaning behavior. For example, adults will clean Manta Rays (*Manta birostris*).

Captive Care: The Blunthead Wrasse occasionally enters the trade and is usually sold as an "assorted wrasse" or the "Indo-Pacific Rainbow Wrasse." It is a very durable species that is well suited to the home aquarium. It will do well in a moderate-size tank and is not as great a threat to fish or ornamental invertebrates as some of its larger congeners. Adult Blunthead Wrasses may pester ornamental crustaceans, but because this species feeds mainly on zooplankton, it is less of a threat if well fed. Keep one terminal phase male per tank, but in a larger aquarium (e.g., 180 gallons or more) a terminal phase individual can be housed with a small group of initial phase conspecifics. If a group of initial phase fish are kept in a tank without a terminal phase male, one of these fish is likely to transform to a "super male." They are proficient jumpers that will leap from an uncovered aquarium.

Aquarium Size: 75 gal. **Temperature:** 23° to 28°C (74° to 82°F).

Aquarium Suitability Index: 5.

Remarks: Initial phase *Thalassoma amblycephalum* are light with a black lateral stripe, while the terminal phase male is reddish purple with a yellow saddle just behind the pectoral base and a blue-green head.

Thalassoma ballieui (Vaillant & Sauvage, 1875)

Common Name: Blacktail Wrasse.

Maximum Length: 40 cm (15.7 in.).

Distribution: Hawaiian Islands and Johnston Island.

Biology: This species is found on rocky and fringing coral reefs off the Hawaiian coast. It is most often found in boulder habitats, on reef flats, and on the reef face. This wrasse occurs at depths of 3 to 24 m (10 to 80 ft.) and feeds on crabs, urchins (both sea urchins and heart urchins), and fishes in about equal amounts. Less important prey items include snails, lobsters, hermit crabs, shrimps, brittle stars, bivalves, snail eggs, damselfish eggs, and sea stars. It is a solitary species that will often approach fishes that disturb the substrate.

Captive Care: This large, less brilliantly colored member of the genus is not highly sought after and rarely makes it into aquarium stores. While hardy, its large size means *T. ballieui* is a great threat to a wider range of fish and invertebrate tankmates. Keep it with larger fishes that have equally boisterous personalities. Juveniles obviously cause less trouble than adults and are more often available in the trade.

Aquarium Size: 180 gal. **Temperature:** 22° to 28°C (72° to 82°F).

Aquarium Suitability Index: 3.

Remarks: Juvenile *T. ballieui* are greenish yellow. Larger terminal phase males are very similar in color to initial phase females, except they may have a black tail. Molecular studies have suggested that this species is the oldest member of the genus, having diverged from the other lines in the family tree about 8 to 13 million years ago.

Thalassoma bifasciatum (Bloch, 1791)

Common Name: Bluehead Wrasse.

Maximum Length: 18 cm (7.1 in).

Distribution: Bermuda, Florida, and southeastern Gulf of Mexico south to northern South America. (It is the most abundant wrasse found over hard substrate in the tropical Atlantic.)

Biology: The Bluehead Wrasse is found in almost every reef habitatæaround rocky or coral reefs, pier pilings, lagoon patch reefs, seagrass beds, reef flats, reef faces, and deep-reef slopes. Initial phase individuals regularly associate with the Giant Sea Anemone (*Condylactis gigantea*) and often swim among the cnidarians' tentacles. This labrid is reported at depths of less than 1 to at least 40 m (3.3 to 132 ft.). Juvenile Bluehead Wrasse form groups that move just over the substrate and pick small benthic invertebrates from rocks, the algae mat, and the surfaces of gorgonians. Loose groups of initial phase adults often swim over the bottom and feed on passing zooplankters (e.g., copepods). These groups often number in the hundreds and may even exceed 1,000 individuals. They are sometimes joined by other zooplankton feeders, like juvenile Sergeant Majors (*Abudefduf saxatilis*). Groups of initial phase fish occasionally raid the nests of demersal spawners, including the Beau Gregory Damselfish (*Stegastes leucostictus*), Sergeant Major, and Saddle Blenny (*Malacoctenus triangulatus*). As a result, they are frequent targets of pomacentrid attacks. Initial phase individuals regularly engage in cleaning behavior. More than one Bluehead Wrasse will clean a posing client, sometimes along with cleaner gobies (*Gobiosoma* spp.) or young Spanish Hogfish (*Bodianus rufus*). *Thalassoma bifasciatum* rarely cleans

Thalassoma bifasciatum, Bluehead Wrasse, initial phase variant.

Thalassoma bifasciatum, Bluehead Wrasse, initial phase.

Thalassoma bifasciatum, Bluehead Wrasse, terminal phase male: a dazzling aquarium species for a Caribbean biotope. Keep one male and several IP fishes.

fish-eating predators because they will often be eaten (especially if the piscivore is young and inexperienced). Known predators of this species include the Trumpetfish (*Aulostomus maculatus*), groupers, and soapfishes. While initial phase individuals are more zooplanktivorous, terminal phase males feed more on benthic invertebrates, including serpent stars, crabs, polychaete worms, sea spiders, shrimps, and the occasional small fish. Terminal phase males are occasionally seen dashing around initial phase groups and often chase consexuals and display to females. When engaged in combat with a consexual, the coloration of the terminal phase *T. bifasciatum* may fade. While the terminal phase individuals are usually dominant over initial phase individuals, large initial phase males may occasionally dominate small terminal phase males.

The Bluehead Wrasse is a protogynous hermaphrodite. If a terminal phase male is removed from a population, a large initial phase female will usually change sex. The female will engage in male reproductive behavior minutes after a terminal phase male is removed, adopting the male role during spawning that same day (although the transforming individual does not have viable sperm at this point). This sex-changing fish will have mature sperm in as few as 8 days after the transformation begins. Some populations of Bluehead Wrasse spawn throughout the year, while others exhibit seasonal spawning. For example, off Barbados, this species spawns primarily between January and August. Most spawning occurs around the new and full moons (spring tides); it usually occurs in the middle of the day, but peaks near the beginning of an ebb tide (i.e., when surface currents would be taking the eggs offshore). This wrasse uses traditional spawning sites; that is, they are utilized consistently from one generation to the next. On barrier reefs, large mating groups may migrate to specific spawning sites that are up to 1.5 km (0.9 mi.) away. It may take the group an average of 52 minutes to get to the site.

Like others in the genus, *T. bifasciatum* engages in two different spawning strategies. Initial phase individuals form groups which rush into the water column and release their gametes. (Initial phase spawning groups usually consist of a single female and 5 to 15 males.) Studies have shown that during group spawnings, large males are selective, more often joining groups that include a large female. (Larger females produce more eggs, increasing the chances the male's sperm will successfully "compete" with the sperm of other males in the group.) A terminal phase male will set up a temporary spawning territory at the down-current edge of the reef and attempt to induce a female to spawn with him by dashing into the water column. His body color will also change from green to opalescent and he will develop spots on the pectoral fins during courtship. A receptive female will join him in the

upward dash and release her gametes. A terminal phase male will spawn with any female that visits his territory. While males typically spawn with 30 to 50 females in a day, some have been reported to have as many as 100 partners in this time period. Initial phase males will sometimes engage in "streaking" (in about 3% to 5% of the pair spawning events). Eggs are pelagic and hatch in 18 to 24 hours. The larvae, which are 12 mm (0.5 in.) in length at hatching, spend from 6 to 8 weeks (and maybe as long as 11 weeks) in the plankton before settling out on the reef or in seagrass meadows. It has been shown that this species can delay metamorphosis while in the larval stage, an adaptation that would allow them to remain in the plankton until they reach coastal habitats.

Captive Care: "Super male" Bluehead Wrasses make dazzling aquarium animals. While initial phase animals feed heavily on zooplankton, and thus are not a threat to ornamental invertebrates (with the exception of more delicate shrimps), large terminal phase males may feed on motile invertebrates like polychaete worms, tiny snails, crustaceans, and small serpent stars. If it is not well fed, a terminal phase individual is more likely to turn its attention to ornamental shrimps and crabs. Initial phase individuals will also clean their tankmates in the home aquarium. You can keep a male with several initial phase individuals if the aquarium is large (preferably 135 gallons or larger). Adult *T. bifasciatum* may pick on more passive fishes introduced after them. They are capable jumpers that will leap from an open tank. Feed them meaty foods two or three times a day.

Aquarium Size: 75 gal. **Temperature:** 23° to 28°C (74° to 82°F).
Aquarium Suitability Index: 5.

Remarks: There are three primary color phases of *T. bifasciatum*. The juveniles have a black mid-lateral stripe which goes onto the head and changes to pale red blotches. In the juvenile, the dorsum above the stripe is yellow on individuals from shallow reef areas and whitish on fishes from seagrass beds and noncoralline environments. The initial phase individuals (which can be male or female) are yellow, often with a dark stripe along the side. The terminal phase males have a bright blue head and a green body.

Thalassoma cupido (Temminck & Schlegel, 1845)
Common Name: Cupido Wrasse.
Maximum Length: 20 cm (7.9 in).
Distribution: Japan to Taiwan.
Biology: The Cupido Wrasse is found on rocky and coral reefs. It has been reported at depths of 3 to at least 10 m (10 to 33 ft.). This wrasse eats benthic invertebrates in order of importance: chitons, isopods, sea cucumbers, errant polychaetes, crabs, and amphipods. Smaller fish feed more on small crustaceans (includ-

Thalassoma cupido, Cupido Wrasse, terminal phase: rarely collected.

Thalassoma duperrey, Saddle Wrasse, juvenile.

ing amphipods, isopods, copepods, and ostracods), which they wrest from the algal mat, but as they get larger they take more worms, snails, chitons, bivalves, crabs, stomatopods, shrimps, and hermit crabs. The adults forage more in areas with heavy coralline algae growth and sometimes associate with feeding parrotfishes. Adults will also forage in the water column on zooplankton, but this is of secondary importance in the diet. Males are solitary and will sometimes lock jaws during bouts of aggression. This wrasse usually forms large breeding assemblages over prominent reef features like large boulders. These groups consist of 1,000 to 3,000 individuals. This fish typically group spawns in the morning until just after midday. In certain areas of Japan, the spawning period is limited to the warmer months of the year (May to August). As the groups of *T. cupido* approach the spawning site, they swim in an unusual bobbing fashion. They will swim in this way above the spawning site for several minutes before they release gametes. From 5 to 40 individuals (one female, the rest males) will break off from the bobbing group and form a milling group in the water column. Some members (1 female and 2 to 20 males) of the agitated mass will then engage in a sudden dash even higher into the water column and jettison their gametes at the apex of the spawning ascent. The group will then dash back toward the substrate.

Captive Care: *Thalassoma cupido* is rare in the aquarium trade. Like others in the genus, it is a durable species that can be pugnacious toward smaller tankmates and fish added to a tank after it. Its husbandry requirements are similar for others in the genus.

Aquarium Size: 75 gal. **Temperature:** 23° to 27°C (74° to 80°F).

Aquarium Suitability Index: 4.

Thalassoma duperrey (Quoy & Gaimard, 1824)

Common Name: Saddle Wrasse.

Maximum Length: 28 cm (11 in).

Distribution: Johnston and Hawaiian Islands.

Biology: This is one of the most common fish on Hawaiian coral reefs. It occurs in almost every reef habitat, including surge-swept reef flats, reef faces, and slopes. *Thalassoma duperrey* is found in areas with rich coral growth, as well as habitats that are devoid of coral coverage. It feeds on zooplankton, often high above the substrate, but also hunts a wide variety of benthic invertebrates. Hobson (1974) lists the following prey items (in order of importance): gastropods, sea urchins, brachyuran crabs, bivalves, amphipods, copepods, tanaids, stony corals, polychaetes, brittle stars, tunicates, isopods, fish eggs, hermit crabs, forams, peanut worms, fish, eggs, and algae fragments. The Saddle Wrasse is very opportunistic, often following fishes that disturb the substrate when they forage. It positions itself close the heads of parrotfishes as they feed, pouncing on small crustaceans that are flushed by the scarids' rasping. It will also engage in cooperative hunting with small goatfishes (the pair stick together and "work" rubble or small coral heads as a team) and will associate with the Day Octopus (*Octopus cyanea*), scavenging on the remains of the octopus's prey. Juveniles set up cleaning stations (usually on large heads of *Porites pukoensis*) and actively pick parasites off other fishes; adults rarely clean, however. The adults move over a large home range that overlaps those of other adult conspecifics. These home ranges are often far from the preferred spawning sites.

Thalassoma duperrey spawns throughout the year in pairs or in groups. Initial phase individuals spawn in groups, while initial

Thalassoma duperrey, Saddle Wrasse, terminal phase: beautiful species that is a common sight on Hawaiian coral reefs. Requires a large aquarium.

phase females and terminal phase males spawn in pairs. It has been suggested that there may be several factors at work to influence sex change in this species. In one study, isolated females did not change sex, while the larger individual in a female pair did. It was determined that sex change is socially controlled—the transformation was stimulated by the presence of a smaller consexual, but inhibited by the company of a larger member of the same sex. Studies have shown that when the ratio of males to females gets too low, the largest female *T. duperrey* will change to a male. This transformation usually takes 6 to 8 weeks. The presence of a conspecific can either stimulate or inhibit growth rates. Subordinates grow more slowly in the presence of a dominant conspecific, while the latter grow faster when kept with a smaller *T. duperrey* than it would if kept on its own.

Captive Care: This is a large species that requires a large tank. Adults can be aggressive in crowded confines, harrying other wrasses and smaller fishes. It will eat any fish or motile inverte-

brate that it can swallow or grasp and bash to pieces against the aquarium decor. Keep it with larger fishes, like large angelfishes, surgeonfishes, triggers, and pufferfishes. (For more on the general husbandry, see the genus Captive Care section.)

Aquarium Size: 100 gal. **Temperature:** 22° to 28°C (72° to 82°F).
Aquarium Suitability Index: 4.

Remarks: Terminal phase individuals are larger, with a white bar behind the orange collar. This species has been reported to hybridize with the Sunset Wrasse (*Thalassoma lutescens*).

Thalassoma hardwicke (Bennett, 1830)
Common Names: Sixbar Wrasse, Hardwicke Wrasse.
Maximum Length: 20 cm (7.9 in).
Distribution: East Africa to the Line and Tuamotu islands, north to southern Japan, and south to the Lord Howe and Austral Islands.
Biology: While it occurs in lagoons, reef flats, and reef faces and

Thalassoma hardwicke, Sixbar Wrasse, terminal male: must be fed frequently.

Thalassoma genivittatum, Redcheek Wrasse, initial phase fish.

Thalassoma genivittatum, Redcheek Wrasse, terminal phase male.

slopes, this species is more common in shallow-water habitats (e.g., reef crests). It is reported from depths of less than 1 to 15 m (3.3 to 50 ft.). Young fish are usually found among branching stony corals.

Crustaceans form the bulk of this species' diet, which includes benthic and planktonic forms: crabs, crab megalops, shrimps, shrimp larvae, copepods, and isopods. It will occasionally take small fishes and forams and feeds off the benthos and in midwater. The Sixbar Wrasse occurs singly (especially large adults) or in small groups. It spawns year-round (at least in American Samoa) and does so during the daytime. Spawning occurs in or near reef channels.

Captive Care: This species is similar to its kin in both hardiness and disposition. It is a relatively durable species that will thin out snails, crustaceans, worms, and serpent stars. Large adults will also eat smaller fishes. The Sixbar Wrasse needs lots of open swimming space and should be fed frequently (at least three times a day) to meet its high metabolic demands. Keep one terminal phase individual per tank. If the aquarium is large enough, you should be able to house several initial phase fish together (one will more than likely transform to a super male).

Aquarium Size: 75 gal. **Temperature:** 23° to 28°C (74° to 82°F).
Aquarium Suitability Index: 4.
Remarks: The terminal phase males are slightly more brilliant in color than initial phase individuals, but the difference is not as striking as it is in some other species.

Thalassoma hebraicum (Lacepède, 1801)

Common Name: Goldbar Wrasse.
Maximum Length: 23 cm (9.1 in).
Distribution: East Africa to the Maldives (not common).
Biology: The Goldbar Wrasse is very common on South African reefs. It occurs on rocky and coral reefs, fringing reefs, lagoon patch reefs, and outer reef faces and slopes. It is found at depths of less than 1 to 30 m (3.3 to 98 ft.). Young fish are often seen in tidepools. Adult male *T. hebraicum* are reported to be territorial and will respond very aggressively to each other. This wrasse may form groups consisting of a single male with a number of females. It feeds on a host of benthic invertebrates, including gastropods, crustaceans, and urchins.
Captive Care: The husbandry requirements of *T. hebraicum* are similar to others in the genus, although it is happy at cooler water temperatures than some congeners. It is also a larger species; therefore, it is a threat to a larger range of invertebrates and small fishes. Like others in the genus, it is a proficient jumper, so make sure you have a secure top on the tank.
Aquarium Size: 100 gal. **Temperature:** 20° to 27°C (68° to 80°F).

Thalassoma hebraicum, Goldbar Wrasse, terminal male: an exceptionally beautiful species, but one requiring ample swimming space.

Aquarium Suitability Index: 4.

Remarks: The **Redcheek Wrasse** (*Thalassoma genivittatum*) (Valenciennes, 1839) is a similar species that is only known from South Africa and the island of Mauritius. This species reaches a length of 20 cm (7.9 in.). This fish lives in small groups on rocky reefs.

Thalassoma jansenii (Bleeker, 1856)

Common Name: Jansen's Wrasse.

Maximum Length: 20 cm (7.9 in).

Distribution: Maldives to Fiji, north to southern Japan, and south to Lord Howe Island.

Biology: Jansen's Wrasse is found at depths of 1 to 15 m (3.3 to 50 ft.) on lagoon patch reefs, exposed outer reef crests, and reef faces. Young fish tend to live among dead coral rubble, while adults occur over a wider range of habitats. Although information does not

Thalassoma jansenii, Jansen's Wrasse, terminal male.

Thalassoma nigrofasciatum, Blackbar Wrasse, terminal male.

Thalassoma lucasanum, Cortez Rainbow Wrasse, initial phase.

exist on its food habits, it no doubt has a polyphagous diet similar to that of other moderate-sized species in the genus.

Captive Care: *Thalassoma jansenii* is a durable species that can be pugnacious in aquarium confines. It has been known to attack and bite newly introduced species (e.g., anemonefishes) and may even attempt to eat smaller fishes. It is a threat to snails, worms, crustaceans, serpent stars, and small sea stars. It may even nip at tridacnid clams.

Aquarium Size: 75 gal. **Temperature:** 23° to 28°C (74° to 82°F).

Aquarium Suitability Index: 4.

Remarks: Initial phase individuals have three black bars. Females are black with a white band and a white area that extends from below the head to the anus. The terminal phase male is yellow between the black bars. A similar species, referred to as the **Blackbar Wrasse (*Thalassoma nigrofasciatum*) Randall, 2003** has been described from the Great Barrier Reef and eastern Papua New Guinea east to the Cook Islands. It is said to differ from *T. jansenii* in having longer pectoral fins and a different color pattern. However, molecular studies conducted by Bernadri et al. (2004) suggest that this "species" is probably just a variant of *T. jansenii*.

Thalassoma lucasanum (Gill, 1862)

Common Name: Cortez Rainbow Wrasse.

Maximum Length: 15 cm (5.9 in).

Distribution: Gulf of California to Panama and the Galapagos Islands.

Biology: The Cortez Rainbow Wrasse is a resident of rocky and coral reefs. It occurs in a variety of different habitats and has been reported at depths of less than 1 to 64 m (3.3 to 211 ft.). It is most common at depths of less than 10 m (33 ft.). On reefs off the west coast of Panama, this species exhibits a population density of 1.92 individuals/m² (or per 10.7 ft.²). It feeds on zooplankton and small benthic invertebrates. Young fish regularly clean other fishes. This species is found singly or, more often, in small groups, usually on the up-current edges of rocky outcrops. At certain times it also forms larger groups which consist mainly of initial phase individuals that facilitate feeding activities. When these fish enter the water column to feed on plankton, the group provides some degree of protection for the individual. *Thalassoma lucasanum* also use groups to overwhelm the defenses of the Panamic Sergeant Major (*Abudefduf troschelii*). Rainbow Wrasse groups will hang above the nesting area of this damsel and occasionally descend into the nesting arena. Once they initiate a raid, the labrid groups are often joined by other damsels, butterflyfishes, angelfishes, and parrotfishes. Foster (1987) reports that there is a positive correlation between *T. lucasanum* group size and the amount of time that an individual is able to feed on eggs before being run off by the defending male *Abudefduf*. The Cortez Rainbow Wrasse will form large groups (100 to 300 individuals) to benefit from this temporary resource (the eggs are usually available during the wet season for 8 days per month). Solitary *T. lucasanum* are unable to get to these nutrient-rich eggs because they are rebuffed by the large pomacentrids. The smallest group observed attempting to raid a nest comprised about 30 individuals.

Warner (1982) conducted an in-depth study on the reproductive behavior of this species. He found that the Cortez Rainbow Wrasse spawns daily (at least over some of its range). Spawning time is related to the tidal cycle (most spawning occurs during the outgoing tide). In Panama it occurs between approximately 10:00 A.M. and 4:00 P.M. About 40 minutes before

Thalassoma lucasanum, Cortez Rainbow Wrasse, terminal phase.

Thalassoma lucasanum, Cortez Rainbow Wrasse, terminal phase variant.

Thalassoma robertsoni, Clipperton's Wrasse, terminal phase.

spawning, initial phase males leave feeding groups and gather at the down-current edge of the reef. These spawning groups can get quite large (as many as 5,000 individuals). When the initial phase females are ready to spawn, they join the initial phase males, spawn, then return to the up-current edge of the reef to continue feeding. The initial phase individuals spawn in groups, typically around 21 individuals, consisting of a single female and multiple males. In some cases, smaller terminal phase males will join these spawning groups. Larger terminal phase males set up temporary spawning territories up-current from the initial phase assemblages. The terminal phase territory measures about 10 m² (107 ft.²) in diameter. Solitary females visit the terminal phase individuals and they pair spawn. Initial phase individuals engage in interference competition (groups of initial phase males try to chase females from terminal phase territories) and "streaking" (initial phase males rush in and attempt to join the pair at the top of the spawning ascent). Streaking occurred during approximately 11% of the pair spawnings. According to Warner, the terminal phase males in the population he studied do not have greater reproductive success than the initial phase males.

Captive Care: Although not as common as its Atlantic congener (i.e., *T. bifasciatum*), this species is smaller and equally colorful. Unfortunately, super-males are prone to color loss if they are not fed a varied diet and kept with conspecific females. The species feeds mostly on zooplankton but will eat small benthic invertebrates (especially if underfed). It has also been known to eat some algae. Initial phase individuals are facultative cleaners. You can keep a male with several initial phase individuals if the aquarium is 135 gallons or larger. The Cortez Rainbow Wrasse is not an overly aggressive species and will usually ignore nonrelated tankmates. They are likely to flip from an open aquarium.

Aquarium Size: 55 gal. **Temperature:** 20° to 28°C (68° to 82°F).

Aquarium Suitability Index: 5.

Remarks: The **Clipperton Wrasse** (*Thalassoma robertsoni*) Allen, 1995 is a similar species that is known only from Clipperton Island. It is found on the rocky and coral reefs at depths of less than 1 to at least 60 m (3.3 to 195 ft.). It attains a maximum length of 12 cm (4.7 in.). Its behavior and aquarium care would be similar to *T. lucasanum*.

Thalassoma lunare (Linnaeus, 1758)

Common Names: Moon Wrasse, Lunar Wrasse, Crescent Wrasse.

Maximum Length: 25 cm (9.8 in).

Distribution: Red Sea and East Africa to the Line Islands and Micronesia, north to southern Japan, and south to the Great

Thalassoma lunare, Moon or Lunar Wrasse, terminal phase: will clean Giant Manta Rays in the wild.

Thalassoma lunare, Moon or Lunar Wrasse, large terminal male: eye-catching, active fish for large aquariums.

also tend to live among or near branching corals or refuge in holes at the bases of large *Acropora* plate corals. This fish feeds heavily on benthic invertebrates, as well as on fish and gastropod eggs and crustaceans, such as crabs, shrimps, stomatopods, amphipods, copepods, hermit crabs, and isopods. Other invertebrates reported in its diet include (listed in order of importance according to Sano et al., 1984): polychaetes, sea urchins, filamentous algae, chitons, barnacles, snails, forams, sea anemones, and sponges. They also feed heavily on fish eggs in certain regions, with individuals and sometimes groups invading damselfish nests. They regularly feed on post-larval fishes that have recently settled out of the plankton. Initial phase individuals will form groups in the water column and feed on zooplankton; these *T. lunare* groups often join heterospecific assemblages. Juveniles of this species will clean small, substrate-bound fishes (e.g., blennies) and fusiliers. Adults will occasionally clean Manta Rays (*Manta birostris*). This species spawns in pairs (a terminal phase fish with a female) or in groups (initial phase individuals). Males set up temporary spawning territories.

Captive Care: This is one of the most popular members of the genus. Young fish are model aquarium residents, but adults can cause behavioral problems, chasing newly introduced fishes and eating (or attempting to eat) more elongated tankmates. For example, I have seen an adult attempt to eat dartfishes (*Ptereleotris* spp.). While initial phase individuals can be kept together, it is prudent to house one per tank to avoid aggression problems. They rarely bury and will jump out of open aquariums. A color-

Barrier Reef, Lord Howe Island, and northern New Zealand.
Biology: The Moon Wrasse is found on inshore and offshore reefs in a variety of reef zones. (It has also been reported from estuarine habitats.) It occurs at depths of less than 1 to at least 20 m (3.3 to 66 ft.). Juveniles tend to prefer shallower water than adults and

Thalassoma lutescens, Sunset Wrasse, terminal male: safe with corals and anemones, but will target a wide array of ornamental reef aquarium invertebrates.

ful terminal phase *T. lunare* makes a stunning addition to the reef tank, but it will eat many ornamental invertebrates, including snails (it will not bother cnidarians).

Aquarium Size: 100 gal. **Temperature:** 23° to 28°C (74° to 82°F).
Aquarium Suitability Index: 4.
Remarks: Juveniles have white bars on an olive-green body, a spot in the middle of the dorsal fin, and one on the caudal peduncle. The white barring is less pronounced in the initial phase fish. Terminal phase males have blue heads and a green body, while the lunate caudal fin is yellow. This species has been reported to hybridize with *Thalassoma rueppellii*.

Thalassoma lutescens (Lay & Bennett, 1839)

Common Names: Sunset Wrasse, Yellow-brown Wrasse.
Maximum Length: 30 cm (11.8 in).
Distribution: Sri Lanka to Ducie Island, north to southern Japan and the Hawaiian Islands, and south to southeastern Australia, Lord Howe Island, the Kermadec Islands, and Rapa Island.

Biology: The Sunset Wrasse is found in various reef zones and habitats including lagoons, back reefs, reef faces, and reef slopes. It is often found in more turbulent reef habitats and will live over open sand, rubble, or rich coral growth. It occurs at depths of 1 to 30 m (3.3 to 98 ft.). This fish feeds heavily on crustaceans (i.e., crabs, shrimps, hermit crabs) and polychaete worms. Other components of the diet include snails, bivalves, sea urchins, brittle stars, fish eggs, sea cucumbers, and algae (probably taken incidentally along with benthic prey). Studies demonstrate that younger fish eat more soft-bodied or smaller prey items which they pluck from the algal mat. As *T. lutescens* grows, it spends more time hunting in crevices and among stony corals for larger, hard-bodied invertebrates (e.g., crustaceans, bivalves, and sea urchins). Larger fish may move over hundreds of meters as they forage, while the young fish will hunt over a much smaller range (5 to 8 m [17 to 26 ft.]). This is an active, solitary species that is

Thalassoma lutescens, Sunset Wrasse, juvenile: great transformations ahead.

Thalassoma lutescens, Sunset Wrasse, initial phase.

Thalassoma lutescens, Sunset Wrasse, terminal male: potential bully.

often seen patrolling just over the substrate. It is especially common around patch reefs, where it hunts among branching corals or on the surrounding sand substrate. In a study conducted on the mating system of this species in Japan, most males were products of sex change, with only 3.6% of individuals in the population being primary males. In the late mornings, terminal phase individuals, who hunt in inshore habitats, move to outer reef areas to set up temporary spawning territories. These "lek-like" spawning territories are formed on conspicuous rocks or coral heads or on the reef face. Females migrate to the spawning area in early afternoon and pair spawn with the terminal phase males. The courtship behavior of terminal phase males includes circling the female, looping, pectoral fluttering, and quivering. The receptive female follows the terminal phase male into the water column and they engage in a rapid spawning ascent. Large terminal phase individuals spawn with more females than smaller terminal phase individuals. The latter often set up territories around the larger males and try to induce females traveling to the large males' territories to spawn with them (they are rarely successful). If something happens to a larger terminal phase male, one of these smaller males attempts to occupy the now-vacant territory. Initial phase males engage in different mating tactics: they will follow the females to the spawning arena and engage in streaking. The time of spawning varies from one location to the next and in at least some areas is dependent on the tidal cycle. In Miyake-jima, Japan, spawning has been observed between 10:30 and 11:30. A.M.

Captive Care: The Sunset Wrasse, especially terminal phase individuals, can make a stunning addition to the larger fish-only aquarium. It can be kept in a reef tank, but is a threat to a wide range of motile invertebrates. Adults can be very aggressive, especially toward smaller tankmates. It is best to keep one individual per tank. *Thalassoma lutescens* will sometimes bury under the sand, but a sand substrate is not essential for keeping this species. Feed it meaty foods, at least twice and preferably three times a day.

Aquarium Size: 135 gal. **Temperature:** 23° to 28°C (74° to 82°F). **Aquarium Suitability Index:** 4.

Remarks: Initial phase individuals are yellow and white, while terminal phase males are blue to blue-green with a pink and green head. For many years the name *T. lutescens* was applied to a similar species, the **Eastern Sunset** or **Green Wrasse** (*Thalassoma grammaticum*) **Gilbert, 1890**, that is found in the Eastern Pacific, from the Central Gulf of California to Panama, including the Galapagos Islands. This wrasse attains a maximum length of 32 cm (12.6 in). Juvenile *T. grammaticum* have a dark stripe along the side of the body and a spot near the base of the caudal fin. The stripe disappears when the fish reaches a length of about 6 cm (2.4 in.). The terminal phase male is spectacular, with a bright green body and a blue-green head adorned with purple lines. *Thalassoma grammaticum* is found on rocky and coral reefs at depths of 3 to 65 m (10 to 215 ft.). It prefers shallow (less than 20 m [65 ft.]), exposed reefs. In the Galapagos Islands, it sometimes joins groups of Cortez Rainbow Wrasse, but *T. grammaticum* rarely feeds on zooplankton. It feeds on benthic prey, in particular polychaetes, mollusks, crustaceans, brittle stars, and fish eggs, and tends to be a solitary species.

Thalassoma noronhanum (Boulenger, 1890)

Common Name: Noronha Wrasse.

Maximum Length: 13.3 cm (5.3 in).

Distribution: Brazil and adjacent oceanic islands.

Biology: This species occurs on rocky and algae covered reefs at depths of less than 1 to at least 60 m (3.3 to 198 ft.). In the deeper parts of its range, it sometimes hides in the lumens of large sponges. It is a diurnal species, being one of the last fish to emerge from the reef in the morning and one of the first to take refuge in the early evening. It feeds mainly on small benthic invertebrates and zooplankton, but juveniles are also parasite-pickers. They have been observed to clean 19 different species, including small groupers, grunts, damsels, parrotfishes, and surgeonfishes, but prefer to clean planktivorous species. The initial phase individuals sometimes perform their cleaning activities in groups (these can number from 10 to 450 individuals). Those *T. noronhanum* in near-shore habitats apparently do not clean. The Coney (*Cephalopholis fulva*) has been observed to feed on these cleaners, especially when they occur singly and have moved away from a defined cleaning station. Like others in the genus, this wrasse is an opportunist and will follow other marine animals that disturb the substrate. For example, young *T. noronhanum* will follow feeding Green Turtles (*Chelonia mydas*), capturing small prey items flushed out by the foraging reptiles. The Noronha Wrasse is often found in large groups comprising mainly initial phase individuals. (A few terminal phase individuals can be found in these groups.) When it is time to spawn, groups of initial phase individuals will assemble near a conspicuous boulder or outcropping. The group will tighten its ranks and then dash into the water column, releasing their gametes at the apex of the ascent (about 2 m [7 ft.] above the bottom). This species will also pair spawn. In these cases, terminal phase individuals will set up small spawning territories, which are visited by females. These males will spawn with multiple females each day. Spawning occurs throughout the year.

Captive Care: The Noronha Wrasse has begun to show up in the

Thalassoma noronhanum, Noronha Wrasse, terminal phase.

aquarium trade in the last decade. It is a durable aquarium fish and its smaller size makes it a better home aquarium choice than some of its congeners. Young fish have been known to clean in the aquarium. See the general Captive Care section for the genus.

Aquarium Size: 55 gal. **Temperature:** 22° to 28°C (72° to 82°F).

Aquarium Suitability Index: 4.

Remarks: The initial phase fish are mainly dark brown and white. Terminal phase males are purple and blue.

Thalassoma purpureum (Forsskål, 1775)

Common Name: Surge Wrasse.

Maximum Length: 46 cm (18.1 in).

Distribution: Red Sea to the southern coast of South Africa, east to the Hawaiian, Marquesas, and Easter Islands, north to southern Japan, and south to Lord Howe, Kermadec, and Rapa Islands.

Biology: The Surge Wrasse, as the name implies, is most often found in turbulent shallow-water habitats (e.g., rocky shorelines, reef flats, and reef crests). It occurs at depths of less than 1 to 10 m (3.3 to 33 ft.). This species preys heavily on decapod crustaceans (crabs and shrimps), stomatopods (mantis shrimps), and small fishes. It also eats sea urchins (including pencil urchins), bivalves, polychaetes, brittle sea stars, and fish eggs. This species is apparently haremic, with a male dominating a loose group of females.

Captive Care: This is a large, very active fish that is not suitable for most home aquariums. That said, if you have an extra-large aquarium (180 gallons or more), this fish can be successfully kept. Because of its large size, *T. purpureum* can eat a wider range of invertebrates and needs plenty of open swimming space, making it a bad choice for most reef aquariums. Try to replicate its

Thalassoma purpureum, Surge Wrasse, terminal male: a spectacular active fish that inhabits the turbulent areas of the reef crest.

Thalassoma purpureum, Surge Wrasse, initial phase.

Thalassoma rueppellii, Klunzinger's Wrasse, terminal phase.

preferred habitat with a surge generating device (wave-maker) and/or plenty of water movement. In a small tank with little water movement, it will nervously swim from one end of the tank to the other. It is a threat to smaller fishes and should not be kept with conspecifics.

Aquarium Size: 180 gal. **Temperature:** 22° to 28°C (72° to 82°F).

Aquarium Suitability Index: 4.

Remarks: Males attain a larger size than females. This species is very similar to the Christmas Wrasse (*Thalassoma trilobatum*). The **Emerald Wrasse** (*Thalassoma virens*), **Gilbert, 1890** is a similar species that occurs around the Revillagigedo Islands.

Thalassoma rueppellii (Klunzinger, 1871)

Common Name: Klunzinger's Wrasse.

Maximum Length: 20 cm (7.9 in).

Distribution: Red Sea.

Biology: This wrasse is a resident of inner barrier reefs, reef flats, outer reef crests, and reef faces. It occurs at depths of less than 1 to at least 25 m (3.3 to 83 ft.). It is an active species with the large males defending a harem of females. Its diet consists of benthic invertebrates and small fishes. It will often follow feeding parrotfishes. It shelters in the reef at night.

Captive Care: Klunzinger's Wrasse is a durable aquarium species. It is best to house one per tank, although it is possible to keep more than one initial phase individual in a large tank. They are active and have a high metabolism; therefore, they will need frequent feedings (preferably three times a day). They also produce prodigious waste, so a good protein skimmer is a valuable piece of equipment for any tank that contains a large adult Klunzinger's Wrasse. Adults can be very aggressive.

Aquarium Size: 75 gal. **Temperature:** 22° to 28°C (72° to 82°F).

Aquarium Suitability Index: 4.

Remarks: Reported to have hybridize with *Thalassoma lunare*. It is a synonym of *Thalassoma klunzingeri*.

Thalassoma quinquevittatum (Lay & Bennett, 1839)

Common Names: Fivestripe Wrasse, Redribbon Wrasse.

Maximum Length: 17 cm (6.7 in).

Distribution: East Africa to the Hawaiian Islands, north to the Ryukyu and Bonin Islands, and south to southeastern Australia and Lord Howe Island.

Biology: The Fivestripe Wrasse is most common in shallow reef zones, such as unprotected fringing reefs, reef flats, surge channels, and reef crests. It occurs to depths of 18 m (59 ft.). It is often found in coral-rich habitats (e.g., among tabular *Acropora* corals), singly or in small groups made up of predominantly females). This species feeds most heavily on crustaceans (e.g., crabs,

Thalassoma quinquevittatum, Fivestripe Wrasse, terminal phase.

including *Trapezia* spp., and shrimps) and small fishes (e.g., cardinalfishes). Minor parts of the diet include snails, sea urchins, tips of *Pocillopora* coral, and filamentous algae (which may be ingested incidentally while hunting prey that lives in the algal mat). It wrests prey from coral crevices and also feeds at the bases of coral heads. This wrasse will hunt with goatfishes (e.g., *Parupeneus heptacanthus*). The two fish will swim together, with the wrasse positioned over the caudal peduncle of the other. It spawns all year round (at least in American Samoa) and does so during the daytime. Spawning occurs in or near reef channels.

Captive Care: This is an active fish that prefers strong turbulence. However, it will thrive in the conditions normally found in the home aquarium. It should be kept in a large tank with plenty of swimming room. Dietary studies indicate an occasional individual may bite the tips off stony corals, although this is not a major food item. It is a threat to a variety of motile invertebrates. For more information on its general husbandry, see the Captive Care suggestions for the genus.

Aquarium Size: 75 gal. **Temperature:** 22° to 28°C (72° to 82°F).

Aquarium Suitability Index: 4.

Remarks: *Thalassoma quinquevittatum* has been reported to hybridize with *T. jansenii* and *T. nigrofasciatum*. It is replaced by *Thalassoma cupido* in southern Japan to Taiwan, **Heiser's Wrasse** (*Thalassoma heiseri*) **Randall & Edwards, 1984** in the Pitcairn Group, and the **Oman Wrasse** (*Thalassoma loxum*) **Randall & Mee, 1994** in the Arabian Sea.

Thalassoma trilobatum, Christmas Wrasse, terminal male: psychedelic colors and an active disposition make this a centerpiece species for large aquariums.

Thalassoma trilobatum (Lacepède, 1801)

Common Name: Christmas Wrasse.

Maximum Length: 30 cm (11.8 in).

Distribution: East Africa to the Pitcairn Group, north to the Ryukyu Islands, and south to Tonga and Rapa Islands.

Biology: This fish is usually seen along exposed rocky shorelines, reef flats, and reef faces at depths of less than 1 to 10 m (3.3 to 33 ft.). It is often found in the surge zone. The Christmas Wrasse feeds during the day on a wide variety of benthic invertebrates. Hobson (1974) lists the following prey (in order of importance): brachyuran crabs, mollusks, octopuses, brittle stars, polychaetes, peanut worms, fish, copepods, and isopods. It does not bury, but hides in reef crevices at night. Initial phase fish will group spawn, while initial phase females and terminal phase fish pair spawn.

Captive Care: The Christmas Wrasse is a large, active wrasse that needs an appropriately large tank with lots of swimming room. It will "enjoy" strong water movements, which are reminiscent of the surge zone where it normally occurs. It can be aggressive toward conspecifics, congeners (especially smaller individuals), and smaller fishes. Like others in the genus, it may harass similar-shaped fishes, especially those introduced after it is an established resident of the tank. Do not confuse this species with the smaller and less pugnacious Ornate Wrasse (*Halichoeres ornatissimus*), which is also called the Christmas Wrasse in the aquarium trade. It will consume ornamental invertebrates like mollusks, crustaceans (smaller shrimps, crabs), and echinoderms (serpent stars, small urchins).

Aquarium Size: 135 gal. **Temperature:** 22° to 28°C (72° to 82°F).

Aquarium Suitability Index: 3.

Remarks: The initial phase of *T. trilobatum* is very similar to the initial phase *T. purpureum* (the latter has a distinct V-shape on the snout). *Thalassoma fuscum* is a synonym.

A sea turtle service station in the Hawaiian Islands: Yellow Tangs and Goldring Bristletooth Surgeonfish scour the algae from the marine reptile's carapace while a Saddleback Wrasse, *Thalassoma duperry*, inspects its plastron (belly shell) for barnacles.

Turtle Service Stations

Fishes are not the only marine organisms that suffer infection by foreign bodies. Sea turtles are often afflicted with external disease and fouling organisms like barnacles and algae. It is difficult for the turtle to rid itself of these problems without the aid of cleaner fishes. Off the coast of the Hawaiian Islands, Saddleback Wrasse (*Thalassoma duperrey*) set up cleaning stations that cater to Green Turtles (*Chelonia mydas*). These wrasses pick parasitic barnacles off the turtles and, in fact, stomach examination has shown that some individuals feed exclusively on these crustaceans. Turtles posture to facilitate the wrasses' cleaning efforts; they stop swimming and extend their flippers and necks while the wrasses pick at their skin. Surgeonfish, like the Yelloweye Bristletooth (*Ctenochaetus strigosus*), the Convict Surgeonfish (*Acanthurus triostegus*), and the Yellow Tang (*Zebrasoma flavescens*), perform a different service: they rasp algae off the turtles' shells and skin.

Other fish species also nip at turtles. For example, a pair of adult French Angelfish (*Pomacanthus paru*) were reported to pick at the flippers of a Hawksbilled Turtle (*Eretmochelys imbricata*) in the Caribbean. The Whitespotted Toby (*Canthigaster jactator*) has been observed picking at turtles in Hawaiian waters, and Moon Wrasses (*Thalassoma lunare*) have been seen removing barnacles from turtles near the Great Barrier Reef. In the Maldives, I have observed Bluestreak Cleaner Wrasses (*Labroides dimidiatus*) picking at the necks and heads of passing turtles and an adult Diana's Hogfish (*Bodianus diana*) picking at the shell of a feeding Hawksbilled Turtle. Whether or not the removal of barnacles benefits the turtle is debatable. Removing crustaceans and algae does reduce drag as the turtle swims, thus decreasing energy expenditure. But the open wounds left where the barnacles are detached may invite bacterial or fungal infection. There is one other potential drawback for the reptiles: A study documented that the Saddleback Wrasse can carry a herpes virus and may transmit the *Fibropapilloma* virus to Green Turtles.

Wetmorella tanakai, Tanaka's Possum Wrasse: extraordinarily good reef aquarium fishes—peaceful and seldom a threat to ornamental invertebrates.

GENUS *WETMORELLA* (POSSUM WRASSES)

In the last few years, several small, secretive wrasses have been showing up in aquarium stores with greater frequency. These are superlative reef wrasses. They particularly enjoy the many reef interstices and caves present in the invertebrate aquarium as well as the natural microfaunal fodder that is typically associated with live substrate. Unlike some of their larger cousins, they are not a threat to ornamental invertebrates. Theses wrasses are the three members of the genus *Wetmorella*.

Biology

Known commonly as the Possum, Pigmy, or Sharpnose Wrasses (I have followed Kuiter [2002] and use the common name, Pos-

sum Wrasse), the three species are the Whitebanded Possum Wrasse (*Wetmorella albofasciata*), the Yellowbanded Possum Wrasse (*W. nigropinnata*), and the Tanaka's Possum Wrasse (*W. tanakai*). Of the three species, I have found the Whitebanded and Yellowbanded to be most common in the aquarium trade. Be sure you do not mistake the juvenile of the Slingjaw Wrasse (*Epibulus insidiator*) for the young *W. albofasciata*—the young slingjaw and this possum wrasse are very similar. The Slingjaw Wrasse gets approximately 35 cm (14 in.) in length and is a voracious predator.

Relatively little is known about the biology of these wrasses. As mentioned above, all three species are quite secretive, spending their days moving within crevices and from hole to hole under overhangs and in caves. These habitats usually have fairly rich sessile invertebrate growth (e.g., sponges, soft corals, and cup corals). One species (*Wetmorella tanakai*) has also been reported from rubble slopes. All three *Wetmorella* spp. tend to occur on reef dropoffs, usually at water depths in excess of 20 m (66 ft.). They are some of the smallest of the wrasses, reaching maximum lengths of 5 to 6.5 cm (2 to 2.6 in.).

These labrids seem to hover, float, and skulk about more than others in the family. Adult *Wetmorella* wrasses are typically found in pairs or in groups. For example, the Yellowbanded Possum Wrasse is usually found in small groups, while the White-banded Possum Wrasse is usually seen in pairs. There is no data available on the food habits of these fishes. Based on what is known about the diets of similar-sized, secretive wrasses, I assume that they eat small crustaceans, polychaetes worms, and possibly foraminiferans (shelled protozoa) and tiny snails (e.g., prosobranch gastropods).

Captive Care

Because of their diminutive size, the possum wrasses can be kept in small to very large tanks. It is possible to keep possum wrasses in a nano-reef tank, but you will need to feed them frequently as there will not be enough natural fodder in a small tank to sustain them. You may not see them frequently if you keep them in a large reef aquarium, especially if it contains loads of live rock.

The major drawback with *Wetmorella* is that they are quite reclusive. They spend most of their time moving among the rockwork. Occasionally you will see them peeking out of a crevice or a cave, or they may swim out to grab a passing morsel. While these wrasses are not likely to parade around the tank, they will become more bold once they have acclimated, if they are not picked on by piscine neighbors.

The possum wrasses are more likely to spend time in the open if kept in relatively quiet surroundings. For example, I had a 90-gallon reef tank in my office that contained two members of the genus. After a fortnight, I started seeing them moving about in the open quite frequently, but usually only when most of the room lights were off and I was working quietly at my desk. The tank had a large overhang and several small caves. I could often see the *Wetmorella* spp. moving along the edge of the overhang roof. If there was movement in the room, they stayed among the catacombs of the reef structure. Unlike some wrasses, the *Wetmorella* spp. do not bury in the sand at night, but simply "hole up" in the reef.

Not only are they shy by nature, they are also potential targets of tank bullies. It is best to avoid keeping them with more pugnacious species that may pick on them or with fishes that will prevent them from getting enough to eat. That said, I have noticed that many fishes simply ignore them. The 90-gallon community tank mentioned above included a fairly pugnacious Redstriped

Pacific Hogfish (*Bodianus* sp.), a Whitebarred Wrasse (*Pseudocheilinus ocellatus*), a Pinkstreaked Wrasse (*Pseudocheilinops ataenia*), and several fairy wrasses (*Cirrhilabrus* spp.). For the most part, the *Wetmorella* spp. did not elicit an aggressive response from their labrid tankmates. This may be due to the odd behavior, small size, and somewhat divergent body shape of the possum wrasses. I did see the *Bodianus* nip at the eyespot on the anal fin of one possum wrasse on several occasions. I am not sure if

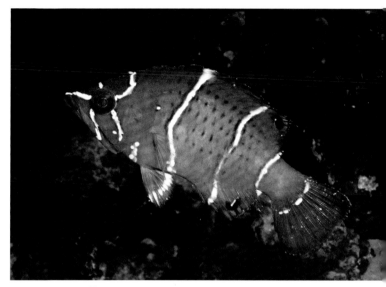

Epibulus insidiator, Slingjaw Wrasse: compare with Possum Wrasse below.

Wetmorella nigropinnata, Yellowbanded Possum Wrasse: members of the genus can be mistaken for the juvenile Slingjaw Wrasse.

Wetmorella albofasciata, Whitebanded Possum Wrasse: cavedweller.

the hogfish mistook the spot for a small prey item or if it was intentionally attacking the possum wrasse. In this fish community, it was obvious that the possum wrasses gave way to larger fishes and were at the bottom of the pecking order. I never saw them behave aggressively toward other fishes in the tank, including a Pinkstreaked Wrasse that was of similar size.

I rarely observed aggression between the two possum wrasses in my 90-gallon tank. However, I have seen larger *Wetmorella* bother smaller conspecifics in smaller tanks. In one case, a large individual continually harassed a smaller congener until the submissive fish spent all of its time cowering in the upper corner of the aquarium. If you plan on keeping more than one individual of the same species, or even congeners in the same tank, make sure the tank is large enough (e.g., 70 gallons or larger) and that it is replete with places for them to hide. Small holes are fine, but they really seem to appreciate caves and ledges. When there are aggression problems, the largest *Wetmorella* in the tank is likely to be the bully, no matter what species it is.

These microcarnivores will feed on tiny worms and crustaceans that associate with live rock. They also readily take aquarium foods, like mysid shrimp, frozen preparations, and flake food. My *Wetmorella* seemed to prefer Cyclop-Eeze, which they picked out of the water column. Even though they will eat introduced fodder, it is still best to house them in a tank with live substrate because they are so reclusive (especially when first added to a tank) and prone to being dominated by tankmates. This will enable the possum wrasses to feed throughout the day on the

minute prey living on the rock. A productive refugium can also help to ensure that they get enough to eat.

Although they are not bullet-proof, I have never had a *Wetmorella* succumb to a parasitic infection. I believe the most likely cause of death would be malnutrition resulting from infrequent feeding and an impoverished micro-invertebrate population in their tank. If their tankmates are too boisterous at feeding time, they may be intimidated and not get enough to eat.

Although I have not had many of these fishes shipped to me, I think possum wrasses are susceptible to shipping stress. I suggest shipping them in a large bag with plenty of water. Once they arrive, they should be placed and acclimated in a quarantine tank as soon as possible. Make sure your quarantine tank has plenty of good hiding places and includes a few bits of live rock for them to pick at.

For those interested in smaller, more secretive fishes, I would highly recommend the possum wrasses. But make sure your tank meets the conditions necessary to successfully house one of these lovely little labrids. These include a relatively passive fish community, lots of appropriate hiding places, and live substrate.

Possum Wrasse Species

Wetmorella albofasciata Schultz & Marshall, 1954
Common Names: Whitebanded Possum Wrasse, White Barred Pygmy Wrasse.
Maximum Length: 6 cm (2.4 in.).
Distribution: East Africa to the Hawaiian and Society Islands, south to the Great Barrier Reef.
Biology: *Wetmorella albofasciata* is found on lagoon patch reefs, reef faces, and slopes at depths of 8 to 42 m (26 to 139 ft.). It is usually found under ledges and in caves and often swims with its belly oriented toward the cave ceiling. This wrasse usually occurs in pairs.
Captive Care: See remarks above for more the general care of members of this genus.
Aquarium Size: 10 gal. **Temperature:** 23 °to 28°C (74° to 82°F).
Aquarium Suitability Index: 3.

Wetmorella nigropinnata (Seale, 1901)
Common Names: Yellowbanded Possum Wrasse, Blackspot Pygmy Wrasse, Sharpnose Wrasse.
Maximum Length: 8 cm (3.1 in.).
Distribution: Red Sea to the Marquesas and Pitcairn Island, north to the Ryukyus, and south to the Great Barrier Reef and New Caledonia.
Biology: This fish is found on lagoon patch reefs and reef faces

Wetmorella nigropinnata, Yellowbanded Possum Wrasse.

Wetmorella tanaka, Tanaka's Possum Wrasse: note eyespots on median fins.

and slopes at depths of 1 to 30 m (3.3 to 98 ft.). It is often found in dropoff caves. Acryptic species, it spends most of its time under ledges or in caves. Adult *W. nigropinnata* sometimes occur in pairs or groups.

Captive Care: The Yellowbanded Possum Wrasse will do best in a passive community tank. It is well suited to the reef tank where it can lurk about in the many hiding places. It may have difficulty competing with more aggressive feeders, so make sure it gets enough to eat.

Aquarium Size: 10 gal. **Temperature:** 23° to 28°C (74° to 82°F).

Aquarium Suitability Index: 3.

Remarks: *Wetmorella nigropinnata* has a yellow band on the head and one at the front of the caudal peduncle. Young individuals (under about 4 cm [0.8 in.] in total length) also have light bands on the body.

Wetmorella tanaka Randall & Kuiter, 2008

Common Names: Pygmy Possum Wrasse, Tanaka's Pygmy Wrasse.

Maximum Length: 5 cm (2 in.).

Distribution: Indonesia (Flores, Sulawesi), Philippines.

Biology: This wrasse has been reported from coastal reefs among coral rubble and algae; probably also in caves. To depths of at least 21m (68 ft.).

Captive Care: The husbandry needs of this fish are similar to those of others in the genus. An individual I kept seemed to be somewhat more aggressive toward congeners than others in the genus.

Wetmorella nigropinnata, Yellowbanded Possum Wrasse: hovering vertically.

(I do not know if this is a species-specific difference or if the individual I had was unusual.)

Aquarium Size: 10 gal. **Temperature:** 23° to 28°C (74° to 82°F).

Aquarium Suitability Index: 3.

Remarks: This species has an oblique white bar behind the eye and two narrow, lightly oblique bars on the middle of the body. It also lacks a black spot on the caudal fin. *Wetmorella tanaka* is thought to be relatively rare.

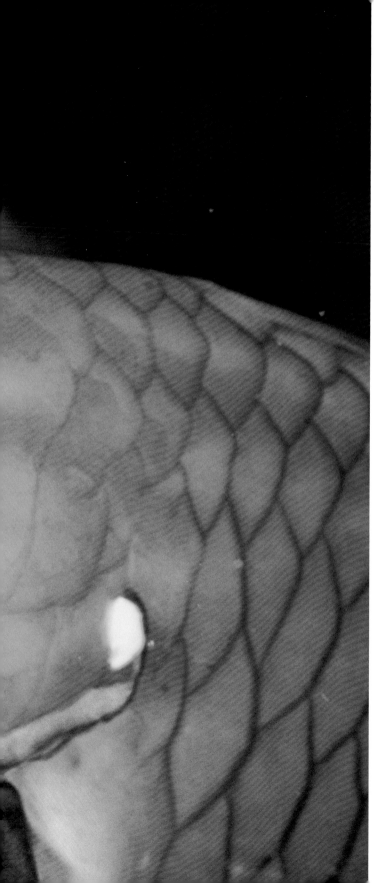

FAMILY SCARIDAE
PARROTFISHES

CORAL REEFS FISHES ARE CHARACTERIZED BY STRIKING COL-ors, and one of the most chromatically blessed of all the piscine groups in this ecosystem are the members of the family Scaridae. This group of fishes, commonly known as parrotfishes, includes some of the most beautiful species in the sea and is also one of the most numerically dominant on coral reefs. Many of the parrotfishes are green or greenish blue with attractive markings on the head and a colorful flash of pigment or a spot on each scale. The common name is not derived from the colorful "plumage" but was given to these fish because of the amazing dentition many scarids possess. In these species, the teeth have fused to form a beak. This family also includes one of the largest fish that roams the reef—the Bumphead Parrotfish (*Bolbometopon muricatum*), which often move through coral communities in small "herds," reaches a length of 1.2 m (47 in.), and can weigh over 46 kg (100 lb.).

While they are wonderful to observe in the wild, the parrotfishes are not typically a good choice for the home aquarium. Most get too large, are too active and have specialized dietary needs—all of these characteristics make them more difficult to maintain in anything but a huge aquarium. For this reason, I have decided to do an overview of the natural history of the family and a relatively brief look at their husbandry requirements. You will note the species account section is by no means exhaustive—I have only included a few species that occasionally show up in the aquarium trade, as well as some types that remain small.

Classification and Biology

The scarids are very closely related to the wrasses (some authors regard them as a subfamily of the family Labridae). There are approximately 90 species in the family in 10 genera, with more than half of the described species belonging to the genus *Scarus*. The earliest parrotfish fossils were found prior to the mid-Miocene (14 to 35 million years ago). These fishes are found in tropical and warm temperate waters around the world. The genera that are found in the Indo-Pacific include the *Cetoscarus* (2 spe-

Sparisoma viride, Stoplight Parrotfish, terminal phase male: favorites of snorkelers and divers worldwide, the parrotfishes sport glorious pigmentation and fascinating behaviors but are mostly unsuited to life in an aquarium.

Bolbometopon muricatum, Bumphead Parrotfish: at 130 cm (51 in.) and 46 kg (101 lb), it is the largest parrotfish species and a favorite target of food fishermen.

cies), *Bolbometopon* (1), *Chlorurus* (17), *Hipposcarus* (2), *Leptoscarus* (1), and *Scarus* (51), while the genera *Cryptotomus* (5), *Nicholsina* (2), and *Sparisoma* (9) are residents of the Atlantic and tropical Eastern Pacific. There are a number of species that have very expansive ranges (e.g., Bluebarred Parrotfish, *Scarus ghobban*). This is due in part to their long pelagic larval stage.

During normal locomotion, parrotfishes keep their bodies rigid and propel themselves with their pectoral fins (this is known as "labriform swimming," named after their relatives the wrasses). When a burst of speed is required, they use their caudal fin and then coast for a distance (this swimming mode results in rapid fatigue so they engage in this type of locomotion only when necessary). At night, most parrotfishes hide in reef crevices and produce a mucous cocoon. (Some labrids [e.g., *Cirrhilabrus* spp.] also produce this "mucus bedding.") It has been suggested that this slime envelope prevents sensory cues from being broadcast to nocturnal predators or that it might prevent parasites from attaching to these fish while their inactive. But others have suggested that the mucus cocoon has no particular function but is simply a byproduct of excessive slime production—this slime is normally washed off the body as the fish moves, but accumulates, forming the cocoon, when the fish is inactive.

There are two distinct groups of parrotfishes—the seagrass group and the coral reef group. The seagrass guild consists of *Cryptotomus*, *Nicholsina*, *Leptoscarus*, *Calotomus*, and *Sparisoma*. The reef group, which contains many more species (about 80% of the total), consists of the other five genera. These two groups are considered by some to be distinct subfamilies—the seagrass group comprises the subfamily Sparisomatinae, while the subfamily Scarinae is made up of the reef-dwelling forms. Some parrotfishes (usually seagrass species) also utilize adjacent mangrove habitats. For example, the young of the reef-dwelling Rainbow Parrotfish (*Scarus guacamaia*) utilize the mangroves as a nursery area.

When it comes to dentition, the seagrass species are more similar to their wrasse relatives. The jaws have discrete teeth in oblique rows and are not cemented or fused together. In the reef group (and some species of *Sparisoma*) the teeth of the jaws consist of vertical and oblique rows with the outer surface being coated with cement to form plates. The tooth plates can have smooth edges (e.g., *Chlorurus*, *Hipposcarus*, and *Scarus*), the outer surface of the tooth plates may be nodular (e.g., *Cetoscarus*), or there may be conical teeth present on the side of the upper or lower dental plate (e.g., *Chlorurus*). In most species the lips do not or only partially cover the tooth plates (e.g., *Chlorurus*, *Scarus*), but there are species where the lip covers most of the dental plates (e.g., *Cetoscarus*).

The parrotfishes also have pharyngeal teeth in the throat that are vital to their normal feeding activities. They have molarlike teeth on three upper pharyngeal bones and on a single lower pharyngeal bone (this is known as the "pharyngeal mill"). Bullock and Monod (1997) looked at the cranial musculature of two scarids and found 50 different muscles associated with the head, including 5 that were unique to this group of fishes. Some of these muscles are important in the functioning of the "pharyngeal mill," which helps masticate substrate and the algae ingested and results in the sediment clouds these fish release when they defecate (more on this later). The parrotfishes also lack a true stomach and instead have a very long intestine.

Food Habits

Scarids are a major constituent of the herbivore fish community on coral reefs. For many years, naturalists thought the primary food of the parrotfishes were stony corals. These fishes are often observed rasping hard reef surfaces. It was thus assumed that these fishes were scraping coral polyps and skeleton from the reef. Now we know that the primary diet of most scarids consists of algae growing on dead reef surfaces (including filamentous and crustose forms) and/or endolithic (boring) algae. Some species also eat detritus that has accumulated in epilithic turf algae. Sponges are a minor constituent in some parrotfish diets. And yes, while they are not as common as once thought, there are a handful of scarids that do feed heavily on stony corals.

Many young parrotfish differ in their dietary preferences to

Scarus taeniopterus, Princess Parrotfish: feeding on algae growing on dead coral surface.

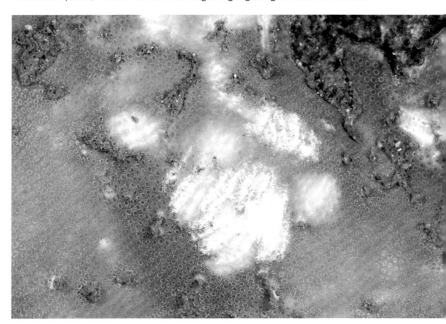

Typical parrotfish bite marks on coral rock, where scarids feed primarily on algae.

adults. The juveniles of herbivorous species tend to be more omnivorous, switching to a plant-dominated diet as they grow. The animal prey that is consumed by juvenile scarids includes foraminiferans and small crustaceans. This is not uncommon in herbivorous fishes, as the young need more protein to augment the growing process. Also, younger scarids also feed more on epilithic algal turfs, but as they grow most feeding is directed at hard substrate and they ingest more endolithic and coralline algae.

Adult parrotfishes can be broken down into three different

groups based on their feeding strategies: the browsers, the scrapers, and the excavators. The browsers use their teeth to procure epilithic algae, macroalgae, and seagrass but do not disturb (i.e., scrap or scar) the substrate when doing so. Scrapers bite at the surface of the substrate, ingesting relatively little inorganic matter, as they ingest epilithic algae. These fishes have complex, relatively moveable jaw articulations and have relatively small jaw muscles.

The excavators are the most specialized of the parrotfishes. These parrotfishes ingest significant amounts of substratum as they feed on both epilithic, endolithic, and crustose algae. They employ robust jaws and powerful jaw muscles to bite off chunks or scrape off bits of the calcium carbonate substrate. As a result of their feeding activity, they also ingest more carbonate sediment than do the scrapers or grazers. For example, the excavating Stoplight Parrotfish (*Sparisoma viride*) ingests more than five times as much sediment per bite than a similar-sized scraper, the Queen Parrotfish (*Scarus vetula*).

Competition for algae on the coral reef is fierce. But with their specialized anatomical characteristics, the excavating scarids are able to utilize microalgae that grows under the surface of stony corals—these are unavailable to other plant-eating fishes. (Most parrotfishes excavate these algae from dead coral substrate, only occasionally nipping at live scleractinians.) If you were to split a hard coral in two, you would see green bands in the skeleton; these are algae growing in the pores of the inert skeleton. It was once thought that these algae weakened the coral's skeleton and hindered its growth, but it seems more likely that a mutualistic relationship exists between the algae and the coral. The coral's metabolism may provide a nitrogen source for the algae, while its hard skeleton serves to protect the algae from most herbivores. The diffusion of organic substances from the algae might benefit the coral by acting as a supplementary nutrient source, and the algae may also raise the pH in the coral's skeleton, reducing calcium carbonate decomposition.

When it comes to taking bites out of the reef, the density of the substrate will impact the morphology of the bite administered by an excavating scarid. If the substrate is of low density, the bite will be larger and deeper and thus there will be more endolithic algae ingested per bite. The density of the substrate also impacts the ability of the parrotfish to assimilate nutrients. The lower the substrate density, the more nutrients the scarid will be able to extract from each bite. As a result, the excavating Stoplight Parrotfish (*Sparisoma viride*) takes more bites (85%) from the lower density Boulder Star Coral (*Montastrea annu-*

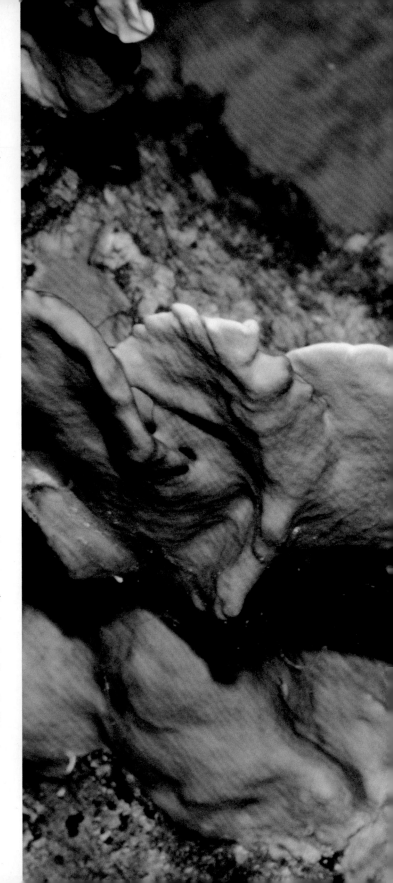

Sparisoma viride, Stoplight Parrotfish, terminal male: taking a bite of fire coral, *Millepora* sp., undeterred by this coral's notorious stinging abilities.

laris) and Boulder Brain Coral (*Colpohyllia natans*) than it does *Acropora* rubble, which has a higher skeletal density and is a more common substrate in some of the habitats this fish lives in. *Acropora* rubble tends to be veneered by more coralline algae, which makes penetrating the calcium carbonate substrate, and getting at the boring algae inside, more difficult. *Acropora* is also more dense and tends to have less epilithic algae than *Montastera* rubble.

Certain parrotfishes are also known to be sponge predators, readily consuming cryptic sponge species that grow under rocks. If a rock that has a veneer of these proliferans on its underside is flipped, parrotfish will join other well-known spongivores (e.g., angelfishes) in feeding on these invertebrates. But not only will scarids prey on these cryptic types, they also feed on larger, more conspicuous species, like barrel sponges (e.g., *Xestospongia muta*). Dunlap and Pawlik (1998) recorded that in 10 hours of observations on 40 different *X. muta*, three different parrotfishes (e.g., *Sparisoma aurofrenatum, Scarus croicensis*, and *S. taeniopterus*) engaged in 45 bites on individuals sponges with normal pigmentation, while they took 527 bites from bleached *X. muta*. In mangrove areas, parrotfishes (e.g., *Scarus guacamaia* and *Sparisoma chrysopterum*) feed heavily on sponges that grow on the prop roots. The sponge, *Geodia gibberosa*, is common in mangrove areas and is common in the stomachs of parrotfish that live in this habitat. This sponge, as well as some of the cryptic forms, does not contain as much of the toxins that are present in sponges living in the open on the coral reef.

There are some parrotfishes that regularly target scleractinians. For example, adult Bicolor Parrotfish (*Cetoscarus bicolor*) will chomp off the tips of live *Acropora* branches, apparently benefiting from the nutrients that both the plant (zooxanthellae) and animal constituents contain. It is not uncommon to see live coral colonies with white scars that result from scarid bites. However, many of these are the work of species that do not regularly eat coral but occasionally bite it. For example, the Stoplight Parrotfish (*Sparisoma viride*) will bite at stony coral colonies (usually *Montastrea annularis*) 4 out of every 100 bites taken at the substrate. In most cases, this parrotfish will spit out the material

Sparisoma viride, Stoplight Parrotfish, initial phase, feeding on a sponge growing on an overturned piece of rock. Its feeding activities have also attracted the attention of a Bluehead Wrasse, *Thalassoma bifasciatum* (right, in photo) and a Smooth Trunkfish, *Lactophrys triqueter* (left, in photo).

Scarus vetula, Queen Parrotfish, terminal phase: display a swooping, gliding swimming style.

initially ingested after biting one of these corals. Some researchers have suggested that they make these marks to communicate with conspecifics (e.g., territorial boundaries).

Feeding Behavior and Antipredation Strategies

All scarids feed during the day, exhibiting little difference in consumption rates between the morning and afternoon. Many scarids make long migrations from slumber sites to feeding grounds. They have a high turn-over rate of the alimentary tract contents: Bruggemann et al. (1996) report a gut turnover rate of about 10 times per day. Scarids begin their days with an empty stomach and feed almost constantly throughout the day (most species spend 80% to 95% of the daylight hours feeding). Bruggemann et al. also found that the Stoplight Parrotfish (*S. viride*) took 12% more bites at the substrate during summer days than during the winter, when day length was shorter.

Some parrotfishes defend defined feeding territories, while others are home ranging. Two territorial Caribbean species (Stoplight Parrotfish and Queen Parrotfish) studied by Bruggemann et al. (1994) utilized a foraging area that is from 250 to 800 m² (299 to 957 ft.²). (A little larger home range than provided by most home aquariums!) In the Redband Parrotfish (*Sparisoma aurofrenatum*) the territory can range in size from 88 to 1,000 m² (105 to 1196 ft.²), depending on a number of different factors (e.g., resource distribution, competitor density).

Feeding territoriality in scarids (as well as other reef fishes) is dependent on the defensibility of a food source. For example, the

Chlorurus gibbus, Steepheaded Parrotfish, initial phase: truly suggestive of avian parrots, this Red Sea and Indian Ocean species is too large for home aquaria.

Stoplight Parrotfish may or may not defend a feeding territory. On dropoffs and reef slopes off the island of Bonaire, this species defends patches of large turf and macroalgae. In the shallows, where algae is less prevalent, the algae that is there exhibits less patchy distribution, and where competing herbivores are more abundant, *S. viride* is nonterritorial. A study by Bruggemann et al. (1994) showed that when defending a territory, this species spends less time foraging (around 70% of its time) and more time defending than nonterritorial conspecifics (these individuals spend over 90% of their time feeding). But the food available to territorial Stoplight Parrots has more protein and energy content than the algae ingested by their nonterritorial counterparts. So, while they may take fewer bites, the nutrient yield is greater per bite taken.

In territorial species, terminal phase males will attack other terminal phase fish with great vigor and may also chase initial phase conspecifics. Bouts of aggression between terminal phase fish, which are typically not common, most often occur due to disputes over territorial boundaries. Territorial parrotfishes might also behave aggressively toward congeners or confamilials, at least in some areas. For example, in the Florida Keys, terminal phase Redband Parrotfish will vigorously chase Redtail Parrotfish (*Sparisoma chrysopterum*) that enter their territories. The Redtail Parrotfish, which is not territorial and spends much of its time in neighboring seagrass beds, will attempt to feed in the territory of *S. aurofrenatum*. Both species feed heavily on the green calcareous algae, *Halimeda opuntia*. But the Redband Parrotfish has been reported to engage in little interspecific aggression in study sites in the Caribbean. Off the island of Bonaire, research has shown that Stoplight Parrotfish that defend a territory from conspecifics will allow five other parrotfishes to enter and feed in their territories, even though they all exhibit significant trophic

Chlorurus gibbus, Steepheaded Parrotfish, terminal phase male: grazing a stony coral reef with attendant *Thalassoma rueppellii*, Klunzinger's Wrasse.

overlap. It may be that it is just to calorically-expensive to try and exclude all of these other food competitors from its territory.

Parrotfish aggression usually involves displaying (erecting the dorsal and spreading the pelvic and caudal fin, tail-standing), chasing, and nipping.

The Redtail Parrotfish does not defend a feeding territory but moves in foraging groups over a home range that greatly exceeds the size of *S. aurofrenatum* territories (in the Florida Keys they were reported to utilize a home range with a mean size of 4372 m² [5229 ft.²]). The males of some nonterritorial species exhibit aggression toward conspecifics or other parrotfishes, but usually it is less intense (e.g., displays, short chases) than seen in the territorial forms. These species may exhibit greater levels of aggression during the spawning period; in fact, some species form temporary spawning territories at this time (see below for more details).

Sympatric parrotfishes may avoid direct competition by feeding on different types of algae or by feeding on the same algae but preferring to ingest this plant material from different microhabitats. For example, the co-occurring Queen and Stoplight Parrotfish demonstrate these foraging differences. *Scarus vetula* prefers to graze off of flat surfaces, while *S. viride* bites at more concave surfaces. The Stoplight Parrotfish also takes smaller bites at the substrate, ingesting macroalgae and leaving crustose and endolithic algae for the Queen Parrotfish to consume. Likewise, five species studied in San Blas Archipelago, Panama, exhibit habitat/trophic partitioning (note: the diets and behavior of these species may vary from one location to the next). The Striped Parrotfish (*Scarus iseri*) scrapes filamentous microalgae from eroded coral pavement on the lower slope of patch reefs, while the Stoplight Parrotfish feeds mostly off of dead coral on the upper slopes of patch reefs, and the Redband Parrotfish has the most diverse diet, feeding on seagrasses and macro and microalgae, which it scraps from dead coral on the lower reef slope. The Redtail Parrotfish feeds in seagrass beds, while the Yellowtail Parrotfish (*Sparisoma rubripinne*) occurs over the largest number of reef zones and habitats and feeds on seagrass, micro and macroalgae. While habitat partitioning has been shown in this study conducted in Panama, this is not the case in other locations.

Some parrotfishes form large foraging groups that swamp the defenses of territorial herbivores (e.g., damsels, surgeonfishes). In this way they can gain access to the otherwise "off limits" algal community that is often farmed by resident territory-holders. Other fish species may join these parrotfish bands. For example, Redtail Parrotfish foraging groups often include Redfin Parrotfish, Blue Tangs (*Acanthurus coeruleus*), Ocean Surgeonfish (*A. bahianus*), and Doctorfish (*A. chirurgus*). These large, roving groups provide a moving blind for some opportunistic predators as well. For example, hamlets (*Hypoplectrus* spp.) will associate with these herbivore bands in order to take advantage of the

Cetoscarus bicolor, Bicolor Parrotfish, taking a bite from an *Acropora* colony. Note Bluestreak Cleaner Wrasse (*Labriodes dimidiatus*) feeding simultaneously.

chaos that they produce when they descend on the territory of a damsel or acanthurid. The feeding activity of parrotfishes can flush hidden prey (e.g., small crustaceans, fishes) that these predators then pounce on. It is not uncommon to see wrasses (e.g., *Bodianus* spp., *Thalassoma* spp.) swimming near large parrotfishes. When the scarid feeds, the wrasse will move near to its head and search for prey that are exposed as a result of the parrotfish's feeding activity.

Young parrotfishes are important prey for a variety of reef piscivores. As a result, many form groups as an antipredation strategy. If there are enough conspecifics in the area, juvenile Striped Parrotfish will form groups, which can number over 100 individuals. If the density of *S. iseri* in a location is low, they will hide in the coral for protection. Groups of juvenile Striped Parrotfish are often joined by young Stoplight Parrotfishes, and young Ocean Surgeonfish (*Acanthurus bahianus*)—this increases the protective value of the group even more. It has been suggested that the similar juvenile color patterns of the many *Chlorurus* and *Scarus* may make heterospecific shoaling a more effective antipredation strategy (because they look alike no one individual is likely to attract the attention of a hungry piscivore). Many young parrotfishes are striped, blotched or spotted, which may help them to blend in among the algae, rubble, and corals in the microhabitats where they feed.

Sexuality and Social Systems
Parrotfishes exhibit a variety of different sexuality patterns. Most parrotfishes are protogynous hermaphrodites (at least some males arise from female sex change), but there is at least one species (*Leptoscarus*) that is gonochoristic (this is where no sex change is involved—a male is a male from hatching to death). The protogynous species can be either monandrous or diandrous. Monandry is the condition in which all males derive from female sex change. All seagrass species studies thus far that exhibit sex change are monandrous (excluding *Calotomus spinidens*). Diandry is where you have both initial phase (or primary) males (males that are born and remain as males) and terminal (or secondary) males (males that result from female sex change). In most diandrous species the primary males are similar in color to the females, which often sport more subdued colors, while the terminal phase is much more colorful. Almost all the reef-dwelling species exhibit this condition. Many of the diandrous species also exhibit strong sexual dimorphism, with males attaining a much larger size than females. Size differences between the sexes tend to be greater in those species that have a longer life span. In the diandrous species, sex change (and associated color transformations) tend to occur at a particular size.

The mating system of the parrotfishes are also somewhat variable and are also related to the habitat utilized. Those genera that are found in seagrass meadows are usually not territorial (with the exception of some of the *Sparisoma* spp.), while the reef-dwelling scarids exhibit a variety of different mating systems. Some species are permanently territorial, while other form temporary territories during the mating period. Some species may exhibit both of these types of territoriality, depending on the population in question.

To demonstrate the differences in the social behavior in disparate populations of a parrotfish species consider the Striped Parrotfish, a smaller, wide-spread species. Buckman and Ogden (1973) described three different "classes" within the Panamanian population of *S. iseri*: the "territorials," the "stationeries," and the "foragers." A "territorial" is a male (usually a terminal phase fish) and a dominate female that defend an area that includes several subordinate females. The females in the territory comprise the males harem, while a size-related dominance hierarchy exists among the females. The harem-master spawns with the females in his territory as well as initial phase foragers (more on these below) that move through his turf. The stationeries are site-attached initial phase males and females and terminal phase males that do not defend an area. Finally, the foragers roam over the reef, often in groups that be composed of as many as 500 individuals. These groups are typically comprised almost entirely of initial phase females, but small foraging groups of terminal phase male *S. iseri* have also been reported from greater depths. The Panamanian members of this species engage in both pair and group spawning. Contrast this will the population of Striped Parrotfish from Puerto Rico. Here, this fish does not form permanent territories, but establishes temporary, lek-like spawning territories, which the females visit. In this area, this parrotfish usually spawn in pairs. In Jamaica, this species was described as typically occurring in foraging assemblages which spawn in groups.

Spawning Behavior and Scarid Larvae
Some species visit traditional spawning sites (e.g., a specific reef pinnacle) every day for many years (e.g., at least 17 years in the Yellowtail Parrotfish). Those that form temporary territories will arrive at the spawning area before the females and engage in a turf battle. The color of the males often intensifies as they chase consexuals in defense of their territory. Initial phase males and females will then arrive at the "lek-like" breeding area and begin to feed. The territorial males will attempt to attract the opposite sex to their spawning area by engaging in "bob-swimming" (this is where they swim up and down with the median fins folded and the caudal fin bent upward). When an initial phase fish

Sparisoma chrysopterum, Redtail Parrotfish: exhibiting typical blotchy nighttime coloration, a nocturnal camouflage adaptation to deter predators' attacks.

enters a male's territory, it will either court with that individual or chase it away. The male may be able to recognize initial phase consexuals and will attempt to exclude these individuals from its breeding area. He courts females by circling around them with the fins spread or by engaging in vigorous bob-swimming. If the female is receptive, he will place his head near her pectoral fin and the two fish will commence in the spawning ascent. In most species, the spawning ascent is quick and can take the pair at least 3 m (10 ft.) above the substrate. The gametes are released at the apex of the rush.

Initial phase males may engage in streaking, where they join the spawning pair as they ascend and release their gametes along with the terminal phase male and female. Initial phase males also engage in group spawning. Groups of initial phase fish will visit a spawning site and begin to mill in the water column in large groups. Small groups break away from the larger gathering an

move about in tight formation, at a greater swimming rate. While it may not be the case in all situations, these small groups often consist of a single female which is trailed by a group of males. The group will dash up into the water column several more meters (yards) and release their gametes. These group spawning ascents often occur in rapid succession.

Spawning occurs year-round in many species, but may peak in the summer months. It typically occurs in the afternoon, but may be impacted by tidal conditions. For example, at Heron Island scarids will spawn at or just after peak high tide to increase the likelihood of gamete dispersal.

The pelagic eggs of the scarids can be spindle-shaped (2.4 to 3.1 mm [.1 in.] long) or spherical (0.6 and 1.1 mm [.02 to .04 in.] in length). Eggs of both shapes include a single yellow or orange oil droplet. The pelagic larval stage of Atlantic scarids ranges from 28 to 53 days. Once they settle, the young parrotfish begin feeding on crustaceans (namely harpacticoid copepods). As they grow, the juveniles begin to ingest more algae.

Bio-erosion

Scarids have a great impact on the structure of reef communities and coral reefs. Because of their size and mobility, and the fact they feed throughout the day, parrotfishes can greatly impact algal communities (both their diversity and biomass). Adult parrotfishes also leave scars on carbonate surfaces as a result of their feeding activities. The boring algae that the parrotfish feed on, along with the scarids feeding activity, can quickly erode portions of a reef. For example, an adult parrotfish that feeds by excavating boring algae may remove more than 12 kg of reef substrate per m²/yr (26 lb. per yd²/yr). Bruggemann et al. (1996) found that *S. vetula* and *S. viride* are likely the main contributors to the bioerosion of fringing reefs around Bonaire. (At one time sea urchins were probably more responsible for bioerosion than scarids, but these echinoderms have been subject to mass die-offs in the Caribbean in 1983.) They have a greater impact on shallow reef zones than on deeper areas because adult scarids tend to be more abundant in the former.

The size of the individual fish and the species feeding behavior will determine how much erosion a scarid will cause. Larger parrotfish will produce more sediment than smaller conspecifics, and excavators will produce more than scrapers, which in turn generate more erosion than browsers. For example, the daily erosion rates by *S. viride* are 3 to 10 times than those of similar size *S. vetula*. In a study conducted on scarids on the reefs of Bonaire, parrotfish-caused erosion rates were highest for dead coral substrates, which harbor endolithic algae (12.3 kg m²/yr on shallow reef), followed by coralline algae-encrusted substrate (4.1 kg m²/yr on shallow reef), followed by live corals (0.4 kg m²/yr on the shallow reef)—the parrotfish studied rarely if ever feed on live coral at this location.

Parrotfishes are a major producer of the sand found around reefs. The bits of limestone ingested when an excavating species

Scarus coeruleus, Blue Parrotfish, juvenile: small specimens are appealing, but have a maximum adult length of 120 cm (47 in.) and hard-to-meet dietary needs.

Emaciated seaweed parrotfish juvenile: although sometimes available to aquarists, small members of the family Scaridae seldom thrive in captivity, usually succumbing to starvation.

feeds is ground up further by the pharyngeal mill. If you shadow a parrotfish around the reef for long enough, you are likely to see it emit a fine cloud of sediment when it defecates. It has been estimated that a large scarid could deposit as much as 2,272 kg (5,000 lb.) of sediment around a reef in a year's time.

Life Span
The scarids are definitely long-lived fishes, with there being a direct correlation between age and size (that is, the larger species live longer). Some species (e.g., Palenose Parrotfish [*Scarus psittacus*]) have a shorter life span of around 5 years, while others (e.g., Blunthead [*Chlorurus sordidus*] and Bridled Parrotfish [*Scarus frenatus*]) may live at least 20 years in the wild. The very large parrotfish species, like the Bumphead Parrotfish (*Bolbometopon muricatum*), may live for decades. Most parrotfish species develop rapidly and reach maturity between 2 and 4 years.

Captive Care
While scarids have been successfully housed in the home aquarium, they are certainly not a good choice for the majority of marine hobbyists. First of all, the majority of species get over 30 cm (12 in.) in length. While that may not seem too big (many angelfish exceed this length), when you consider how active these fishes are, it means a tank of at least 8 ft. in length (that is for the species in the 30 cm [12 in.] range). There are a number of species that exceed 50 cm (20 in.) and will need an immense aquarium. Some scarids do well as juveniles, but most will out-

grow the home aquarium.

These fish only rest at night. During the day most species are on the move most of the time. They will swim, stop and take some bites at the substrate, then they swim again. There are some species found in seagrass beds and macroalgae stands that do spend much of their time resting among plant material. These species tend to do best in the home aquarium; however, they are also the most drably colored members of the family (I can guarantee you they will never take the hobby by storm as a result).

Because they are so active, parrotfishes also have very high basal metabolic needs. Most aquarium keepers will not be able to provide enough food to keep these active species going. A mature aquarium that has abundant algae growth is going to be imperative to keep a scarid healthy. The addition of dried algae sheets will also be important to supplement the diet (algae sheets should be introduced at least once a day). While younger parrotfishes are more likely to acclimate to the confines of captivity, they also have even high metabolic needs than adults. Feed them often (small amounts, numerous times a day). Any prepared foods should include algal materials. Make sure you have adequate filtration and a good protein skimmer to take care of the high nutrient loads. Thresher (1980) states that scarid keepers may get annoyed with the constant fecal clouds regularly excreted by a healthy parrotfish. Make sure you have a good external, mechanical filter to help remove some of this material.

While there are many parrotfishes that do not regularly feed on coral, many of the grazers and especially the excavators may occasionally nip at live corals. As mentioned above, studies in the field documented that *S. viride* takes 95% of its bites from dead coral substrate, but 3.6% of its bites are taken from live corals. In the confines of a reef tank, a parrotfish taking three or four bites at your scleractinians for every 100 bites taken could be disastrous to your stony coral community.

There is one other reason to think twice about purchasing a scarid for your aquarium. The scarids are some of the most important herbivores on all tropical coral reefs. These fish are essential to reduce algae growth in coral reef ecosystems. If they are overcollected, either for food fishes or for the aquarium trade, their absence will impact the health of the coral reef. If there are not enough herbivores on a reef, prolific algae growth will inhabit coral larvae from settling and growing on hard substrates, or if they settle these recruits are sometimes overgrown by algae.

Scarus chameleon, Chameleon Parrotfish: terminal male, resting in a shroud of mucus.

Cocooning Parrotfishes:
A New Sleeping Bag Every Night

Slumbering on the reef at night is a dangerous thing. Marauding morays and roving reef sharks (namely the Whitetip Reef Shark, *Triaenodon obesus*) hunt reef crevices after dark, looking for slumbering fishes. These predators utilize their keen olfactory senses to locate torpid prey.

As the sun sinks on the horizon, solitary and shoaling parrotfish species will disperse over the reef and find holes and crevices in which to slumber. After finding a nocturnal refuge, some of these scarids will exude a slimy sleeping bag that envelopes the fish.

This phenomenon was first noted in the scientific literature in parrotfishes back in 1955. Winn described it as "a thin transparent and gelatinous mucoid substance which starts to fold at the mouth and progresses backwards in folds to surround the body." The mucus is apparently secreted by glandular tissue present in the buccal cavity. It is usually completely formed within 20 to 40 minutes after night falls on the reef, and becomes more viscous and almost "rubbery" as it

"cures" in the surrounding seawater. An aperture remains at the posterior end of the cocoon to allow for circulation of fresh water into the sleeping chamber.

So what is the purpose of this mucus cocoon? It has been suggested that it serves to prevent olfactory stimuli, and possibly other attractants, from reaching the sensory systems of foraging piscivores. If a moray should locate the mucus-clad scarid and begins to probe the covering, the scarid will erupt from its sleeping quarters and rapidly swim off, leaving the mucus behind to distract the hungry eel.

The mucus cocoon may also serve another function. It is thought to have anti-bacterial properties that could protect the fish from infections and possibly even parasites that often attack resting fish at night.

Some wrasses, including fairy, cleaner and flasher wrasses, also produce a mucus cocoon at night, at least some of the time. It has been suggested that these fish tend to be more likely to create this structure when stressed or injured.

Cetoscarus ocellatus, Spotted Parrotfish, terminal phase: Red Sea species similar to the Bicolor Parrotfish, *Cetoscarus bicolor*, that grows to 90 cm (35 in.).

GENUS *CETOSCARUS* (PARROTFISH)

Until recently, only one species was recognized in this genus (i.e., *Cetoscarus bicolor*), but now a second species (*C. ocellatus*) from the Red Sea is considered to be distinct. The members of this genus have nodular edges on the tooth plates, lack conical teeth on these plates, and the lips cover most of the tooth plates. The caudal fin of the adults is emarginate. They feed by excavating algae and also eat stony corals. They also are reported to set up spawning territories, are haremic, and exhibit diandry. The juvenile Spotted Parrotfish is probably the most frequently encountered scarid in the aquarium trade.

Cetoscarus ocellatus (Bloch & Schneider, 1801)
Common Names: Spotted Parrotfish, Bicolor Parrotfish.

Maximum Length: 80 cm (31.5 in.).
Distribution: East Africa east to the Society Islands, Tuamotus, and Micronesia.
Biology: The Spotted Parrotfish is found on clear lagoons and outer reef faces at depths of 1 to 30 m (3.3 to 99 ft.). This species will eat stony corals. It has been observed biting chunks from branching corals (e.g., *Acropora*). Juveniles are solitary and often is shallow water among stands of soft corals (e.g., *Sinularia*, *Xenia*). Some terminal phase of the similar *Cetoscarus bicolor* are reported to be territorial and haremic. (They may hold territories just before and during reproductive bouts [lek-like mating system], ranging over larger areas of the reef during other parts of the day.) This species is sometimes attacked by territory-holding Lined Surgeonfish (*Acanthurus lineatus*). *Cetoscarus* have been observed group spawning, but probably pair spawn as well.
Captive Care: While the juveniles of this species are not uncommon in the aquarium trade, they are not really suitable for most

Cetoscarus ocellatus, Spotted Parrotfish, older juvenile.

Cetoscarus ocellatus, Spotted Parrotfish, initial phase.

Cetoscarus ocellatus, Spotted Parrotfish, juvenile: one of the more commonly seen scarids in the aquarium trade, but with poor survival prospects in captivity.

home aquariums because of their large size and active lifestyle. They need lots of unencumbered swimming room as an adult.

Aquarium Size: 500 gal. **Temperature:** 23° to 28°C (74° to 82°F).

Aquarium Suitability: 4.

Remarks: Juvenile *C. ocellatus* are white with an orange band around the head and on the caudal fin and an ocellus on the dorsal fin. The initial phase fish is grayish brown with spots on the scales, a lighter dorsum and red margins on the dorsal, anal, and caudal fin. The terminal male is spectacular. It is bluegreen overall with pink spots and highlights on the head and scales. *Cetoscarus bicolor* is a distinct species that is limited in distribution to the Red Sea.

GENUS *CHLORURUS* (PARROTFISH)

There are 17 species in this genus, most of which are most often associate with coral reefs. The members of this genus have dental plates that are fused at the center by a median suture. They feed by excavating algal material, tend to set up temporary breeding territories, are haremic, and exhibit diandry.

Chlorurus bleekeri (de Beaufort in Weber & de Beaufort, 1940)

Common Name: Bleeker's Parrotfish.

Maximum Length: 30 cm (11.8 in.) according to Randall (2006). Others report this species reaches 49 cm (19.3 in.).

Distribution: Philippines to the Great Barrier Reef, east to Fiji, Samoa, and Micronesia.

Biology: This fish is found in clear lagoons, coastal fringing reefs, reef channels, and outer reef faces (often on dropoffs) at depths of 3 to 35 m (10 to 116 ft.). Terminal males are solitary animals, while females are sometimes found in groups and may form mixed feeding assemblages with other scarids.

Captive Care: As per other parrotfishes (see the general family discussion). It is not often available to hobbyists.

Aquarium Size: 180 gal. **Temperature:** 23° to 28°C (74° to 82°F).

Chlorurus bleekeri, Bleeker's Parrotfish, terminal phase male: near-fluorescent colors, in this case vivid green scales edged in pink, typify many scarids.

Aquarium Suitability: 4.

Remarks: The juveniles of this species are dark gray with horizontal light stripes and a white caudal peduncle and caudal fin. The initial phase of this species is dark brown with red highlighting on the scale and often with white bars on the body (which can be turned off and on). The terminal phase is green with a pink bar on each scale and a large white to yellowish patch on the cheek that is bordered by blue-green.

Chlorurus sordidus (Forsskål, 1775)

Common Name: Bullethead Parrotfish.

Maximum Length: 40 cm (15.7 in.).

Distribution: Red Sea to the Hawaiian and Line Islands, north to the Ryukus, south to Rowley Shoals, the Great Barrier Reef, and New Caledonia.

Biology: The Bullethead Parrotfish is found in lagoons, reef flats and outer reef faces at depths of 2 to 25 m (7 to 83 ft.). Young *C. sordidus* are often in shallow water in lagoons or reef flats. This species is often found in areas with rich coral growth. This species feeds mainly on filamentous algae, but also occasionally eats sponges; its stomach also contain lots of calcareous powder, detritus, and sand. This is a solitary species. In Aldabra, this species is reported to spawn all year round. Spawning typically occurs during high tide and for a couple hours after the tide begins to fall. This is one of the most common parrotfishes over much of its range.

Captive Care: As per other parrotfishes (see general family discussion). It is not often available to hobbyists.

Aquarium Size: 240 gal. **Temperature:** 23° to 28°C (74° to 82°F).

Aquarium Suitability: 4.

Remarks: Juveniles are light gray to dark brown in color with a light area on the caudal peduncle or dark with light stripes. Initial phase *C. sordidus* is reddish brown with red on the ventral portion of the snout and around the jaws. Terminal phase individuals are green with a pink bar on each scale. Some terminal phase fish have yellow suffused on a portion of the body. Because of its great variability in color and its wide geographical range, there are 16 synonyms of this fish.

GENUS SCARUS (PARROTFISH)

This is the largest genus with at least 51 species. The *Scarus* species are circumtropical in distribution. Like the *Chlorurus*, these parrotfishes have dental plates that are fused at the center by a median suture. They are coral reef associated fishes, most of

Chlorurus sordidus, Bullethead Parrotfish, terminal phase.

Chlorurus sordidus, Bullethead Parrotfish, terminal phase: gold variant.

which tend to be scrapers (that is, they remove algae by scraping the surface of the substrate, but do not remove pieces of the substrate). They form breeding territories, are haremic, and are diandrous.

Scarus dimidiatus, Yellowbarred Parrotfish, terminal phase: at this size, the fish is mostly solitary, while younger scarids usually form social groups.

Scarus dimidiatus, Yellowbarred Parrotfish, initial phase.

Scarus dimidiatus Bleeker, 1859

Common Name: Yellowbarred Parrotfish.

Maximum Length: 30 cm (11.8 in.).

Distribution: Ryuku Islands south to Great Barrier Reef, east to Samoa Islands and Micronesia (excluding the Mariana Islands).

Biology: This lively parrotfish occurs in lagoons and reef faces, often in coral-rich areas. It is found at depths of 1 to at least 25 m (3.3 to 83 ft.). Initial phase *S. dimidiatus* form groups, while terminal phase fish are often solitary.

Captive Care: As per other parrotfishes (see the general family discussion). It is not often available to hobbyists.

Aquarium Size: 180 gal. **Temperature:** 23° to 28°C (74° to 82°F).

Aquarium Suitability: 3.

Remarks: The initial phase fish is yellow with a gray head and three gray bars on the back. The terminal phase is blue-green on the top of the head onto the back, while the rest of the body is green with lavender edges on the scales.

Scarus iseri, Striped Parrotfish, initial phase juvenile in foreground.

Scarus globiceps, Violet-lined Parrotfish, initial phase.

Scarus globiceps Valenciennes in Cuvier & Valenciennes, 1840

Common Name: Violet-lined Parrotfish.

Maximum Length: 27 cm (10.6 in.).

Distribution: East Africa to Line Islands, north to the Ryukus, south to Great Barrier Reef, Lord Howe Island, and New Caledonia.

Biology: The Violet-lined Parrotfish is found in lagoons, on reef flats, and outer reef faces and slopes at depths of less than 2 to at least 30 m (7 to 99 ft.). This species engages in pair and group spawning. Gametes are typically shed on an outgoing tide.

Captive Care: As per other parrotfishes (see the general family discussion). It is not often available to hobbyists.

Aquarium Size: 180 gal. **Temperature:** 23° to 28°C (74° to 82°F).

Aquarium Suitability: 3.

Remarks: The initial phase *S. globiceps* is brownish gray and has three white lines on the ventrum (it is difficult to distinguish from two other scarids—*Scarus psittacus* and *S. rivulatus*). The terminal phase fish is green with pink edges on the scales, and there are two to three pink stripes on the ventrum.

Scarus iseri (Bloch, 1789)

Common Name: Striped Parrotfish.

Maximum Length: 35 cm (14 in.).

Distribution: Bermuda and Florida, Gulf of Mexico, and throughout the Caribbean.

Biology: The Striped Parrotfish is found in lagoons, on reef flats, and reef faces at depths of less than 1 to 25 m (3 to 83 ft.). It is occasionally found in seagrass meadows. This species feeds on algae (including members of the genus *Calothrix*, *Centroceras*,

Scarus globiceps, Violet-lined Parrotfish, terminal phase, Papua New Guinea.

Coelothrix, *Enteromorpha*, *Gelidium*, *Lyngbya*, and *Polysiphonia*). It also ingests lots of inorganic matter (calcium carbonate, sand) and detritus. This species often forages on mixed sand-rubble substrates or on coral pavement. The Striped Parrotfish exhibits several different behavioral "states": stationary (striped and terminal phase individuals that occur singly or in small groups and remain in the same area that could cover several to 50 m² [539 ft.²], but do not defend this area), territorial (usually terminal phase male, with one or more females, that actively defends an area that averages from 10 to 12 m² [108 to 129 ft.²]), and foraging (groups, numbering up to 500 individuals, which consist mainly of initial phase fish and fewer terminal phase individuals, that move about the reef and feed). Foraging groups form in the morning and feed in an area of approximately 1.2 ha. Group

Scarus iseri, Striped Parrotfish, terminal phase: formerly known as *Scarus croicensis*, this is a smaller species sometimes available from Caribbean collectors.

cohesion is tighter on bright, sunlit days, especially if the group foraged in clear water, while individuals were more loosely associated on cloudy days or in more turbid conditions. These scarid groups are often joined by Doctorfish (*Acanthurus chirurgus*), Blue Tang (*A. coeruleus*), Spotted Goatfish (*Pseudupeneus maculatus*), and Barred Hamlet (*Hypoplectrus unicolor*). The latter two species feed on invertebrates and small fishes stirred up by the parrotfish's feeding activities. These mixed-species groups often overwhelm the defense of aggressive damsels (*Stegastes* spp.) and feed in the pomacentrids more productive territory. The young and initial phase individuals often associate with similar-sized Princess Parrotfish (*Scarus taeniopterus*). Individuals move a considerable distance (up to at least several hundred meters [yards]) from feeding area to sleeping sites (which tend to be in deeper water), consistently following the same migration route when moving from the nocturnal resting site to their feeding grounds. Groups of *S. iseri* are attacked by groupers and jacks. This species visits goby (*Gobiosoma*) or Bluehead Wrasse (*Thalassoma bifasciatum*) cleaning stations as it forages or during their daily migrations. Initial phase males often group spawn with females, while terminal phase males pair spawn.

Captive Care: As per other parrotfishes (see the general family discussion). It is not often available to hobbyists.

Aquarium Size: 200 gal. **Temperature:** 23° to 28°C (74° to 82°F).

Aquarium Suitability: 3.

Remarks: The initial phase *S. ineri* are brown above with white stripes along the side and a while ventrum. Terminal phase males are bluish green with an orange band on the side. This species was formerly known as *Scarus croicensis*.

Scarus niger Forsskål, 1775
Common Name: Swarthy Parrotfish.
Maximum Length: 35 cm (13.8 in.).
Distribution: Red Sea and East Africa east to the Society and Tuamotu Islands, north the Ryukus, and south to the Great Barrier Reef, Lord Howe Island, and New Caledonia.
Biology: The Swarthy Parrotfish is found in clear lagoons, reef channels, and outer reef faces and slopes, at depths of 2 to 20 m (7 to 66 ft.). It is usually found in coral-rich habitats. Males are haremic and spawn in pairs.
Captive Care: As per other parrotfishes (see the general family discussion). It is not often available to hobbyists.
Aquarium Size: 200 gal. **Temperature:** 23° to 28°C (74° to 82°F).
Aquarium Suitability: 3.
Remarks: The initial phase *S. niger* has black and white stripes on the body and tail and a red head, dorsal, anal, and pelvic fins. Terminal phase males are dark green to purplish with reddish brown trim on the scales. There is a green patch behind the eye and bands around the mouth. The rear margin of the caudal fin is also yellow and the pectoral fins are magenta to red.

Scarus schlegeli (Bleeker, 1861)
Common Name: Yellowbar Parrotfish.
Maximum Length: 38 cm (15.0 in.).
Distribution: Cocos Keeling Island and Western Australia, east to the Tuamotu and Austral Islands, north to the Ryukus and Bonin Islands, south to Lord Howe and Rapa Islands.
Biology: The Yellowbar Parrotfish is found in lagoons to the outer reef face and slope, at depths of 1 to 50 m (3.3 to 165 ft.). The adults are most abundant around reef pinnacles and outer walls, often in areas with rich stony coral growth. Myers (1999) reports that feed in groups on ruble and mixed rubble-coral slopes. Terminal males may establish temporary spawning territories.
Captive Care: As per other parrotfishes (see the general family discussion). It is not often available to hobbyists.
Aquarium Size: 200 gal. **Temperature:** 23° to 28°C (74° to 82°F).
Aquarium Suitability: 3.
Remarks: Initial phase individuals are reddish brown with lighter bars on the body and a black spot at the base of the pectoral fin. Terminal phase males are green, pink, and purple with a bright yellow bar in the middle of the back (the color of the terminal phase fish varies by region; in the Philippines, it has a yellow and light green bar anterior to the principal yellow bar).

Scarus niger, Swarthy Parrotfish, initial phase, Great Barrier Reef.

Scarus niger, Swarthy Parrotfish, terminal phase.

Scarus schlegeli, Yellowbar Parrotfish, terminal phase.

Scarus spinus (Kner, 1868)
Common Name: Greencap Parrotfish.
Maximum Length: 30 cm (11.8 in.).
Distribution: Northwestern Australia (Scott Reef) east to Fiji, Samoa and Caroline Islands, north to the Ryukus, south to the Great Barrier Reef and Lord Howe Island.

Biology: This smaller parrotfish is often seen on inner barrier reefs and reef faces, at depths of 2 to 25 m (7 to 83 ft.). It tends to occur in habitats with coral-rich habitats. Terminal phase males are solitary.
Captive Care: As per other parrotfishes (see the general family discussion). It is not often available to hobbyists.
Aquarium Size: 180 gal. **Temperature:** 23° to 28°C (74° to 82°F). **Aquarium Suitability:** 4.
Remarks: Initial phase *S. spinus* are dark brown with pale body bars. Terminal phase Greencap Parrotfish are green with pinkish lavender scale trim, the top of the head and snout are green, and there is a large patch of yellow on the cheek and behind the eye.

Scarus taeniopterus Desmarest, 1831
Common Name: Princess Parrotfish.
Maximum Length: 35 cm (13.8 in.).
Distribution: Bermuda, southern Florida, Bahamas, south to Brazil, and throughout the Caribbean.
Biology: The Princess Parrotfish is found at depths of 2 to 25 m (7 to 83 ft.); it is most common at depths of 15 to 50 ft. It is most often found in areas of rich-coral growth, although juveniles sometimes occur in seagrass (*Thalassia*) beds. This species feeds heavily on algae (genera include *Centroceras*, *Enteromorpha*, *Gelidium*, *Microcoleus*, *Polysiphonia*, and *Rhizoclonium*) and occasionally on seagrass and sponges. It also consumes detritus. The terminal phase males are territorial, defending an area 100 to 500 m² (1,076 to 5,380 ft.²). The male's territory will contain a harem of three to five females. The males will vigorously defend their mates and territory. Initial phase fish are often found in foraging groups. DeLoach (1999) observed males will adopt an unusual, and unexplained, tail-stand position, remaining with heads up and tails directed toward the seafloor for up to 5 minutes at a time. During this posturing, the male becomes darker, and the fish turns in circles while opening and closing its mouth. As the sun begins to set, most *S. taeniopterus* migrate (up to several hundred meters [yards]) to sleeping areas. The Princess Parrotfish court and spawn early to midmorning. Terminal phase males dash about their territories, with fins down, for approximately 20 minutes, displaying to potential mates and

Scarus schlegeli, Yellowbar Parrotfish, terminal phase.

Scarus spinus, Greencap Parrotfish, terminal phase.

Scarus taeniopterus, Princess Parrotfish, terminal phase: common species familiar to all divers and snorkelers in South Florida, the Bahamas, and Caribbean.

challenging possible rivals. When the females are ready to spawn, they change color (from striped to solid brown) and rise up in the water column (usually about 1.8 to 2.5 m [6 to 8 ft.]). Males circle around their mate and then the pair dashes several meters (yards) higher into the water column and release their gametes.

Captive Care: As per other parrotfishes (see the general family discussion). This is one of the more common species in the North American aquarium trade. Aquarists who have tried keeping them even in larger home systems (300 gal./1,136 L) report that they seldom live more than a year, eventually going into decline probably owing to malnutrition and confinement.

Aquarium Size: 200 gal. **Temperature:** 23° to 28°C (74° to 82°F). **Aquarium Suitability:** 4.

Scarus taeniopterus, Princess Parrotfish, initial phase.

Scarus taeniopterus, Princess Parrotfish, juvenile.

Sparisoma aurofrenatum, Redband Parrotfish, initial phase.

Sparisoma aurofrenatum, Redband Parrotfish, terminal phase.

GENUS *SPARISOMA* (PARROTFISH)

This genus consists of nine species. When it comes to habitat preferences and feeding behavior, this is the most diverse genus. As a result, they are often considered to be transitional between the more seagrass inhabiting genera (e.g., *Cryptotomus, Leptoscarus*) and the reef-dwellers (e.g., *Chlorurus, Scarus*). The genus *Sparisoma* includes browsers, excavators, and scrapers. This genus is limited in distribution to the Atlantic Ocean (most are limited to the Western Atlantic). It exhibits functional diandry—that is, all males result from sex change; however, some of these males maintain the coloration of initial phase individuals, while most take on the terminal color phase upon engaging in sex change.

Sparisoma aurofrenatum (Valenciennes, 1840)
Common Name: Redband Parrotfish.
Maximum Length: 28 cm (11 in.).
Distribution: Bermuda, Florida (USA), and Bahamas to Central America and Brazil; throughout the Caribbean Sea.
Biology: This species is most often found on outer reef faces or slopes, at depths of 2 to 20 m (7 to 66 ft.). It is primarily a herbivore, ingesting a variety of plant species (including *Centroceras, Coelothrix, Gelidium, Herposiphonia,* and *Polysiphonia*). But this parrotfish also ingests sponges, crabs, brittle stars, and sea urchins on occasion. On rare instances, they may even consume some stony corals and gorgonians. Males are territorial, vigorously attacking and chasing consexuals intruders. All males are derived from female sex change, many of which, but not, become terminal males. This fish does not produce a mucus cocoon nor does it migrate to a slumber site, but rather shelters in its daytime home range or territory. It is preyed upon by groupers, snappers, and jacks. *Sparisoma aurofrenatum* pairs spawns late in the afternoon.
Captive Care: As per other parrotfishes (see the general family discussion). It is not often available to hobbyists.
Aquarium Size: 180 gal. **Temperature:** 23° to 28°C (74° to 82°F).
Aquarium Suitability: 4.
Remarks: Juvenile *S. aurofrenatum* are often coppery orange with a black spot behind the gill cover and they have two white stripes down the body (juveniles can also be brown overall with dark and light mottling). Initial phase fish range from metallic green overall with red fins, to mottled brown with longitudinal stripes. These initial phase fish adopt the dappled pattern to enhance their camouflage. Adults have a white spot at the rear end of the dorsal fin. Terminal phase fish are green dorsally and white ventrally, with a red anal fin and black-tipped caudal lobes.

Chlorurus gibbus, Steepheaded Parrotfish, initial phase.

Chlorurus bowersi, Bower's Parrotfish, terminal phase.

Chlorurus microrhinus, Pacific Steephead Parrotfish, terminal phase.

Scarus ferrugineus, Rusty Parrotfish, terminal phase.

Chlorurus strongylocephalus, Roundhead Parrotfish, initial phase.

Scarus forsteni, Rainbow Parrotfish, initial phase, Bali.

Scarus frenatus, Bridled Parrotfish, initial phase.

Scarus prasiognathos, Greenthroat Parrotfish, terminal phase.

Scarus ghobban, Blue-barred Parrotfish, initial phase.

Scarus psittacus, Palenose Parrotfish, terminal phase.

Scarus ghobban, Blue-barred Parrotfish, initial phase.

Scarus quoyi, Quoy's Parrotfish, terminal phase.

Scarus rivulatus, Surf Parrotfish, terminal phase.

Scarus xanthopleura, Red Parrotfish, initial phase.

Scarus tricolor, Tricolor Parrotfish, initial phase, swimming.

Scarus vetula, Queen Parrotfish, initial phase.

Sparisoma viride, Stoplight Parrotfish, initial phase, swimming.

Sparisoma viride, Stoplight Parrotfish, terminal phase, feeding.

Bibliography

Achterkamp, A. 1987. Bewust kiezen...een serie praktische aquariumtips/6. *Het-Zee Aquarium*, Januari (1987): 4-8.

Allen , G. R. 1999. Descriptions of a new wrasse (Pisces: Labridae: *Cirrhilabrus*) from north-western Australia. *Rev. Fr. Aquariol.* 119–122.

———. 2000. Description of a new wrasse (Pisces: Labridae: *Cirrhilabrus*) from northern Sumatra, Indonesia. *Aqua - J. Ichthyol. Aquat. Biol.* 4:45–50.

Allen, G. R. and M. V. Erdmann. 2006a. *Paracheilinus walton*, a new species of flasher wrasse (Perciformes: Labridae) from Papua, Indonesia with a key to the species of *Paracheilinus*. *Aqua - J. Ichthyol. Aquat. Biol.* 12:11–18.

———. 2006b. *Cirrhilabrus cenderawasih*, a new wrasse (Pisces: Labridae) from Papua, Indonesia. *Aqua - J. Ichthyol. Aquat. Biol.* 11:125–131.

———. 2008. *Paracheilinus nursalim*, a new species of flasher wrasse (Perciformes: Labridae) from the Bird's Head Peninsula of western new Guinea with a key to the species of *Paracheilinus*. *Aqua - J. Ichthyol. Aquat. Biol.* 13:179–188.

Allen, G. R. and J. E. Randall. 1996. Three new species of wrasses (Labridae: *Cirrhilabrus*) from Papua New Guinea and the Solomon Islands. *Revue. Fr. Aquariol.*, 23:101–111.

Allen, G. R., J. E. Randall, and B. A. Carlson. 2003. *Cirrhilabrus marjorie*, a new wrasse (Pisces: Labridae) from Fiji. *Aqua - J. Ichthy. Aquat. Biol.* 7:113–118.

Allen, G. R. and R. H. Kuiter. 1999. Descriptions of two new wrasses of the genus *Cirrhilabrus* (Labridae) from Indonesia. *Aqua - J. Ichthyol. Aquat. Biol.* 4:133–140.

Allen, G. R., R. Steene, P. Humann, and N. DeLoach. 2003. *Reef Fish Identification: Tropical Pacific*. New World Publ./ Odyssey Publ., 457 pp.

Arnal, C., S. Morand, and M. Kulbicki. 1999. Patterns of cleaner wrasse density among three regions of the Pacific. *Mar. Ecol. Prog. Ser.* 177:213–220.

Ayling, T. 1982. *Collins Guide to Sea Fishes of New Zealand*. Collins, Auckland, 343 pp.

Baird, T. A. 1993. A new heterospecific foraging association between the Puddingwife Wrasse, *Halichoeres radiatus*, and the Bar Jack, *Caranx ruber*: evaluation of the foraging consequences. *Env. Biol. Fish.* 38:393–397.

Bansemer, C., A. S. Grutter, and S. Poulin. 2002. Geographic variation in the cheating behaviour of the cleaner fish *Labroides dimidiatus*. *Ethology* 108:353–366.

Bell, L. J. 1983. Aspects of the reproductive biology of the wrasse, *Cirrhilabrus temminckii*, at Miyake-jima, Jap. *Jap. Jour. Ichthyol.* 30:158–167.

Bellwood, D. R. and J. E. Randall. 2000. *Pseudojuloides severnsi*, a new species of wrasse from Indonesia and Sri Lanka (Perciformes: Labridae). *J. South Asian Nat. Hist.* 5:1–5.

Bernadri, G., G. Bucciarelli, D. Costagliola, D. R. Roberstson, and J. B. Heiser. 2004. Evolution of coral reef fish *Thalassoma* spp. (Labridae). 1. Molecular phylogeny and biogeography. *Mar. Biol.* 144:369–375.

Bruckner, A. W. and R. J. Bruckner. 1998a. Destruction of coral by *Sparisoma viride*. *Coral Reefs* 17:350.

———. 1998b. Rapid wasting syndrome or coral predation by Stoplight Parrotfish? *Reef Encounter* 23:18–22.

———. 2000. Parrotfish predation on live coral: "spot biting" and "focused biting." *Coral Reefs* 19:50.

Bruggemann, J. H., A. M. Van Kessel, J. M. Van Roiji, and A. M. Breeman. 1994c. A parrotfish bioerosion model: implications of fish size, feeding mode and habitat use for the destruction of reef substrates, p. 131¬152. In J. H. Bruggemann (ed.). *Parrotfish grazing on coral reefs: a trophic novelty*. Ponsen and Looijen, Holanda.

———. 1996. Bioerosion and sediment ingestion by the Caribbean Parrotfish *Scarus vetula* and *Sparisoma viride*: Implications of fish size, feeding mode and habitat use. *Mar. Ecol. Progr. Ser.* 134:59¬71.

Bruggemann, J. H., M. J. H. Van Oppen, and A. M. Breeman. 1994b. Foraging by the Stoplight Parrotfish *Sparisoma viride* .I. Food selection in different, socially determined habitats, p. 29-52. In J. H. Bruggemann (ed.). *Parrotfish grazing on coral reefs: A trophic novelty.* Ponsen and Looijen, Holanda.

Bruggemann, J. H., M. Kuiper, and A. M. Breeman. 1994a. Comparative analysis of foraging and habitat use by the sympatric Caribbean Parrotfish *Scarus vetula* and *Sparisoma viride* (Scaridae), p. 105–130. In J. H. Bruggemann (ed.). *Parrotfish grazing on coral reefs: a trophic novelty.* Ponsen and Looijen, Holanda.

Bshary, R. 2002. Biting cleaner fish use altruism to deceive image-scoring client reef fish. *Proc. Roy. Soc. London Series B—Biol. Sci.* 269:2087–2093.

Bshary, R. and A. S. Grutter. 2002a. Experimental evidence that partner choice is a driving force in the payoff distribution among cooperators or mutualists: the cleaner fish case. *Ecol. Let.* 5:130–136.

———. 2002b. Asymmetric cheating opportunities and partner control in the cleaner fish mutualism. *Anim. Behav.* 63: 547–555.

———. 2002c. Parasite distribution on client fish determines cleaner foraging patterns. *Mar. Ecol. Prog. Ser.* 235:217–222.

———. 2005. Punishment and partner switching cause cooperative behaviour in a cleaning mutualism. *Biol. Let.* 1:396–399.

Bshray, R. and D. Schaffer, D. 2002. Choosy reef fish select cleaner fish that provide high-quality service. *Anim. Behav.* 63:557–564.

Bshary, R. and M. Würth. 2003. Cleaner fish *Labroides dimidiatus* manipulate client reef fish by providing tactile stimulation. *Proc. Roy. Soc. London Series B—Biol. Sci.,* 268:1495–1501.

Bshary, R. and R. Noe. 2003. Biological markets: the ubiquitous influence of partner choice on the dynamics of cleaner fish ¬ client reef fish interactions. From *Genetic and Cultural Evolution of Cooperation.* P. Hammerstein (ed.). *Dahlem Workshop report.* Cambridge, MA: MIT Press, pp. 167–184.

Bullock, A. E. and T. Monod. 1997. Cephalic myology of two parrotfishes (Teleostei: Scaridae). *Cybium* 21:173–199.

Carlson, B. A., J. E. Randall, and M. D. Dawson. 2008. A New Species of *Epibulus* (Perciformes: Labridae) from the West Pacific. *Copeia* 2008:476–483.

Castriota, L, M. P. Scarabello, M. G. Finoia, M. Sinopoli, and F. Andaloro. 2005. Food and feeding habits of Pearly Razorfish, *Xyrichtys novacula* (Linnaeus, 1758), in the southern Tyrrhenian Sea: variation by sex and size. *Env. Biol. Fish.* 72:123–133.

Chave, E.H. and B.C. Mundy. 1994. Deep-sea benthic fishes of the Hawaiian Archipelago, Cross Seamount and Johnston Atoll. *Pac. Sci.* 48:367–409.

Cheney, K. L and I. M. Cote. 2003. Do ectoparasites determine cleaner fish abundance? Evidence on two spatial scales. *Mar. Ecol. Prog. Ser.* 263:177–188.

Clark, E. 1988. Reproductive behavior and social organization in the sand tilefish, *Malacanthus plumieri. Env. Biol. Fish.* 22:273–286.

———. 1998. Spawning behavior of the Collared Knifefish, *Cymolutes torquatus* (Labridae) in Papua New Guinea. *Env. Biol. Fish.* 53:459–464.

Clavijo, I. E. and P. L. Donaldson. 1994. Spawning behavior in the labrid, *Halichoeres bivittatus,* on artificial and natural substrates in Onslow Bay, North Carolina, with notes on early life history. *Bull. Mar. Sci.* 55:383–387.

Cornish, A. 2003. Diadema sea urchins and the Black-spot Tuskfish. *Porcupine* 98:5–6.

Coyer, J. A. 1995. Use of a rock as an anvil for breaking scallops by the Yellowhead Wrasse, *Halichoeres garnoti* (Labridae). *Bull. Mar. Sci.* 57:548–549.

Darcy, G. H., E. Maisel, and J. C. Ogden. 1974. Cleaning preferences of the gobies *Gobiosoma evelynae* and *G. prochilos* and the juvenile wrasse *Thalassoma bifasciatum. Copeia* 1974:375–379.

Debelius, H. and H. A. Baensch. 1994. *Marine Atlas.* Melle, Germany: Mergus-Verlag Gmbh, 1215 pp.

De Bernado, J. P. 1975. *Anampses cuvieri:* the firefish from Hawaii. *TFH Publications Inc.* 24:60–65.

de Graff, F. 1973. *Marine Aquarium Guide.* Harrison, N.J.: The Pet Library Ltd., 284 pp.

Delbeek, J. C. and J. Sprung. 1994. *The Reef Aquarium. Volume 1.* Coconut Grove, FL: Ricordea Publishing, 544 pp.

DeLoach, N. 1999. *Reef Fish Behavior. Florida, Caribbean, Bahamas.* Jacksonville, FL: New World Pub. Inc., 359 pp.

Donaldson, T. J. 1995. Courtship and spawning of nine species of wrasses (Labridae) from the western Pacific. *Jap. J. Ichthyol.* 42:311–319.

Dunlop, M. and J. R. Pawlik. 1998. Spongivory by parrotfish in Florida mangrove/reef habitats. *Mar. Ecol.*, 19: 325–337

Ebisawa, A., K. Kanashiro, T. Kyan, and F. Motonaga. 1992. Aspects of reproduction and sexuality in the Black-spot Tuskfish, *Choerodon schoenleinii. Jap. J. Ichthyol.* 42:121–130.

Eckert, G. J. 1987. Spawning in *Anampses* (Pisces: Labridae). *Copeia* 1987:789–790.

Feder, H. M. 1966. Cleaning symbiosis in the marine environment. *Symbiosis* 1:327–380.

Feitoza, B. M., T. L. P. Dias, L. A. Rocha, and J. L. Gasparini, 2002. First record of cleaning activity in the Slippery Dick, *Halichoeres bivittatus* (Perciformes: Labridae), off northeastern Brazil. *Aqua - J. Ichthyol. Aquat. Biol.* 5:73–76.

Feitoza, C. V., M. E. de Araújo, and L.B. Correa. 2003. Cleaning activity of *Bodianus rufus* on *Clepticus brasiliensis* (Actinopterygii-Perciformes). *Coral Reefs* 22:10.

Foster S. A. 1985. Wound healing: a possible role of cleaning stations. *Copeia* 1985: 875–880.

———. 1987. Acquisition of a defended resource: a benefit of group foraging for the neotropical wrasse, *Thalassoma lucasanum. Env. Biol. Fish.* 19:215–222.

Francini–Filho, R. B., R. L. Moura, and I. Sazima. 2000. Cleaning by the wrasse *Thalassoma noronhanum*, with two records of predation by its grouper client *Cephalopholis fulva. J. Fish Biol.* 56:802–809.

Frydl, P. and C. W. Stearn. 1978. Rate of bioerosion by parrotfish in Barbados reef environments. *J. Sed. Petrol.* 48:1149–1158.

Garrison, G. 2000. *Peces de la Isla del Coco*. Costa Rica: Instituto Nacional de Biodeversidad, 393 pp.

Gomon, M. F. 2006. A revision of the labrid fish genus *Bodianus* with descriptions of eight new species. *Rec. Austral. Mus. Suppl.* 30 (2006):1–133.

Gorlick, D. L. 1980. Ingestion of host fish surface mucus by the Hawaiian cleaning wrasse, *Labroides phthirophagus* (Labridae), and its effect on host species preference. *Copeia* 4: 863–868.

———. 1984. Preference for ectoparasite-infected host fishes by the Hawaiian cleaning wrasse, *Labroides phthirophagus* (Labridae). *Copeia* 3:758–762.

Gorlick, D. L., P. D. Atkins, and G. S. Losey Jr. 1987. Effect of cleaning by *Labroides dimidiatus* (Labridae) on an ectoparasite population infecting *Pomacentrus vaiuli* (Pomacentridae) at Enewetak Atoll. *Copeia* 1:41–45.

Green, A. L. 1996. Spatial, temporal and ontogenetic patterns of habitat use by coral reef fishes (Family Labridae). *Mar. Ecol. Prog. Ser.* 133:1–11.

Greenfield, D. W. 1975. *Clepticus parrae*, an Additional Sponge-Dwelling Fish. *Copeia* 1975:381–382.

Grove, J. S. and R. J. Lavenberg. 1997. *The Fishes of the Galapagos Islands*. Stanford, CA: Stanford University Press, 863 pp.

Grutter, A. 1994. Spatial and temporal variations of the ectoparasites of seven coral reef fish from Lizard Island and Heron Island, Australia. *Mar. Ecol. Prog. Ser.* 115:21¬30.

———. 1995. The relationship between cleaning rates and ectoparasite loads in coral reef fishes. *Mar. Ecol. Prog. Ser.* 118:51–58.

———. 1996a. Experimental demonstration of no effect by the cleaner wrasse *Labroides dimidiatus* (Cuvier and Valenciennes) on the host fish *Pomacentrus moluccensis* (Bleeker). *J. Exp. Mar. Biol. Ecol.* 196:285–298.

———. 1996b. Parasite removal rates by the cleaner wrasse *Labroides dimidiatus. Mar. Ecol. Prog. Ser.* 130:61–70.

———. 1997. Size-selective predation by the cleaner fish *Labroides dimidiatus. J. Fish. Biol.* 50:1303–1308.

———. 2001. Parasite infection rather than tactile stimulation is the proximate cause of cleaning behaviour in reef fish. *Proc. Roy. Soc. Lond.* 268:1361–1365.

———. 2002. Cleaning behaviour: from the parasite's perspective. *Parasit.* 124(Supplement):S65–S81.

Grutter, A. S. and J. Hendrikz. 1999. Diurnal variation in the abundance of parasitic gnathiid isopod larvae on coral reef fish: it's implications in cleaning interactions. *Coral Reefs* 18:187–191.

Grutter, A. S., and R. Bshary. 2003. Cleaner fish prefer client mucus: support for partner control mechanisms in cleaning interactions. *Proc. Roy. Soc. London B, Biology Letters. Supp.* 2:S242–S244.

———. 2004. Cleaner fish, *Labroides dimidiatus*, diet preferences for different types of mucus and parasitic gnathiid isopods. *Anim. Behav.* 68:583–588.

Grutter, A. S., M. R. Deveney, I. D. Whittington, and R. J. G. Lester. 2002. The effect of the cleaner fish *Labroides dimidiatus* on the capsalid monogenean *Benedenia lolo* parasite of the labrid fish *Hemigymnus melapterus*. *J. Fish Biol.* 61:1098–1108.

Gushima, K. 1981. Study on the ecology of reef fishes in Kuchierabu Island. *J. Fac. Appl. Biol. Sci. Hiroshima Univ.* 20(1):35–63. (Japanese with English summary)

Heiser, J., B. Moura, R. L., and D. R. Robertson. 2000. Two new species of Creole wrasse (Labridae: Clepticus) from opposite sides of the Atlantic. *Aqua - J. Ichthyol. Aquat. Biol.* 4:67–76.

Hiatt, R. W. and D. W. Strasburg. 1960. Ecological relationships of the fish fauna on coral reefs of the Marshall Islands. *Ecol. Monogr.* 30:65–127.

Hobson, E. S. 1968. Predatory behavior of some shore fishes in the Gulf of California. *Fish. & Wildlife Res. Rpt.* 73, 92 pp.

———. 1974. Feeding relationships of the teleosteon fishes on coral reefs in Kona. *Fishery Bull.* 72:915–1031.

Hoffman, S. G. 1983. Sex-related foraging behavior in sequentially hermaphroditic hogfishes (*Bodianus* spp.). *Ecology* 64:798–808.

———. 1985. Effects of size and sex on the social organization of reef-associated hogfishes, *Bodianus* spp. *Env. Biol. Fish.* 14(2/3):185–197.

Hoover, J. 1993. *Hawaii's Fishes*. Honolulu, HI: Mutual Publ., 163 pp.

———. 2000. Expedition to the Marquesas. www.coralrealm.com

Humann, P. and N. DeLoach. 2002. *Reef Fish Identification (Third Edition)*. Jacksonville, FL: New World Publ. Inc., 481 pp.

Itzkowitz, M. 1974. A behavioral reconnaissance of some Jamaican reef fishes. *Zool. J. Linn. Soc.* 55:87–118.

———. 1979. The feeding strategies of a facultative cleanerfish, *Thalassoma bifasciatum* (Pisces: Labridae). *J. Zool. Lond.* 187:403–413.

Jones, C. and A. S. Grutter. 2005. Parasitic isopods (*Gnathia* sp.) reduce haematocrit in captive *Hemigymnus melapterus* (Bloch) (Pisces: Labridae) on the Great Barrier Reef. *J. Fish Biol.* 66:860–864.

Jones, C., A. S. Grutter, and T. H. Cribb. 2004. Cleaner fish become hosts: a novel form of parasite transmission. *Coral Reefs* 23:520–521.

Jones, H., L. Lefebvre, and J. K. Duryea. 2002. Mechanism for co-existence of two cleaner wrasses in Moorea, French Polynesia: *Labroides dimidiatus* and *Labroides bicolor*. http://bio.classes.ucsc.edu/bio162/Publications/Moorea2002.pdf

Kobayashi, K. and K. Suzuki. 1990. Gonadogenesis and sex succession in the protogynous wrasse, *Cirrhilabrus temminckii*, in Suruga Bay, Central Japan. *Jap. Jour. Ichthyol.* 37:256–264.

Kohen, K. Personal communication.

Kuiter, R. H. 1992. *Tropical reef fishes of the Western Pacific: Indonesia and Adjacent waters*. Jakarta: PT Gramedia Pustaka Utama, 314 pp.

———. 1993. *Guide to Sea Fishes of Australia*. Sydney, Australia:

New Holland Publ., 433 pp.

———. 1995. The juvenile Vermicular Cod, *Plectropomus oligacanthus*, a mimic of the Slender Maori Wrasse, *Cheilinus celebicus*. *Rev. fr. Aquariol.* 21:77–78.

———. 2002. *Fairy and Rainbow Wrasses and their relatives*. Chorleywood, England: TMC Publishing, 208 pp.

Kuiter, R. H. and G. R. Allen, 1999. Descriptions of three new wrasses (Teleostoi [sic]: Perciformes: Labridae: *Paracheilinus*) from Indonesia and north-western Australia with evidence of possible hybridization. *Aqua - J. Ichthyol. Aquat. Biol.* 3(3):119–132.

Kuiter, R. H. and H. Debelius. 1994. *Southeast Asia tropical fish guide*. Frankfurt: IKAN-Underwasserarchiv, 321 pp.

Kuiter, R. H. and J. E. Randall, 1981. Three look-alike Indo-Pacific labrid fishes, *Halichoeres margaritaceus*, *H. nebulosus* and *H. miniatus*. *Rev. Fr. Aquariol.* 8:13–18.

———. 1995. Four new Indo-Pacific wrasses (Perciformes: Labridae). *Rev. Fr. Aquariol.* 21:107–118.

Kuiter, R. H. and T. Tonozuka, 2001. *Pictorial guide to Indonesian reef fishes. Part 2. Fusiliers - Dragonets, Caesionidae - Callionymidae*. Australia: Zoonetics, p. 304–622.

Kuwamura, T. 1981. Diurnal periodicity of spawning activity in free-spawning labrid fishes. *Jap. J. Ichthyol.* 28:343–347.

Lieske, E. and R. Myers. 1994. *Collins Pocket Guide. Coral Reef Fishes: Indo-Pacific and Caribbean.* London: Harper Collins Publ., 400 pp.

Lobel, P. S. 1976. Predation on a cleanerfish (Labroides) by a hawkfish (*Cirrhites*). *Copeia* 1976:384-385.

———. 1981. *Bodianus prognathus* (Labridae, Pisces), a new longnose hogfish from the Central Pacific. *Pac. Sci.* 35:45–50.

Losey, G. S. 1972. The ecological importance of cleaning symbiosis. *Copeia* 1972:820–833.

Losey, G. S., G. H. Balazs, and L. A. Privitera. 1994. Cleaning symbiosis between the wrasse, *Thalassoma duperry*, and the Green Turtle, *Chelonia mydas. Copeia* 1994:684–690.

Mahon, J. L. 1994. Advantage of flexible juvenile coloration in two species of *Labroides* (Pisces: Labridae). *Copeia* 1994:520–524.

Marconato, A., V. Tessari, and G. Marin. 1995. The mating system of *Xyrichthys novacula*: sperm economy and fertilization success. *J. Fish Biol.* 47:292–301.

McIlwain J. L. and G. P. Jones. 1997. Prey selection by an obligate/coral-feeding wrasse and its response to small-scale disturbance. *Mar. Ecol. Prog. Ser.* 155:189–198.

Michael, S. W. 1999. *Marine Fishes.* Neptune City, NJ: TFH Publications, 447 pp.

Moe, M. A. 1992. *The Marine Aquarium Handbook: Beginner to Breeder.* Plantation, FL: Green Turtle Publications, 318 pp.

Moyer, J. T. 1987. Quantitative observations of predation during spawning rushes of the labrid fish *Thalassoma cupido* at Miyake-jima, Japan. *Jap. J. Ichthyol.* 34:76–81.

Moyer, J. T. and J. W. Shepard. 1975. Notes on the spawning behavior of the wrasse, *Cirrhilabrus temminckii. Jap. Jour. Ichthyol.* 22:40–42.

Munoz, G. and T. H. Cribb. 2005. Infracommunity structure of parasites of *Hemigymnus melapterus* (Pisces: Labridae) from Lizard Island, Australia: the importance of habitat and parasite body size. *J Parasitol.* 91:38–44.

Myers, R. F. 1999. *Micronesian Reef Fishes: A Comprehensive Guide to the Coral Reef Fishes of Micronesia, 3rd revised and expanded edition.* Barrigada, Guam: Coral Graphics, 330 pp.

Nemtzov, S. C. 1985. Social control of sex change in the Red Sea razorfish *Xyrichtys pentadactylus* (Teleoseti: Labridae). *Env. Biol. Fish.* 14:199–211.

———. 1994. Intraspecific variation in sand-diving and predator avoidance behavior of Green Razorfish, *Xyrichtys splendens* (Pisces Labridae): effect on courtship and mating success. *Env. Biol. Fish.* 41:403–414.

Nemtzov, S. C. and E. Clark. 1994. Intraspecific egg predation by male razorfishes (Labridae) during broadcast spawning: Filial cannibalism of intra-pair parasitism? *Bull. Mar. Sci.* 55:133–141.

Nishi, G. 1989. Locomotor activity rhythm in two wrasses, *Halichoeres tenuispinnis* and *Pteragogus flagellifera*, under various light conditions. *Jap. J. Ichthyol.* 36:350–356.

Ogden, J. C. and N. S. Buckman. 1973. Movements foraging groups, and diurnal migrations of the striped parrotfish *Scarus croicensis* Bloch (Scaridae). *Ecology* 54:589–596.

Ormond, R. F. G. 1980. Aggressive mimicry and other interspecific feeding associations among Red Sea coral reef predators. *Zool. Soc. Lond.* 191:247–262.

Parenti, P. and J. E. Randall. 2000. An annotated checklist of the species of the labroid fish families Labridae and Scaridae. *Ichthyol. Bull. J .L .B. Smith Inst. Ichthyol.* (68):1–97.

Potts, G. W. 1973. The ethology of *Labroides dimidiatus* (Cuv. and Val.) (Labridae, Pisces) on Aldabra. *Anim. Behav.* 21:250–291.

Randall, J. E. 1967. Food habits of reef fishes of the East Indies. *Stud. Trop. Ocean., Univ. of Miami* 5:665–847.

———. 1972. A revision of the labrid fish genus *Anampses. Micronesica* 8(1–2):151–190.

———. 1976. A review of the Hawaiian labrid fishes of the genus *Coris. U O. Japan. Soc. Of Ichthy. Tokyo* 26:1–10.

———. 1978. A revision of the Indo-Pacific labrid genus *Macropharyngodon*, with descriptions of five new species. *Bull. Mar. Sci.* 28:742–770.

———. 1980. Two new Indo-Pacific labrid fishes of the genus *Halichoeres*, with notes on other species of the genus. *Pac. Sci.* 34(4):415-432.

———. 1981. Revision of the labrid fish genus *Labropsis* with descriptions of five new species. *Micronesica* 17:125–155.

———. 1982. A review of the labrid fish genus *Hologymnosus. Rev. fr. Aquariol.* 9:13–20.

————. 1985. *Guide to Hawaiian Reef Fishes*. Newton, PA: Harrowood Books, 79 pp.

————. 1988. Five new wrasses of the genera *Cirrhilabrus* and *Paracheilinus* (Perciformes: Labridae) from the Marshall Islands. *Micronesica* 21:199–226.

————. 1992. A review of the labrid fishes of the genus *Cirrhilabrus* from Japan, Taiwan and the Mariana Islands, with descriptions of two new species. *Micronesica* 25:99–121.

————. 1995. *Coastal Fishes of Oman*. Honolulu, HI: University of Hawaii Press, 439 pp.

————. 1996. *Shore Fishes of Hawaii*. Vida, OR: Natural World Publ., 216 pp.

————. 1999a. Revision of the Indo-Pacific labrid fishes of the genus *Coris*, with descriptions of five new species. *Indo-Pacific Fishes* (29):74 pp.

————. 1999b. Revision of the Indo-Pacific labrid fishes of the genus *Pseudocheilinus*, with descriptions of three new species. *Indo-Pacific Fishes* (28):34 pp.

————. 1999c. *Paracheilinus attenuatus*, a new labrid fish from the western Indian Ocean, with a redescription of *P. piscilineatus*. *J. South Asian Nat. Hist.* 4:29–38.

————. 2003. *Thalassoma nigrofasciatum*, a new species of labrid fish from the southwest Pacific. *Aqua - J. Ichthyol. Aquat. Biol.* 7:1–8.

————. 2005. *Reef and shore fishes of the South Pacific. New Caledonia to Tahiti and the Pitcairn Islands*. Honolulu, HI: University of Hawaii Press, 720 p.

Randall, E. R. and G. R. Allen. 2003. *Paracheilinus rubricaudalis*, a new species of flasher wrasse (Perciformes: Labridae) from Fiji. *Aqua - J. Ichthyol. Aquat. Biol.* 7:103–112.

————. 2004a. *Gomphosus varius* x *Thalassoma lunare*, a hybrid labrid fish from Australia. *Aqua - J. Ichthyol. Aquat. Biol.* 8:135–139.

————. 2004b. *Xyrichtys koteamea*, a new razorfish (Perciformes: Labridae) from Easter Island. *Raffles Bull. Zool.* 52:251–255.

Randall, J. E. and A. Kunzmann. 1998. *Cirrhilabrus adornatus*, a new species of labrid fish from Sumatra. *Rev. Fr. Aquariol.* 25:31–39.

Randall, J. E. and A. Miroz. 2001. *Thalassoma lunare* x *Thalassoma rueppellii*, a hybrid labrid fish from the Red Sea. *Aqua - J. Ichthyol. Aquat. Biol.* 4(4):131–134.

Randall, J. E. and A. S. Andrew. 2000. *Xyrichtys trivittatus*, a new species of razorfish (Perciformes: Labridae) from Hong Kong and Taiwan. *Zool. Stud.* 39:18–22.

Randall, J. E. and B. H. Nagareda. 2002. *Cirrhilabrus bathyphilus*, a new deep-dwelling labrid fish from the Coral Sea. *Cybium* 26(2):123–127.

Randall J. E. and F. Walsh, 2008. A pictorial review of the Indo-Pacific labrid fish genus *Pseudocoris*, with description of a new species from the Coral Sea. *Aqua - J. Ichthy. Aquat. Biol.* 14:45–58.

Randall, J. E. and H. A. Randall, 1981. A revision of the labrid fish genus *Pseudojuloides*, with descriptions of five new species. *Pac. Sci.* 35(1):51–74.

Randall, J. E. and G. Helfman. 1972. *Diprocanthus xanthurus*, a cleaner wrasse from the Palau Islands, with notes on other cleaning fishes. *Trop. Fish Hobby.* 20:87–95.

Randall, J. E and J. L. Earle. 2002. Review of Hawaiian Razorfishes of the Genus *Iniistius* (Perciformes: Labridae). *Pac. Sci.* 56:389–402.

Randall, J. E. and K. E Carpenter. 1980. Three new labrid fishes of the genus *Cirrhilabrus* from the Philippines. *Rev. Fr. Aquariol.* 17–26.

Randall, J. E. and P. Fourmanoir. 1998. *Terelabrus rubrovittatus*, a new genus and species of labrid fish from New Caledonia and New Guinea. *Bull. Mar. Sci.* 62:247–252.

Randall, J. E. and P. S. Lobel. 2003. *Xyrichtys halsteadi*, a new labrid fish from the central and western Pacific. *Bull. Mar. Sci.* 72:971–977.

Randall, J. E. and R. H. Kuiter. 1982. Three new labrid fishes of the genus *Coris* from the Western Pacific. *Pac. Sci.* 159–173.

————. 2007. *Wetmorella tanakai*, a new wrasse (Perciformes: Labridae) from Indonesia and the Philippines. *Aqua - J. Ichthyol. Aquat. Biol.* 13(1):1–6.

Randall, J. E. and R. Lubbock. 1981. Labrid fishes of the genus *Paracheilinus*, with descriptions of three new species from the Philippines. *Jap. J. Ichthyol.* 28:19–30.

Randall, J. E. and H. Masuda. 1991. Two new labrid fishes of the genus *Cirrhilabrus* from Japan. *Rev. Fr. Aquariol.* 53–60.

Wrasse References

GENERAL
Allen et al. (2003), Debelius & Baensch (1994), Delbeek & Sprung (1994), de Graff (1973), Garrison (2000), Green (1996), Grove & Lavenberg (1997), Gushima (1981), Hoover (1993), Humann & DeLoach (2002), K. Kohen (personal communication), Kuiter (1992, 1993), Kuiter & Debelius (1994), Kuiter & Tonozuka (2001), Lieske & Myers (1994), Myers (1999), Parenti & Randall (1995, 1996, 2000, 2005), Randall et al. (1990), Sprung & Delbeek (1997), Thomson et al. (1979), Thresher (1980, 1984) , Victor (1986), Warner and Roberston (1978).

ANAMPSES
De Bernado (1975), Eckert (1987), Hobson (1974), Randall (1972, 2005), Sano et. al. (1984).

BODIANUS
Debelius & Baensch (1994), DeLoach (1999), Gomon (2006), Hoffman (1983, 1985), Hobson (1968, 1974), Kuiter (1993), Kuiter & Debelius (1994), Lobel (1981), Myers (1999), Randall (1967), Randall (2005), Randall & Fourmanoir (1998), Randall et. al. (1990), Rocha (2000), Sazima & Gasparini (1999); Thomson et. al. (1979).

CHEILINUS AND OXYCHEILINUS
Donaldson (1995), Hiatt & Stratsburg (1960), Hobson (1974), Kuiter (1995, 2000), Kuiter and Debelius (1994), McClanahan (1995), Myers (1989), Ormond (1980), Randall (1978), Randall (1985, 2005), Randall et al. (1978); Robertson (1982), Sano et al. (1984).

CHEILIO
Sano et al. (1984)

CHOERODON

Cornish (2003); Donaldson (1995); Ebisawa et al. (1992); Kuiter & Tonozuka (2001); Randall (2005); Sano et al. (1984).

CIRRHILABRUS
Allen (1999, 2000), Allen & Erdmann (2006b, 2008), Allen & Kuiter (1999), Allen & Randall (1996), Allen et al. (2003), Bell, (1983), Donaldson (1995), Kobayashi & Suzuki (1990), K. Kohen (personal communication), Kuiter (1992, 2002), Myers (1999), Moyer & Shepard (1975), Randall (1988, 1992, 2005), Randall & Carpenter (1980), Randall & Kunzmann (1998), Randall & Masuda (1991), Randall & Nagareda (2002), Randall & Pyle (1989); Randall & Pyle (2001), Randall et al. (1989), O. Suarez (personal communication about *Cirrhilabrus* husbandry); Senou & Hirata (2000), Springer & Randall (1974), Tanaka (2007), Tanaka (personal communication).

CLEPTICUS
DeLoach (1999), Feitoza et al. (2003), Greenfield (1975), Heiser et al. (2000), Randall (1967), Sazima et al. (2006), Thresher (1980).

CORIS
Ayling (1982), Hiatt and Stratsburg (1960), Hobson (1974), Hoover (2000), Kuiter (2002) Randall (1976, 1985, 1999a), Randall & Kuiter (1982), Sano et al. (1984), Shibuno et al. (1994).

EPIBULUS
Carlson et al. (2008), Donaldson (1995), Hiatt & Stratsburg (1960), Ormond (1980), Myers (1999), Robertson & Foster (1982), Sano et al. (1984).

GOMPHOSUS
Bernardi et al. (2004), Hiatt and Stratsburg (1960), Hobson (1974), Randall (1985, 2005), Randall & Allen (2004a).

HALICHOERES
Baird (1993), Clavijo & Donaldson (1994), Coyer (1995), DeLoach (1999), Feitoza et al. (2002), Hiatt & Stratsburg (1960), Kuiter & Randall (1981, 1995), Randall (1967, 1980, 2005), Sano et al. (1984), Shibuno et al. (1993), Shibuno et al. (1993), Sazima et al. 1998), Thresher (1979, 1980).

HEMIGYMNUS
DeGraf (1968), Grutter & Hendrikz (1999), Grutter et al. (2002), Haywood (1982), Hiatt & Stratsburg (1960), Jones et al. (2005), Madsen (1975), Michael (2001), Munoz & Cribb (2005), Sano et al. (1984)

HOLOGYMNOSUS
Allen et al. (2003), Myers (1999), Randall (1982, 2005), Randall & Yamakawa (1988).

TRIBE LABRICHTHYINI
McIlwain & Jones (1997), Randall (1981), Randall & Helfman (1972), Randall & Springer (1973), Sano et al. (1984)

LABROIDES
Arnal et al. (1999), Bansemer et al. (2002), Bshary (2002), Bshary & Grutter (2002a, 2002b, 2002c, 2005), Bshary & Noe (2003), Bshray & Schaffer (2002), Bshray & Würth (2003), Cheney & Cote (2003), Feder (1966), Foster (1985), Gorlick (1980, 1984), Gorlick et al. (1987), Grutter (1994, 1995, 1996a, 1996b, 1997, 2001, 2002), Grutter & Bshary (2003, 2004), Grutter & Hendrikz (1999), Grutter et al. (2002), Jones & Grutter (2005), Jones et al. (2002), Jones et al. (2004), Lobel (1972), Losey (1972), Mahon (1994), Potts (1973), Robertson (1972), Sano et al. (1984), Tebbich et al. (2002), Youngbluth (1968).

MACROPHARYNGODON
Delbeek (1989), Hiatt & Stratsburg (1960), Hobson (1974), Myers (1999), Randall (1978, 1985, 1995), Sano et al. (1984), Thresher (1984).

TRIBE NOVACULINI
Castriota et al. (2005), Clark (1988, 1998), DeLoach (1999), Hiatt & Stratsburg (1960), Marconato et al. (1995), Myers (1999), Nemtzov (1985, 1994), Nemtzov & Clark (1994), Randall (1967), Randall & Allen (2004), Randall & Andrew (2000), Randall & Earle (2002), Randall & Lobel (2003), Randall et al. (2002), Tanayanagi et al. (2003), Victor (1987), Victor et al. (2001),.

PARACHEILINUS
Allen (2008), Allen & Erdmann (2006a), Debelius (1987, 1993), Kuiter (1992, 2002), Kuiter & Allen (1999), Myers (1999), Randall (1988, 1999c), Randall & Allen (2003), Randall & Harmelin-Vivien (1977), Randall & Lubbock (1981), Roux-Esteve & Fourmanoir (1955), Tanaka (2007), Tanaka (personal communication).

PSEUDOCHEILINUS AND PSEUDOCHEILINOPS
Delbeek & Sprung (1994), Hiatt & Stratsburg (1960), Hobson (1974), Kuiter (2002), Myers (1999), Randall (1999b), Randall (2005), Sano et al. (1984).

PSEUDOCORIS
Kuiter (2002), Myers (1999), Randall & Walsh (2008)

PSEUDODAX
Myers (1999), Randall (2005)

PSEUDOJULOIDES
Bellwood & Randall (2000), Myers (1999), Randall & Randall (1981)

PTERAGOGUS
Donaldson (1995), Kuiter (2002), Myers (1999), Nishi (1989), Randall (2005)

STETHOJULIS
Hiatt & Stratsburg (1960), Kuiter (2002), Myers (1999), Randall (2005), Sano et al. (1984).

THALASSOMA
Bernadri et al. (2004), Darcy et al. (1974), DeLoach (1999), Donaldson (1995), Feddern (1965), Foster (1987), Francini-Filho et al. (2000), Hiatt & Stratsburg (1960), Hobson (1974), Itzkowitz (1974, 1979), Kuwamura (1981), Losey et al. (1994), Moyer (1987), Myers (1999), Shibuno et al. (1994), Randall (1967, 1985, 2003, 2005), Randall & Allen (2004a), Randall & Miroz (2001), Reinboth (1973), Robertson & Choat (1974), Robertson & Hoffman (1977), Rocha et al. (2001), Ross (1981), Sano et al. (1984), Snyder (1999), Walsh & Randall (2004), Warner (1982), Warner & Hoffman (1980), Warner & Robertson (1978).

WETMORELLA
Kuiter (2002), Myers (1999), Randall & Kuiter (2007).

SCARIDAE
Bruckner & Bruckner (1998a, 1998b, 2000), Bruggemann et al. (1994a), Bruggemann et al. (1994b), Bruggemann et al. (1994c), Bruggemann et al. (1996), Frydl & Stearn (1978), Ogden & Buckman (1973), Robertson & Hoffman (1977), Randall (1967, 1995), Robertson & Choat 91974), Sano et al. (1984).

Glossary

aggregation: a social group consisting of members of the same or different species that are not attracted to each other but to some other mutually attractive stimulus (e.g., food, shelter).

aggressive mimicry: a type of imitation wherein a predatory species resembles a nonpredatory form to gain a hunting advantage over its prey.

alpheid shrimp: a member of the family Alpheidae, with greatly enlarged pincers that are used to produce a snapping sound, hence their common name, snapping shrimp. Many engage in commensal relationships.

amphipod: a group of small crustaceans belonging to the order Amphipoda, including the genus *Gammarus*, used as a common aquarium fish food.

band: a thick, pigmented vertical marking that encircles the circumference of the fish's body.

bar: a thick, pigmented vertical marking that does not encircle the body.

Batesian mimicry: a type of imitation wherein an innocuous species resembles a noxious species to gain protection from predators.

benthic: pertaining to organisms that live on or just over the seafloor.

bivalve: a member of the mollusk class Bivalvia, having a dorsally hinged, calcareous shell comprised of two valves; includes the oysters, clams, and mussels.

blotch: a patch or spot of pigment with irregular edges.

branchial: related to the gills.

buccal: related to the mouth.

canine teeth: pointed, conical teeth located at the front or edge of the jaws.

carapace: a rigid shell or exoskeleton that encases the body.

caudal: referring to the tail.

caudal peduncle: the narrow portion of the body of a fish located just before the caudal fin.

cephalopods: members of the class Cephalopoda, including the squids, octopuses, cuttlefishes, and nautiloids.

chitons: members of the mollusk class Polyplacophora, which adhere tightly to the substrate and have flattened, ovoid bodies and shells comprised of eight overlapping plates.

commensalism: a relationship between members of different species in which one member benefits while the other is unaffected (compare to **parasitism**).

congeners: of the same genus.

consexual: of the same sex.

conspecific: of the same species.

copepods: very small crustaceans that belong to the extremely large class Copepoda. Some are ectoparasites of fishes, while others are planktonic.

cumaceans: small, mysidlike crustaceans that belong to the order Cumacea, many of which burrow in bottom sediments.

diurnal: active during the day (compare to **nocturnal**).

echinoderms: members of the phylum Echinodermata, which encompasses radially symmetrical invertebrates, some of which have sharp spines; includes sea stars, serpent stars, sea cucumbers, and sea urchins.

echinoids: members of the class Echinoidea, including sea urchins, heart urchins, and sand urchins.

emarginate: having a notched margin, but not so deeply as to be forked.

endemic: restricted in distribution to a specific area or region.

facultative: capable of living in varying conditions; e.g., facultative cleaners do not rely strictly on parasites for food (compare to **obligatory**).

filamentous: long and thin.

gastropod: members of the mollusk class Gastropoda, including the limpets, top shells, snails, cowries, moon shells, whelks, bubble shells, sea hares, nudibranchs, and sea slugs.

gonochorism: the condition wherein the sexes are separate, predetermined at birth or hatching, and do not change throughout the individual's lifetime.

gorgonian: a soft coral of the order Gorgonacea, having a horny, organic skeleton; includes sea whips and sea fans.

grass shrimp: a species of small, transparent shrimp often sold for freshwater aquariums and as food for other fishes; also called ghost shrimp.

group spawning: reproductive behavior in which a group of individuals simultaneously release their gametes; these groups usually consist of one female and several males.

infaunal: pertaining to organisms that live in the sediment of the seafloor.

initial phase: in a sequentially hermaphroditic species, the color exhibited before the sex change (compare to **terminal phase**).

isopods: crustaceans belonging to the order Isopoda (including the gnathid isopods, some of which are ectoparasites on coral reef fishes); most are quite small (less than 1.5 cm [0.6 in.]).

lanceolate: shaped like a spear head, being tapered at each end.

line: a narrow, straight-sided chromatic marking (thinner than a stripe or bar), that radiates from the eyes, runs longitudinally or vertically on the body or tail, or appears as a chevron shape on the fish's side.

lunate: shaped like a crescent.

marginal: just along the fin edge.

molariform: describing molarlike or pebblelike teeth.

mutualism: a relationship between members of different species in which both members benefit (compare to **commensalism** and **parasitism**).

mysid shrimp: a member of the crustacean order Mysidacea; often called possum shrimps because of the pouch on the ventrum. Most reef-dwelling mysid species are small and swarm near the ocean floor.

nape: area behind the back of the head, extending from the back of the skull to the dorsal fin origin.

nocturnal: active at night (compare to **diurnal**).

obligatory: obligate or required; e.g., an obligatory cleaner fish relies entirely on this feeding mode to obtain nutrients (compare to **facultative**).

ocellus (*pl.*, **ocelli**)**:** a spot with a lighter outer margin (also known as an eyespot).

ontogenetic: referring to a change that occurs with age.

operculum: a bony gill cover.

ostracod: a member of the crustacean subclass Ostracoda, with a body encased in a bivalve shell; resembles a minute clam.

papillae: small, fleshy protuberances.

parasitism: a relationship between members of different species in which one benefits while the other is harmed (compare to **commensalism**).

pelagic: pertaining to the open sea and to the organisms that inhabit it.

pharyngeal teeth: teeth located on the bones in the pharynx, which is located between the mouth and the esophagus.

piscivorous: fish-eating.

poisonous: an organism that contains poison (a substance causing illness or death) in its tissues that can be harmful if the organism is ingested (compare to **venomous**).

polychaetes: worms in the class Polychaeta, many of which are marine and infaunal; are part of the phylum Annelida (the segmented worms).

primary male or female: a male or female whose sex is genetically determined at birth or hatching and which is not the result of a sex change.

protandry: sequential hermaphroditism in which individuals transform from male to female (compare to **protogyny**).

protogyny: sequential hermaphroditism in which individuals transform from female to male (compare to **protandry**).

protractile: capable of being protruded or thrust out.

proximal: nearest to the point of origin (compare to **distal**).

rostrum: an elongate or extended snout.

school: a social group consisting of individuals of the same species, with individuals being similar in size, equal in their social status, and moving in a highly coordinated fashion (compare to **shoal**).

secondary male or female: a male or female that is the result of a sex change; a secondary male would be derived from a protogynous female, while a secondary female would be derived from a protandrous male (compare to **primary male or female**).

sequential hermaphroditism: a form of hermaphroditism in which individuals can change sex, but the sexes are separate (compare to **simultaneous hermaphroditism**).

sessile: attached to the substrate; stationary.

sexual dichromatism: color differences between the sexes.

sexual dimorphism: structural or size differences between the sexes.

shoal: a social group consisting of individuals of the same species that are not always similar in size, not equal in social status, and that usually do not move in a highly coordinated fashion (compare to **school**).

simultaneous hermaphroditism: a form of hermaphroditism in which individuals have functional testes and ovaries at the same time and can release either sperm or eggs during spawning (compare to **sequential hermaphroditism**).

snout: the portion of the head that is just in front of the eyeball.

spot: a circular area of pigment.

stripes: a straight area of pigment that can vary in width (wider than a line), and can be oriented vertically, horizontally, or obliquely on the head, body, or fins.

supraorbital: above the eye.

sympatric: having a similar geographical and/or bathymetric distribution.

terminal phase: in sequentially hermaphroditic species, the color pattern developed after sex change (compare to **initial phase**).

truncate: having the end squared off.

vermiculations: fine, wavy lines.

zooplankton: free-floating, typically minute animals (e.g., protozoans, copepods, crustacean larvae, fish larvae).

zooxanthellae: dinoflagellate photosynthetic algae living within the tissues of corals and other organisms.

Index

Photo Credits

All photographs by **Scott W. Michael** *unless otherwise indicated*

Roger Steene: 22, 44, 69(TR), 70(B), 77(R, L), 86(L), 97, 100 (T), 104(B), 117(BL), 118(C), 130(B), 135(B), 137, 162(TR), 172, 203, 209 (L), 218, 229, 247 (TL, TR), 261, 272 (TR), 288 (BR), 301 (TL), 310 (BR), 320, 322 (C), 332 (T, C, B), 333 (T), 334 (R), 335 (TR), 336 (B), 337, 338 (B), 340 (T), 356, 357, 363, 375 (CL, BL), 376 (TR, CL, BL)

Keoki Stender: 48-49, 50, 52(C, B), 65(B), 163(R), 166(B), 168, 169(BL), 170(TR, M, B), 173, 176(B, T), 204, 212 (T), 255 (T, BL, BR), 256 (TL), 262, 268 (BL, BR), 269 (TL, TR), 270 (B), 299 (TL), 301 (TR), 309 (C), 311, 314 (B), 317 (L), 324, 326 (T, BL, BR), 330 (R), 331, 342

John E. Randall: 54(TR, TL), 55 (TR), 66(B), 70(T), 73(B), 134(TR), 143(BR), 162(B), 165(B), 167(B), 171, 198 (B), 203 (B), 221 (R), 305, 306 (B), 308 (L, R), 318 (TR), 319 (B), 335 (TL), 365 (TR), 368 (B), 369 (TR, B), 371 (T, C), 372 (T), 375 (BR), 377 (TR)

Rudie Kuiter: 57 (T), 92(C), 101(L), 155(BL), 162(TL), 185 (TR), 190 (L), 202 (TR, B), 206 (C), 210 (TL, B), 211 (B), 212 (BR), 219 (B), 256 (TR), 263 (TL), 268 (TR), 291 (BL, BR), 309 (B), 314 (C), 340 (BL), 341, 346, 375 (TR)

Robert F. Myers: 92(TL), 104 (C), 221 (L), 226 (T), 248 (TR), 316, 364, 368 (T), 371 (B), 377 (TL)

Gerald R. Allen: 72(R), 135 (B), 155 (BR), 162 (TL), 170 (TL), 205 (T), 284, 335 (B), 339

Liveaquaria: 47 (TL, TR), 151 (TL), 256 (BL, BR), 280 (B), 286 (BR)

Takamasa Tonozuka: 93(B), 214, 215(B), 248 (TL), 263 (TR), 277 (B), 286 (TL)

Fenton Walsh: 58 (C), 107, 115(BL), 118(B), 265 (T), 302

Fred Bavendam: 40, 80, 177, 223, 350

Alf Jacob Nielsen: 11, 41, 76(R), 78-79, 85

Tomonori Hirata: 129(B), 144 (B), 310 (TL)

John Hoover: Back Cover (B), 43 (BR), 271 (BR)

Keisuke Imai: 67, 143(CR), 153(BR)

Hiroshi Nagano: 121(R, L), 281 (TR)

Hiroyuki Tanaka: Back Cover (C), 132 (T), 148(TR)

Janine Cairns-Michael: 220 (BR), 230

Paul Humann: 206 (B), 271 (B)

Larry Jackson: 81 (L), 213

Tomoshibi Mizutani: 151 (CL, CR)

Ned DeLoach: 280 (T)

Andre Seale: 343

Toshio Tsubota: 55 (CR)

About the Author

SCOTT W. MICHAEL is an internationally recognized writer, underwater photographer, and marine biology researcher specializing in reef fishes. He is a regular contributor to *Aquarium Fish Magazine* and is the author of the *PocketExpertGuide to Marine Fishes* (Microcosm/TFH), the *Reef Fishes Series* (Microcosm/TFH), *Reef Sharks & Rays of the World* (Sea Challengers), and *Aquarium Sharks & Rays* (Microcosm/TFH).

Having studied biology at the University of Nebraska, he has been involved in research projects on sharks, rays, frogfishes, and the behavior of reef fishes. He has also served as scientific consultant for National Geographic Explorer and the Discovery Channel. His research and photographic en-

Author Scott W. Michael in Bonaire.

deavors have led him from Cocos Island in the Eastern Pacific to various points in the Indo-Pacific, including the Maldive Islands, Sulawesi, the Fiji Islands, Papua New Guinea, Australia's Great Barrier Reef, and Japan, as well as the Red Sea, the Gulf of Mexico, and many Caribbean reefs.

A marine aquarist since boyhood, he has kept tropical fishes for more than 30 years, with many years of extensive involvement in the aquarium world, including a period of retail store ownership. He is a partner in an extensive educational website on the coral reef environment, **www.coralrealm.com.**

Scott lives with his wife, underwater photographer Janine Cairns-Michael, and their Golden Retriever, Ruby, in Lincoln, Nebraska.

Author's Camera Equipment

Nexus F4 camera housing; Nikon F4 camera; Nikkor 60 and 105 mm macro lenses; TLC and Oceanic strobe arms; Nikon V with 20 mm lens; SB 105 Speedlights.

Future Editions

The author and editor are committed to making all future editions of this series as complete, accurate, and up-to-date as possible. Readers with suggestions, information, or photographs for possible publication are encouraged to contact one of the following in writing:

Reef Impressions
Scott W. Michael
4310 Garfield Street
Lincoln, NE 68506

Microcosm, Ltd.
James M. Lawrence, Editor
Charlotte, VT 05445
jml@microcosm-books.com

The World's Leading Aquarium Magazine
from the publishers of the world's finest aquarium books

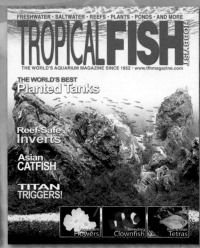

FRESHWATER • SALTWATER • REEFS • PLANTS • PONDS • AND MORE

FREE Gifts With Your Subscription:

• **FREE** *TFH* Aquatic Life Calendar • **FREE** Access to *TFH* Digital
• **FREE** book with 2-year subscription
Choose either *The 101 Best Saltwater Fishes* or *The 101 Best Tropical Fishes*
from the Microcosm/TFH Professional Series

Call for your FREE Trial Issue! 1-888-859-9034
www.tfhmagazine.com